The Father of Virginia
Military Institute

The Father of Virginia Military Institute

A Biography of Colonel J.T.L. Preston, CSA

RANDOLPH P. SHAFFNER

McFarland & Company, Inc., Publishers
Jefferson, North Carolina

Frontispiece: Colonel J.T.L. Preston, ca. 1870 (courtesy Louisa Berger Cofer).

Library of Congress Cataloguing-in-Publication Data

Shaffner, Randolph P., 1940–
The father of Virginia Military Institute : a biography of Colonel J.T.L. Preston, CSA / Randolph P. Shaffner.
 p. cm.
Includes bibliographical references and index.

ISBN 978-0-7864-9395-1 (softcover : acid free paper) ♾
ISBN 978-1-4766-1723-7 (ebook)

1. Preston, John Thomas Lewis, 1811–1890. 2. Virginia Military Institute—Biography. 3. College teachers—Virginia—Biography. 4. Confederate States of America. Army—Officers—Biography. 5. Virginia Military Institute—History—19th century. 6. Lexington (Va.)—Biography. I. Title. II. Title: Biography of Colonel J.T.L. Preston, CSA.
U430.V8S55 2014   355.0092—dc23   [B]   2014030335

British Library cataloguing data are available

© 2014 Randolph P. Shaffner. All rights reserved

No part of this book may be reproduced or transmitted in any form or by any means, electronic or mechanical, including photocopying or recording, or by any information storage and retrieval system, without permission in writing from the publisher.

On the cover: John Thomas Lewis Preston, portrait by Adele Williams ca. 1902, drawn from an ambrotype made ca. 1851 when Preston was forty (Virginia Military Institute Archives); present day Virginia Military Institute (iStock/Thinkstock)

Printed in the United States of America

McFarland & Company, Inc., Publishers
Box 611, Jefferson, North Carolina 28640
www.mcfarlandpub.com

To my son Tom,
who wears the ring

Table of Contents

Acknowledgments ix
Preface 1
Prologue: "A Day I Will Never Forget" 5

Part I: In the Beginning
1. The Growth of the Mind   14
2. A Classical Education   25

Part II: Father of the Dream
3. The Cives Letters   36
4. The Battle of the Arsenal Bills   47
5. From Dream to Reality   59

Part III: The First Decade
6. Professor of Modern Languages   76
7. Classical and Practical   79
8. VMI Under Attack   85
9. Fluctuations   89
10. The Challenge of Discipline   96

Part IV: Morning and Evening Star
11. A New Physics Professor   104
12. Irreparable Loss   108
13. Venus   115
14. A Grave Question of Educational Reform   119

Part V: Reluctant Confederates
15. Shades of Conflict   126
16. Virginia First and Last   134

17. Jackson's Chief of Staff   140
18. Craney Island   145
19. He Cannot Be Spared   149

Part VI: The Gloom and the Glory

20. Slain in Battle   156
21. The Shuddering Horror of Death   162
22. This Savage and Ferocious War   167
23. It Made Our Hearts Leap   171

Part VII: Twilight

24. Like a Bolt of Lightning   182
25. God and Slavery   189
26. Beyond the Sunset   197
27. Brigadier General and Doctor of Laws   204
28. Finis Opus Coronat   209

Epilogue   215
Chapter Notes   223
Bibliography   249
Index   263

Acknowledgments

This study has been greatly aided by the following individuals:
- in Norwich, Connecticut: Archivist and Special Collections Librarian Kelly Nolin at the Kreitzberg Library of Norwich University and Assistant Archivists Gail Weise and Mary Margaret Fletcher;
- in West Palm Beach, Florida: James R. Stockton, Jr.;
- in Louisville, Kentucky: Lois Strange;
- in Baltimore, Maryland: Former Archivist of the McDonogh School Frayda Salkin and current Archivist MaryLu Greenwood;
- in Hunt Valley, Maryland: Administrative Law Judge in the Office of Administrative Hearings William "Will" Somerville;
- in Asheville, North Carolina: Mary White Dorris;
- in Cary, North Carolina: Judge Anne Berger Salisbury;
- in Chapel Hill at the University of North Carolina: Curator of the Southern Historical Collection Walter C. "Tim" West, University Archivist Jay Gaidmore, Student Assistant Megan Martin, and Manuscripts Research Librarian in Special Collections Matthew Turi;
- in Charlotte, North Carolina: Jimmy White, Lucy White Moore Butler, and Louisa Berger Cofer;
- in Durham, North Carolina, at Duke University: Research Services Librarian at the David M. Rubenstein Rare Book and Manuscript Library and Elizabeth Dunn;
- in Winston-Salem, North Carolina: John Spach Creech, Jr., Juliana Christian Creech;
- in Bala Cynwyd, Pennsylvania: Henry and Roberta Shaffner;
- in West Chester, Pennsylvania: Chester County Historical Society Librarian Diane P. Rofini;
- in Arlington, Virginia: Army National Guard Planner Lt. Col. William McKern;
- in Buena Vista, Virginia, at Southern Virginia University: Professor of Art Dr. Barbara Crawford;
- in Blacksburg, Virginia, at the Virginia Polytechnic Institute Newman Library: Public Services and Reference Archivist Marc Brodsky, Library Assistant Christopher Barb, and Special Collections Archives Assistant John M. Jackson;
- in Blacksburg, Virginia, at the Historic Smithfield Plantation: *Smithfield Review* Editor Hugh Campbell, Head Interpreter April Danner, Board of Directors member Diane Hoover, Museum Administrator David McKissack, Ray Scott of the Smithfield Preston Foundation, and Smithfield volunteer Candi Kelly;
- in Charlottesville at the University of Virginia Albert and Shirley Small Special Collections Library: Director Nicole L. Bouché, Head of Reference and Research Services Heather Riser, Reference Coordinator Margaret Hrabe, and Sean Gleason;

- in Lexington, Virginia: President of the Rockbridge County Public Schools Foundation Richard C. Halseth, President of the Historic Lexington Foundation Skip Ravenhorst and Executive Director Don Hasfurther, Pastor of the Lexington Presbyterian Church the Rev. William "Bill" M. Klein and Administrative Assistant Lila G. Rogers, Rockbridge County Clerk of Court D. Bruce Patterson, Rockbridge Historical Society Executive Director George Warren, Stonewall Jackson Memorial Cemetery Supervisor Nicky Keen, author William G. Bean, Jr., Lexington Heritage Tour Guide Fred Bloom, and Patrick MacNamara;
- in Lexington, Virginia, at the Stonewall Jackson House: Executive Director Michael Anne Lynn and Curator Heidi Wing Sheldon;
- in Lexington at the Virginia Military Institute: Assistant to the Superintendent Col. Edwin L. Dooley, Jr., Instructor of History David W. Coffee, Executive Director of Museum Programs Col. Keith E. Gibson, Archivist and Records Manager Col. Diane B. Jacob and Assistant Mary Laura Kludy, Head Librarian Col. Donald Samdahl, Jr., head of Access Services Lt. Col. Susie Hastings, Interlibrary Loan Manager Valerie Gaylard, Reference Librarians Lt. Col. Janet Holly and Major Accacia Flanagan, and Director of Communications and Marketing Col. Stewart D. MacInnis;
- in Lexington, Virginia, at Washington and Lee University: Classics Department head Dr. Miriam Carlisle and Art History Professor Pamela H. Simpson; at the James G. Leyburn Library: Former Special Collections Librarian Vaughan Stanley and Current Librarian Tom Camden, Senior Special Collections Assistant Lisa McCown, in particular, as well as Senior Assistant Seth Goodhart and Assistant Edna Milliner;
- in Norfolk, Virginia: Norfolk Navy Yard Historian and Archivist Marcus Robbins;
- in Quantico, Virginia, at Marine Corps Command and Staff College: Professor of Military History Bradford A. Weinman;
- in Radford, Virginia, at Radford University McConnell Library: Lester Capon;
- in Richmond, Virginia: retired General Council for the Federal Reserve Bank of Richmond James B. McAfee, Jr., Page McLemore;
- in Richmond at the Library of Virginia: Archives Research Services Manager Virginia S. Dunn, Reference Services Coordinator William "Bill" Luebke, Reference Archivists Chris Colby, Tom Crew, Cara Griggs, and Tricia Noel, and Reference Coordinator Minor Weisiger;
- in Richmond at the Virginia Historical Society: Museum Collections Manager Heather Beattie, Assistant Librarian Sarah Bouchey, and Library Clerk Katherine Wilkins;
- in Staunton, Virginia, at Mary Baldwin College: Professor of History and Art Katharine Brown; R. Tucker Shields;
- and in Washington, D.C., at the Library of Congress: Lia Kerwin in the Manuscript Division and Tomeka Myers in Duplication Services.

I am indebted to Colonel Tho W. Davis, retired professor of history at VMI and president of the Rockbridge Historical Society, for his encouragement and support of this project, and to former VMI Assistant Archivist Patricia Gibson for her valuable suggestions regarding the book's appeal and style. I owe special thanks to Stuart Ferguson for his astute and incisive editing, his suggestions of structural arrangement for impact and relevance, and his recommendations concerning what to excise without excluding critical parts of Preston's story.

Lastly, for her unwavering support, assistance in research, and judicious evaluation of the book's form and content, as well as putting up with me while engrossed in my fascinating task, no words are sufficient to convey my gratitude to my wife Margaret. Similarly, I owe my son Tom high praise for the critical acumen he applied to assuring that the book be as near accurate and its author as near objective as is practicable. This book could not have been created without the considerable assistance of all the individuals credited in these acknowledgments.

For the whole earth is the sepulcher of famous men, and their story is not graven only on stone over their native earth, but lives on without visible symbol, woven into the hearts and minds of other men.
—Thucydides, Pericles' Funeral Oration, 430 BC

Preface

Colonel John Thomas Lewis Preston was born, lived, and died in Lexington, Virginia. His life from 1811 until 1890 encompassed much of the nineteenth century. At the time of his death no one in his hometown knew its history as intimately and thoroughly as he had lived it, and few played as widespread a role in forging it. But his influence extended far beyond the limits of his small town to the broader interests of his state and the nation.

With his talents he could have entered almost any profession, but he settled on education as the child of his heart. Education was not a particularly renowned or prestigious profession, but it was what he loved and found best suited to his needs and capabilities, much to the benefit of the thousands of young men and ultimately women whom he influenced. At the end of his long life what he considered his most valued accomplishment was the child of his brain: the Virginia Military Institute.

The biography of a military or political leader depicts his astonishing actions or decrees. The biography of an author more properly centers on the creation and reception of his masterpieces. But the biography of an educator, even a master educator, frequently contains little that is new or unusual to those outside his profession, apart from the progression of his thoughts and his influence on others. Socrates is known not for his actions but for his thoughts, yet Socrates taught Plato who taught Aristotle who taught Alexander the Great who conquered the world. J.T.L. Preston's influence would extend, in the words of Thucydides, "without visible symbol" through nineteenth-century America into the twenty-first century, "woven into the hearts and minds of other men."[1] If "the energy of mind is the essence of life," as Aristotle would have it, then this account of the life of J.T.L. Preston is a study of the essence of a brilliant and fertile mind.

The library on the VMI post bears Preston's name above its entrance. A metal nameplate beneath his portrait identifies him as "Founder of VMI and Faculty Member." Beyond that, there is little to indicate who this founder was. In my research I have discovered to date no book-length biography of Preston. Brief sketches of his life exist by his close friend Dr. William Ruffner among the Washington and Lee University Historical Papers, by Henry Wise in his *Military History of the Virginia Military Institute,* and by former VMI Museum director June Cunningham in Thomas Davis, ed., *A Crowd of Honorable Youths.* Bradford Wineman's "J.T.L. Preston and the Origins of the Virginia Military Institute" in *Virginia Magazine of History and Biography* offers the best account of the years 1834–42.

Occasional allusions to Preston are made in biographies of well-known individuals relevant to his life. These include his boyhood friend Edgar Allan Poe; his second wife, Poet of the Confederacy Margaret Junkin Preston; his brother-in-law General Thomas

Jonathan "Stonewall" Jackson; his relationships to the extensive Preston and Randolph families in Virginia; and his colleagues on the faculty of VMI: Superintendent Francis Smith, Colonel Claudius Crozet, Commodore Matthew Maury, and Colonel John Mercer Brooke.

Among all these notable individuals associated with him or with the institute, Preston remains the least familiar. Yet in his time he was an ever-present figure, a *primum mobile* of new ideas that pervade the world of education today. He was a pioneer of free schooling for the poor, practical education for the common people, and training for technical careers in engineering and science together with the learned professions of law, medicine, education, and the ministry. He fought for the study of mathematics, natural philosophy (physics), chemistry, and the military arts, which he considered essential to a basic education that had formerly focused exclusively on the classics.

In his battle for change, he championed the transformation of a state arsenal into the first state-supported military institute in the nation, a new kind of school that offered "academic study of the highest possible quality conducted in and facilitated by a rigorous system of military discipline." Under the twofold concept of the "citizen-soldier," he promoted a civilian alternative to the military whereby many graduates would select a civilian rather than military career but still be qualified for service to their country in case of need. He supported two years of teaching in exchange for free tuition and board at state-supported VMI, which helped provide competent teachers in the schools of Virginia while improving the quality of the educational curriculum throughout the state.

Apart from his contributions to the field of American education, Preston displayed by his character and worldview enough contradictions to afford a fascinating study of the man himself. Bits and pieces of his life in letters, speeches, articles, book reviews, journals, reports, and memoirs are scattered throughout college and university libraries and public institutions. Taken together, they define his eclectic thinking within the realms of literature, language, science, law, history, religion, and philosophy. They address the controversial issues of his era—slavery, secession, and war—in the historical context of a universal striving for freedom and civilization. While the chapter on slavery expounds a view that few people would endorse today, it nonetheless endeavors to paint Preston, as Cromwell ordered, warts and all, for a completely authentic portrait of the man.

Even so, no biography can presume to be complete for what it must necessarily omit due to lack of space or interest. Many of Preston's thoughts, which could fill another book, were omitted from this account as not crucial to a basic understanding of his character and worldview. Within his educational philosophy and religious beliefs, which guided his actions throughout his long career, his steadfast aim remained the development of a young man's character. For that high purpose, even his opponents could not fail to give him credit. With all his inherent contradictions, eccentricities, and new ideas, he was above all an innovative pioneer of modern American education.

In a work that purports to be scholarly, the subject of bias must always be addressed; more so when the author is a descendent of the subject. It would be unreasonable to claim that such a familial connection can ever exert no influence. The subject of this work is one that has been relatively unknown to prior research, and while I have always been aware of my family connection, it was on visiting the VMI post and seeing the portrait of Preston in the library, which bears his name, that I became interested in the man, for family lore had little to say of him. As such the research for this book has been an exploration into unknown territory on both the personal and professional levels, and the result has been as new to the Preston family as to the world at large.

But the risk of bias could not be ignored, and in recognition of this I have endeavored to address it on several fronts. First, in the creation of this work I have attempted to ensure all statements are supported by the evidence. I have not shied away from discussing all sides of Preston, including difficult ones. Second, I have asked several independent parties to review the work, including my wife, who had more to say than the historical authorities in ensuring I was being objective. And third, I have been extremely careful to document at length the research underlying the text. This is particularly true in areas that might prove controversial, in which I strove to ensure that the research could speak for itself. Not to address this topic would constitute a deception of omission, but in the end it is my belief that the assertions of the final work result from the facts as documented, independent of the identity of the documenter.

Perhaps most contentious is the statement that Preston was the "father of VMI." I expect it to provoke some debate, especially among those who favor a particular time-honored alternative for that claim. Other than the supportive role that he played in helping to found the institute, Preston is often overlooked or disregarded as its originator. In all humility he himself eschewed the honor, which further served to perpetuate the oversight.

It is not the intent of this biography to detract in the least from the substantial contributions made to the founding of VMI by such praiseworthy men as Francis Smith, Claudius Crozet, John Caruthers, Hugh Barclay, and others, who are frequently cited as the institute's parents. But the lack of public information about Preston has left him so little understood for who he was and what he strove to accomplish that a whole section of this book is devoted to his unique role as "Father of the Dream." The three chapters of the section grew beyond the scope I first envisioned. But in light of the number of conflicting claims on the institute's parentage, it seemed advisable to settle the issue as conclusively as possible and to leave the task of refuting it or restoring the debate to later generations.

The chapters of this book were

John Thomas Lewis Preston. Portrait by Adele Williams ca. 1902, drawn from an ambrotype made ca. 1851 when Preston was forty. Preston's daughter Libbie had to instruct the artist concerning the appropriate coloring, since the positive image on the glass didn't show "the very dark blue" of his cap and uniform and the "dark brown" of his hair. This portrait now hangs in the Preston Library (**Virginia Military Institute Archives, No. 0002021**).

undertaken on the basis of distinct periods in Preston's life. Apart from the opening flash-forward, the first section describes his education before his decision to define a new type of school. The next twenty years present him as an educator, crusader, husband, father, sportsman, traveler, and philosopher before the onset of the Civil War that ripped apart his life. The final twenty-five years complete the picture of a man of lofty principles that earned him the respect of all who knew him well.

As a modest man, Preston would have abjured any monuments to honor his achievements. But a library is a proper tribute to the scholar he chose to become, making him a man worthy of a long overdue life story. At the least this biography may help dispel some of the questions that spring from a name above a door and a metal plate beneath a portrait.

I wish to acknowledge the invaluable help of the individuals listed in the Acknowledgments, without whose aid this book would not have been possible. And to other friends and colleagues, who have given assistance and encouragement, I am deeply grateful.

Prologue:
"A Day I Will Never Forget"

They set fire to the institute about nine o'clock; the flames are now enveloping it; the towers have fallen; the arsenal is exploding as I write.
—Margaret J. Preston, June 12, 1864

The Battle of New Market had been a glorious Confederate victory, which Union General David Hunter meant to avenge. Fresh on his mind, as he advanced into the Shenandoah Valley, was fellow General Franz Sigel's humiliating defeat, aided by a ragtag army of young cadets from the Virginia Military Institute. General Ulysses S. Grant had immediately replaced Sigel with Hunter, who was ordered to do what Sigel had failed to do. He was to destroy the Virginia and Tennessee and the Virginia Central railroads at their junction in Staunton and open the valley to Lynchburg. Both Lexington and VMI would rue Sigel's replacement by a man far more vengeful. Hunter would make the town and institute pay for their role in the Confederate success at New Market.

On June 7, 1864, the same Corps of Cadets that had fought so valiantly at New Market was abruptly recalled from their camp in Richmond to help stop Hunter's looming raid. The previous day, Hunter's troops had entered Staunton, having plundered homes along the way and taken clothes, lard, butter, potatoes, colts, cattle and sheep. One witness reported they brought with them "a very respectable man named David Creigh, of Greenbrier" and hung him in the Rev. James Morrison's yard "for killing a Yankee near Lewisburg. Mr. Creigh, it is said, did it in defense of his family and himself."[1] In Staunton, Hunter joined General George Crook's infantry and General William Averell's cavalry from West Virginia with the intent of taking Lexington and then Lynchburg.

Word reached Lexington that Averell was advancing from North Mountain, only twenty to thirty miles to the west. Colonel J.T.L. Preston set out immediately to secure whatever valuables could be transported to Washington College, especially from the library of the Virginia Military Institute. The institute had been the child of his brain and heart. He had invested too much of himself into its survival since the day it was painstakingly created to have invaders trample its treasures underfoot. A quarter century had passed since he, in his mid-twenties, and Francis Smith, Claudius Crozet, and a whole host of staunch supporters both within and outside its hallowed walls had struggled to assure its existence and secure its future. The institute had succeeded in providing Virginia not only with many of its finest citizens but also its finest soldiers.

But now it stood on the brink of destruction by those who had felt the far-reaching impact of its military might. Was it not a Union general or President Abraham Lincoln himself who had blamed that small military school in Virginia for prolonging this war with its inexhaustible supply of officers and fighters for the Confederacy? As the institute was government property, the enemy would most likely burn it, which was Colonel Preston's apprehension. He had just learned of Hunter's burning of a woolen factory, which he himself partly owned, in Port Republic.[2] Already this war had cost Preston much of what was most dear to him. As he would later confess, he had known the "anguish beyond remedy" of a father, uncle, and cousin each time "the bloody, remorseless hand of war" tore from his heart what, to him, was more precious than liberty, home, or anything but heaven.[3] Among the wounded or killed were three of his sons, several nephews, more cousins, fellow citizens he had known since childhood, countless soldiers he had taught as cadets, and faculty associates. This included his brother-in-law and best friend T. J. "Stonewall" Jackson, whose irreplaceable loss the entire Confederacy had mourned after Chancellorsville. Still remaining were family, relatives, and friends, all imperiled by the horrors of this war, but especially VMI. Hunter meant to invade the "hornet's nest" to exact retribution for what its cadets had inspired at the Battle of New Market.

On June 8, Preston was given charge of loading six canal boats with artillery and ammunition, commissary stores, and vital records of VMI for safekeeping in Lynchburg.[4] People throughout Lexington were hiding their valuables, moving flour and goods, driving out their cows, and running about in a high state of excitement. Preston himself was having his bacon hauled into the mountains and his cattle driven off from the farm. The Corps of Cadets arrived from Richmond on June 9, allowing Preston's son Frank to join his family. Word came that Crook's infantry had reached Brownsburg before turning back to Staunton. This seemed inconsistent, since all that stood between them and Lexington were the remnants of Confederate regiments. But by evening on the 10th, Crook's command had turned south again in full force.

General John McCausland, Class of 1857 and VMI's professor of mathematics, retreated with his 1,500 Confederates. He knew that he'd be able only to delay but not stop Hunter's combined 18,000 troops from entering Lexington.[5] Shortly after midnight on June 11, Preston and two officers rode out to see McCausland, returning around three in the morning. By ten o'clock, with the enemy not yet in sight, McCausland burned the venerable fifty-four-year-old covered bridge across the North River and began to fire on Union forces as they approached. During the ensuing counter fire, Preston remained with the cadets on the hill at the institute until the shot and shell drove them back. John Thompson, a wounded cadet who was on the cusp of death, was removed from the VMI hospital during the barrage to Preston's home on the south side of town.[6] Knowing that his wife Maggie and the younger children would not be harmed, Preston left them with the wounded cadet and retreated farther south with the cadet corps to Balcony Falls, where the James River passed through the Blue Ridge Mountains.

By evening, Maggie Preston reported in her journal that Hunter's artillery was still shelling the town with vengeful fury from across the North River. One shell exploded in the Prestons' orchard. First the cavalry and then the infantry poured into town. Soldiers invaded the Prestons' yard and kitchen so that Maggie found herself ordering them "out of the kitchen, half a dozen at a time." She had contented them with slices of bacon, but when they demanded entry into the smokehouse "with a score of them surrounding me, with guns in their hands," she entreated them "by the respect they had for their wives, mothers, and sisters, to leave me a little meat." They responded like "wild beasts," swearing at her and leaving nothing in the smokehouse. Barely successful in keeping them out of her home, she had all the windows nailed shut and wrote a courteous note to Union General Averell, asking in vain that he send a guard. He was headquartered in the yard of the Rev. William White's Presbyterian manse. "At ten we went to bed," she wrote, "feeling that we had nothing between these ravagers and us but God's protecting arm."[7]

Sunday morning, June 12, Maggie described as "a day I will never forget." A throng of soldiers were demanding entry into the house. She again appealed to them "as a lone woman who had nobody to protect her." But she "might as well have appealed to the bricks." Her pleas fell on deaf ears, as they tried to carry away the china in the dining room. As she described it, "I told them all I was a Northern woman, but confessed that I was ashamed of my Northern lineage when I saw them come on such an errand." When she wouldn't give them the key to the cellar, they threatened to burn the house. She replied, "Yes, we are at your mercy—burn it down—but I won't give you the key." They demanded arms and broke into the cellar, carrying off everything they could find. They seized the breakfast while the children cried for something to eat. She had nothing left to give them but crackers. Soldiers "set fire to the institute about nine o'clock," for she could see the flames enveloping it, the towers falling, and the arsenal exploding from her window.[8]

General Hunter had ordered the burning of Governor John Letcher's home and "all the V. M. I. professors' houses," namely those of Thomas Williamson and William Gilham at the institute, but including Preston's home off post.[9] At the governor's home, "Mrs. Letcher was given only five minutes notice."[10] It was enough time to open a drawer to get a dress for the four-month-old baby before the provost marshal threw lighted matches into the clothes and set the cradle aflame. Superintendent Francis Smith's home escaped being torched because his daughter was desperately ill with a child only two days old, so Hunter made Smith's home his headquarters.[11] General Crook headquartered in Preston's first home, then owned by schoolmaster Jacob Fuller, on the high hill east of the institute.[12]

Hunter had all but two buildings of VMI shelled and burned. Barracks, officers' quarters, mess hall, and all academic facilities were burned, including laboratories and equipment. Also in flames were the hospital and what remained of the library after 10,000 books were confiscated or burned. Only the walls of Barracks, Smith's house, and the quarters of the ordnance sergeant were left standing. Several of Hunter's own officers opposed the destruction of the institute. They included future U.S. Senator Henry duPont and future U.S. Presidents William McKinley, Jr., and Rutherford B. Hayes. Colonel Hayes wrote in his diary on June 12: "General Hunter burns the Virginia Military Institute. This does not suit many of us…. General Hunter will be as odious as Butler or Pope to the Rebels and not gain our good opinion either."[13]

Colonel James Schoonmaker of Pennsylvania not only opposed but "positively refused" to carry out Hunter's general order to set the institute ablaze. Its defenders had already abandoned it, he reasoned, and "he had not enlisted in the army for that purpose."[14] He was subsequently placed under arrest for insubordination. He was later acquitted because what he had refused was Hunter's "regular policy" of burning, rather than a direct order. The only potential charge against him was that in Hunter's opinion, according to Schoonmaker, "my judgment was poor and that is why he released me from arrest."[15]

Captain duPont, on the contrary, as artillery commander, had direct orders "to bombard the V.M.I." But seeing it vacated, he too had decided not to follow through. Sympathizing with duPont's dilemma, Colonel Schoonmaker advised him to fire just a few rounds so that technically he would have obeyed orders, which he did. Hence "the two solid shot," which a later alumnus explained, were "still sticking in the walls" of Barracks.[16] Almost a decade earlier, duPont had tried to be admitted to VMI. But before 1858 only Virginians were allowed to attend. So he had attended West Point instead and served the Union at New Market. In 1914, fifty years after his having fired token shots at Barracks, then–Senator duPont would sponsor a bill compensating the institute $100,000 for Hunter's destruction. The money would be used to construct Jackson Memorial Hall, and Henry duPont would be made an honorary alumnus, Class of 1864, in appreciation of his "sound judgment" during the raid.

During the rest of Sunday, Union troops slaughtered every sheep and cow and carried off the horses, placing Maggie in despair. The next day her home, like other homes in town, was searched for arms and cadet trunks and clothing. She was forced to tear up and burn seven trunk loads of uniforms belonging to VMI officers and cadets that had just been delivered for safekeeping. They included Frank's outside clothes and Mr. P's (Preston's) new $300 coat. Fearing for Stonewall Jackson's sword, which she had previously concealed in Anna Jackson's piano, she now hid it under her clothing. Many women in town wore the contraband uniforms of their cadets under their own clothing to prevent their being found.[17] Like mother hens guarding their nests, they scolded the raiders like children. They ordered them out of their private homes, away from their children, and out of their larders, often in vain. In Maggie's case in particular, as one cavalryman told her, if all the women talked as she did, the Yankees "would fire the entire town."[18] Maggie decided to show her Yankee guard the wounded cadet in the library. She knew he would eventually discover the youth anyway. But she was surprised when the guard spoke compassionately, "Well, in the other world there will surely be somebody made to suffer for all this!"[19]

Maggie's misgivings grew with rumors that VMI officers and cadets had been taken prisoners. She worried for her husband and Frank. Hearing that 40,000 troops were marching on Richmond through Lexington, she further feared for the Confederacy itself. But she knew "there was a deadly earnestness among our men which would make the last remnant of them fly to our mountain fastnesses and fight like tigers till the last inch of ground was taken from them: that then the women and children would be swept into the Ocean on one side, and into the wilds of Mexico on the other, but there *could* be no yielding."[20]

By June 13, Confederate forces had cut off Hunter's supply line to Staunton. He received word that Union General Philip Sheridan had been beaten back in one of the largest all-cavalry battles of the war at Trevilian Station near Charlottesville. Confederate Generals Wade Hampton and Fitzhugh Lee had blocked Sheridan's attempt to follow Grant's grand scheme and unite with Hunter. This left Hunter no hope of aid from east of the Blue Ridge. His only escape was a grueling march over the mountains to Lynchburg. On June 14 the women of Lexington heaved an uncertain sigh of relief, as though a storm had passed, when the entire Union army evacuated Lexington. Owing to their emotional absorption in their suffering from the moment the bombardment had commenced until the soldiers were gone, they had "forgot to eat." Maggie quickly realized, "Four days we went from morning till dark without food."[21]

Hunter's terrifying raid on her town and home, which Maggie recorded in graphic detail in her journal, gave first-hand insights into the intense suffering that this savage and ferocious war was inflicting on so many hapless victims in her homeland. Her sympathy with the grief that put almost everyone in the community in tears would eventually find its most powerful expression in the ballad *Beechenbrook: A Rhyme of the War* that would earn her the accolade "Poetess of the Confederacy." But for now, her heart overflowed with sorrow for the inhumanity she had witnessed. Her immediate concern was for the return of her husband, whom she thought it very possible she might never see again.

The news of Hunter's unjust burning of VMI so infuriated Confederate General Jubal Early that he vowed "to open the eyes of the people of the North to this enormity, by example in the way of retaliation."[22] On July 28 he ordered McCausland's cavalry to retaliate by crossing the Potomac into Maryland and Pennsylvania. McCausland entered Chambersburg, Pennsylvania, and demanded $100,000 in gold or $500,000 in U.S. currency to compensate Hunter's victims for their loss of property or he would burn their town.[23] Early himself had made previous demands on Hagerstown, Maryland, where he received a ransom of $20,000 for sparing the town. His demands on Frederick had netted $200,000.

On July 31, McCausland took possession of Chambersburg, giving its citizens six hours to comply. When they failed to take it seriously, they were herded out of their homes, and the town was set ablaze. The fire consumed 550 buildings, left 3,000 people homeless, and caused $1.6 million in damages.[24] In the aftermath, McCausland's name was as hated above the Mason-Dixon line as the name of Hunter was below it. Known as "the Hun of Chambersburg," he would flee the country after the war until President Grant offered him amnesty, contending that acts of war must be forgotten and forgiven. Declining to return to his professorship at VMI, he would choose instead farming in the Kanawha Valley of West Virginia until his death in 1927.

Virginia Military Institute after Hunter's raid, July 12, 1864. Photograph by Boude and McClellan (Virginia Military Institute Archives, No. 0001047).

Main Street, Lexington, after Hunter's Raid. Photograph by A. H. Plecker, 1865–66. View of Main Street shortly after the end of the Civil War. The ruins of the Virginia Military Institute Barracks, extensively damaged during the raid, are visible in the background (Virginia Military Institute Archives, No. 0003049).

While McCausland was wreaking revenge in Pennsylvania, Generals John Breckinridge and Early were repulsing Hunter west of Lynchburg. Here the Corps of Cadets, including Preston and his son Frank, were in the trenches, but not in action. They left Lynchburg by canal boat on June 24, arriving the following day in Lexington. Owing to the destruction of the Virginia Military Institute, fourteen veterans of the Battle of New Market were graduated, and the corps was furloughed. At the beginning of October the corps was reassembled at Camp Lee[25] in Richmond and sent to Poe's Farm in support of the infantry's defense of the capital.

In the Shenandoah Valley, General Sheridan was busy carrying out Grant's order to destroy the vast food resources there "so that crows flying over it for the balance of the season will have to carry their provender with them."[26] Fortunately Lexington was spared, but Sheridan destroyed crops and livestock between Winchester and Staunton. He burned flour mills and barns filled with wheat, hay, and farm equipment and killed sheep to feed his army. Far from winding down to a long anticipated close, this war of three years and hundreds of thousands of casualties raged on unabated.

Maggie despaired that "the cause of the Confederacy was finished for the present." Or at least it had become a hopeless struggle in which prayers had not been heard. But the one gleam of brightness that dispelled all her gloom and raised her spirits was Mr.

Opposite: Map of the Shenandoah Valley. The Shenandoah Valley stretches 200 miles across the Blue Ridge and Allegheny mountains. It is bounded on the east by the Blue Ridge Mountains, on the west by the eastern front of the Ridge-and-Valley Appalachians (excluding Massanutten Mountain), and on the south by the James River. It slopes downward to the Potomac River in the north. During the Civil War it was known as "the breadbasket of the Confederacy" (map by George Skoch).

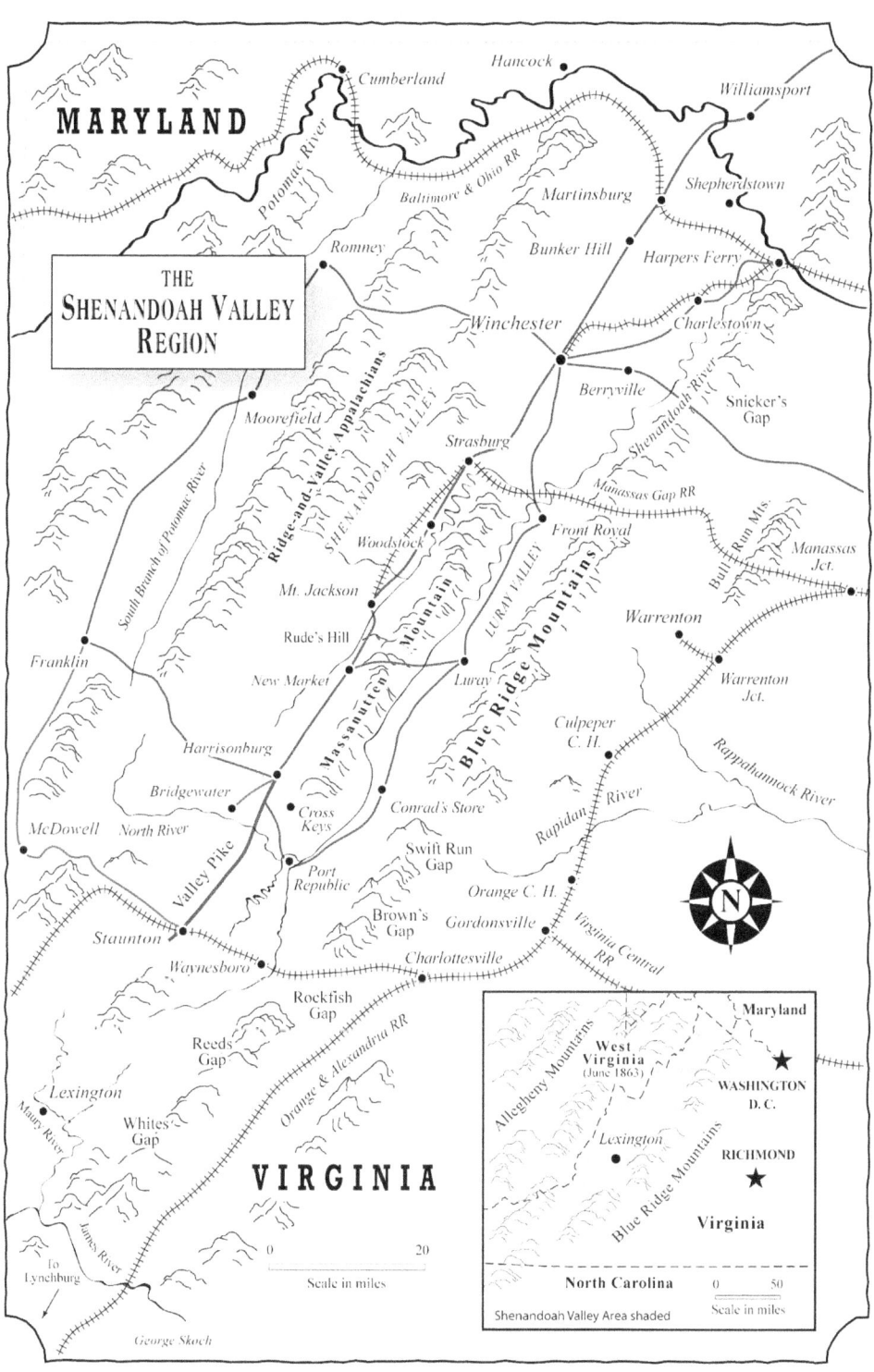

P.'s return home. She was overjoyed with thanks to God for his deliverance, feeling herself blessed beyond all she dared to hope. Preston too was thankful on his return, despite the realization in short order that "$30,000 would scarcely cover what he has lost" by Hunter's invasion. Maggie noted how, without complaint, he resigned himself to live as "a poor man now for the rest of his days."[27] The prospects for any means of subsistence grew dimmer and narrower with each passing day.

The town in which Preston had lived all his life had been bombarded and pillaged almost beyond recognition. Not since the Great Fire had Lexington looked so destitute. More than forty houses had been struck during Hunter's initial barrage. A dozen barns lay in ashes. Acres of farmland had been stripped of their crops, and every sheep, cow, and horse had been carried away. Very little in the way of food remained in the homes. Governor Letcher's home was gone, and the institute, which Preston had fathered and where he taught, including almost all the faculty houses, lay in total ruins. Moreover, before abandoning Lexington, Hunter's troops had removed from VMI, as a trophy of war, William Hubbard's treasured statue of George Washington.[28]

Walking the streets of his hometown, Preston surveyed the extent of the damage done. He wondered if he would live to see the day that the scattered remnants of his and his neighbors' lives might be reassembled enough to recognize them again. There were irreplaceable pieces that were forever lost: homes, stores, relatives, and friends that made a village a home. He gazed at the charred remains of VMI, which showed no signs of life, and wondered if his dream, to which he had devoted half his existence, was finished.

Part I:
In the Beginning

She teaches her two little children exclusively and they are much further advanced in grammar and geography than any of their age I have ever seen.

—Eliza Madison about
Edmonia Preston

1

The Growth of the Mind

With pride and amazement I saw myself where I never was before and never was afterwards,—above Nat Howard and Edgar Poe.
— J.T.L. Preston

Lexington would rebuild, as it had after the Great Fire of April 11, 1796, when all but two of its hundred buildings were consumed in a single night. After that conflagration the town's grief-stricken residents, from the ashes of their log houses, cabins, and frame dwellings, had resurrected buildings of brick and stone. But they would carry to their graves a hereditary dread of fire. It was during this earlier rebirth of the town from the misfortunes of its infancy that Preston's father had arrived in 1801 to attend what was then Washington Academy. It was the only institution of higher learning in the isolated mountainous region of western Virginia.

Lexington itself was little more than a remote outpost west of the Blue Ridge. It was founded by Scots-Irish refugees scarcely a year after America's Declaration of Independence. Seeking freedom from English persecution, these founders had chosen to settle at the upper end of the valley through which the Shenandoah River swept down between the Blue Ridge and Allegheny mountains to join the Potomac River at Harpers Ferry in the north. Perched on the north fork of the James River, their new home took its name from the town in Massachusetts where was shed the first blood of America's revolution against oppression.

On January 12, 1778, a legislative decree had established the boundaries of Lexington on twenty-seven acres near the center of the newly created Rockbridge County. Partly donated by Isaac Campbell, a Scots-Irish farmer, the new town measured 900 by 1,300 feet. It encompassed thirty-six half lots on rolling farmland too steep to appear on a flat map, which is how the rectangle was drawn by the statute. The dirt streets were so precipitous that horse-drawn wagons slid into muddy intersections for many years before the town would slice off ten feet from its hills to make them more negotiable. Even so, the hills would remain exceptionally steep. Four of the major streets on them were named for Virginia's leaders during the Revolution: Peyton Randolph, Thomas Jefferson, Patrick Henry, and George Washington.

It's not surprising that so much of Lexington's focus was on the heroes of Virginia. Long before the United States, there had been Virginia. From its establishment as an English colony in the 16th century, it had grown to embrace the entire Eastern coast of North America from the 34th to the 48th parallel, including the shores of Arcadia and a large part of inland Canada. Eventually the colony was extended over the Blue Ridge Mountains to claim the great Northwest Territory, reaching as far as was known toward the Pacific Ocean. Virginia's history as a colony spanned nearly one and three-quarters

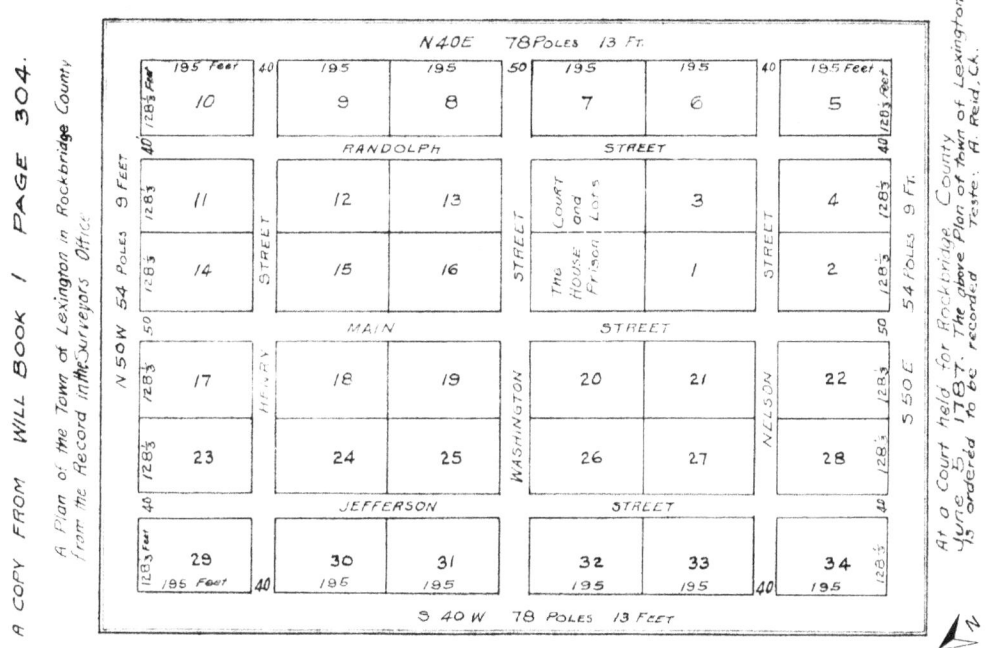

Plat of Lexington, June 5, 1787. Reprinted from Will Book 1, 304, in the Rockbridge County Courthouse. All surveyor records were destroyed by General Hunter's army during the Civil War.

Sketch of Lexington in December 1849, by local resident Seth Eastman. (President and Fellows of Harvard University, Peabody Museum of Archaeology and Ethnology, PM# 41–72–10/191 [digital file# 98420013]).

Antique map of Virginia and Florida. Drawing in 1632 of *Virginiae Item et Floridae Americae Provinciarum nova Descriptio* by Gerard Mercator, copper-engraved by Pieter van der Keere.

centuries before its eventual integration into the United States. Although many of its statesmen had helped create the fledgling nation and many states of that nation would be born on its land, the inextricable bond between Virginia and its residents would remain strong in the event the new nation might fail. Especially in the west, where the Scots-Irish had originally sought refuge from a powerful central government, the loyalties of these free and independent people were first and foremost to their newfound home in the Shenandoah Valley of Virginia.

Into this environment J.T.L. Preston was born in 1811. He was not yet two when Major Thomas Preston died, so he never knew his father. If the old adage "like father, like son" were to relate at all to young John's life, which would follow closely in the footsteps of the man he never knew, it would serve only to confirm that nature rather than nurture drove him to accomplish many of the same goals his father had set for himself in Lexington. Even the boy's name, like the name of the town itself, was dictated by an inherited past. The marriage of his parents, Thomas Lewis Preston and Edmonia Madison Randolph, had united two of the most prolific, if not most prominent, families of Virginia. Theirs was a union of hereditary wealth and property, but also deep-seated family values and traditions.

Genealogically as well as historically, this marriage of a Preston with a Randolph was destined to produce a soldier, politician, lawyer, minister, professor, doctor, or landowner. But which of the political or religious leanings would prevail in such a union of family opposites would depend on whether the boy shared the Preston fire of a rebel, like his ancestral Covenanters of Lowland Scotland, or the Randolph passion of a loyalist, like his ancestral Cavaliers of Northern England. The Prestons of Virginia sprang from Scots-Irish insurgents; the Randolphs, from British royalists. The Prestons were essentially uncompromising Calvinists; the Randolphs, high-church Anglicans.

The Prestons populated western Virginia to the same extent that the Randolphs inhabited eastern Virginia. Indeed, both families were so prolific that Dr. William Ruffner, Virginia's first superintendent of public instruction, once remarked about the Preston descendants: "They are greater in number than those of Abraham in the same length of time, and there is every prospect that in less than 400 years, they will be as numerous as the children of Israel when they started for the promised land, which will be of great advantage to this republic."[1]

In like manner, the Randolph descendants, many of whom did not bear the family name but still acknowledged kinship, inspired a Virginia adage that nothing was good enough for a Randolph but another Randolph. This produced a clever corollary that the Randolph family had so intermingled in their marital relationships that it was like "a tangle of fishhooks, so closely interlocked that it is impossible to pick up one without drawing three or four after it."[2] In uniting the Preston and Randolph families through their marriage, Thomas and Edmonia established kinships with what seemed like almost everyone in Virginia. So when their first child, a daughter, was born in 1808, she was named Elizabeth Randolph Preston, after Edmonia's mother, Elizabeth Nicholas, and the pervasive Randolph and Preston family names.[3] When their second child, a boy, arrived in 1811, he was named for his father, Thomas Lewis Preston, but also for his great-grandfather, John Preston, the progenitor of all the Prestons in Virginia. The boy was destined to carry all four names, John Thomas Lewis Preston, and be known as J.T.L.[4]

Elizabeth had been born when her father was still serving in the state legislature in Richmond. But Thomas's term had expired by the time John was born in Lexington. Thomas and Edmonia were boarding in a house on East Washington Street not far from the county courthouse.[5] Built in 1801, it was a modest, two-story brick Valley I–house with two rooms separated by a central hallway. Known today as the Stonewall Jackson House, it was owned and run by the jailor, Cornelius Dorman, a stooped old man with long gray hair flowing to his waist. The Rockbridge County Jail where he worked nearby had only recently been rebuilt after the Great Fire.

When John arrived on the scene, Dorman's son Charles, at age seventeen, was helping his father manage the house. At the time he had no idea of the crucial role he would play in the far-off future as a delegate to the General Assembly in support of this new arrival's petition to establish a military school in Lexington. But on April 25 in 1811 the focus of the entire Dorman household, far from dwelling on the distant future, was centered instead on Elizabeth Preston's new baby brother and the sunlit hopes of spring.

On August 11, 1812, when John was not yet two, his father died of typhoid fever he had contracted while stationed near Norfolk.[6] He was serving there on active duty as a major in the militia at the beginning of the War of 1812. His death at thirty struck his young widow, Edmonia, with inconsolable grief and plunged her into a despondency from which she never fully recovered. As a consequence, neither John nor his sister Elizabeth ever knew their father or even knew about him. Edmonia in her private and prolonged grief over her husband's early demise never mentioned him to her children.

Left with two children to rear, ages three and one, she retreated to the Virginia home of her mother-in-law, Susanna Preston, at Smithfield. There she numbly cared for them and struggled with practical and legal demands that her husband had always handled for her. The daughter of Edmund Randolph, Virginia's former attorney general and first attorney general of the United States, she might have turned to her esteemed father for legal advice. But her father's health was fading fast so that he too was in her care. Like many women of her time, she owed her education to her parents, which in her case had been directed by her father. Under his tutelage in Richmond she had acquired the literary taste and cultivation of one of the most aristocratic cities in America.

Edmonia's mind proved to be exceptional. Although she possessed an adequate knowledge of the usual subjects of a woman in her day, she had also acquired a remarkable mastery of history and English literature, a polished fluency in French, and outstanding proficiency in music. She kept an album of hand-copied piano and voice scores, including English, Scottish, Irish, and French love songs, songs of the Cherokee, military airs and marches, and works of Haydn, Mozart, Muzio Clementi, Camille Pleyel, Rodolph Kreutzer, Stephen Storace, and Metastasio.[7] Her manners, typical of refined polite society, were impeccable.

Despite the scope of her education, she found herself suddenly called upon to assume her deceased husband's responsibilities. Thomas had died before completing the sale of her father's farm in Richmond, which would have funded her father's last years. Although totally unfamiliar with the mechanics of the commercial world, she was nonetheless proficient in expressing her need for help. In this regard, her father had prepared her well. In the most exquisitely refined manners imaginable, she addressed a letter to her brother-in-law, General John Preston, asking for his advice.

She began the letter with a disarmingly undemanding greeting: "Knowing how much your time is occupied, this letter would demand an apology for its intrusion upon your attention, necessarily employed in your many and important avocations. I am encouraged, however, by the affectionate and parental attention you have hitherto shown to me and those most dear to me, to hope that you will not deem this letter intrusive."[8] Like her husband, who had always consulted his older brother for guidance, she too now asked General Preston's opinion about selling the house and investing the proceeds in bank stock.

Edmonia's primary concern was for her family: her children and her father. When Edmund Randolph died in 1813, she again wrote to General Preston. She and her children were now staying with her sister, Susan Randolph Taylor, at Avon Hill in western Virginia. "I am now so far removed from those of my friends who are acquainted with my business, and so totally ignorant of it myself, that I feel a peculiar anxiety on that account. But above all other occurrences I dread that the separation of myself and my children from the family may produce an estrangement, which would pain me more than I can express."[9]

By July 1814, almost two years after Thomas's death, Edmonia was still living in relative isolation at Avon Hill. She wrote to Thomas's oldest sister, Eliza Preston Madison, whose son-in-law John Peyton was administering Thomas's estate. Edmonia lamented,

> My life is a scene of perfect uniformity. There is nothing like society here, and even of the few persons who visit the house, I rarely see anybody. I sit constantly in one spot in

my own room, solely occupied in the instruction of my children, in working for them, and in reading such books as may best qualify me for fulfilling my duties towards them. My mind has sunk into the only calm I can ever feel—that of entire despondency. I feel that I am very ungrateful to my God who has left me so many blessings. I pray to him to pardon my discontent and resign me to his will, but I fear I never shall bring my heart to say as I ought to do "Thy will be done."[10]

In 1816, for much needed income, Edmonia rented the town lot that her husband had bought eight years earlier just beyond the eastern boundary of Lexington.[11] Consisting of twenty-one acres, it lacked only six acres of equaling the entire size of Lexington, as platted when the town was founded. The rent would help provide for her immediate needs.

By early 1818 she had moved with her children back to Smithfield to live with her mother-in-law. Susanna's separation from her last child had left her essentially alone at age seventy-nine. Edmonia was all duty, attention, and tenderness to her needs, as Eliza would report, but "there is still a melancholy [that] hangs over her which she has not yet been able to conquer, notwithstanding all her fine sense, which is certainly very superior. She teaches her two little children exclusively and they are much further advanced in grammar & geography than any of their age I have ever seen. They are also a great comfort to our dear Mother."[12] What John and Elizabeth lost in the premature death of their father, they gained in the exclusive attention of their mother. She gave

J.T.L. Preston's birthplace, today's Stonewall Jackson House (Rockbridge Historical Society Photograph, Washington and Lee University, Leyburn Library Special Collections).

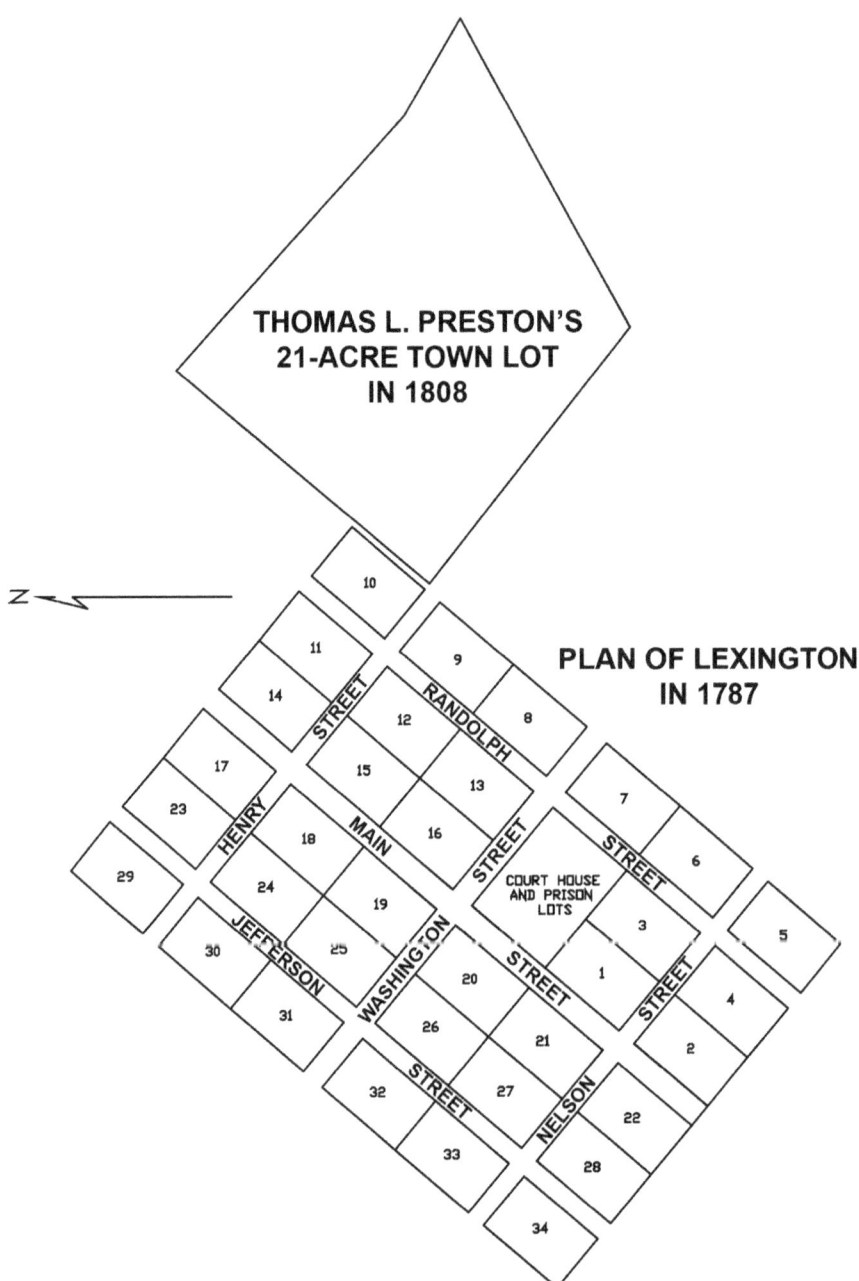

Thomas L. Preston's 21-acre town lot in 1808. This is today's Diamond Hill in northeast Lexington (courtesy Jim Green).

them a classical education at a very young age. When the family returned to Lexington in 1819, Elizabeth at eleven and John at eight had been thoroughly home schooled and were fully prepared for more structured learning. Edmonia placed John in what he would later describe as a "mixed school" of boys and girls run by Mr. Dame.

He described his teacher, Charles Tidd, as a "tall, raw boned, high cheeked Connecticut Yankee, with sandy hair and a nasal tone." Captain John Leyburn, a Lexington merchant, had found him destitute in Richmond and brought him to Lexington for a chance to try his hand at teaching for income. "He had been brought up on a farm, and had never been taught," and revealed his ignorance by speaking ungrammatically, spelling incorrectly, reading in a high-pitched monotone, and writing in a painful scrawl. But he could add and subtract. He performed his duties conscientiously and made no pretense to knowledge, which had not been prerequisite to his being hired for the task.[13]

Mr. Tidd's chief virtue was disciplinarian. He'd punish a wrongdoer by setting him "on a high table with a long switch" hanging from his nose. Or he'd place him on a bench zealously rocked by two comrades or compel him to stand in the center of the room wearing a paper cap. He was not opposed to physical persuasion. When the occasion was appropriate—and it was surprising to John how frequent that was—"he did not spare the rod, and added thereto the ferule and the leather strap." He wasn't crabbed or cruel, since he considered severe flogging "a custom not even to be honored in the breach." He practiced instead "trapping," changing places, to avoid problems. And he rewarded the head boy or girl with a silver quarter strung on a ribbon. If they earned it, at the close of the session they owned it. "Thus, one way or another, by punishing or encouraging, by hook or by crook, though he knew little himself," John concluded, "he taught us a good deal of what was to be found in Murray's *Grammar;* Walker's *Dictionary;* Webster's *Spelling Book;* Adam's *Geography,* and Pike's *Arithmetic;* to say nothing of the requirements of courtesy, inculcated by the obligatory bow on entering and leaving the classroom."[14]

What young John learned from Mr. Tidd wasn't limited to the classroom. Years later he would hunt with his teacher in the hills and fields surrounding Lexington. As a legendary sportsman, Tidd "knew little about the battle of Marathon or of Waterloo, but he did know how to shoot a shotgun" and impressed John with the first percussion gun he'd ever seen and the first pointer dog to hunt in the county. "He lived and died a bachelor, and his gun and his dog were his only household treasures, and they seemed sufficient for his simple tastes." He remained in town until his limited method of teaching was replaced by new ideas, which he couldn't master. Then he retired to the country.[15]

It was in Mr. Tidd's classroom, during John's eighth year, that fate played a significant role in assuring his future. While learning the rudiments of language and mathematics solely through discipline rather than informed teaching, he chanced to meet the ideal of his boyhood, Sarah Caruthers, known to everyone as Sally.[16] Sally's father, Colonel William Caruthers, was a respected Lexington merchant and wealthy land owner who had recently died. He owned more than 30,000 acres in Rockbridge County. Before his death, as a service to Virginia Governor Wilson Nicholas, he had located the land in western Virginia where the Lexington Arsenal would be built, the same that would later become the home of VMI. When he died, his wife Phoebe placed Sally, their sixth child, in Dame's School. Sally was tall for her eight years, but she was also notable for her bright blue eyes, abundant and waving chestnut-brown hair, and healthy, radiant complexion. Seated next to John, she quickly became, as he would later describe her, "the joy of his heart and light of his life."[17] At a very impressionable age they conversed easily and formed a bond that would last for the next eight years, each indelibly imprinted on the other's memory when they were apart.

At the end of the school year, in 1820, John's mother took him and his sister for the summer to the town of Fairfield. Lexington had no classical school, he would later remark, where he might learn "the rudiments of Latin" that Edmonia considered essential to her son's education.[18] She herself had achieved a mastery of the language under the careful tutelage of Edmund Randolph. In Fairfield, John studied under a young Irish teacher "who was master of the humanities." Apart from the basic grammar of declensions and conjugations, John was tutored in the rhythm, stress, and intonation of Latin. In the fall his mother took him and Elizabeth to live in Richmond, where Sally Caruthers receded into the back corners of his memory. Little more than a large village with gracious homes, expansive green lawns, and wide verandahs overhanging multi-flowered gardens, Richmond was the home where his mother had been reared and where the schools were among the best in the nation.

Edmonia enrolled her son in Richmond Academy. It was a classical preparatory school with whitewashed walls and large-paned windows open to the light of the sun. At the time, John recalled, "it was the one of highest repute in the metropolis." The headmaster was John Clarke, "a hot-tempered, pedantic bachelor Irishman" from Trinity College in Dublin. Unlike Mr. Tidd, he stood as a Latin scholar of the first order. He had a high opinion of what boys might become and a great tolerance of their shortcomings. Master Clarke pompously assured John's mother that her son would be taught "only the pure Latinity of the Augustan age."[19]

True to Master Clarke's word, the boy was drilled in the language until even the minutiae of its irregularities, inflections, and pronunciation were committed to perpetual memory. For the first two years John, who became known at the academy as Jack, was thoroughly grounded in the basics of reading with proper emphasis and modulation. These were practiced on selections from Addison's *Spectator*. He was drilled in English grammar, spelling, and the meaning of sentences. He learned the elements of rhetoric and how to speak properly and gracefully. He was introduced to the logic of mathematics and taught the lessons of ancient Roman and modern English history.

In 1822 he was just beginning classes in composition, penmanship, ethics, and geography when a youth of thirteen, two and a half years his senior, joined his form. The newcomer had recently returned from school in England. John was captivated by the boy's "power and accomplishments," and the attraction was promptly reciprocated. Like John, the boy had lost his father. He had also lost his mother when he was not quite two.[20] His adopted father, John Allan, a Scottish merchant, had sent him to a venerable academy in England for five years before his return to school in Richmond, where he now sat with Preston.

What impressed John most about Edgar Allan Poe, as he called himself, were "his *facile princeps*" in sports. He ran swiftly, leapt wonderfully, and boxed instinctually. He confided in John, whom he called Jack, "the secret" of his ability to withstand the blow of the strongest boy in the school, whom he allowed "to strike him with full force in the chest." He would fill his lungs to their maximum and, at the exact moment of taking the blow, exhale. It astonished onlookers and, despite some discomfort, wasn't hard to endure. Jack even tried it himself with some success. Poe was also a champion swimmer. Like Byron's swimming the Dardanelles, he dared to challenge "the rapids of the James River" in a six-mile stretch from Richmond to Warwick Bar, which no other student would venture to risk.[21]

Poe's performance in Latin exercises found only two worthy competitors: his new friend Jack Preston and the studious Nat Howard. A favorite competition in class was called "capping verses," similar to today's spelling bees. All the Latinists at the end of the school session lined up beginning with the best scholar, who quoted from memory a Latin verse to be "capped." The challenge was for anyone in the line to quote another verse in Latin beginning with the same letter. Whoever succeeded would replace him as leader, and the "capping" would continue.

This was "simple capping," but "double capping" was far more difficult. It required that the second verse both begin and end with the same letters as the first verse. For example, where both Nat Howard and Edgar Poe found themselves bested, was when Nat Howard offered for double capping a verse beginning with *d* and ending with *m*. It passed Edgar Poe and other competent scholars until it reached Jack Preston, as he admitted, "a tyro, away down the line." To the surprise of everyone including Preston, a line from Virgil popped into his head, which he cited, "*Ducite ad urbe domum, mea carmina, ducite Daphnim*"[22] (Daphnis from the town, bring Daphnis home to me). "With pride and amazement," Preston marveled, "I saw myself where I never was before and never was afterwards,—above Nat Howard and Edgar Poe."[23]

Edgar Allan Poe, 1809–49. Daguerreotype by Edwin H. Manchester, November 9, 1848 (Library of Congress, RN: LC-USZ62–104482 [b&w film copy neg.], CN Lot 4457 [P&P]).

This practice, taught by Master Clarke, filled Preston's memory, as he admitted, "with many good quotations for ready use." Poe too learned them by rote. Preston learned, almost by osmosis, the *Odes of Horace* and the lilting rhythm of the Sapphics and iambics from Poe's constant repetition of them. Two of these, he claimed, hummed in his ear all his life in the musical way Poe recited them:

Jam satis terris nivis atque dirae	Enough of snow and hail at last
Grandinis misit Pater, et rubente	The sire has sent in vengeance down

and

Non abur neque aureum	Carven ivory have I none
Mea renidet in domo lacunar	No golden cornice in my dwelling shines

Years later Preston would compose an epitaph for his boyhood friend, whose poetry he first heard from his own lips long before reading it in print. His tribute would lament his tragic end:

Ille, mordaci velut icta ferro	He, like a pine by axes sped,
Pinus, aut impulsa cupressus Euro,	Or cypress sway'd by angry gust,
Prodicit late, posuitque collum in	Fell ruining, and laid his head
Pulvere Teucro.	In Trojan dust.[24]

Preston remembered Poe also as a very fine French scholar. Poe spent as much time out of school as in it writing verses. "As we sat together," Preston recalled, "he would show them to me, and even sometimes ask my opinion, and now and then my assistance." Preston admired his talent so highly that he "requested his permission to carry his portfolio home for the inspection" of Preston's mother. The boy poet came to value her criticism as much as her praise. Unfortunately, Poe's adopted father, Mr. Allan, sought to suppress the child's trials at poetry, which he regarded as signs of idleness. When he caught Edgar engaged in such foolishness, he sternly reprimanded him for it and ordered him not to repeat it. So it was Preston's mother whom Preston would later describe as "the first critic to whom were submitted the verses of our world-famed poet."[25] Indeed, Poe's genius benefited as much from her intimate familiarity with the English classics as from her critical but appreciative acumen.

In 1823 Preston left Richmond Academy, returning with his sister and mother to Lexington. Without the encouragement and literary advice of Preston's mother, Poe now turned to the gentle and gracious mother of another schoolmate. She became the first love of his life whom he idolized as a guiding light in his literary endeavors. But he was devastated when she succumbed to a brain tumor, leaving the forsaken boy to mourn her again and again in lovelorn verse as the classic Helen, the lady Irene, and the forever-flown Lenore.

Like Preston, Poe would leave Richmond Academy when he entered "Jefferson's University" of Virginia in 1826. But drinking and gambling soon left him out of school and penniless. When his adopted father exposed his indulgences in his application to West Point in 1829 and then disowned him, it was his old friend Jack Preston who came to his defense in a letter to the secretary of war. He described Poe as a young man of genius who had established his reputation as a writer at the University of Virginia and in the publication of his first book of poems. And he concluded, "I would not write this recommendation if I did not believe he would remunerate the government at some future day by his services and talents, for whatever may be done for him."[26]

Ten years later, when Poe composed his tale of "William Wilson," his old friend Preston appears by name as Wilson's classmate. Literarily Poe sets the scene of a pivotal incident of his short story at Oxford University. But autobiographically he merely transposes Mr. Clarke's Richmond Academy to England. He portrays Wilson as a card shark whose skill at gambling targets a young nobleman and triumphs with huge monetary gains in the chambers of his classmate, "Jack Preston."[27] At the dramatic moment that Wilson is unmasked as a scam artist by his own doppelganger, it is Jack Preston who hands him his duplicate fur cloak on his departure from Oxford and his exile from Britain. This unique psychological study is celebrated because it anticipated the major theories of Sigmund Freud, the father of psychoanalysis and one of the twentieth century's most important psychologists. Poe's notion of the rivalrous double predated Freud's concept of the repressed, unconscious alter ego by at least half a century.

2

A Classical Education

If that part of his biography is omitted, it will just be too bad for Yale.
—William Couper

In 1823 Preston embarked on five years of study at Washington College, from which his father had graduated in 1800.[1] Although students at the college were generally between the ages of sixteen and twenty-one, he entered its grammar school at age twelve. There were only three professors, none trained as teachers, but two were ministers and the third a lawyer, plus one tutor. The Rev. Dr. George Baxter, called "Old Rex" by his students, had taught Preston's father and was now president of the college. He specialized in Calvinistic theology in addition to philosophy and the ancient classics. Henry Ruffner taught languages, and the Rev. Edward Graham, natural philosophy and chemistry.

The demanding curriculum was prescribed without any electives. The text for natural philosophy (physics) was Tiberius Cavallo's *Elements of Natural Philosophy*, newly published in 1808. For chemistry, Preston studied Mrs. B's *Conversations,* a fictional dialogue between two inquisitive teenagers—the thoughtful Emily and lively Caroline—and their knowledgeable mother, Mrs. Bryant. Published by Jane Marcet in 1805 and originally intended for girls, the book made chemistry eminently readable and universally popular.

Preston's progress was remarkable. During his year of grammar school he translated with facility all of the *Collectanae Graeca Minora* and was examined on the nine orations of Cicero.[2] The next year, as a college freshman at age thirteen, he earned top grades in reading the Greek works of Xenophon and the Latin works of Livy and Tacitus. He mastered Lacroix's arithmetic, Euler's algebra, two semesters of French, and Worcester's geography.

In his sophomore year he studied the fifth and sixth books of Euclid and began translating selections from the greatest Greek writers in the *Collectanae Graeca Majora*, including Herodotus, Thucydides, Xenophon, Lysias, Socrates, Demosthenes, Plato, Polyanus, and Aelian. He read Latin verse and Horace and studied plain and spherical trigonometry and surveying. His junior year at age sixteen entailed translating Aristotle, Longinus, Homer, Hesiod, Apollonius, and Sophocles from the *Graeca Majora*. Included was science with courses in physics (Cavallo's *Natural Philosophy*), astronomy, and the general principles of chemistry.

His senior term would culminate with Blair's lectures and Campbell's philosophy of rhetoric, Hedge's logic, and Jean-Jacques Burlamaqui's theories of natural and civil law. Throughout his five years the primary focus of his classical education heavily favored language over science, namely foreign languages, criticism, rhetoric, and ora-

The colonnade at Washington College. Photograph in 1867 by Michael Miley (Washington and Lee University, Leyburn Library Special Collections, 024 Tucker Family, Johnston Scrapbook).

Daniel Blain house on Washington Street. Photograph by James W. McClung for Virginia Historical Inventory. Built by the Rev. Blain in 1900, the house is now known as the Estill House in Davidson Park (Washington and Lee University, Leyburn Library Special Collections, RG41, WPA).

tory. On reaching seventeen in the spring of 1828, he would receive his bachelor of arts degree, three years before the customary age of graduation.[3]

Preston's mother could not have known how much her son would benefit from attending Washington College. His return to Lexington in 1823 to finish grammar school was not what she had originally preferred. She knew that Richmond offered far wider opportunities than the secluded mountain town of Lexington could afford. But General John Preston, who became her benefactor after her husband's death, had resigned as treasurer of Virginia when his accounts were found to be in arrears. A judgment against him of $87,000 had thrown him into severe debt. So he could no longer afford to support Edmonia and her children in Richmond. Instead, he offered to pay her board in cheaper quarters somewhere else. So in 1823 she arranged to board in Lexington with Mary "Polly" Hanna Blain, the widow of the Rev. Daniel Blain, professor of languages and mathematics. He had taught at Washington Academy since its inception in 1798, including the years when her husband had studied there.[4]

Polly Blain lived with her five daughters and a son but took in boarders for income. As the intellectual widow of a minister and professor, she nonetheless displayed practical judgment if not innately then by necessity. She had learned to spin and weave, feed and milk the cows, cook, and wash in addition to rearing children. Up before dawn, she knew no rest during the day, and she finished late at night. In addition, she taught her children the value of cooperation as they, along with a few servants, helped her manage the household. Polly was somewhat older than Edmonia. Although they had grown up worlds apart in origin and opportunity, they shared the bonds of widowhood and children, becoming steadfast friends for the lasting benefit of their offspring.

Two years would pass in this cheerful household of two adults and eight children before another boarder arrived, herself a member of a large family of eight orphans. For John, it was the return of Sally Lyle Caruthers, who was six when she had lost her father, eight when she met John at Dame's School in Lexington, and ten when her mother died in 1821 of tuberculosis. She had lived as an orphan for two years with her mother's sister, the charming Aunt Elizabeth Alexander McClung, and her husband, Henry, a Rockbridge captain of artillery during the War of 1812. For two more years she had boarded with Henry Ruffner, professor of ancient languages at Washington College, and his wife Sally Lyle, a gifted and cultivated lady of commanding appearance, who radiated conversational persuasiveness, warm sympathies, and cordial manners. It was after her that Sally had been named.[5] She had also spent several winters with her Uncle Archibald (pronounced at that time "Ursuble") Alexander, professor and founder of Princeton Theological Seminary, whose influence on her intellectual and religious life had been extraordinary.

Now in 1825, Sally's unmarried older brother John Caruthers was administrator of the $70,000 fortune that his father William had left from his mercantile trade for the care and education of his fatherless children. John placed Sally in Mrs. Blain's Boarding House for the "piety and culture of the two older women living there."[6] Since the Blain and Caruthers families had been close friends from the time the Reverend taught at Washington College, Polly felt a strong desire to care for the orphaned girl. Sally was now fourteen, still large for her age, with "a remarkable good figure, erect, with good shoulders," and "a certain air of distinction," for she usually "dressed in white."[7] Her Uncle Alexander had noted in a letter to his sister, Margaret Graham, the sterling qualities of his favorite niece.[8] Her radiant beauty reawakened in Preston the indelible impression she had made on him that first year at Dame's School.

When Preston wasn't translating Horace or Herodotus, he was escorting Sally to parties and balls. With his friends he sported in wrestling, running, jumping, ball playing, and especially hunting. He took part in shooting matches for beef and turkeys in the country and in town. He pursued foxes behind a choir of Mr. Tidd's hounds, their baying echoing in the Bushy Hills and against the cliffs of the North River. And he flushed whirring coveys of partridges with his friends Jacob Ruff and John Haugawout, both future mayors of Lexington. He and Sally joined crowds in town attending celebrations of the 4th of July and the 22 of February, weddings, and wakes. His adolescence was spent, he admitted, with "much noise, fuss, fighting and rampaging generally. It was a rare frolic for boys, a scary time for mothers, and a busy day for magistrates and constables."[9]

In 1828, when he was seventeen, Preston entered the University of Virginia in only its fifth session to study modern languages and philosophy.[10] For a year he pursued his studies assiduously, but nagging at the back of his mind was an acute awareness that what a classical education lacked was practicality. During his junior year at Washington College he had studied natural philosophy, astronomy, and chemistry. But he'd felt a single semester of practical science woefully insufficient. So in 1829 he traveled to Yale College, where he spent a year as a "resident graduate" auditing science courses under Benjamin Silliman.[11]

A lawyer by training, Silliman had been appointed professor of chemistry and natural history in 1802. He soon became the country's leading pioneer in the teaching of modern chemistry, geology, mineralogy, and botany. His mineral and rock collection was the nucleus of Yale's museum. It would later become the first Peabody Museum, which houses today over twelve million specimens and objects. He published the first documented fall of a meteorite in America, which occurred in 1807 near New Haven and became the first exhibit in the Yale collection of meteorites. He also founded the oldest continuing journal of natural science in the U.S.: *The American Journal of Science.*

Preston was drawn to Silliman for his excellence as a teacher but also for his solid, up-to-date knowledge of the natural sciences. As one of America's first professors of science, Silliman had been innovative in establishing laboratory and field programs at Yale. In addition to sitting in on Professor Silliman's courses, Preston studied law on the side. He departed at the end of one year without a diploma but with an improved legal grounding.

Preston's attendance at Yale has been questioned by skeptics who claimed they searched in vain for any record of his having studied there. In 1936 VMI's historiographer, Colonel William Couper, received an enquiry from George Derby, managing editor of the *National Cyclopedia of American Biography,* claiming that he couldn't verify Preston's matriculation either at the University of Virginia or at Yale. Derby threatened to delete these statements from Preston's biography if Couper couldn't substantiate them. Couper obligingly documented Preston's attendance at the University of Virginia but regretted he lacked the time to research his Yale connection. He then responded, "If that part of his biography is omitted, it will just be too bad for Yale."[12] When the *Cyclopedia* finally appeared, Preston's biography included the Yale entry and has since been verified.[13]

In 1830 Preston took the customary grand tour of Europe.[14] If he kept a journal of his first trip to the Old World, as he would for his second in 1851 and third in 1884, it hasn't survived. Indeed, the little that is known of his grand tour comes from an incident he remembered in his second journal about the practical value of a dead language. At one point he found himself stranded on a platform in a Prussian train station during a transportation breakdown. Surrounded by Slovaks and Hungarians speaking in incomprehensible tongues, he felt stymied in trying to get directions to continue his trip. He tried communicating in English and French and with the little German he'd learned, but all to no avail. At last, jumping up onto a truck, he cried out in the only other language he knew, "*Adestne aliquis qui loqui aut intellegere Latine potest?*" (Can anyone here speak or understand Latin?) To his amazement, a man nodded and was able to help him locate the connection he needed.[15]

On his return to Lexington from his grand tour, Preston immediately set the stage for his future by purchasing a large house on the hill overlooking VMI. Located east of Randolph Street, it would be known later as Blandome.[16] He had not intended to take on such a large expense and would not occupy the house for the next two years. But he made the purchase in three installments to save Sally's older brother William from financial ruin.

William Caruthers, after graduating from medical school in 1823, had married the wealthy heiress and belle Louisa Catherine Gibson of Savannah and laid claim to her considerable estate, in addition to his own inheritance from his father. This allowed him to purchase six acres on a hillside just outside the limits of Lexington from the Rev. Andrew Davidson for $4,500. This land, which Davidson had bought the previous year from John A. Cumings, a Caruthers family friend, included a home that Cumings had built in 1820–21. It bordered the twenty-one-acre town lot that Preston and his sister Elizabeth had inherited from their father.

William set about making "great improvements" to the old home. He added a circular three-story piazza with white pillars and surrounding gardens, about which his Aunt Margaret remarked, "He is making it a very pretty place."[17] In time he would acquire a library of 150 volumes, a significant collection for the times, to which he added parlor chairs done in green and finished in gilt, dining tables and a sideboard of mahogany, and an expensive phaeton or barouche carriage. Between 1824 and 1829 this elegant Federal-Greek Revival home was the scene of gay and happy parties graced with typical Virginian hospitality.

But by late 1829, William was earning little income from his medical practice for which he had no heart. He received even less income from his aspirations to write historical romances, and he had a penchant for extensive travel. Not only had he overdrawn his and his wife's inheritance, but he had also amassed considerable debts. His stylish home was scheduled to be sold at auction on July 1, 1830, to retire his obligations.

Preston bought William's house and lot in three installments for $4,000 to allow William to satisfy his debts. For another $150 he also bought two back lots with a stone spring house and a small brick tenement adjoining his own and his sister's acreage. When William left Lexington in early 1832 to repair his fortune in New York, Preston decided to occupy the mansion with his sister and mother.[18] It was a plan that Edmonia strongly opposed because she had been urging her son not to settle in Lexington. She wrote her sister-in-law Susan Preston McDowell in January 1832 that John and Elizabeth "have determined that we shall go to house-keeping, as soon as Dr. Caruthers's house is vacant—a poor plan, in my opinion. They may say what they please about 'lasses' and a certain august personage [herself] driving people as they will, but I think children can drive pretty well too."[19] Despite her reservations, Preston had made up his mind, so he and his sister moved in along with their mother.

As it turned out for a physician and writer, William was wise to seek a more cosmopolitan environment for his medical practice with ready access to publishers in New

J.T.L. Preston's first home, 1832–44. This is today's Blandome at 101 Tucker Street, built by John A. Cumings in 1820–21 and greatly enlarged by William A. Caruthers ca. 1823 (Washington and Lee University, Leyburn Library Special Collections, Rockbridge Historical Society Photograph, 294 Walker-Wood Family).

York. Between 1834 and 1841 he produced three very successful romances celebrating Virginian history. Indeed, in 1840, while Preston was away from Lexington checking on property, Sally wrote to express her excitement about a future book her brother would be publishing, called *The Knights of the Golden Horseshoe*.[20] In fact, it was destined to become one of the most notable Southern romances of the first half of the nineteenth century. It stood as the crowning achievement of a trilogy of novels that began with *The Kentuckian in New York* (1834) and *The Cavaliers of Virginia* (1835). And it established him as the earliest significant novelist of Virginia.

Although the custom of the times was for young couples in Virginia to keep their engagements secret, John and Sally's betrothal was generally known and approved by both the Preston and the Caruthers families. Two months before their marriage John had traveled to look after his and his sister's Kentucky estate, which Jefferson had awarded their grandfather and they now owned by inheritance.[21] Sally admitted in one of her letters, "I have made no announcement of our wedding plans, but doubtless they know something of them. I am in no sense leaving my people behind in entering the new life, but I stand on the threshold of womanhood, and look tenderly back on the kindly faces which have smiled upon me, all my life, as I walk forward into the happy fulfillment of girlhood's dreams. Come back quickly, my dearest, that we may set up the home we long for, hallowed by love human and Divine. Your Sally."[22]

August 2, 1832, would become what Preston considered one of the two happiest days of his life. At age twenty-one he married his childhood sweetheart, Sarah "Sally" Lyle Caruthers, in the home of her brother John. Church weddings were not common in Lexington at this period. Since family life centered in the home, great events, such as birth, marriage, and death, found their settings within the family. The date so joyously fixed itself in his mind that twenty-five years hence it would threaten to dissolve the second great day of his life. But for now, it was the day, as Preston described, that "an angel gave me her hand when hardly more than a boy. I stepped forth into the world."[23] Unlike Sally's brother William, John had managed the Caruthers fortune so well that he would turn over $10,000 to Preston upon his marriage to Sally.[24] It facilitated her move into her brother William's former home with Preston, his mother, and his sister. The home was large enough to house all four comfortably.

For John, Sally was Aphrodite, the morning star of his life. He bestowed on her the reverence that only a goddess could inspire. She was for him, "one of the loveliest women in the world."[25] So blindly smitten was he that he never noticed the silent suitor who stepped aside and, slipping into the shadows, departed Lexington after Sally's wedding day. But on that day and every day for the next twenty-three and a half years, his all-embracing focus would rest exclusively on this noble woman of devoted affection and infinite tact. She would mother eight of his children while serving as "his best counsellor, as well as his best friend."[26] From the perspective of compatibility, Sally was the ideal mate for Preston. Both stemmed from Scottish ancestry that had settled the wilderness between the Blue Ridge and the Alleghenies, built churches, established schools, reared God-fearing families as diligently as they were economical, and based their religious beliefs on the Bible and the Shorter Catechism.

Sally had been spared the austerity of Calvinism by the winters she spent with her Princetonian uncle, Dr. Archibald Alexander. His intuitive simplicity, directness, and knowledge of the human heart had imbued his strong beliefs with a sweetness that washed over her like the rays of the warm sun. It was reflected in her cordial manner, never despondent, always content and cheerful. Dr. Henry Ruffner, who had helped raise her as a child, once described her as "a perennial fountain of happiness to others."[27] One unnamed gentleman is recorded to have said, "She was the only woman he had ever known who could talk incessantly without ever a word that was not worth hearing."[28]

Preston's frequent departures from Lexington to check on his Kentucky properties would prove difficult for Sally. For the first two years of their marriage he remained at home. But his absences, when they occurred, were not brief. During their first separation as a couple in October 1834, her letter expressed the misery of a woman desperately in love. She began,

> I feel so wretched that I must relieve myself by writing to you. I cannot express the lonely, miserable, forlorn creature I feel myself to be. I want to scream when I see other people's husbands at home, and just want to put my bundle on my back and follow you. I am resolved that no earthly power shall again separate me from you. Yesterday for about half of the day I sat thinking of you, dying and being buried out of my sight—of my going out and having you disinterred, and your portrait painted—but why try to express such misery as mine? ... I am a burden to myself and all around me.... I sleep none at night, I mope all day—indeed I feel sometimes as if my reason would fail me. But you will say "How selfish of Sally to fill her letters with complaints and repinings—she ought to be trying to comfort me." I wish I could, but I have forgotten the meaning of the word![29]

Outwardly Sally could be a model of calm propriety. But inwardly she suffered the extravagant emotions and inconsolable anxiety of vulnerable love. Fully aware that travel in those times was fraught with danger, she found relief only in his reassuring replies. On one of his trips to property in Ohio, she wrote, "What a joy, my dearest, to have a letter from you in Cincinnati, arriving in *eight days!* It soothes my lonely heart to feel in such close contact with you, for I am fortunate if a letter reaches me in a fortnight. It alarms me to hear in how much danger you have been—and I hope you will not venture on those horrid Western boats again—they are almost certain death, and I was almost afraid to open your letter, lest it tell of some dreadful explosion or accident."[30]

Among the real dangers she feared, with good reason, was the dread of disease. Hearing of the death of two Lexingtonians from a fever that had spread to the South and West, she feared for John in the North. "My love, I charge you in the name of God we worship, if this fever is in Kentucky, to bend your steps homeward as fast as possible." She begged, "Do inquire before you go further, as to the health of the towns lying ahead of you."[31] Travel at the time exposed travelers to "brain fever," scarlet fever, tuberculosis, and many mysterious diseases that yet had no name so that Sally was forever and perhaps legitimately concerned about the welfare and return of her lifelong companion. Indeed, on one visit in Missouri, John contracted malaria and suffered from severe chills and fever. But typical of her husband, when the fever raged, "he would get in a tub of cold water." Mrs. John Moore remembered, "The old ladies thought that it would kill him; for at that time all fever patients were kept as warm as possible, not even allowed a drink of cold water."[32] But no ill effects were recorded.

The Lexington Arsenal, December 1, 1849. Drawing by Seth Eastman. This scene, probably drawn from Superintendent Francis H. Smith's front porch, shows the west side of the original 1816 arsenal in front of Barracks and Major William Gilham's residence on the right. The cupola crowned the center barracks building (Virginia Military Institute Archives, No. 0003147).

When Preston wasn't traveling afar, he was practicing law. This challenged his intellect and gave him the satisfaction of recognized success, but his heart wasn't in his work. He relieved his mind regularly by attending the debates of the Franklin Society, where he met the most enlightened citizens of Lexington. Every Saturday night these intellectuals passionately tackled the most significant local, national, and international issues, both secular and religious, that loomed on the horizons of their lives. The debates, which included lectures, were being held in John Ruff's hatter's shop and were announced to the town by the blowing of a horn.

Whether Preston knew it or not, he was following in the footsteps of his father, who had co-founded the society three decades earlier.[33] Its stated mission was to provide a place where "people met, discussed the designs of their enemies, contrived the means of defeating them, encouraged each other in the good fight for liberty, directed and concentrated public opinion so as to make it more effectual."[34] Indeed, its motto was, "We snatched the lightning from the heavens and the scepter from the tyrants."[35] On being admitted as a shareholding member in late 1832 and elected secretary in early 1833, Preston threw himself wholeheartedly into the preparation and delivery of personal views on vital current issues.

In December 1834, a hotly contested debate erupted at the society over the proper use and mission of the detested arsenal that dominated Lexington's skyline. It flooded the community with the unsavory behavior of its idle and self-indulgent soldiery. Preston found himself engaged in a personal crusade that would dominate the rest of his life and redefine his future as much as that of the town, the state, and the nation. What began as a passionate intellectual exchange of ideas would end with the establishment of the Virginia Military Institute, the first state-supported military school in the United States.

Part II:
Father of the Dream

The healthful and pleasant abode of a crowd of honorable youths....
—J.T.L. Preston

3

The Cives Letters

Genius knows no fixed locality, and is as often born under a cottage roof as the dome of a palace; and there are hundreds of young men whose minds thirst for an education which they have not the means of obtaining.
—J.T.L. Preston

In 1816, the year that Preston's uncle, James Patton Preston, became governor of Virginia, an arsenal was erected in the small town of Lexington. It was one of three such structures built by the state that would house 30,000 arms and munitions accumulated from America's recently concluded War of 1812. Authorized by the legislature and James Preston's predecessor, Governor Wilson C. Nicholas, it was constructed within a year on a high bluff overlooking the valley of the North branch of the James River.

The superintendent of the state arms factory in Richmond, Major John Staples, designed it as a three-story box-like structure of 200,000 handmade bricks surrounded by a 90,000-brick wall ten feet high and one foot thick. It was surrounded by five acres to protect houses in the neighborhood from the risk of fire and accessed by a road across three more acres to the crest of a hill. Aesthetically it stood like a red clay fortress dominating any view of the town. Oren Morton, in his *History of Rockbridge County*, characterized it as an unattractive structure that neither the town nor the county wanted. He described it as "a substantial brick building, four stories high, from which every architectural beauty was scrupulously excluded."[1] Superintendent Francis Smith would later recall, the windows of the first story of the barracks were guarded by stout iron bars, giving the whole complex "the appearance of a prison, and such it was to the old soldiers."[2]

The arsenal began operation on January 27, 1818, with a detachment of twenty-four enlisted militiamen headed by Captain James Paxton of Lexington, himself a noted leader and scholar. But it soon degenerated into a nuisance and a burden for the thrifty people of the community. Faced with tedious and boring work and tri-monthly musters, its guards suffered from idleness and squandered their wages on drink and revelry in town. "The soldiers," as Cadet Boyd would later describe them, "having nothing else to do beyond a little guard duty, fell into bad habits, committed petty depredations and became drunken and worthless."[3] Several years of frequent confrontations with townspeople and among themselves eventually resulted in deadly violence when in 1826 a quarrel sparked a fight between two soldiers at the arsenal. Daniel Mills struck John Moseley "with a rock and afterwards kicked and stamped him" to death.[4]

Soon after the brutal affair, Lexington's own Captain David E. Moore replaced Captain Paxton. But by the mid–1830s dissatisfaction with the arsenal and its guardsmen had evolved all the more into full-blown opposition. What to do with the arsenal and how to control the behavior of its "inmates" became a critical problem for the Franklin Society to address. On December 5, 1834, Hugh Barclay and attorney James D. Davidson proposed a topic for debate the following week: "Would it be politic for the state to establish a military school, at the arsenal, near Lexington, in connection with Washington College, on the plan of the West Point Academy?"[5]

Mr. Barclay, a Lexington merchant, was particularly interested in proposing the topic because he had recently visited West Point, then in the third decade of its formative years. He was enthralled by "the splendid drills and training" of its cadets. On his return to Lexington he told his business associates and friends at the Franklin Society with great enthusiasm what he had witnessed. He envisioned solving the problem of the objectionable arsenal by turning it "into a military school patterned after West Point."[6] On December 12, Captain Moore, now the arsenal's superintendent, and James Davidson, co-proposer of the topic, debated the issue. We aren't told who took which side, but the members of the society voted "unanimously in the negative." They were not persuaded to replace the arsenal, as objectionable as it might be, with another West Point.

The Franklin Society, 1800–1915. Photograph by Michael Miley. A group of leading intellectual citizens of Lexington met weekly at the building on the corner of Jefferson and Nelson streets to debate pressing local, state, national, and international issues of the times (Washington and Lee University, Leyburn Library Special Collections, Harper and Agnor Miley Store).

However, neither were they content to let the matter rest. On December 20, James Rockwood and Matthew Kahle proposed a second debate—"Would it be politic for the state to establish a military school at the arsenal near Lexington in connection with Washington College?"—where the phrase "on the plan of the West Point Academy" was intentionally deleted. Two days after Christmas four members of the Society—J.T.L. Preston, who had been absent from the first debate while purchasing land in Indiana, James D. Davidson, Hugh Barclay, and William C. Lewis—squared off. The vote on the second question, unlike the vote on the first, was decided unanimously in the affirmative. Preston would later remark, "So earnest was the sentiment, that before the members left the Hall, it was agreed to give the matter a practical shape."[7]

The mission of giving the matter a practical shape fell naturally to Preston. As spokesman for the affirmative in the second debate, he had publicly demonstrated his grasp of the issues involved. And his thorough training in rhetoric and oratory had prepared him even at the young age of twenty-three to propose on paper what he had successfully defended in the public forum. It's for this reason that he would soon be known as "Lexington's Demosthenes."[8] Like his prototype, he employed similar techniques of eloquent persuasion. His contemporary model was John Peyton, his cousin and administrator of his father's estate, whom he admired for his excellence in oratory as the complete lawyer. A lawyer himself, Preston derived his power of rhetoric from what he described in Peyton as "energy, reality, and efficiency." What he most esteemed in Peyton, he practiced in his own ability "to comprehend the subject as a whole, and shed its light upon each detail belonging to it." And like Peyton, "He spoke as a lawyer, he spoke for the verdict, and expected to gain it by showing that he was entitled to it."[9]

Preston knew from his own experience, as much as from Peyton's example, that to gain the desired verdict, he "must mould, and sway, and lead, and this to be effected by continued, persistent pressure, rather than by *tours de force*." He must determine in his own mind "not only the order of the different parts of his discourse, but also their relative importance in producing the general impression." His audience, like Peyton's juries, inevitably "came away satisfied with the whole, rather than treasuring up memorable points and passages."[10] Rarely, if ever, did Preston lapse into colloquialism—or if he did and if anyone challenged him, he would reply serenely, "I use an elegant laxity when I find it more nearly suited to my meaning."[11]

With these rhetorical talents at his disposal, the task Preston now set before himself was to persuade the general public to support the type of comprehensive school that he envisioned should replace the detested arsenal. He labored for eight long months to compose three letters, the first of which appeared in the *Lexington Gazette* at the end of August 1835. From exordium to peroration, with every trope and figure at his disposal, he structured his argument as he would a formal oration to gain his readers' unanimous endorsement.

Like Demosthenes, however, he was convinced that "all speech is vain and empty unless it be accompanied by action." So he published his letters, pseudonymously under the nom de plume Cives (the Latin plural of *civis*), meaning "citizens."[12] Directing his appeal to the general public of Lexington, he set out to represent in one voice all the members of the Franklin Society collectively, not under his own name, but under the editorial "we" and "our." The letters appeared on August 28, September 4, and September 11 requesting public consideration of a proposal the Franklin Society wished to present to the Virginia Legislature for their enactment.

The First Letter of August 28, 1835

In the first letter Preston cast the proposal as a clear topic for debate: "Whether it be practicable, so to organize the Lexington Arsenal, that it shall preserve its present character and uses as a military establishment, and be at the same time a Literary Institution for the education of youths."[13] It's intriguing to follow how the young orator marshaled his case. Approaching the subject directly in a natural and tranquil style, he began his exordium without show of emotion by setting the stage for a balanced discussion. He proposed that the Lexington Arsenal retain its uses "as a military establishment, and be at the same time a Literary Institution for the education of youth." He sought to gain the good will and attention of "those who may think differently from us" by promising that the society would relinquish its opinions, "if we can be convinced that they are erroneous." He avowed that "no political, nor party, nor personal feeling has induced this discussion," so the proposal would not lose any of its force "from the suspicion that it proceeds from interested motives." Instead, he pledged to show how the proposal would be "beneficial at once to the state, to this community, and to the cause of education" in the nation.

It would later prove noteworthy that in his personal role as formulator of the plan under the editorial "we" in the Cives letters, he played down any personal claim of originality for the idea: "This project of a literary institution, instead of one of a purely military character, is not new, nor are we by any means, the first to suggest it; and we are glad that we are not; for we willingly forego the merit of originality, to escape the objections and difficulties which must be met by those who assume to be wiser than their fathers." With disarming modesty, he admitted that some of the most intelligent citizens of Lexington had favored such a plan since the arsenal was first erected.

The Plan

His exordium complete, Preston proceeded immediately to the plan, which he characterized as one plan among many that had been only partially considered in the past. He offered it "not as that which ought to be adopted," but as the beginning of a full discussion of "the practicality of the scheme in general." Knowing that first impressions are lasting, he stated the plan succinctly and simply at the outset. The proposal was to replace the current guard of the arsenal by a body of "young men from sixteen to twenty-four years of age, engaged for four years," who would perform the same duties without pay in exchange for "the opportunities of a liberal education."

Their education would be guided by a faculty of three instructors: a teacher of the classics, a professor of the sciences, and a captain to carry out the present duties as an officer. The four-year structure would begin with first-year cadets engaged mainly in military exercises. Second-year cadets would supervise them as members of the guard. Third-year cadets "would be more devoted to study." And fourth-year cadets would be "released from military duty" as far as possible to attend lectures at Washington College.

For course study, the first year would focus on English and Latin, or its substitute. The second year would continue Latin but add mathematics. The third year, continuing mathematics, would introduce physics, then known as natural philosophy. And the final year would supplement natural philosophy with chemistry and military science. Preston cautioned that such a program "does not comprise the drill of a complete education." But it would be "sufficiently liberal" to prepare a young man to pursue his own interests unassisted, or to begin "the study of any of the learned professions," such as law, medicine, education, or the ministry.

The institution would be under military discipline, which would not only fulfill its obligations to the state but also produce diligent, consistent, and healthy young men. The youths would be selected from senatorial districts, each senator having "the privilege of nominating a candidate," whom the faculty would be permitted to accept or reject upon personal interview. And the institution itself would be evaluated annually by a board of examination that would report to the governor.

Preston concluded his first letter by offering the society's plan, subject to better ones if one could be suggested, whether specifically or in general. He hastened to add that the scheme was not a charitable or religious plan to benefit the poor at the expense of the state. It was rather a reorganization of the arsenal so that "young men may be enabled to earn an education there." He remarked that the current guardsmen gave their services for money, but the new guard would be "willing to receive their wages in *an education.*" This being the first of three letters to the citizens of Lexington, Preston promised two more on the topic: one showing the advantages of the proposed change, the other answering potential objections of those who might oppose it.

The Second Letter of September 4, 1835

Having defined the literary institution in his first letter, Preston proposed in his second to show the many benefits "which, in our opinion, would result from the change proposed."[14] It would benefit first the state of Virginia, then the community of Lexington, and finally the young men who would attend. But before addressing the benefits of the plan, he hastened to cover "any objections which may be urged against it" as being exaggerated or too ambitious. The Franklin Society, he declared, had proposed the sensible and practical goal of graduating as few as "eight or ten young men" a year—no more—"with highly respectable attainments in literature and science" and a thorough acquaintance with "the military art" and "the principles of the science of war."

Advantages to the State

This unpretentious goal of graduating "eight or ten young men," Preston affirmed, would satisfy the state's minimum requirement on which the arsenal was founded— that it "secure preservation of the arms deposited there." It would also expand and improve on this requirement by providing a source of qualified officers to guarantee the arsenal's efficiency. He admitted that the "inefficiency of militia organizations" had long been the complaint of state legislatures, including Virginia's. This had led Virginia to reduce its annual inspections from four to two, since arsenals were viewed at the time as little more than numbers for tabulating the country's military strength.

This waning faith in militia organizations had evolved from infrequent military training exercises but also "the want of suitable officers" to direct them. The current state of the military, Preston summarized, was comprised of captains lacking the skill to lead their companies effectively. Even their superiors knew little of "the science of tactics." The problem would be remedied, he proposed, by the institute's "annual supply of young men" fully qualified for subordinate commands, some of whom might advance to distinguished military careers.

Of course, not all "would be desirous of a command in the militia." But if actual service were required, "all would be put into requisition" to defend their respective counties or the state effectively. This was Preston's first allusion, although not by name, to the citizen-soldier, who could choose to accept active service upon graduation or remain inactive until needed, like minutemen, in times of crisis or war. While making restored faith in an improved militia an advantage to the state, Preston had introduced a vital distinction between the proposed literary institution and just another West Point.

Besides these two advantages to the state of Virginia—the creation of a more secure storeroom for arms and a ready source of qualified military officers—Preston suggested a third benefit: the expansion of public education. Much of the state's budget, he argued, was spent on educating "her future voters and her future statesmen, in primary schools, and at the University." Few of them, he added, would convincingly dispute the truth that "in the intelligence and virtue of the people, is the hope of Liberty."

He gave prime examples of what education could contribute individually to "developing the wealth of a country, or adding by inventions, to its capabilities." He cited Richard Arkwright, creator of the factory system of mass production in the U.S.; Robert Fulton, inventor of the steamboat and the first practical submarine; and DeWitt Clinton, father of the Erie Canal, which had connected the Atlantic Ocean with the Great Lakes. "One such mind rescued from the thrall of ignorance," Preston intoned, "would richly repay the State for all the money ever expended for Public Education."

Advantages to the Community

Apart from these significant benefits, Preston pointed out for his local readers what giving up the arsenal would mean for the people of Lexington and its surroundings. He diplomatically exonerated "the gentleman at the head of that establishment," his Franklin Society associate Captain David Moore. He contended Moore was "not responsible for the moral character of the inmates" since he could only supervise duties performed on site. But reflecting the prevailing opinion of his fellow Lexingtonians, Preston cited the arsenal's soldiers as "the most unpleasant part of our population."

While acknowledging a few exceptions, he vividly characterized them collectively as "men of idle, dissipated dispositions, to whom the easy duties, and licentious morals of a barracks, offer greater charms than the laborious, regular life of the artisan or farmer." He blamed their idleness for encouraging vice and their wages for facilitating it. They saved "nothing of their earnings" and "squandered their allowance in advance" so that in the end they departed the arsenal as paupers, as penniless as when they arrived. Preston harshly concluded that in the community's view, they merited no sympathy: "In short, as a body, they are respected by none, considered obnoxious by some, and disliked by all."

Against this specter of a hopeless situation and in an emotional appeal to his readers' higher instincts, Preston painted an inspired vision of a promising future. He pictured "a corps of young men, guided by virtuous principles, ennobled by the ardor of patriotism, and cheered by the proud consciousness that they were, by their own exertions, preparing themselves for the highest posts under their own free government, of which they should be capable." He envisioned these corpsmen, unlike the guardsmen, intermingling with the citizens of Lexington "upon the equality of gentlemen, ready to aid on every enterprise of patriotism or philanthropy." In the end they would graduate, sad to go and sadly missed by a community "whose confidence and regard they had secured, and whose sympathies and best wishes would continue to follow them in after life."

Without doubt, he concluded, "the substitution of such a corps" would be genuinely appreciated by a community like Lexington, which had suffered for nearly two decades under the flagrant abuses of the present guard. But any community, he summarized by appealing to all factions of the town, would definitely benefit from having a literary institution in its midst, such as Washington College, from which the town derived much of its character "for intelligence and virtue." He held up Washington College as the unblemished example of what could be realistically expected in a town such as Lexington. But he further averred that the town's female seminary, Ann Smith Academy, with its recent increase in student body, might also achieve its former literary eminence. The town as a whole, with such support of higher learning, would then qualify as "the Athens or Boston of Western Virginia."

Advantages to the Cadets

In stark contrast to this heightened portrayal of what the community stood to gain in the future, Preston abruptly lowered his sights to the deplorable state of education in contemporary Virginia and the nation. He argued that what the institute stood to offer its cadets was rooted in the melancholy state of the world, the energy of which was "crippled up by poverty" and its power "wasted in obscurity." Ostensibly drawing from Gray's inspired *Elegy*, he lamented how many a fine-spirited individual struggled in vain, "like a generous steed degraded to the service of a hack," to rise above his inferior station in life.[15] Some few individuals "have, after severe struggles, forced their way up through opposing difficulties, and gained for themselves noble names in the world's history, but for everyone who has succeeded, what unnumbered and unnamed multitudes have sunk heartbroken under the effort."

He wrote, "Genius knows no fixed locality, and is as often born under a cottage roof as the dome of a palace; and there are hundreds of young men whose minds thirst for an education which they have not the means of obtaining." He admitted that governments and charitable societies, including individuals, were more "engaged in assisting the deserving." But even their increased help couldn't begin to accommodate the vast demand. Government favors were "a matter of patronage, falling too often upon those who do not stand in need of them." Colleges were obliged to charge tuition, and many who ought to attend couldn't afford to pay for boarding. A prerequisite to receiving any help from most societies was religious qualifications. And aid from individuals was considered "a mere charity, which all do not like to receive."

The alternative to these inequities in the system, Preston contended, was the establishment of an institution "where, though opportunities are offered, no gratuity is conferred, but an education is given a compensation of valuable services rendered." This was Preston's first suggestion that VMI could serve as a normal school, where young men who are assisted "are willing to help themselves." A further benefit, with the addition of military discipline, would be the development of "good habits and the exercise to health."

Preston launched his broader appeal to many a parent who would surely be "anxious about the morals or the constitution of his son." He suggested that a parent might prefer sending his son to a literary institution such as this rather than exposing him to the "collegiate institutions of the country." If such an institution were established, it shouldn't surprise anyone "to see students there upon their own expense" in addition to the guard supported by the state, which in the end would benefit all three: the individual, the community, and the state.

The Third Letter of September 11, 1835

As promised in his first letter to the *Gazette,* Preston addressed, in his third and final letter, "some points upon which objections might be raised" against converting the arsenal into a literary institution.[16] By anticipating potential arguments against the plan before they were even voiced, he sought to preempt the necessity of refuting them.

The Need for Approval by the State

The first objection he anticipated from a purely practical perspective. Would the state be agreeable to such a conversion? He acknowledged that the physical strength of the current guard might exceed that of most students. So admission to the institution "might be granted only to those more than sixteen or even eighteen years of age" and of sufficient muscular strength to meet a required standard. On the other hand, he pointed out, the intent of the state in establishing the arsenal was that it be "a mere magazine, or depository of arms, and the Guard only sentinels over it." It was not meant to be "a fort commanding some important position, and manned with a garrison for its occupation and defence." The legislative act that created the depository made it "a proper receptacle for the public arms" from which "they could be distributed to the militia when the occasion should demand."

Preston declared he couldn't imagine "any invading army" willing to penetrate so far into the mountainous region of western Virginia "where the fruits of victory would be so few." Moreover, such an army must soon discover itself wholly vulnerable to "attack from the inhabitants, who might make harassing irruptions, and then retreat amid impregnable fastnesses." And what would an enemy want with our arsenal other than "possession of the arms there?" Long before he could possibly march from his landing on the coast "thus far into the interior," all the arms in the arsenal would have been "distributed among the inhabitants of the State for its defence."

Even if it were attacked, Preston insisted, the thirty guardsmen, "whether men or boys," would be woefully inadequate "to oppose any force that might be sent against it." And their being physically strong would prove less important in this instance than if they were morally qualified to safeguard their public responsibility. In summary, "We would not hesitate to prefer to the present illiterate band, a corps composed of virtuous, educated, honorable young men, in whom would be found, that incorruptible integrity, and that spirit of patriotism more valuable than the size and strength of grenadiers."

The Need for Qualified Students

Preston anticipated a second objection to the arsenal's conversion. From where might young men be recruited? He held no doubts that a larger number of young men desirous of what the institution had to offer would seek admission than could be accepted. He was also certain that each of the thirty-two senatorial districts would want to submit "at least one young man anxious to receive an education, and willing by honorable means, to earn it for himself." While he admitted that the arsenal was currently in disrepute and "there was a prejudice against enlistment," he attributed its poor reputation to the deficient character of the arsenal's soldiers. He advocated they should be "disbanded, and the institution changed in its character" to the point that students would actually compete for admission rather than shun it.

The Expense of the Conversion

A third objection to the arsenal's conversion might compare the lower expense of sustaining it to that of a literary institution. But he pointed out that the physical structures of the campus were already in place. "The salary of the Captain would be the same in either case." And the cost of boarding and clothing thirty students couldn't differ significantly from that of boarding and clothing the same number of soldiers. Better uniforms might be more appropriate, but the added expense could be offset by the savings gained from boarding students together rather than in separate housing. The main savings would derive from suspending "the wages now given" to twenty-eight soldiers in exchange "for the salaries of two additional instructors."

He even itemized the difference to demonstrate the actual savings by a literary institution:

The Arsenal	The Literary Institution
Annual wages/soldier: $108 (at $9/month)	Annual salary/instructor: $900
times 28 men = $3,024 per year	times 2 instructors = $1,800 per year
	An annual savings of $1,224

Preston pointed out that the state would have the same service performed for less money and the difference "placed in her coffers, for any other expenditure. The State would in ten years, save $12,240, a sum surely worth looking after." But a better use of the additional money, rather than stockpiling it in savings, would be to spend it on "increasing the number of students, and perhaps of instructors, or in founding a library; or perhaps better than either, a large part of it would be given to the class that would leave the institution as graduates, to enable them to prosecute their studies for a session at College or to support them until they could find some occupation."

There would be a slight additional expense if the number of students at the institute were increased from thirty "to at least thirty-two," since that was the number of senatorial districts in the state. But the cost would still be less than increasing the paid guard to the same number. Indeed, increasing the guardsmen to fifty, if circumstances ever required it, would cost the state in wages "more than $5,000 a year." But increasing the number of students to fifty would add "no more cost than their support, which would be about the same as that of hired soldiers." Based on these figures, Preston summarized, it would be "cheaper to maintain a body of men without wages, than to support them, and give them $9 per month—which we consider sufficiently obvious, without any further illustration."

The Conclusion

In his peroration Preston brought his articles to an arousing finish. He appealed to the political emotions of all people whose taxes supported the arsenal. Claiming that taxpayers "have a right to demand that these taxes be so expended as to produce the greatest benefit in return," he equally declared, "We will be right in asking the Legislature to take this matter into consideration, and they will do wrong, without cause, to disregard our wishes." Then riding the wave of patriotic sentiment, he elevated the thought and diction of his argument to ask rhetorically, "Who would not wish to see the change if it would be as practicable and advantageous as we have represented—who would not wish to see those really handsome buildings, which upon their commanding site, adorn the approach to our village, no longer the receptacle to drones, obliged to be restrained

The Parapet at Virginia Military Institute ca. 1935. View of the inscription on the Parapet below Washington Arch and Statue (Virginia Military Institute Archives, No. 0001001).

by the coercion of military rule, a discordant element in our social system," but rather "the healthful and pleasant abode of a crowd of honorable youths, pressing up the hill of science with noble emulation, a gratifying spectacle, an honor to our county and State, objects of honest pride to their instructors, and fair specimens of citizen-soldiers, attached to their native State, and proud of her fame, and ready, in every time of deepest peril to vindicate her honor, or defend her rights."[17]

This transforming incantation would become the mantra of VMI. It is committed to memory by every cadet who enters the institute as the definition of the "citizen-soldier." It appears in the cadet's Rat Bible and in 1927 was inscribed on the parapet across from William H. Cocke Hall. Preston might have been right to end his appeal at its emotional summit. But he wisely attached a calmer and milder denouement, modestly apologizing for any shortfall in his "feeble" presentation of the plan. "We cannot hope," he admitted, "that in the course of our remarks, we have escaped giving offence to any—but this, while it is to be regretted, could not be avoided, nor will it deter us from pursuing our object, by all proper means. We have made no statement which we did not conscientiously believe to be true, and none which in our view was uncalled for, nor have we 'aught set down in malice' in the way of opinion, but as we believe, fairly and honestly and with proper motives set forth the reasons supporting our opinion and our wish upon this subject."

He wrote in conclusion, "If we are right, then none ought to be offended. If wrong, no one is more solicitous than ourselves, to have our error pointed out, that we may abandon our scheme if it is impracticable or remedy our plan if it be defective."

4.

The Battle of the Arsenal Bills

As a tax paying citizen, I enter my solemn protest against such a foolish expenditure of public treasure as that proposed by Cives.
—A Citizen of Lexington

In the history of the Virginia Military Institute, few defining events would have as profound an effect on its establishment in Lexington as J.T.L. Preston's three "Cives" articles. They defined the school as it would eventually come to exist. Three months passed without a single objection or alternative to his proposal. That's not to say objections weren't brewing beneath the general public's wish to replace their reviled arsenal. But none were actually expressed until after a brief notice appeared in the December 11, 1835, issue of the *Lexington Gazette*. The notice announced, "A petition will be presented to the Legislature, praying the re-organization of the Lexington Arsenal so as to substitute, in lieu of the present Guard, a Guard of young men who are to receive literary, scientific and military instruction, in place of money wages. Memorials will be prepared, in a few days, for signatures."[1]

A Simpler Plan

The following week the first of two anonymous communications from "A Citizen of Lexington" appeared in the *Gazette* under the heading "Lexington Arsenal." Citizen readily admitted, "I can perceive no well founded objection to it, compared with the present system. On the contrary, it possesses many decided advantages over it." But he begged leave to offer a much simpler alternative for securing the public arms. His plan, he submitted, "renders any guard entirely unnecessary." He proposed to erect instead in town "a very substantial fire-proof building" to house the arms.[2]

He asked, "Who could doubt that they would be perfectly secure?" Providing lodging for three or four respectable men who could ring a bell in an emergency would save the state about $4,000 a year. The obnoxious arsenal could then be torn down "for a private residence—a literary or humane institution or some other purpose." He calculated the savings to the state would be more appropriately spent, at $10 per child, to "educate 400 CHILDREN WHO ARE NOW GROWING UP IN OUR STATE, ALMOST AS IGNORANT AS THE BRUTES THAT PERISH!" This use of the savings would be far preferable to squandering it on some twenty young men "pretty well instructed in the elements of education." In a P.S. he requested that other newspapers, like the Richmond *Whig, Enquirer,* and *Compiler,* publish his proposal to give the legislature a choice.[3]

A week later the editor of the *Gazette,* Cornelius C. Baldwin, lent his support to

Citizen's simpler plan. He agreed it "would combine perfect security to the public arms, with the greatest possible economy to the State." But he also agreed with Citizen that Cives' plan would be "infinitely better than the current system," if the state "is determined to sustain a guard at the Arsenal." He hoped that both plans would be submitted to the legislature.[4]

The Problem of Fire

Unlike the detailed plan of Cives, the simpler plan of Citizen provoked immediate protests in the public forum. On New Year's Day, Citizen felt compelled "to reply to some objections I have heard."[5] One objection claimed that arms stored in town, as he had proposed, would be at risk to destruction by fire. So he proposed making the new arsenal "completely fire proof" so that "the conflagration of every building in town would not injure it." It could be located some distance from all other buildings. He spoke to the terrible memory of many Lexingtonians of the Great Fire that had turned the entire population out of doors, leaving their homes in ashes.

The Problem of Security

A second objection argued that the stored arms would be exposed to domestic foes. So he advised posting "two sentinels at night" and ringing "the Alarm Bell, at a moment's warning," night or day, if needed, to alert the entire village to action. Cives' plan, he contended, "is all fudge for effective defence." It offered far less security: "What resistance I pray you, would some 20 white livered, chicken hearted, raw chaps, who had never smelt burnt gunpowder in their lives, oppose to an assailing foe in the consternation and dismay of a sudden midnight assault?" Furthermore, who would dare attack an arsenal positioned "in town" versus one isolated "half a mile from town," as it now existed?

The Problem of Cost

A third objection questioned the cost of Citizen's simple plan. But Citizen contended that a solid structure could be built for an initial cost of $5,000 or $6,000. He figured this was the same amount that Cives would spend every year on graduating fewer than ten cadets. But Citizen's plan would involve only "two sentinels," each earning a dollar a night, and a captain of the guard receiving $100, for a total of $830. So the state, he concluded, "would then *save annually upwards of $5,000 by adopting my plan.*" Or let the sentinels be the town's police, and have the state "pay half of this charge" to protect "both arsenal and town."

Citizen argued that realistically it's a waste of money to spend $5,000 a year to educate "some six or eight young men," since that's about how many would graduate annually under Cives' plan. Since Cives himself had argued that public funding should produce the greatest public benefit, Citizen was led "to ask most triumphantly, which is the greater benefit ... the education of some twenty young men who, at all events will be pretty well instructed, or the rescuing of *five hundred immortal minds from the palsying grasp of total ignorance,* by establishing common schools?" The money would be better spent on a manual labor school for educating "*five times* that number."

In his peroration, Citizen targeted the lofty idealism of Cives' definition of the citizen-soldier. He claimed sardonically that his simpler plan made no pretensions to "assemble in our village, a noble band of high minded, chivalrous youths, panting for honorable distinction, and mingling on terms of equality with our citizens!" He contended that such grandiloquence would be better suited for a legislative bill with a different title: "An act for promoting the social enjoyments of the citizens of Lexington and to make that village the 'Athens or Boston of Western Virginia.'"

Academy vs. Asylum

Not content to rest on his laurels, Citizen posted a "Communication" the following week on January 8.[6] Addressing it to "the honorable Senate and House of Delegates of Virginia," he repeated the same simple plan he had outlined earlier of "a substantial *fire proof* building" in town for an annual savings to the state of $5,000. He suggested that the old arsenal be converted into "a deaf and dumb asylum" under the state's patronage. This would benefit a class of society "with the benevolence which characterized the Saviour of the world, as it were, unloosing the tongues of the dumb and unstopping the ears of the deaf." Since only 50 of the 400 deaf-mutes currently living in Virginia were of suitable age to receive instruction in such an asylum, many would be "supported by themselves, friends, and by charitable associations," leaving only a few in need of public assistance, for which the $5,000 would amply serve.

Citizen argued that military academies, other than West Point, "could not be sustained." He cited Captain Alden Partridge's "entirely unsuccessful" academy at Middletown, Connecticut, and his further attempt at Middleburg, Virginia. He contended that "only one-third of all the cadets" who entered West Point actually graduated. In addition, he accused Cives of underestimating the cost of supporting his thirty cadets and two professors. "Each cadet would cost for his support, very nearly $200 a year," whereas at West Point the annual pay was $336. So Citizen recalculated the cost for thirty cadets at $200 and two professors at $1,000 each for a total of $8,000 to produce four or five "high souled warriors, to 'invigorate our militia system,' and to lead our armies on to conquest and to *glory*!!!" He then voiced, as a tax-paying citizen, his "solemn protest against such a foolish expenditure of public treasure as that proposed by Cives." He begged the Legislature to adopt his simpler plan rather than convert the Lexington arsenal into "a military nursery" for Cives to serve as "the adopted god father and kind nursing mother."

On January 13, Alfred Leyburn presented to the House of Delegates the formal petition "praying a change in the organization of the Lexington arsenal, so as to give that institution a collegiate as well as a military character." It was signed by ninety-four citizens of Lexington and worded to appeal to the legislators on the same three levels that Preston had expressed in his Cives articles. The petition described the plan as "highly advantageous to the cause of learning, to the community in which it is hosted, and to some important interests of the state at large."[7] Leyburn submitted a second petition, signed by eighteen citizens of neighboring Fairfield.[8] And on January 16, Delegate Charles Dorman introduced a resolution, instructing the Committee of Schools and Colleges to report on establishing a military school, in lieu of the Arsenal, as part of Washington College.[9]

Three days later a new petition rejecting Cives' plan in favor of Citizen's proposal arrived from Lexington. It bore only four signatures but included *Gazette* editor Cornelius Baldwin. It contended that a fireproof building without a day guard and two sentinels at a dollar a night would suffice, or else turn the arsenal over to the local militia or to the town as trustee.[10] The following day an article in the *Advocate* in neighboring Buchanan objected that no one could feel safe if his security were entrusted to "frolicsome, inconsiderate boys with the duty of guarding instruments of death." Complaining that the youth of Virginia were proverbially indiscreet and shamefully insubordinate, it asked rhetorically, "Who would rest secure if his own life and that of his wife and children were perpetually dependent upon the vigilance and prudence of a boy ... especially a Virginia boy?"[11]

On January 22 the *Gazette* published a letter from Captain Alden Partridge, addressed to Lexington's Charles Dorman. Delegate Dorman had written Partridge to ask if an arsenal would be equally safe under guard by a military school as by enlisted soldiers. In his reply Partridge contended that a military school was far better equipped to protect public arms than any arsenal under "the protection of any guard of enlisted soldiers whatever." He spoke "from many years of experience as an instructor." The core of his argument was that "correct and efficient instruction," which a military school would provide, was what state legislatures had failed to give the enlisted soldiers of their militias. But "with competent and well instructed officers" and "in case of war or any other emergency," militias could be assembled on very short notice to serve in "a state of mechanical discipline as would render them superior to any troops in the world."[12] In his support of military schools, Partridge reinforced Cives' argument for converting the arsenal.

But on January 26, Citizen's cheaper plan found a further advocate, who published under the pseudonym "Rockbridge," the name of the county, in the *Richmond Whig and Public Advertiser*. Rockbridge endorsed Citizen's plan as "much superior" to either alternative, whether the arsenal as it existed or a military school. Twenty "citizens of the town" could guard the arms in shifts. With "two sentinels posted each night, each man would be required to perform duty but once in ten days, and then only for a few hours at night. In exchange they would be "exempted from military duty" and paid a dollar for each night served. Rockbridge argued that there were respectable young men in Lexington "who would be very glad to enter the guard for a dollar a night." He recalculated Citizen's plan to cost $7,150 less than a military school annually and $5,150 less than the present arsenal. The money thus saved could establish "a military professorship in each" of Virginia's five colleges as well as educate over half the state's "deaf and dumb, who might require public assistance."[13]

On February 5, the *Gazette*'s editor reprinted Rockbridge's cheaper plan and commended his views "to the serious consideration of our Delegates."[14] On February 12, Partridge published his rebuttal. Appealing to the pride of Virginia to take the lead in establishing a military school, he contended it would blend "the citizen with the soldier and thereby set an example well worthy of being followed by all her sister states."[15] By the end of February, the *Gazette* was quoting the *Danville Observer* as "decidedly in favor" of an asylum for the deaf and dumb instead of a military academy. In the same issue it quoted the *Richmond Compiler*'s appeal to Virginian pride in support of an asylum, which would enlist "the kindly feelings of the heart, and ... reflect honor upon the state. To what purpose could a portion of the surplus of the Literary Fund be better applied, than to an institution so truly noble and benevolent? Virginia should not lag behind her sisters, in a measure calculated to add so much to her true glory."[16]

The First Bill

By the beginning of March, Preston's plan for a military school was by no means assured passage in the legislature. Determined to leave no stone unturned, he attended the 1835–36 session to solicit support. Republishing in a single sheet all three Cives articles, he personally placed a copy on the desk of each and every member of the House of Delegates. On March 3 a bill to reorganize the arsenal was introduced by Oscar M. Crutchfield (whose son would later become a professor of mathematics at VMI).[17] On March 9 the Committee on Militia Laws endorsed the military academy as a "reasonable" alternative to the arsenal and rejected the asylum plan.[18] And finally, on March 22, 1836, the arsenal bill, having been read twice more, was passed as "an act reorganizing the Lexington arsenal, and establishing a military school in connexion with Washington College."[19]

The matter should have ended there with the passage of this first act, but it didn't. The legislature properly issued a joint resolution to disband the arsenal, establish a military school, and elect a board of visitors to govern the new institution. But its session ended before a quorum could be raised to authorize an election, so no board was created.[20] The arsenal act died intestate!

The Second Bill

An entire year would pass before the legislature could revisit the issue at its next session. On January 13, 1837, a letter to the *Gazette* signed merely by "C" complained, "How happens it that nothing has yet been done by our representatives in the legislature in regard to the bill passed at the last session, for the reorganization of the arsenal? ... I would call the attention of our senator and representatives to the subject and press them to delay no longer, the necessary steps in the matter."[21] Whether "C" was Preston writing as Cives or one of Preston's supporters, Delegate Dorman resolved in the legislature on the same day that the complaint appeared "that this house will, by joint vote with the senate, proceed ... to the election of four visitors to the military school in connexion with Washington College, as provided for under an act passed March 22, 1836."[22]

Auspiciously, Dorman's resolution preempted by a few days the opposition's attempts to repeal the entire arsenal act. By the end of March, when one of the bills to repeal it was in the midst of heated discussion, Dorman introduced an amendment to the bill that would "strike out the word 'repealed' and insert 'amended' in the second section thereof." This would "authorize and empower the governor of the commonwealth, instead of the general assembly, to appoint the four visitors therein provided for." The amendment was accepted, and on March 22, 1837, this second arsenal bill passed, assuring no further delays.[23]

On May 30, Governor David Campbell appointed Colonel Claudius Crozet, General William Ligon of Powhatan, General Peter Johnston of Washington County, and General George Rust of Loudoun to the new institution's first board of visitors, with Adjutant General Bernard Peyton serving *ex officio*. An enthusiastic board met on August 7, 1837, and elected Colonel Crozet its first president. A logical choice, Crozet was a native of France who had served under Napoleon. A graduate of the *L'École Polytechnique*, he taught engineering at West Point.

As its first order of business, the board drafted a letter to the trustees of Washington College inquiring if they would accept the new military school as specified in the act "as a part and branch of the college."[24] At the time the college was in a state of transition. In 1830 Louis Marshall, an education reformer, had assumed its presidency and replaced traditional classes with faculty-assisted but liberal, self-directed studies. As a consequence, Washington College had reached the verge of collapse, which only Henry Ruffner's election as its president in 1836 had begun to prevent.[25] Aware, as the board of visitors was, of the recent decline in the college's reputation and enrollment, its members naturally expected its trustees to welcome a union with VMI.

But Washington College had other concerns. If the fledgling VMI via its board of visitors had high hopes of flying, it was destined to an aborted liftoff. On the third day of meetings the board received a letter that would derail all that Preston, the legislature, and the governor had achieved over the past two and a half years. In the letter John F. Caruthers, Preston's brother-in-law and chairman of the college's board of trustees, expressed the trustees' support of the idea of "an auxiliary connection between the college and the arsenal." But the legislature had no right to make the school a "branch of the college" due to its private status.[26]

As Preston would later explain, the act, as presently worded, would assume "an illegal control over the college," which the trustees could not endorse.[27] By way of consolation, the trustees welcomed a reciprocal arrangement with the proposed military academy for instruction without charge. But their reluctance to accept it as a branch had rendered the entire act null and void. And in the meantime, the board of visitors had discovered that the old arsenal buildings were unsuitable for thirty cadets and two professors. So they promptly notified Governor Campbell that, considering their need of $2,500 to repair dilapidated the buildings, they felt compelled by the circumstances "to suspend for a while the organization of the military school," to which Governor Campbell agreed.[28]

Claudius Crozet, 1790–1864. Photograph ca. 1860 by William G. Brown. Crozet was the first president of the Virginia Military Institute Board of Visitors, 1837–45. His portrait hangs in the Virginia Military Institute Museum (Virginia Military Institute Archives, No. 0000245).

The Third Bill

Six more months would pass before James McDowell, later Governor McDowell, could introduce a third arsenal bill at the 1838–39 session. On February 24, 1838, the House of Delegates passed "an act amending and reducing the several acts concerning the re-organization of the Lexington Arsenal and the establishment therewith a military school at Washington College."[29] Preston wrote McDowell to express his delight at the bill's passage by the House.[30] But with its failure in the Senate, another year would be lost before it could become law. Despite the failure of this third bill, Governor Campbell was still authorized by the second bill to create a second board of visitors, which he did on April 17, 1838.

This second board differed significantly from the first since it now included a civilian. As time was passing and interest was waning, Campbell decided to replace General Rust with Preston, the project's strongest advocate. As a result, the mission gained renewed momentum. The board met on May 18, and at James McDowell's request Preston was asked to give the proposed school a name that would define it as precisely as his Cives letters had outlined. A skilled wordsmith, Preston chose three expressions that would clearly distinguish the school from all other schools, each word denoting a separate but primary function: "VIRGINIA—A state institution, neither sectional nor denominational. MILITARY—its characteristic feature. INSTITUTE—something different from either a college or university. The three elements thus indicated are the basis of a triangular pyramid, of which the sides will preserve their mutual relation to whatever height the structure may rise."[31]

The Fourth Bill

At the 1839–40 session of the legislature, Leyburn introduced the final "petition of sundry citizens of the county of Rockbridge, asking for certain amendments to the act providing for the re-organization of the Lexington arsenal and for establishing a military school thereat."[32] No mention was made at all of Washington College since this act, as introduced by Delegate Dorman and passed on March 29, 1839, would create by name the "Virginia Military Institute" as an independent organization funded by the state. This final act, successfully establishing VMI, read,

> Whereas it is represented to the General Assembly, that the State Arsenal situated near the town of Lexington, in the County of Rockbridge, can be advantageously converted into a public military school without endangering the public arms, or other property, thereto belonging, and without imposing any additional expense upon the Commonwealth,
>
> Be it therefore enacted, that the sum of six thousand dollars be and the same is hereby appropriated annually from the public treasury for the establishment and support of a military school at the said arsenal, as per the plan hereinafter provided for, which said school shall be called the "Virginia Military Institute."[33]

In mid–April, Governor Campbell created the third and final board of visitors. He increased its membership to ten by adding four more citizens of Lexington: local merchant Hugh Barclay and the three legislators who had introduced the various bills, Dr. Leyburn, Colonel Dorman, and James McDowell.[34]

If Preston was elated that the dream of a military institution was at last on the threshold of reality, Governor Campbell was equally thrilled. Within a month he was addressing the legislature about the importance of free schools in "an efficient system of education" designed for "the whole population" of Virginia. Like Preston, he saw the urgency of improving "the education of poor children" who could not read and write.[35]

Preston himself had received his education at a time in Virginia's—indeed America's—history when only the fortunate could afford to attend a college or university. While he was learning Greek and Latin at Washington College, a pathetic number of his fellow Virginians were doomed to illiteracy. In 1810 the Virginia Legislature had created the Literary Fund under "An Act to Provide for the Education of the Poor." As Governor Campbell reported, it had discovered a quarter of those who applied for marriage licenses "were unable to write their names." It was a percentage that would remain essentially the same for the next forty years, despite an annual expense of $45,000 collected from fines, forfeitures, and repaid loans to educate the poor. "The education of females," Campbell contended, had suffered "a condition of much greater neglect" than that of males.[36]

The governor deplored the failure of the Literary Fund to affect in the slightest the "deplorable extent of ignorance" among the generation just rising into manhood. He cited statistics showing that 40,000 of the 200,000 children between the ages of five and fifteen lived in poverty, and "of them only one half" attended school.[37] Indeed, the census of 1840, as the editor of the *Richmond Times-Dispatch* would confirm, showed the number of white illiterates in Virginia was almost 60,000 or approximately one in thirteen.[38] All too many of them derived little or no instruction "in miserable huts scarcely more comfortable than those you provide for your cattle," owing in part to the incapacity and inexperience of their teachers.[39] It was a situation that Preston's proposal for VMI had sought to help correct. Like Preston, Governor Campbell foresaw what VMI would later provide as long-term state-supported education "to the class whose revenues are insufficient to educate their children without some assistance from the state." It would also supply "a gradual increase of the number of experienced and qualified teachers."[40]

The Search for a Superintendent

A month before VMI's newly appointed board of visitors could meet, Preston launched the search for a principal professor and commandant to head the new school. According to historian William Couper, "Who suggested the name of Francis Henney Smith for the position is not known."[41] But on April 29, Preston addressed a letter to Smith, a twenty-seven-year-old graduate of West Point and teacher of mathematics at Hampden-Sydney. He wrote "as an individual" to ascertain if Smith "would be willing that [his] name should be placed before the board at its meeting" on May 30 "as a candidate for the selection of commandant or principal professor." He thoughtfully noted that the future character of the military school would be determined by the one who will preside over it. In the same breath he described the Lexington population as "intelligent, moral & religious." With three quality schools—Washington College, the revival of the female Ann Smith Academy, and Virginia Military Institute—Lexington would become for education "the most favored spot in the state."[42]

Before responding, Smith wrote to several friends, including the Rev. Dr. William M. Atkinson, for advice. He told Atkinson he was tempted by the offer of $1,500 a year with a house, because his salary at Hampden-Sydney was "barely $1,000—last year it was only a trifle over $800 and so dear is living here that it is almost impossible with such a sum to get along respectably." While admitting that he was young, he now felt a duty to his family to provide better support. He knew nothing of Lexington but thought the letter from Preston worthy of consideration. In conclusion, he wrote, "I trust that Providence will guide me and not have to determine for myself."[43] Smith would later confess he was reluctant to leave Hampden-Sydney, where he had taught for only three years but already loved his work and friends. "I did not know there was an Arsenal in Lexington. I had not heard of the scheme to convert it into a Military School until these facts had been made known to me by the letter of Mr. Preston."[44]

As persistent in soliciting Smith as he'd been in promoting his plan, Preston wrote Smith again on May 17 to give further details about the institute. Among them were that two professors would be in charge. A commandant would give "instruction in the military art, and also in mathematics, with particular reference to its application to civil engineering." A chair of modern languages would be filled later. Preston mentioned that "an outline of regulations for the military institute" had been prepared by a member of the board, presumably Crozet. And he confirmed that the principal professor would receive $1,500 per annum, payable quarterly.[45] On May 30 the board convened and elected Smith, offering him the additional title of major, pending approval by the legislature. Preston informed him of his election and invited him to visit Lexington before making his decision. He added that no professor of modern languages had been elected yet, but he himself expected to apply for the job.[46] Three weeks later Smith answered Preston, accepting the appointment and expressing his appreciation to the board for the honor.[47]

As straightforward as the board's minutes show the election of Smith to have been, the unofficial account suggests less unanimity. Both Jennings Wise and William Couper relate that Crozet's first assistant engineer, fellow West Pointer, and friend Joseph R. Anderson was also considered for the position. But the board members, finding themselves unable to choose between Anderson and Smith, "devoted most of their time to singing the praises of Mrs. Anderson and Mrs. Smith." When it appeared the discussion would continue without cease, Crozet rose and facetiously "called for a vote as to which one of the ladies should be superintendent!"[48]

Francis Henney Smith, 1812–90. Photograph ca. 1860 by Richmond Minnis. Superintendent Smith was the builder and rebuilder of Virginia Military Institute. His signature appears below his image, photographed during the Civil War (Virginia Military Institute Archives, No. 0001856).

The Task of the Board of Visitors

Apart from electing Smith, the board spent ten days establishing the main outlines of the new institute, a rather formidable task. As Preston would later recount in his fifty-year history of VMI, the temptation of the members, six of whom were gallant officers and soldiers, was simply to copy West Point exactly as a model. But to do so would prove impracticable. West Point had "a single object, viz., to give the best possible military education to army officers" with the "prospect of promotion in a brilliant service." In addition, "the entire support of the cadet was assumed by the government." On the contrary, VMI "must begin with a very meager endowment" and would need to prove itself "worthy of fuller support from the state, and larger patronage from the public." It would also have the enlarged goal of "preparing young men for the varied work of civil life."[49]

In the end West Point would serve only as a model for VMI's Code of Regulations and its prescribed uniform because the course of education at VMI would differ significantly in its "necessary variations" from that of the national academy. This fact would be confirmed by its first graduating class in 1842. Their educational curriculum consisted of mathematics, mechanics, chemistry, engineering and tactics, French and German language, English and German literature, and drawing, with Latin substituted the following year for German.[50]

Preston summarized, "The general controlling purpose of the board" was to furnish the institute's graduates with an education that would not upset "the established system of classical education" while focusing on "the practical pursuits of life." Since military discipline had been required for the establishment of the institute, he explained, it "might be of great importance in some possible emergencies of the state." But it also "had special advantages in promoting the health of its pupils, in training them in habits of subordination to lawful authority, to industry and punctuality, and to accustoming them to prompt obedience to every call of duty, small or great, without regard to preference or self-indulgence."[51]

Preston concluded, "In my opinion, just in proportion as these fundamental principles have been adhered to, the institute has prospered; if at any time they have been departed from, weakening more or less serious has been the consequence." To illustrate his point, he quoted statistics of VMI's graduates from the Report of General Smith to the Governor on November 11, 1881, at the end of the school's forty-second year:

200 killed in battle	94 farmers and planters
175 professors and teachers	59 physicians
135 civil and mining engineers	30 clergymen
120 merchants	19 bankers

Preston contended that what the board of visitors contributed to the original outlines of VMI during the ten days it convened in June 1839 was "staunch firmness with flexibility to meet conditions that could not be anticipated, and which were, when they actually occurred, so critical that had the foundation been less broad and strong the whole structure would have fallen in ruins."[52]

Not quite five years after the Franklin Society's first debate over the fate of its controversial arsenal, Preston joined Alfred Leyburn, Hugh Barclay, and Charles Dorman in a letter to Governor Campbell, certifying that VMI was ready to begin operation as a military school. It was Preston's last act on the board. On November 12 he was elected professor of modern languages and acting superintendent in the superintendent's absence, which required his resignation from the board. His annual salary was set at $700.[53]

November 11, 1839

Despite the freezing cold and drifting snow, twenty-three of the first thirty-one young cadets arrived at the Virginia Military Institute for the first day of school. Preston must have felt the same rush of emotion that washed over John Bowie Strange, Class of 1842, the first cadet sentinel to mount guard in front of the disbanded state arsenal.[54] Sixteen years would pass before this same young man would father his own Albemarle Military Institute, modeled after VMI.[55] But for now his arrival announced the formal changing of the guard as the long hard struggle from plan to reality approached its goal.

There remained, of course, some misgivings about untried youth commanding an arsenal, especially among the old guards being replaced by the new cadets. One eyewitness would later recall, "The evening of the eleventh was a memorable one. As the disbanded soldiers passed the body of youthful Virginians who THEY REGARDED AS MERE BOYS, some were so audacious as to cast a contemptuous look upon their successors and 'muttered loud and deep.'"[56] VMI would have to prove itself not only to the public but to itself, if it were to survive the obstacles that still lay in its immediate path.

Nevertheless, on this first day, a handful of youthful actors, including Preston at twenty-eight and Smith at twenty-seven, stood on history's stage during a cold, snow-white Monday morning in November. As pioneers, they launched an educational system that scores of subsequent military programs would adopt across the South. Many of them, including VMI as prototype, survive intact today. By 1861 "ninety-six schools with military programs" would be founded throughout the South, and each state, excluding Texas, would have "its own state-supported military academy."[57] These schools would educate approximately 11,000 young men.[58]

There was one characteristic of the new school that opened on November 11, 1839, as the first state-supported military institute in the United States, which Preston, Smith, the cadets, the board of visitors, the legislature, the governor, and the people of Virginia could all appreciate with justifiable pride. It was that VMI was distinctively democratic. Dressed in the same uniform, each of its cadets, whether the son of a poor farmer or artist or a rich lawyer or doctor, could enjoy the same opportunities on an equal plane without regard to economic or class status.

This feature of VMI would be eloquently eulogized seventy years later by former Cadet John S. Wise, Class of 1866, when he described the career of a cadet:

> Upon his matriculation he promptly learns that he left at the sallyport any fictitious benefit which he hoped for from wealth or antecedents. That no adventitious circumstance of birth or fortune will avail him here. That rich and poor—patrician and plebeian—stand for judgment in this tribunal, naked as they came into this world, equal as when they shall lie side by side in the grave. That they are to begin, with others, a life wherein the food, the dress, the discipline, and the opportunity of all will be the same. That for any good their names will do them they might as well have numbers or fictitious characters attached to designate them. That after a year of fair and equal

competition their relative merits will be decided by impartial judges solely upon their intrinsic moral, mental and physical worth, as compared with that of others of their class.

No man can watch the transformation which takes place in body, mind and manner of the cadet during his course here, without recognizing the powerful influence of the school upon the lives of its pupils.[59]

Wise drew a vivid contrast "between the pert overconfidence of the town-boy, when he enters, and his consideration and respected reserve, at leaving; between the awkward, slouchy, embarrassment of the country lad, at entering, and the alert, self-poised, and mannerly bearing of the same boy, when he leaves." At the time Wise's characterization of the cadet served to authenticate what Preston had envisioned in the second of his Cives articles as "a corps of young men, guided by virtuous principles, ennobled by the ardor of patriotism, and cheered by the proud consciousness that they were, by their own exertions, preparing themselves for the highest posts under their own free government, of which they should be capable—mingling with the citizens as their duty might permit upon the equality of gentlemen."[60]

5

From Dream to Reality

Just who first thought of V. M. I. seems to have been lost beyond recovery. Several people have claimed to know.
—Colonel James Anderson

By the old adage that failure is an orphan but success has many fathers, if VMI had died in the throes of childbirth, as it almost did in the early 1840s, there would be no question today about its originator. But the problem has been the institution's successful birth, growth, and extraordinary achievements in fulfilling its original mission, currently defined as "Building Leaders in All Walks of Life." Many individuals have sought credit for VMI's remarkable success, evoking the question of who was the Institute's father.

John T. L. Preston was the father of VMI. This statement stands today as a challenge to the claims of a squadron of alternative fathers. In 1937 Colonel James Anderson summarized the problem as it had haunted the institute since its inception almost a century

Virginia Military Institute ca. 1840–1842. Drawing by Cadet Charles P. Deyerle, the earliest known view of Virginia Military Institute. Deyerle, Class of 1842, was among the institute's first cadets. His drawing shows the original Barracks and Arsenal buildings, none of which exist today (Virginia Military Institute Archives, No. 0003455).

earlier. In his article "The Founding of VMI and Its Early Years," Anderson concluded, "Just who first thought of V. M. I. seems to have been lost beyond recovery. Several people have claimed to know."[1] Even today the question baffles historians faced with multiple claims on the institution's parentage.

James Robertson, Jr., as recently as 1997, made the bold assertion in his definitive biography of Stonewall Jackson that John T. L. Preston was the originator of VMI. He declared, "In 1836, Preston had originated the idea of converting the Western Arsenal in Lexington into a military and scientific college."[2] And this might be true, were it not for all the other claimants of the same title, which Anderson felt rendered the issue irreconcilable.

The First Claim

The first to stake a claim was someone who chose to remain anonymous. He called himself "Knox" in a long letter to the editor of the *Lexington Gazette* in May of 1841, only three years after VMI's founding.[3] Headlining his communication "Virginia Military Institute," he cleared the public stage for his proposal by declaring, "The dread of *change* is a fear that is, perhaps, more general than any other." He then warned, "When once a community receives an impression, I care not of what kind or how it may be produced, it is the most difficult thing imaginable to wipe this away."

Appealing to reason, Knox proposed a new view of VMI's originators to wipe away the "clouds of error" that had fed the public's mistaken impression and "set it right." Without stating the public's impression, he offered his "humble testimony of respect and veneration" to the true originators of VMI, one of whom he claimed had just died. In a footnote to his article, he declared his candidate, without naming any others, to be J. F. Caruthers.[4] John Caruthers was a highly respected merchant, Washington College trustee, and early member of the VMI Board of Visitors. He had strongly advocated the establishment of a military school in Lexington, even when he headed the trustees of Washington College in 1837 and had to oppose it as a branch of the college.[5] Knox was satisfied with the mere naming of such "a distinguished citizen of Lexington and a steadfast friend of the institute" to prove his case. He declared, "Tho' he sleeps beneath the silent clods of the earth, like 'the bread that is thrown upon the waters,' *his deeds* survive, and shall gather additional glory as time rolls on."

In Knox's view, John F. Caruthers, Preston's brother-in-law, was an originator of VMI. He went on to extol the success of VMI as a welcome replacement for the Lexington Arsenal, whose "band of hired soldiers were a nuisance to the community." He added, "Nothing could check the torrent of immorality that hurried them to the commission of acts of the most unblushing effrontery." He credited the Franklin Society in part for having unanimously endorsed and emboldened the idea of replacing the offensive arsenal in 1835, and he conceded that the three "Cives" articles had put forward the proposal for public discussion. He then devoted the rest of his letter to quoting Preston's plan for the school but dismissed it, without elaboration, as vastly different from the VMI of 1841 and the legislative acts of 1837 and 1839 that officially created the institution.

In his last paragraph, almost as an afterthought, Knox credited F. H. Smith with being the institute's "pilot" and J.T.L. Preston as "his associate in command." But the true originator was the footnoted Caruthers, now resurrected by Knox into the public's awareness as the man who launched "the little bark … upon the waters of an untried ocean." He concluded his argument with Preston's stirring tribute to "honorable youths," the eloquent definition of the VMI cadet, which was recognizable by anyone familiar with the institute.

The Disclaimer

For the next quarter century no one else staked a claim to the title of VMI's originator. But in 1889 the man who opened the floodgates to a host of willing candidates was Preston himself. Despite his talent and considerable accomplishments, Preston was a disarmingly modest individual. If he ever took credit for originating or organizing anything, he almost invariably shared it with someone else. And he was always the first to disavow any honors as undeserved that others might want to bestow on him. In the course of time he would turn down promotions in rank to inspector general and brigadier general as unmerited. He would routinely deny the very characteristics that markedly distinguished him from others: his talents in the military, "in business, in oratory, in scholarship, and many other things."[6] His innate modesty, indeed his faith before God, saw all assumption of credit as pretentious and "inexcusable egotism."[7]

So it's not surprising or out of character at all that Preston would have foregone any role he might have played as the father of VMI. At the request of the VMI Board of Visitors for its semi-centennial jubilee on July 4, 1889, he composed a "Historical Sketch of the Establishment and Organization of the Virginia Military Institute." He felt compelled to apologize for the number of times he would, of necessity, have to name himself:

> The board has done me the honor to request that I should undertake the preparation of this sketch. It involves what was done by the citizens of the town and county to bring the subject before the General Assembly of Virginia, the preliminaries, and final action of that body, and the work of the first, or organizing, board of visitors.
>
> Except incompetency for the execution of the task, I am the person upon whom it most naturally devolves. I was closely associated with the most prominent movers and agents of the enterprise, of whom few now remain on earth. I am the only survivor of the original board.
>
> I was one of the two original professors of the institute, the honored superintendent being the other. As such I lived with it almost the whole of its fifty years, as I did the whole of my active life, and have the honor of having my name still borne on the roll of its officers. As I stand thus, almost solitary in my position, I must be excused for what would otherwise be inexcusable egotism, in the necessarily frequent reference to myself.[8]

Preston began his history with the two proposals at the Franklin Society in 1834 when the question of replacing the arsenal was initially debated. He reported that the society's vote on the first proposal to model the new school after West Point had failed. But the vote on the second proposal had been "unanimous in favor of making the change" by linking the new school with Washington College. As a consequence, he confirmed, "The three articles, written by myself, under the signature of 'Cives'" deliberately avoided any mention of the national academy. "It is somewhat singular," he remarked, "that the author nowhere makes any reference to West Point, either as an example of the value of a military school, or as a model for the organization of the one proposed." The new school would combine the military function of the arsenal with the education of young men. Preston knew this idea of a military education system would be revolutionary if successfully applied in the world of academia. But he had admitted in his "Cives" articles that the idea itself was not new.

Now in his semi-centennial history, he similarly played down himself as the originator of the idea. In a well-known and oft repeated admission, he asserted, "It is not necessary to refer to the arguments by which the writer [of the Cives letters] maintained the affirmative of the question, but it may not be irrelevant to state that he disclaims being the first to suggest the idea, and that he announces it to be the purpose of the friends of the measure to endeavor by all proper means to effect the change."[9] VMI historiographer William Couper has argued, "Were it not for Colonel Preston's repeated denial of his having been the originator of the idea there would be little doubt that the honor belonged to him."[10] In 1939 the week before the dedication of the Preston Library, Couper declared,

> History is obscure on the point of who it was who originated this argument, but J.T.L. Preston, a man of considerable stature in the community, got behind it from the start. His excellent, intelligent and judicial mind, his consuming energy, and his sense of the value of education and abhorrence of elements represented by the soldiers guarding the arsenal, were the moving force which brought V.M.I. into existence.
>
> Preston held the affirmative side of this debate with such poise, such intelligent argument that the society, when the debate was concluded, was unanimous in favor of the idea.[11]

The Second Claim

As Couper suggested, it was due to Preston's repeated denial of having originated the idea that others leapt in to fill the void and don the mantle appropriate to the honor. The year after Preston offered his history of VMI and just before his own death in 1890, the most likely alternate to displace him as father and founder of the school was Superintendent Francis Smith. Smith had devoted more years to VMI's building and rebuilding than the memories of almost all those associated with the institution encompassed.

Smith had just died in the spring of 1890, and his young replacement as superintendent, Brigadier General Scott Shipp, rightfully regarded him with high esteem for his fifty years of devoted service to the school. Consequently, Shipp issued General Order No. 14, entitled, "In Memoriam: Francis H. Smith, Father and Founder of the Virginia Military Institute." In his memoriam Shipp called Smith not only "the organizer, and for fifty years the superintendent" of VMI, but also "the father and founder."[12] He quoted Governor James McDonald's Order No. 16 that also called Smith "the Organizer." Preston was relegated to the seventh page of his document, where he conceded, "True, it had its origin in the unique conception of Colonel J.T.L. Preston, but there can be no doubt as to the genius that presided at its birth, nurtured it, and guarded it during its infantile struggle for existence."[13]

Ironically, Smith employed the same arguments as Shipp in naming Preston as the originator of VMI. In his Superintendent's Report of 1854, he gave a sketch of the early history of the school:

It is due to truth as well as justice to record, that for the initial steps toward its organization, for the untiring energy and perseverance with which the subject was kept before the public mind up to the period of its final triumphant establishment on the 11th November 1839, the credit belongs exclusively to the gentleman first named John T. L. Preston Esq. Major Preston is then in truth the <u>father of the Virginia Mil Institute</u> [Smith's underlining], and in his unwavering devotion to its interests, and incessant labor in its behalf, as a professor, he has justly proved himself worthy of this high distinction.[14]

Thirteen years later, on the occasion of the twenty-eighth anniversary of VMI, Smith again credited Preston with the distinction of being the "Father of the Virginia Military Institute." On November 11, 1867, he dedicated the textbook he would publish the following year, *Elements of Descriptive Geometry,* to Preston. He singled him out from his associate professors as "the originator of the scheme, by which the public guard of a State Arsenal was converted into a Military School" (see Figure 1).

<blockquote>
TO

COLONEL JOHN T. L. PRESTON,

Professor of Latin Language and English Literature, Virginia Military Institute.

I AM sure my associate Professors will vindicate the grounds upon which you are singled out, as one to whom I may appropriately dedicate this work.

As the originator of the scheme, by which the public guard of a State Arsenal was converted into a Military School, you have the proud distinction of being the "*Father of the Virginia Military Institute.*" You were a member of the first Board of Visitors, which gave form to the organization of the Institution; you were my only colleague during the two first and trying years of its being; and you have, for a period of twenty-eight years, given your labors and your influence, in no stinted measure, not only in directing the special department of instruction assigned to you, but in promoting those general plans of development, which have given marked character and widespread reputation to the school.

Nor is it without reason that *this* work, more than any other of my mathematical series, is dedicated to *you*. *Descriptive Geometry* was scarcely known in the schools and colleges of Virginia, when the Virginia Military Institute, by its distinctive *scientific* character, made instruction in a full course of Descriptive Geometry and its applications, a necessary part of
</blockquote>

Figure 1: Francis Smith's Dedication to J.T.L. Preston.

In a personal addendum to Preston, Smith concluded,

> Nor is it without reason that this work, more than any other of my mathematical series, is dedicated to you. Descriptive geometry was scarcely known in the schools and colleges of Virginia, when the Virginia Military Institute, by its distinctive scientific character, made instruction in a full course of descriptive geometry and its applications, a necessary part of its programme of studies. It was thus that it was proposed, in part, to qualify the young men of Virginia for honorable industrial pursuits; that they might, as civil engineers, architects, machinists, and manufacturers, lend their aid in developing the wealth and industry of this Old Dominion.[15]

Smith's final tribute to Preston as originator of the school appeared in his memoirs, posthumously published in 1912. He began his account with Preston's semi-centennial history of the institution, which outlined VMI's birth before Smith's involvement with the experiment. He included Preston's letters inviting and convincing him to serve as the fledgling institution's first superintendent.[16] And in naming the earliest members of VMI's board of visitors, he concluded, "To these must be added John T. L. Preston, Esq., who had originated the enterprise, had supported it by his pen and by his influence, and would naturally watch every step in its organization."[17]

Despite Smith's repeated assertions that Preston was VMI's originator and father, it was Shipp's memorial to Smith that would creep instead into the popular history of the town. Henry Boley's *Lexington in Old Virginia,* a charming book filled with sketches of people, places, and events connected with Lexington, became a well-read source of local history. Published in 1936, it served to perpetuate Shipp's regard for Smith in its biographical sketch of "Old Specks," whom Boley acclaimed as "the father and founder of Virginia Military Institute."[18]

The Third Claim

The notion that this memorialized old patriarch was VMI's father and founder held sway among Smith's many admirers for at least a quarter century until 1915, when Colonel Jennings C. Wise published his *Military History of the V.M.I.* A prominent attorney and former professor and commandant of cadets at VMI, Wise had a passionate interest in the institute. He proposed an entirely new founder of VMI. He argued that the true originator of the idea was the former chief engineer of Napoleon Bonaparte and the subsequent head of the U.S. Army Corps of Engineers, who had supervised tunnel construction through the Blue Ridge and Allegheny mountains into the Shenandoah and Ohio river valleys prior to his association with the institute.

Wise credited Captain Claudius Crozet with having visited Lexington frequently during construction of the James River and Kanawha Canal. As state engineer, Crozet "knew of the arsenal ... and, in all probability, discussed with some of [Virginia's] principal citizens the project of founding a military school in Lexington long ere it take tangible form." Wise surmised that when the Franklin Society first endorsed the plan in December 1834, "Crozet had been away from Virginia less than two years, and it seems reasonable to conclude that he was one of the originators of the plan, if not solely responsible for its first suggestion."[19]

Wise drew his conclusions from evidence that he considered probable and reasonable to trust and from Preston's express declaration "that he was not the originator of the idea." He dismissed Preston as a man who lacked military training and who failed, in fact, to mention West Point in his "Cives" letters. While allowing for Preston's brilliance and capability, he concluded,

> In the elaboration of the plan, however, Preston, who was not a soldier by education and training, took the leading part. This undoubtedly accounts for the fact that little mention was at first made of West Point. He stated the object of the proposed measure to be "to supply the place of the present guard by another, composed of young men from seventeen to twenty-four years of age, to perform the necessary duties of a guard, who would receive no pay, but, in lieu, have afforded to them the opportunities of a liberal education." In other words, he lost sight, through lack of understanding of the needs of the country and the state, of the primary concept of the originator of the idea.

In addition, Wise ruled out Superintendent Smith, declaring, "Honoring General Smith for his superb executive ability, we must in justice to truth deny him both the titles of 'father' and of 'founder' of the institute, for such was Claude Crozet."[20]

Having ruled out Smith, Wise made the additional and remarkable claim that Crozet not only fathered VMI but actually formulated the school's name. To prove his point, he reproduced from Smith's memoirs a letter that Crozet had written to Smith, dated September 12, 1829, ten years prior to VMI's founding. In the letter Crozet had cited by name "Virginia Military Institute." Noting Crozet's use of the word "Institute," Wise explained, "That was the term he applied by habit to his own alma mater [West Point Academy]. Can it be doubted that he proposed the name to Preston?"[21] Crozet, according to Wise, was the originator both of the school and its name, as verified by the letter that Wise reproduced on page 41 of his book, adding his own commentary (see Figure 2).

It's probably due to an unfortunate misreading of the year of the original document that Wise misdated Crozet's letter to Smith. Wise had used Smith's memoirs as his source, but the date of the letter in that source was not September 12, 1829, but 1839, when VMI already had a name and Crozet was acting as president of its second board of visitors.[22] The original letter in Smith's memoirs commenced with the correct date (see Figure 3).

Despite Wise's misprint of the date in his history, his general notion that it was Crozet who originated VMI would persist unchallenged. Within five years Oren Morton's 1920 *History of Rockbridge County, Virginia* was claiming Crozet as "the real originator."[23] And in 1936, Henry Boley, having previously quoted Shipp's tribute to Smith as the "father and founder," also repeated Wise's tribute to Crozet. In his chapter on VMI, he remarked, "The real originator of Virginia Military Institute seems to have been Claude Crozet, a native of France, a soldier under Napoleon and a wearer of the Cross of the Legion of Honor, received at the hand of the Emperor himself."[24] Boley made this claim on the same page that he also credited Colonel J.T.L. Preston with the school's establishment. He concluded that VMI was "the brilliant result" of Preston's advocating "a military school instead of the arsenal and the State Guard." Thus, by 1936 one father of VMI had blossomed into three.

Wise's choice of Crozet enjoyed further support in 1961, when Dr. James G. Leyburn proposed that Preston acted solely on Crozet's suggestion. He speculated,

> Early in the 1830s Claudius Crozet, a native of France, who had taught mathematics at West Point before coming to Virginia to undertake various large engineering enterprises, seems to have made the suggestion that the state should replace its arsenals by a

> THE VIRGINIA MILITARY INSTITUTE 41
>
> "LEXINGTON, September 12, 1829.
>
> "MAJOR FRANCIS H. SMITH.
>
> "DEAR SIR—You will receive by mail a printed copy of the Regulations adopted by the Board of Visitors for the government of the Virginia Military Institute.
>
> "We understand that it is your intention to take a trip to the North previous to your coming to this place: in this event, you might assist the Board in procuring several things which will be wanted at, or shortly after, the opening of the Institute. Among them are some parts of the uniform and accoutrements, which, you will observe, are similar to those used at West Point.
>
> "Would it be convenient to you, while there, to inquire what prospect there would be of obtaining 100 such muskets and complete accoutrements as are used there, and to take such steps as will secure this object speedily, as also from fifty to one hundred caps introduced by Major Delafield without the plate, of course? The muskets and equipment will be obtained from the U. S. Government, free of charge. It will, consequently, be sufficient to apply for them in the proper quarter, and correspond with General Peyton, if necessary, on the subject, as regards the caps. If you can purchase them, you can draw, or direct the merchant to draw, on Mr. Hugh Barclay, the Treasurer of the Institution."*
>
> Observe how Crozet used the word, "Institute." That was the term he applied by habit to his own Alma Mater. Can it be doubted that he proposed the name to Preston? Also, observe that he is in Lexington busying himself with his pet hobby. Honoring General Smith for his superb executive ability, we must in justice to truth deny him both the titles of "father" and of "founder" of the Institute, *for such was Claude Crozet.*

Figure 2: Jennings Wise's claim that Claudius Crozet coined the institute's name.

> LEXINGTON, September 12, 1839.
>
> MAJ. FRANCIS H. SMITH.
>
> DEAR SIR—You will receive by mail a printed copy of the Regulations adopted by the Board of Visitors for the government of the Virginia Military Institute.

Figure 3: Claudius Crozet's original letter to Francis Smith.

military school on the order of West Point. Alfred Leyburn and particularly his closest friend and brother-in-law, J.T.L. Preston, a lawyer, thought this idea an excellent one.... The bill was introduced into the legislature.[25]

A final claim that Crozet was the one and only father of VMI appeared as late as 1974, when Senior Historian Benjamin Levy of the National Park Service nominated the VMI Historic District for the National Register of Historic Places. He described the institute as the "West Point of the South" and declared that Colonel Claude Crozet "is justly known as the father of the VMI, for he, more than any other individual, moulded the character of the school."[26] Levy's National Register nomination made no mention at all of J.T.L. Preston.

In 1926, less than a decade after Wise's choice of Crozet as VMI's originator, Superintendent Emeritus General Edward West Nichols, Class of 1878, openly denied the claim. In his book, *Fifty Years of Service*, he countered, "It has been intimated by a very enthusiastic writer on institute affairs that credit for the origin of the Virginia Military Institute is largely due to Colonel Claude Crozet, president of the Institute's first board of visitors. This is not true, although ... he originated the courses of instruction and the disciplinary feature of the Institute."[27]

Nichols argued that, despite Crozet's valuable contributions to military discipline, VMI was not a West Point of the South:

> We should never lose sight of the fact—indeed we should be unceasing in emphasizing the fact—that our training system is not intended to prepare young men for the profession of arms as a profession; that our aim is to prepare our graduates by a system of discipline for the practical affairs of life. In a word, our system of training fits our graduates for the vocations of civil life, and, if you please, for the profession of arms as an avocation—and as an avocation only.
>
> The terms "West Point of the South," "The Southern School of the Soldier" have been frequently used in connection with the institute. These names are misleading and may prove exceedingly mischievous. They arose during the Civil War. At that time their use was justified.[28]

Nichols's contention *sui generis* was that VMI was "not the professional school of the soldier; it never has been! It is not a university nor even a college for high cultural attainments; it never has been! It is simply 'The Virginia Military Institute' with all that the name implies!"[29] He advised, "We should use, as we have used, the soft pedal when playing to the tune of 'The West Point of the South' or to the tune of 'The Southern School of The Soldier' in times of peace. When there are war or rumors of war we can then open the stops and employ a brass band as an additional accompaniment!"[30]

The Fourth Claim

In reality, General Nichols was fighting an uphill and ever-widening battle. By 1920, six years before his own history of VMI, *Fifty Years of Service*, appeared, a fourth claim on the title of VMI's originator had been staked by Mrs. John H. Moore. Her charming *Memories of a Long Life in Virginia* contained stories about growing up in Lexington. She remembered her grandfather Andrew Alexander's suggesting, "It would be better to have a military school like West Point, and let the cadets guard the arsenal." She also recalled, "Colonel Thomas L. Preston brought the subject up in the Franklin Society, where it was discussed."[31]

Here Moore confused J.T.L. Preston with his father, Major Thomas L. Preston, who had helped found the Franklin Society. But her contention was that her grandfather Andrew Alexander, surveyor of Rockbridge County in 1816 when the arsenal was built, was the earliest originator of the idea of a military school as replacement for the arsenal. In his history General Nichols acknowledged that he'd heard this same story from Major William A. Anderson, Civil War hero and long-time resident of the vicinity, who had heard it in his youth. But as William Couper has concluded about such rumors, "No contemporary written document has yet been discovered which gives the name of the originator of the basic idea."[32]

The Fifth Claim

In reviewing General Nichols's history and his rejection of Crozet as VMI's originator, Matthew W. Paxton, son of Confederate General Frank Paxton and editor of the *Rockbridge County News,* took the occasion to suggest yet a fifth claim on the title. In his editorial, "Rockbridge when the Virginia Military Institute was Founded," he announced on October 14, 1926, "The *County News* will now put into print for the first time a story it has heard from a trustworthy source of an incident of the time which brought to a head this private discussion, if it did not originate it."[33]

Paxton's candidate was Hugh Barclay, a Lexington merchant who had visited West Point in the early 1830s. He was fascinated by the splendid drills and training of the cadets that he witnessed, so he told his friends at the Franklin Society with great enthusiasm what he had seen. Paxton contended that Barclay started the discussion of turning the old arsenal into a military school modeled on West Point: "If what he [Barclay] said was not the beginning of the discussion to turn 'The Old Arsenal' into a military school patterned after West Point, it probably brought the subject to a head."

Paxton cited Barclay's overriding interest in the founding of the institute. This was evidenced by his being appointed to the original board of visitors and made treasurer upon VMI's establishment. He recalled Barclay as a man of education and intelligence. He was a popular and successful businessman and at one time presiding justice of the county court. And he took great interest in the welfare of his county and country. Since the focus of Paxton's article was actually on Rockbridge County, he hastened to expand his tribute to all those associated with the school's founding for their being Rockbridge men: governors, senators, representatives, soldiers, clergymen, professors, doctors, merchants, and "other outstanding figures whose influence was doubtless sympathetic in founding V.M.I."

It's true that on August 7, 1835, three weeks prior to Preston's "Cives" articles, a report about "West Point Academy" by its own board of visitors had appeared in the *Lexington Gazette*.[34] And were it not for the Franklin Society's rejection of VMI as a second West Point and the deliberate omission of West Point as a model in Preston's articles, Barclay might very well qualify as the originator of the idea. He was as much an originator as Crozet or Alexander or anyone else who envisioned the school as primarily military rather than more broadly defined as a scientific and literary institution. But its goal, as Preston reported in his semi-centennial history, was "not to fit its graduates to a single profession ... but to prepare young men for the varied work of civil life."

In 1939, William Couper reaffirmed Preston as the institute's originator, founder, and father in both his centennial history of VMI and his dedication of the Preston Library. Perhaps he meant to bar the door against more fathers who would step in where Preston had left it ajar. His *One Hundred Years at V.M.I.* called Preston the individual "who was most instrumental in the foundation of the institute," "who had more to do with advocating the establishment of the institute than any other man," "who was the leader in the establishment of the institute," and "the original champion of the foundation of the Virginia Military Institute."[35]

In his Dedication of the Preston Library, Couper concluded,

> Virginia Military Institute is not essentially a fighting school, no more than was the man who fathered it a fighting man. It is and was an educational institution first and the man who founded it was an educated and educational man first, also.
>
> Let it be added hastily, before some of the grand old ghosts of the institute turn over in their honored graves, that Virginia Military Institute can and will fight when it is called upon. It has fought, gallantly and courageously, and a revered portion of American history hallows its heroes.
>
> The same thing can be said of its originator, Col. John Thomas Lewis Preston. Making war was not this man of paradoxical nature's business but when the step seemed the most intelligent for him to take, he took it resolutely with never a backward or regretful glance, regardless of the cost which, more often than not, was heavy, quite heavy.[36]

The Sixth Claim

If Couper thought his arguments had finally laid the issue to rest, he would be sadly mistaken. Colonel James Morgan, Jr., in his 1966 article "Changing Face of VMI," revisited the matter with an entirely new originator. Morgan speculated, "I like to feel that the VMI was first conceived, although tangentially, in a letter of 1 April 1816 from Governor Wilson Cary Nichols *[Morgan's spelling]*, and addressed to the Honorable Samuel McD. Moore, a citizen of Lexington. In his letter, Governor Nichols requested Mr. Moore to be the chairman of a five-man body of local inhabitants who would recommend to him the location of an arsenal to be constructed in the western part of the state. Mr. Moore lived in a dwelling located on what is now the VMI Post."[37] Morgan's candidate for the school's father was the nineteenth governor of Virginia, Wilson Cary Nicholas, whose term from 1814 to 1816 preceded the construction of the original Lexington Arsenal.

In September 2003, Bradford Wineman presented a paper at the Shenandoah Valley Regional Studies Seminar. Like Couper, he sought to settle the continuing argument by detailing Preston's role during the eight years it took to found the school. He titled his paper "J.T.L. Preston, VMI and the Revolution in Virginia Education, 1834–1839."[38] It re-appeared in the *Virginia Magazine of History and Biography* in 2006 under the revised title "J.T.L. Preston and the Origins of the Virginia Military Institute, 1834–42."

Singling out the "Cives" articles that defined the school, Wineman credited Preston with "taking what had been a debate topic and shepherding it into life as a functioning military academy."[39] Wineman used the narrow term "academy," which Preston had rejected in favor of "institute." But he depicted its goal, as Preston had envisioned it, to be broadly social, political, and cultural in its influence. He described the southern military education that Preston fathered at VMI as replicated "throughout the antebellum South."[40] It was not intended as a preparation for Civil War, though it contributed significantly to the leaders of that war. Nor was it designed to train for the military profession, as at West Point. Moreover, it was not even meant entirely for the improvement of the individual. Wineman argued,

> Preston intended for the benefits of his proposed military school to extend beyond the betterment of the individual young men who attended. Indeed, the young lawyer envisioned this new institution benefiting his entire state—its economy, society, and even its democratic values. The process of VMI's establishment included such variables unique to Preston's time and setting as Virginia's political party system, community activism, reform movements, and concepts of state service, in addition to the broader reconciliation of militarism and republicanism.[41]

Wineman credited Preston, as founder of the school, for having articulated the ideas that serve today as the fundamentals of a military education instead of an education for the military: "What began as a solution to curb the irreverent behavior of a small detachment of soldiers resulted in an academic revolution that made military academies the most popular form of higher education in the American South in little more than two decades. The ideas Preston presented in his 'Cives' articles laid the foundations of the southern military education system, which survives in much the same form today."[42]

A Seventh Candidate

Alden Partridge, 1785–1854. Steel engraving by H. W. Smith. Partridge was a pioneer of literary, scientific, and military academies in early America (Norwich University Archives, Kreitzberg Library, Northfield, Vermont, Alden Partridge Records, Box 1, Non-Photographic Images file).

It's true that Preston disclaimed being the first to suggest the notion of VMI. But it's almost certain he was not referring to previous ideas of Crozet, Barclay, Alexander, and others who were primarily focused on military training. Preston's goal was a disciplined education in literary, practical, scientific, and military instruction. Well read and highly educated, he would have looked beyond the confines of Lexington and even Virginia for the origin of such an idea. And he would have found it in the enlightened and far-reaching views of a controversial pioneer in educational reform, Captain Alden Partridge in Vermont. His "Plan of Establishing Additional Military Academies," published in 1815, was a true source of many ideas that would find their realization at VMI.[43]

Partridge had graduated from West Point in 1806 and even served as its fourth superintendent in 1814–17. He originated the uniforms that have since identified its cadets and graduates as "The Long Gray Line." But he also questioned West Point's prevailing goal of producing what he saw as "a military aristocracy that was a threat to republican institutions."[44] He conceived of great generals, like George Washington and Andrew Jackson, as more broadly educated than the soldiers West Point was producing. Since "a well-trained citizen soldiery was the best protection for the republic," he believed training the militia was an urgent necessity. Rejecting West Point as a model for his 1815 "General Plan" to meet the necessity, Partridge was ultimately forced to resign from the Academy and from the army. He promptly proposed, as alternatives to West Point, "a comprehensive national system of military education."[45]

Partridge adopted the ideal of the "citizen-soldier" as the driving force behind his intention "to prepare his students for useful and responsible roles as civilians but, when necessary, they could assume duty as military officers in a citizen army." His school would instill in his young men the education and character traits necessary to serve their country both in and out of uniform. Instead of a "purely military" education, he recommended "one in which military instruction would only be an 'appendage' to civil education." And he sought to expand "the classical curriculum to include modern languages and history as well as political economy, agriculture, engineering, and physical education," thus making the traditional curriculum "more practical, scientific, and liberal."[46]

Between 1819 and 1853, the year before his death, he founded eight literary, scientific, and military institutions. These were not state-based schools, as he would have preferred, but private, beginning with the American Literary, Scientific, and Military College in Vermont. In 1834 it became Norwich University, recognized today as the oldest private military school in the U.S. Prior to 1839 his plan spawned several short-lived imitators in New York, New Jersey, North Carolina, Mississippi, and South Carolina. All of them would incorporate his ideas of a broadly based, disciplined education as depicted in his 1826 *Discourse on Education*.[47] His other literary, scientific, and military academies, all of which were also short lived, were established during or after 1839 in Virginia, Pennsylvania, Delaware, and New Hampshire.[48] His National Scientific and Military Academy was destroyed by fire and closed the same year it opened.

Being familiar with Partridge's ideas, Preston would have rightly disavowed any originality in his own application of many of them to the founding of VMI. In fact, it was Partridge who had lent support to Preston's efforts to found VMI with his open letter in 1836 to the *Lexington Gazette* about the establishment of a military institution at the arsenal in Lexington. He had assured Delegate Dorman that a depository of public arms was "more safe under the protection of a military school properly organized than under the protection of any guard of enlisted soldiers whatever."[49]

An Eighth Candidate

In addition to Partridge, another early advocate of ideas that found their way into the creation of VMI was Thomas Jefferson, with whose writings Preston was familiar.

If the originator of an idea makes an individual the father of an institution, then perhaps Jefferson would qualify as the father of VMI for the same reason that he became the father of the University of Virginia. He favored a general plan of state-supported education for all classes based on the democratic idea that the education of the people was a proper concern of government.[50] Although Jefferson's idea was at first rejected by the Virginia legislature as incurring too great a tax upon the people, it was ultimately accepted when the university was founded on his principle in 1819. But he had pointed out fields which the university had not addressed, such as military, technical, mechanical, and agricultural training. Preston would have felt fully prepared to rectify these deficiencies in his own creation of VMI without having to credit Jefferson in his "Cives" articles nor claim any of Jefferson's ideas as his own.

A Ninth Candidate

Unknown to Preston, one of the earliest advocates of setting up a military school in Lexington had been his own father. In 1810 Thomas Preston had asked the patronage of Congress for "a military school at Washington Academy."[51] But at the time Washington Academy rescinded its petition, leaving Lexington to wait another quarter century for a military school entirely separate from the college.[52]

It's entirely conceivable that Preston's diplomatic disclaimer to being the first to suggest the idea of VMI wisely left unnamed its rival originators. He would not have wished to detract from the significant contributions of men like Smith, Crozet, Barclay, Alexander, and others who were also close friends. But if asked to name the true originators of the idea, he neither could, nor would, have denied the direct or indirect influence of men like Partridge and Jefferson. Many of their notions he had passionately advocated at the Franklin Society, persuasively articulated in his "Cives" articles, and then spent the next four years defining, defending, refining, and promoting in order to assure the ultimate success of a truly unique experiment.

The Father

As Robert W. Jeffrey, historian and public relations director for VMI in 1952, remarked in his brief history of VMI for *The Iron Worker*, "Colonel Preston repeatedly disclaimed credit for originating the idea of creating V.M.I. from the arsenal, although others—including the institute's first superintendent—singled out the author of "Cives" as conceiver of the plan. But even if the original idea did not come from the fertile mind of Colonel Preston, it was he who championed the cause during the institute's incipiency and provided the impetus which resulted in its foundation."[53]

In line with Jeffrey's conclusion, when the Franklin Society first introduced the issue of replacing the arsenal, it was Preston who opposed converting it into another West Point and then won the argument for linking it instead with Washington College. When his oral argument before the Franklin Society needed written expression, it was Preston who synthesized in his Cives articles the classics and the sciences into a militarily disciplined liberal education of young men preparing for civil, ecclesiastical, or military careers. When the proposed school needed legislative support to make it official, it was Preston who had his Cives articles republished on a single sheet, took them to the state legislature, and personally laid a copy on the desk of each member of the House of Delegates.

When the school needed a name, it was Preston who formulated one. When it needed an administrator, it was Preston as a member of its board of visitors who invited and convinced Francis Smith to serve as its first superintendent. And when the school risked straying off the track of a balanced education, which distinguished it from all other schools that lacked either the classical or the practical approach to learning, it was Preston who helped shape and reshape the school's core curriculum over the first half century of its efforts to turn the ideal of the complete citizen-soldier into reality. More important than all these individual accomplishments, however, was Preston's believing in, formulating, promoting, advocating, and molding the character of a school so fundamentally different from West Point and other normal schools that it helped begin an educational revolution. He was not the father for having had the idea, since who had it first cannot be definitively established. And he was not the father for having shaped every aspect of its application. But he was the father for having envisioned the living spirit of an institute made real by his work, which was the embodiment of his mind and heart.

It's ironic but revealing that in 2013, the popular online Wikipedia associates Major General Francis Henney Smith and Colonel Claudius Crozet with VMI but makes no mention at all of J.T.L. Preston, as though he played no role in its founding. In his dedication speech at the Preston Library in 1939, historian William Couper drew a vital distinction between the man and his creation when he concluded, "Col. J.T.L. Preston, the original spirit of Virginia Military Institute, died. The spirit, however, which this grand old gentleman instilled into the school, still lives, a tribute to his vision, a memorial to his intelligence."[54]

Preston would have been content to live anonymously within this spirit that still thrives at VMI. Indeed, he'd have considered a chapter such as this one in an account of his life and its many accomplishments as pretentious. It's little wonder he dodged the appellation of Father of VMI as inexcusably egocentric. But he took great pride in what he had in fact fathered. He confessed at the end of his semi-centennial history of the institute his delight and amazement that after fifty years and a great Civil War his vision of the VMI cadet had been fully realized. "The writer," he marveled as author of the Cives articles, "little supposed that he should live to see the unconscious prophecy of his last lines fulfilled in blood, and recorded in glory."[55]

A postcard of Virginia Military Institute, 1919–20 (Washington and Lee University, Leyburn Library Special Collections, Rockbridge Historical Society Photograph).

Part III:
The First Decade

The Trustees of Washington College have no desire for any change in the present location of the Virginia Military Institute.
—Samuel McD. Reid,
Secretary, 21st of June
1849

6

Professor of Modern Languages

He taught Latin in the good old fashion, with none of the frills and furbelows of the modern Latinist.
— Colonel Joseph Anderson

Three months before the first of the celebrated Cives articles appeared in the *Lexington Gazette* and three years into John's and Sally's marriage, when both his mother, Edmonia, and sister, Elizabeth, were still boarding in the home on the hill, Sally gave birth on June 2, 1835, to their first child: a boy. John promptly named him after the father he himself had never known: Thomas Lewis Preston, to be known as Tom. This thoroughly pleased Edmonia for the honor bestowed on her departed husband, but it was the only time Preston would pay tribute to his father. Indeed, it was his lifelong silence about his father that would lead his grandson to call it "a rather curious thing."[1] And Preston's son, George, admitted he never in his life heard Preston mention his own father's name or anything about him.

This mystery might be rather curious were it not for the fact that Preston knew practically nothing of his father. Apart from his being too young at sixteen months when his father died to remember him, it's significant that his mother's prolonged grief over her husband's death rendered her, in the words of one of Preston's great-grandsons, "unable to talk to her children of their father, hence they knew very little of him." Edmonia was only twenty-five when he died, and so deep was her grief over her loss that it bordered on morbidity. "She would never drive past the cemetery where her husband was buried, and if her coachman inadvertently turned down that stretch of street, she would cower down, and hide her eyes!" Invariably she would direct the carriage away from the south end of Main Street, even if it entailed circling by a longer route. During thirty-five years of widowhood, she made no mention of her husband to her own children. As a consequence, it's a poignant fact that J.T.L. Preston's father "was only a name to his descendants."[2] He would exist no more in his children's memories than in his own.

Instead, Preston regarded his uncle, James McDowell, as "the only father he knew."[3] Colonel McDowell owned Cherry Grove Mansion, a large, two-story, white frame house in a full lawn shaded by giant oak trees near Fairfield. He was a man of strong common sense and unflinching integrity, which he applied to keeping his plantation in good order, including the distillation of large quantities of cherry brandy. The dwelling had the reputation of a happy, cultured, bountiful country home. It was here that Preston's father had once stayed, for like Preston, he too had lost his father when he was not yet two. The stately figure of Colonel McDowell had impressed both Preston and his father like the father that neither of them knew in the absence of their own. But now, three months after the birth of Preston's first child, Colonel McDowell at sixty-five was on the verge of death.

On September 12, 1835, Preston wrote James, Jr., "The mournful event which we have long dreaded, is now alas, we have but too certain reason to believe, at hand. Your dear Father was this morning about 10 a.m. visited with a stroke of paralysis, so deathlike in its character, as to leave in the opinion of the physician little hope that he will ever awake from it." Preston expressed the fervent wish that his letter would reach James "early enough to stand with us around his bedside." He added, "My dear cousin, I will not attempt to inspire your heart with a hope that does not exist in mine, the only consolation I can offer, is the heartfelt sympathy under the bereavement which takes away one who in affection has been to me as well as to you a father."[4] The revered Colonel McDowell, natural father of James and surrogate father of John, died three days later with both "sons" at his bedside.

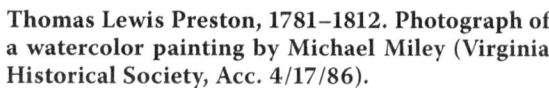

Thomas Lewis Preston, 1781–1812. Photograph of a watercolor painting by Michael Miley (Virginia Historical Society, Acc. 4/17/86).

On October 8, 1835, a month after Colonel McDowell's death, Preston's sister Elizabeth married William Armistead Cocke. She sold her half-interest in the town lot to her brother and moved to William's 2,400-acre colonial home, known as Oakland, forty miles north of Richmond.[5] Their mother, Edmonia, then divided her time between the homes of her children, spending six months at Oakland and six months in Lexington. But rather than posing a burden, she was readily welcomed in both houses. So devoted were her children to her that the only disagreement that ever arose between them, according to Elizabeth, "was caused by each one thinking the beloved mother ought to spend the whole time in their respective homes."[6]

In late May of 1836, Preston traveled to Port William (now Carrollton) to sell land at the mouth of the Kentucky River. In northern Indiana he bought a plot of land for little Tom, not quite a year old, "just as our grandfather did for us," he wrote his cousin James McDowell from Louisville.[7] By late 1837 he had bought a seventy-eight-acre farm two and a half miles southwest of Lexington on the Plank Road, which he named Foxwood.[8] His purchase would satisfy a love he had for physical exercise, manual labor, and agriculture, "a favorite subject with him."[9] He checked out from the Franklin Society's library issues of the *New York Farmer* and, over time, experimented with great success on combinations of fertilizer for use on his plants.

The farm helped supply the family as much as it gave him enjoyment during hours of leisure. He became quite proficient at growing crops, feed, and livestock. He employed a large number of strong horses, which he meticulously groomed, and utilized the best agricultural tools available. Even after his death his farm would still produce lucrative sales of hay, wheat, corn, cattle, hogs, and wood. He attributed his success in agriculture to three things: "The blessing of God, deep ploughing, and clover seed," which he sowed abundantly as supplements to manure for fertilizer.[10]

When his and Sally's second child, a girl, was born on November 27, 1837, Preston honored her with the name of his devoted mother, Edmonia Madison Randolph. More than anyone else, Preston had his mother to thank for his forceful intellect, sustaining faith, and resolute character that had stood him in such good stead when he most needed direction in life. Another girl, born two years after Edmonia on August 12, 1839, they named in remembrance of Sally's mother, Phoebe Alexander, who had died when Sally was only ten.

The family was now poised on the threshold of an extremely promising future. Preston had a successful law practice, a seat on the board of visitors of an emerging school, a stately home, three young children, a farm, and property that he had inherited or purchased. This included his father's twenty-one-acre town lot adjacent to his hilltop home and 1,000 acres in Louisville, Kentucky, as well as land he had bought bordering his Kentucky holdings and property in and near Lexington. Since 1834 he had been developing lots along Randolph Street, adjacent to his home, which provided housing for working-class carpenters, stone and brick masons, shoemakers, chairmakers, and blacksmiths.[11]

This land after the Civil War would become known as Diamond Hill.[12] In 1883, because of Preston's presence as a developer of much of Diamond Hill, the town council almost named a new street for him. But the next year, with Matthew Maury's death in need of commemoration, the road was christened Maury Street instead. Preston Street became the name for the road where Preston then lived in south Lexington, known at the time as Lewis Street.[13] The name Lewis Street was then applied to the road along the crest of Diamond Hill above Maury Street. Where Preston Street was first proposed on Diamond Hill, there was a growing interest after the war by many blacks for settlement across from VMI. So a new neighborhood called Freedman's Hill was developed where Preston had provided so much land and had rented vernacular wood-frame housing to black tenants. Even on North Main Street near the intersection of Diamond Lane, Preston would create a subdivision of modest frame houses in the late 1870s, known as Preston Row, that blacks would occupy from the outset.[14]

At twenty-eight and with so many lucrative projects under way, Preston may have felt he could afford to change careers midstream. In 1839 he considered abandoning eight years of success as a shrewd and incisive attorney with decent earnings to embark on a profession that drew far less pay and risked a far more uncertain future for himself and his family. He knew he possessed all the qualities prerequisite to a successful future in the legal world. But when he came to admit his feelings, he didn't relish the lawyer's "contact with wrong doers," nor did he sanction "some sharp practice on certain legal levels."[15]

For some time now, he had been actively seeking other ways to use his considerable talents more completely and more acceptable to himself. Then, on November 13, 1839, the board of visitors at the Virginia Military Institute elected him to the newly established occupation he himself had created and for which he felt himself more properly fitted: professor of modern languages. And for the next forty years teaching would be the career he would passionately pursue, finding far more delight and meaning in inspiring young men than in defending offenders of the law.

7

Classical and Practical

An education which, while not antagonizing the established system of classical education, should have a strict bearing upon ... the practical pursuits of life.

—J.T.L. Preston

As a professor of rhetoric, literature, and language, Preston provided the necessary academic balance for the otherwise scientific focus of the school. For him, a classical education in these three areas provided the keys to social success for the citizen side of the soldier. He would teach his students Blair's axiom, "To speak or to write perspicuously and agreeably, with purity, with grace and strength, are attainments of the utmost consequence to all who propose, either by speech or writing, to address the Public. For without being master of those attainments, no man can do justice to his own conception."[1]

But for a citizen to achieve lasting success in the social order of the time, Preston felt he had to have more than just a solid knowledge of the belles lettres and a facility in rhetoric. A prerequisite to having something to say and the skill to say it would be the possession of virtue and personal character. Blair's second axiom advised, "Without possessing the virtuous affections in a strong degree, no man can attain eminence in the sublime parts of eloquence. He must feel what a good man feels, if he expects greatly to move, or to interest mankind."[2] For the citizen side of the soldier, an education in rhetoric, literature, and language had not only the capacity to provide upward mobility in society but also the ability to promote morality.

Helping to instill these qualities in his students was all that was needed to give permanent meaning to Preston's choice of a life's work. He embarked on his new career as the only liberal arts teacher at the institute, earning an annual salary of $700 for teaching French and English. Francis Smith, at $1,500, would cover the science of mathematics and military tactics.

On the day that the school opened, however, Preston's dream nearly collapsed. The winter of 1839 proved to be brutally harsh. So intense was the cold, facing twenty-nine cadets crammed into four half-finished sixteen-square-foot rooms, some without roofing, that Superintendent Smith admitted "it was impossible to write with chalk on the blackboard."[3] The roads and ground were covered with heavy snow, there was no fuel supply, and there were no uniforms apart from the clothes that the cadets had brought with them. So intolerable were the frigid conditions that they held a secret meeting and, according to Cadet Edmund Pendleton, "angrily discussed the question whether they would not disband and return to their homes. This action, on being put to the vote, very narrowly escaped being decided in the affirmative."[4]

Their young superintendent, just twenty-six at the time, implored them to stay.

But it was what Preston had predicted in his Cives letters that ultimately rescued the school from immediate failure. As Bradford Wineman observed in his article about Preston's plan for the institute, "If these young men had enrolled at VMI solely for the purpose of receiving a college education, they most assuredly would have immediately abandoned the school. Instead, their belief that they were pursuing something higher than mere schooling, that they were developing character and serving their state, allowed them to bear the suffering. The prospect of achieving the goals set by Preston made them, and all of those who followed, believe they were part of something unique, different from any other endeavor in higher education."[5]

Only three incidents of disorderly conduct marred VMI's initial year. For profane language Cadet Carter was confined to the institute limits, as were Cadets Forbes and Crump for fighting. But it was the conduct of Cadets Forbes and Crump, who had appeared at parade intoxicated, that introduced a long-standing tradition at VMI. They would have been dismissed instead of confined if their entire class hadn't pledged to abstain from all intoxicating liquors for the remainder of their tenure at the institute, a pledge that was dutifully honored.[6]

With only two professors supervising thirty-two cadets and only Smith living at the institute, Preston grew concerned that he too should live on post. He proposed to the board of visitors that he "erect at his own expense a house" for $3,500 to be reimbursed in three years interest free, which the board readily accepted and conferred upon him the rank of captain.[7] How Sally felt about his generous offer would emerge only later. A decade hence Preston recorded in his journal that, for himself, he would have been willing to live in a "staff house." It would be quite small and far from luxurious but romantic in style. But Sally had objected to "going to live upon the V.M.I. Hill, because the quarters of the cadets are so near." In retrospect Preston would muse roguishly, "Let her know that Queen Victoria is content to have common soldiers just next door!"[8] But Sally saw no humor in the proposal and no reason to sacrifice their family's grand home on the hill for a shack, however romantic, near Barracks. So the family remained in their preferred home.

At the end of the first year of precise and rigid class work, examinations were conducted orally and in public before the board of visitors. The results convincingly validated the method of teaching employed at the new school. Preston taught as he had always learned, not from books and lectures but from debating and arguing in the classroom. As one student recalled, "Col. Preston did not lecture. He held a colloquium."[9] He favored small sections and daily recitations that involved the cadets directly in the learning process. These recitations developed their powers of logic and persuasion, allowing them to communicate their thoughts and ideas effectively and convincingly.

In due course the success that attended this method of teaching would gain public attention. As a result, in 1851 Smith would publish *College Reform*, a book based on "the system of discipline and instruction here introduced" at VMI "with a view to a reform of the college system, as it has existed in some of the oldest institutions of our country."[10] The practice at VMI, as Smith would confirm, had replaced the college system of "lecturing" a student by a method of "examining him upon the text." It divided "the classes in each department of study into sections of fifteen each, each section to recite separately for one hour or one hour and a half.... Lessons should as far as practicable be *learned from the text-book,* and each student thoroughly examined each day upon the lessons of the day."[11]

During the second year Preston added German to his list of courses, while continuing to emphasize the importance of taste, style, and eloquence in public speaking. Thomas H. Williamson, Major Smith's former roommate at West Point, was appointed the school's third professor, teaching engineering, drawing, and tactics. Smith introduced into the curriculum trigonometry, descriptive and analytic geometry, and calculus. As a sign of the times, he added Bible recitations every Sunday, conducted by himself and Preston. And to assure that abstract learning was accompanied by practical application, the cadets were assigned to Professor George Armstrong's class in chemistry at Washington College. This was done in exchange for military training of Washington College students at VMI.

The course exchange was financed by the Cincinnati Fund, an endowment that had been promised to Washington College by the Society of the Cincinnati. Formed in 1783 by a group of surviving officers of the American Revolution, the society had been named after its role model Lucius Quinctius Cincinnatus, the ideal citizen-soldier who left his farm in 458 B.C. to lead Rome to victory over the Aequi.[12] Cincinnatus then returned power to the Senate and resumed plowing his fields, very much like the American Revolutionaries who founded the society. George Washington, having set the example, was the patriotic society's first president. In 1802, after his death, the Virginia branch of the society offered its entire treasury of $15,000 to Washington Academy, to which General Washington had previously donated his James River shares of stock.[13] The funds could be given only on the "express condition" that "there shall be established, & continued, at the said seminary, a military school, in which shall be taught (at least) the Sciences of Fortification, and Gunnery."[14]

It was Preston's father, Thomas Lewis Preston, who had been sent to Washington in 1807 as the academy's agent to petition the support of Congress for "a military school" in Lexington.[15] But it wasn't until 1840, when the fund had accrued to around $23,000 and a military school existed, that Washington College became eligible to draw from it in cooperation with VMI. Washington College students began drilling with VMI cadets.[16] Legend has it that these joint drills prompted the students of Washington College to disparage the cadets as "rats." The cadets returned the favor by dubbing the college students "minks" since they appeared to the cadets as mean and sly.[17] It would be the mid 1850s before the VMI cadets would apply the term "rats" to their own freshly matriculated fourth class.[18]

Near the beginning of the third year of VMI's infancy, Virginia and its legislature were given the chance to witness firsthand the success of its and the South's first military school. Adjutant General William Richardson invited the cadet corps to Richmond to escort the funeral of Lexington's Revolutionary War hero, Captain William Moore. When the cadets paraded through Capital Square, headed by General Richardson's son, William, Jr., members of the House of Delegates and the public at large were thoroughly impressed by their grey uniforms "with black stripes down the sides of the pantaloons, with a glazed cap," their precision drill, and their "fine martial air—Young as they are, they look the soldier. We have no doubt that they are admirably taught and trained, and will do high honor to the state."[19] But even more impressive was their stellar performance on semester examinations carried out in front of the entire legislative body. At their next opportunity, the legislators increased the institute's yearly annuity by $1,500 and provided an annual $500 for the next five years to establish a library.

One of the requirements of the act of March 1842, which granted VMI a share of the Literary Fund revenue, was its mandate that every cadet "shall be required to act in the capacity of a teacher in some one of the schools within the commonwealth, for the term of two years after finishing his course at the institute," without requiring military service.[20] In one official stroke the state had endorsed Preston's growing intent that VMI be a normal school. If it didn't become the nation's first, it certainly became Virginia's first normal school, giving its citizens a generous return on their tax dollar by providing teachers for its academies and private schools and improving education in Virginia.[21] "Credit for this," as Edwin Dooley has pointed out, "must be given to the institute's state cadet program, the brainchild of Adjutant General of Virginia William Harvie Richardson, and VMI professor of Latin Colonel J.T.L. Preston."[22]

The following year Superintendent Smith was lauding the initial success of the program in his annual report. He declared, "Many graduates from this school are fully engaged in instruction in our academies and primary schools and have in every case given great satisfaction. The academies in Richmond, Norfolk, Petersburg, Fredericksburg, and Winchester are supplied with them and others are teaching in Amherst, Buckingham, Gloucester, Roanoke, Botetourt and Rockbridge."[23] The focus on July 4, 1842, was on the demonstrated accomplishments of the first graduating class of sixteen cadets. Their diplomas represented three years of mathematics, mechanics, chemistry, engineering and tactics, French, English, German and German literature, and drawing.[24]

Due to a legislative act during the fourth year, Latin was substituted for German in the school's basic curriculum. The Virginia House of Delegates felt that German, which was originally introduced to meet the demands of a large and increasing German population, was no longer as vital as Latin to prepare graduates for teaching. French was still the language of science, but Latin was the language of education, particularly for the learned professions. In short time, Smith would report VMI's being "regarded by the public as having reformed elementary education" in Virginia through its graduation of well-trained native teachers who were in high demand.[25] Consequently Preston, as professor of modern languages, was now being asked to teach his favorite course, the ancient language of Latin. He was further instructed to teach rhetoric and logic, which would help preserve the essential balance within the curriculum between the sciences and the arts.

Years later Colonel Joseph R. Anderson, Class of 1870, would recall learning Latin, rhetoric, and logic under the "dear old Roman" and never experiencing a dull moment. Anderson reported that he "had studied Latin under one Dublin University graduate and three University of Virginia graduates—all Masters of Arts, and all called famous instructors, but ... not one of them could be compared with Colonel Preston. He taught Latin in the good old fashion, with none of the frills and furbelows of the modern Latinist."[26]

Anderson remembered that "Colonel Preston was so enthusiastic as a teacher that he imparted unconsciously, but none the less surely, his own spirit and *fire* to all who sat under him." His students were always kept interested and continually on the alert. Anderson himself was so inspired that he would return in 1872 as assistant professor of Latin under then–Colonel Preston. Indeed, on returning for his final visit during the year that Preston died in 1890, Anderson still regarded him as "one of God's elect—a saint" for what Preston had contributed to his character as much as his intellect. For Preston, half if not most of teaching was essentially character development.

By 1844, Preston's classes were reciting daily in Latin and in English. His first sections finished Virgil's *Eclogues* and *Georgics* as well as all the orations of Cicero and completed Horace. They studied Lindley Murray's prescriptive *English Grammar* for structure and the Scotsman Hugh Blair's equally prescriptive *Lectures on Rhetoric and Belles Lettres* for effective oral and written discourse. Preston lectured solely on English literature.[27]

In his second sections he alternated recitations in Latin and French. The cadets read Virgil's *Aeneid,* Cicero, Horace as far as the *Satires,* and Caesar and then translated English into French. His only disappointment was that most of the cadets were sons of common merchants, farmers, and planters, as he discovered, "who have never studied any of the subjects taught at the institute, and whose minds have not been trained by previous education. As soon as they enter, they are put upon a very trying course of mathematics, are required to learn two languages, each entirely new, and after January spend two hours every other day in drawing—add to this occasional exercises in composition and declamation. To do all this as it ought to be done requires uncommon capacity or uncommon diligence."[28]

The problem was the alternation of Latin and French recitations in the second sections. The cadets would have fared better in one uninterrupted course that retained continuity. Indeed, the second year compounded the problem, disappointing Preston even further. Second-section cadets could see the obvious gap between themselves and their first-section classmates. Preston foresaw no problem in his first sections, since these cadets performed well and were "only stimulated by difficulties which depress others less favoured."[29] But his dream to educate the common man, who was usually poor and "under great disadvantage," rather than just the wealthy and the elite, was in jeopardy.

As it turned out, what was being tested was not the disciplined curriculum itself but Preston's faith in its effectiveness. The following year, to his gratification, the second-section cadets found French classes too easy. They translated French into English without the least difficulty. And the third-section cadets were the best he had ever had in French, even finishing Lesage's picaresque masterpiece *Gil Blas* before the end of the year. By 1846 his second-year Latin course proved that a competent knowledge of Latin could be acquired through uninterrupted daily recitation, even by those who had never studied it before.

Expanding his courses, Preston taught the newly published Augustus Mitchell's *Geography,* the Scotsman Robert Chambers' *History of English Literature,* and a history of Virginia. What was lacking was a history of the United States, which the board of visitors preferred to teaching statistics of Virginia. So by cadet request, Preston was able to add to his first class (senior) curriculum a military history of the Revolutionary War and the War of 1812 as part of a U.S. history course. By now his work load had increased considerably to six or seven sections of English grammar, elementary and philosophical rhetoric, English literature, history, French, and Latin, so he requested and received an assistant.[30]

While he was strengthening the department of language and literature, he was also pressing for a professor of physical sciences. The board of visitors had learned in early 1846 that Washington College would be separating from VMI in February. This meant cadet loss of access to chemistry instruction through the Cincinnati exchange with the college. So in April Preston wrote his cousin George Frederick Holmes, professor of ancient languages at Richmond College (now the University of Richmond), for his recommendation of a science professor to take to the board of visitors.[31]

As a result, the board appointed in July its fourth professor, Lieutenant William T. Gilham, a West Point graduate who was then serving with the U.S. Army in the recently declared Mexican War. His charge was to organize a new department of natural and experimental philosophy, chemistry, mineralogy, and geology. The upshot was that VMI would now offer within its own walls, under its own discipline, and according to its own methods of teaching, every classical and practical course that Preston had envisioned when he sought to broadly define the school in his Cives articles more than a decade past. His original intent, as his "Historical Sketch" to the board of visitors would later confirm, was to furnish its graduates with "an education which, while not antagonizing the established system of classical education, should have a strict bearing upon what, for want of a more distinctive term, may be designated the practical pursuits of life."[32]

8

VMI Under Attack

The friends of the institute in the General Assembly, in the passage of the act, were seriously contemplating the question of moving the institute from so unfriendly a community.
—Francis H. Smith

Despite VMI's internal progress in establishing a balanced academic curriculum, political problems were mounting externally that would threaten not only the school's reputation in the community but also its continued existence as a public institution. Washington College's determination to separate from VMI had been led the previous year, in 1845, by chemistry professor George Armstrong. He had complained to a legislative committee that the institute was engaging in direct rivalry with the college. He contended that it was "not good policy in the state to establish at Lexington a rival institution to the college." He added that "the legislature never intended to establish such an institution as the V.M.I. is becoming."[1]

As though a direct threat to the institute were not enough, the Reverend Professor Armstrong proceeded to attack its superintendent. He resurrected charges, first raised in June of 1844, that Colonel Smith was trying "to give a sectarian bias to this institution."[2] The issue first erupted during the laying of the cornerstone of the new Presbyterian Church in Lexington. Unavoidably Governor James McDowell had been prevented from keynoting the historic ceremony. His impartial role had been filled by a minister who spoke instead on behalf of Presbyterianism.

As Preston described the fiasco to the governor, the minister "gave a discourse of nearly an hour's length, which has created something of a sensation. It was strong, very— a trifle too strong, I think. His eulogy of the Presbyterian Church was fine and appropriate, but not content with this, he attacked the Episcopalians in such a manner as to overstep, in my opinion, the privileges of the occasion. In particular, he made what I consider as an open attack upon the institute, and a personal one upon Colonel Smith, as using the public funds and his official influence for the advancement of his church." Preston felt compelled to ask the governor for his aid as soon as convenient in order to reinvest the occasion "ex post facto" with dignity and help restore the institute's and Colonel Smith's good name.[3]

In the meantime, he found himself summoned before the board of visitors and the legislature to clear both the institute and Colonel Smith of all charges. Particularly with regard to the superintendent, various rumors had been circulating for more than a year that he was "securing the appointment of the sons of Episcopal parents to the exclusion of others." It was further rumored that in the institute's dealings with the merchants of the town he "conferred the patronage of the institute upon those who belong to the Episcopal Church alone" and that he was inducing cadets to become Episcopalians.[4]

Preston fashioned his defense of Smith like a court case. He marshaled his arguments to show that the board of visitors always appointed cadets "without the slightest regard for the religious preference of their parents," and any attempt to influence their decision "would not only be ineffective but would be resented by the members as an insult." Furthermore, the institute purchased only from those merchants "who have furnished supplies on the best terms, and to no others." He testified that all cadets were "allowed entire freedom" in their dealings, and he knew of no instance where Smith had tired "to induce the cadets to give their custom to Episcopalians."

While admitting that the cadets "attended the Methodist and Baptist churches less frequently than the Presbyterian and Episcopal churches," he attributed the imbalance to the zeal of "the present Episcopal minister," who visited the school more often than other ministers in the community. Indeed, Preston knew of no effort on Smith's part to control cadet access to the ministers which would have been as ineffective and insulting as trying to influence members of the board of visitors or the governor. Smith's conduct at the institute, he concluded, had been "not only correct, but scrupulous."

Fully persuaded by Preston's defense, the board voted not to investigate the charges against Smith since no complaint had been made except "through the traceless whisperings of rumor."[5] Smith himself, in addressing the rumors, denied exerting an Episcopalian influence and admitted only to being a devout member of the Episcopal Church. He promptly established a quartermaster's store to forestall any suspicion of misappropriating the $300 that he received from the board to provide cadets with supplies.

Having cleared Smith's name, Preston then turned to Armstrong's charge that VMI was competing directly with Washington College. At stake was the reputation of the institute as a public school. Preston convinced the committee of the legislature not to consider the complaint. So Armstrong took his grievance to the Lexington press. The newspapers printed a pseudonymous attack by "Alumnus" that slandered both Smith and Preston. Preston demanded the identity of Alumnus, but the editors denied knowing it. Smith asked the board of visitors to examine the complaints because it needed to act. The purpose, he argued, was not to convince "Alumnus," since "none are so blind as those who will not see," but for the sake of VMI's reputation as a public school. As embroiled as he himself was in the battle, Smith still upheld the view that, although "the law of love has been somewhat violated by our sister institution, and anonymous scribblers taunt us with sectarianism, no one has been bold enough to question the character of the school, or to reflect upon the eminent service it is now rendering to the cause of education."[6]

At Washington College, President Henry Ruffner proposed a compromise, which called for combining the college and the military school under the single title: "The Washington Institute of Virginia."[7] But the controversy had tarnished the institute's image, so much so that in 1846 the speaker of the House of Delegates felt bound to consider the advisability of removing VMI from Lexington. Perhaps "some village in the Valley" might be willing to erect a building "with a similar value with the present" to house it, rather than risk bitter feelings and disharmony between the two schools.[8]

When Philip St. George Cocke, a West Point graduate and president of the board of visitors, proposed to upgrade VMI's buildings in 1848 to the architectural scale of his own turreted and castellated Gothic villa, Belmead, on the James River, the legislature expressed its reservations. The proposal would cost $50,000 over the next three years. So on March 16, 1849, the General Assembly passed an act requiring the institute to consider the cost of moving to "a more suitable location" rather than incur the "expense of repairing the present buildings."[9] In his history of VMI, Smith summarized the intent of the act: "The friends of the institute in the General Assembly, in the passage of the act, were seriously contemplating the question of moving the institute from so unfriendly a community."[10] Accordingly, the board of visitors spent two weeks investigating relocation sites for the institute at Winchester, New Market, Harrisonburg, Waynesboro, Buchanan, and Salem.

Now Lexington, which had witnessed the rise of a rival to its college and had charged its superintendent with selling goods without a license and promoting sectarianism, suddenly saw itself at risk of losing a valuable asset. The existence of VMI had enabled Washington College to retain its Cincinnati Fund. It had induced the college to improve itself through rivalry. It had provided the merchants and farmers of the town with considerable income and attracted cadet fees and state funding to the community. Abruptly Rockbridge County citizens began offering resolutions at public meetings that "there is not, and can not be, any conflict of interest between it [the institute] and Washington College."[11] So the trustees of the College resolved that, there being no conflict, "the Trustees of Washington College have no desire for any change in the present location of the Virginia Military Institute."[12]

Ultimately the board of visitors, having completed its study of alternative locations, concluded on September 15, 1849, that it would be "inexpedient to remove the institute from its present location." It recommended building new barracks according to Cocke's plan, and it requested adding two professors' homes, five acres to the parade ground, and twenty-five more acres for drill and encampment, for a total expenditure of $46,300.[13] Not until early the following year would the fate of the board's recommendation and request for funding from the legislature be announced.

The request in the bill was for $50,000. On March 10 Smith returned from Richmond, inviting Preston and his friend John Lyle to join him and his wife for supper. Both men readily accepted, expecting news of the bill's progress. But Smith made no mention of it during supper, nor during a smoke and a discussion of the budget afterwards. Another half hour passed during which he related the particulars of his trip to Richmond, and their hopes began to wane. Preston had wished for good news, but Lyle had thought from the start that asking the legislature for that amount of money was ridiculous. When Smith still showed no signs of mentioning the bill, both men begged him to tell them when it might be considered. Smith ended his drama by pulling a bag from his pocket, which he claimed contained "the neat little sum of forty-six thousand dollars." When Preston and Lyle refused to believe him, he displayed a certified copy of the act of March 8, 1850, astounding them both. "Nothing," Smith recalled, "could exceed the joy of this little company."[14]

Ironically, the act that had threatened relocation of the institute proved to be a godsend. Today's castellated Gothic structure of flue limestone was constructed over the next five years. It was designed by Alexander J. Davis, whom Preston invited as one of the foremost architects in the country to plan the barracks.[15] What had begun as the first experiment in applying military discipline to a state-supported educational institution would celebrate its tenth birthday under the seal of the state as a certified success.

At the very moment that Preston's dream was enjoying full realization and widespread acceptance by the Lexington community, he himself fell victim to a mysterious attack. Someone posted his purported obituary in the *Richmond Enquirer*. On April 27, 1849, an announcement claimed he had died "of an internal expansion, on the 18th April, in the 49th year of his age."[16] Whether a disgruntled cadet, political adversary, or hoaxer, the obituary's author was severely reprimanded by the paper's editors. William and Thomas Ritchie were sons of the *Enquirer*'s cofounder Thomas Ritchie, Sr., who had been a close friend of Preston's father.[17] They themselves were former classmates of Preston at Richmond Academy.

Chagrined at having been duped, they took great pains to excoriate the ruse by publishing a retraction the following day under the headline "Gross and Malicious Imposition." Apologizing profusely, they explained, "We yesterday, upon the authority of a letter signed 'Lewis McDowell Preston,' and dated Lexington, Va., April 19th, published an obituary of Major J.T.L. Preston, Professor at the Military Institute. We are delighted to hear from the relatives of Major P. in this city, that the whole affair is a *hoax*, there being no such person as L. McD. Preston. While we rejoice to have this opportunity of publishing in time for our country circulation this correction of the reported death of Major P., for whom, as a schoolmate, friend and man of talents, we feel the highest regard, we cannot too strongly condemn the author of so silly and miserable an attempt to make mischief. Whoever he be, he merits the scorn of the community."[18]

9

Fluctuations

At least let me know whether you have sold the house over my head.
—Sally Caruthers Preston

On September 1, 1841, as VMI entered its third year with just over fifty new cadets, more than doubling the size of the corps to ninety, John and Sally celebrated the birth of their second son. Sally's brother, John Franklin Caruthers, had recently died. As her guardian, he had cared for her when he placed her in Dame's School, where she first met John. In loving remembrance of him they named their son Franklin, calling him Frank.[1] On the heels of his birth, hardly another year passed before little Edmonia, who was not yet five, passed away.[2] Of what she died was not known and would remain an unfathomable mystery, but the words carved on her gravestone reflected her parents' Christian belief that she was "Gone but not lost."

By 1843, with a wife and three children, Preston no longer felt inclined to live at the institute to be near the cadets. At his request the board of visitors canceled and rescinded his agreement to erect a dwelling on the institute's grounds, granting him instead a $100 annual raise.[3] He and Sally were content—or so she thought—to live on the hill within sight and walking distance of the post. But during the summer of 1844, while pregnant with her fifth child, Sally discovered to her consternation and astonishment that plans were underway without her knowledge that would severely affect the family.

Ordinarily, as her daughter Libbie would later confirm, Sally looked up to her husband "as a person of much greater intelligence and advantages than herself" and was readily inclined to accept his decisions.[4] But his recurrent absence on long trips had accustomed her to acting quite efficiently as the chief executive of the household. She attended to the needs of the children, bought winter clothes for the servants, assured that the horses, cattle, and sheep were fed, and killed a calf to have leather shoes made when old ones wore out. In addition, she entertained visiting relatives who naturally expected Virginian hospitality. She had always managed her tasks with intelligence, refinement, marked wisdom, and reasoned judgment. Preston would admit to Libbie that, although he somewhat underrated his wife's "natural mentality, so he afterwards thought, he had an almost superstitious regard for her judgment, which he seemed to consider intuitive and almost infallible."[5]

Libbie herself admitted that "now and then he made decisions without sufficient reference to her opinion." And on this particular occasion when he was away, Sally had learned from a chance encounter with his cousin Susan Taylor that her husband intended to move the family to a new home. She immediately wrote to him that Susan was "full of your exchanging houses; she told me you had nearly closed your bargain."

Sally had had no advance notice in the slightest that her life for the past twelve years might be about to change, not only precipitously but radically. She lamented, "This would necessitate many changes. We will not need as many servants in a smaller house, for we will have no room for company. Mr. Taylor has just been up to say that he was writing you he would take the house. I feel badly about it, but will say no more if this is your decision. Please say in your next letter whether the bargain is concluded, and whether you intend giving possession in the fall. At least let me know whether you have sold the house over my head."[6]

There is no record of Preston's reply, but as their daughter Libbie would later describe this "imperious act" by her father, there was indeed an exchange of homes occurring on the heels of their third son's arrival. On October 26, 1844, Sally gave birth to William Caruthers, whom she named after her father, calling him "Willie."[7] But hardly a month passed before the entire family—parents, servants, and four children, including Willie—were whisked away to new and smaller quarters. Preston's cousins William and Susan Taylor moved into the house on the hill, and the Preston family relocated—all of them—into what Libbie would later describe as "a rather small and far less attractive one on Main Street."[8]

Preston had acquired the Main Street home, known later as the Campbell-Jordan House between the Troubadour Theatre and the Willson-Walker House, for $2,000.[9] It was a two-story frame building with a large basement. "Between the weatherboarding and the laths was a filling of broken bricks and plaster, a primitive type of insulation. At each of the four corners, there were solid wooden corner-pieces, extending from the foundation to the eaves."[10] From Libbie's impressionable perspective, the house would have naturally appeared "far less attractive" owing to the fact that it was the oldest building in Lexington.[11]

Originally it had been an old log farmhouse belonging to Isaac Campbell, part donor of the land on which Lexington was built. Considering its rather sordid history, Preston might have thought twice before moving his pious family into this one time home of ruffians. Sally's Uncle Archibald Alexander was familiar with its infamous reputation. After the Revolutionary War the state of morals and religion had degenerated and the

> old continental soldiers, many of whom in that quarter were convicts, now returned, and having received certificates for their wages, were able to live for a while in idleness and dissipation. Robert ***, a shrewd, intelligent man, who was one of this number, had acquired a house in Lexington, the old farm-house of Isaac Campbell, who owned the land. Here he collected all the vagrants in the country, and a drunken bout would be kept up for weeks. They called themselves the Congress, and made Bob their president. Hard battles were fought here. The better class of people were as much injured by the profane and licentious manners of the officers of the disbanded army, as the lower classes by the soldiery.[12]

The Rev. Alexander's description of early life at Preston's new home ran a close parallel to the unsavory history of the Lexington Arsenal that Preston had just recently fought to replace with VMI.

Actually, the house was better built than Libbie's assessment of it would imply. A century later it was dismantled by Washington and Lee University, despite unsuccessful attempts by local preservationists to save it. During the dismantling it was seen to contain base sills of yellow poplar, 4 × 4 studding, and handmade nails and hand-hewn corner studding extending up two stories. Its mortises were so tight that even after the pins were removed, the uprights had to be dismantled by block-and-tackle attached to a large tree. Dr. Leslie Campbell would confirm at the time that "the whole house could have been easily rolled away, so firm were all the timbers in the frame work."[13]

Indeed, the failure of local efforts to save this house in 1939 would spark the founding of the Rockbridge Historical Society. Preservation advocate Ruth A. McCulloch lamented this destruction of Lexington's oldest pre–Revolutionary building, claiming, "So many persons were truly interested in this really historical landmark, and it was much talked-of, everyone wishing it could be preserved; but no one had the money to restore it."[14]

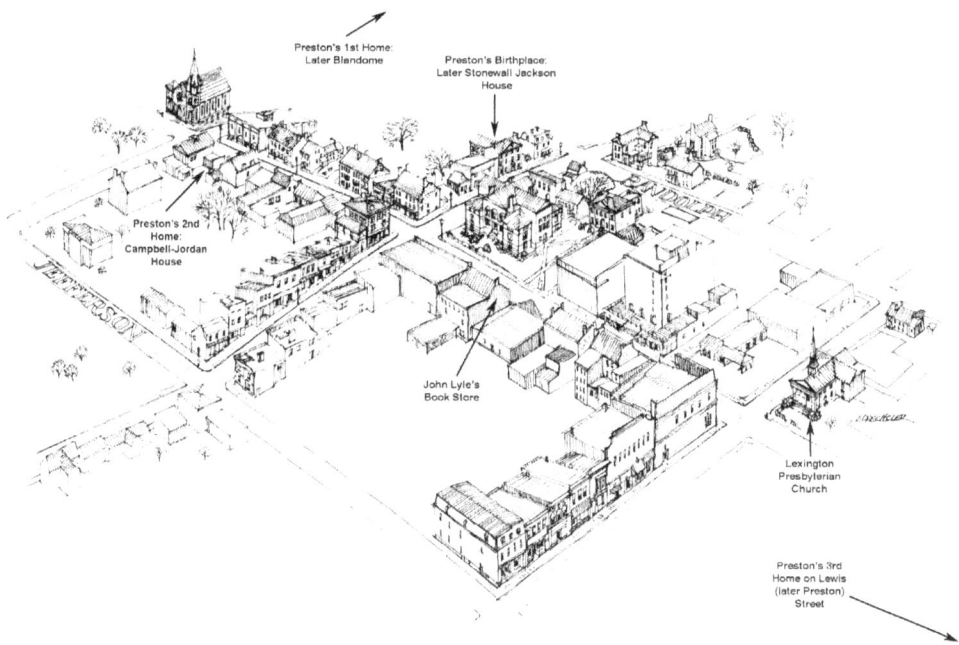

Drawing of historic Lexington showing Preston's homes. Adapted from "Historic Lexington" in Lyle and Simpson's *Architecture of Historic Lexington* (courtesy Historic Lexington Foundation).

The family's move into the Campbell House represented a definite downgrade from their more comfortable home on the hill. But it also typified Preston's inclination to rule his family, including his wife, with what Libbie described as "an imperious—high minded, dominant nature."[15] She avowed that "he belonged to the old regime which was almost feudal in its relation to women, children, and dependents."[16] Closely associated with military discipline, which he considered essential to the success of the institute, he expected instant and unquestioning obedience to authority, just as he himself placed his faith in "the requirement of perfect obedience" to God.[17]

But discipline and self-discipline meant balancing two powerful forces within his character. As Libbie admitted, her father had a temper that was "by no means lamblike." More profoundly, she hastened to add, "I do not believe that father was by nature a good tempered person, but that his temper was both quick and violent. His reverence

Preston's second home in 1844, the Campbell-Jordan House. No longer in existence, this house was centered between Glasgow House and Odd Fellows (Troubadour Theatre) on Main Street (Washington and Lee University, Leyburn Library Special Collections, Rockbridge Historical Society Photograph).

for God's law, his sense of responsibility for setting his children a good example, however, was so great, that he maintained perfect control over his tongue." In the short time that the family lived in the Campbell House on Main Street, Preston's control of his temper sparked a family legend that Libbie heard retold again and again by her older siblings. On one occasion he had grown so frustrated with a pair of twisting fire tongs that, in a towering rage without a cuss or curse, "he flung them out of an upper window on to the sidewalk at the risk of knocking a passerby on the head!" Even at his early age of thirty-three, he was an established "elder in the church, and could not afford to give vent to his wrath by the use of strong language."[18]

Libbie and her siblings used to speculate "(safely out of his hearing), whether it might not be worse to run the risk of manslaughter, than to 'say a few bad words!'" Libbie would later confirm that in her forty years of associating with her father, "I never heard him use a word even of mild profanity, or an irreverent or unseemly expression." She attributed this aspect of his character to "a stern self-control" that kept the underlying fires "banked down." He always balanced his anger with restraint out of a "reverence for God's law" and his "sense of responsibility for setting his children a good example."[19]

Whatever the Preston family's concern about their loss of comfortable living quarters, it was happily short lived. No sooner had they occupied their new home on Main Street than they abandoned it for a far more attractive home on the edge of town. It's conceivable that Preston had intended from the outset that his family occupy the smaller Main Street house only temporarily. Ten months prior to his purchasing it, he had also

9. Fluctuations

Preston's third home, 1845–90, at 110 Preston Street, formerly Lewis Street. This photograph shows Maggie, age fifty, with her sons George, age eleven (standing), and Herbert, age nine (sitting on a bench), in the orchard on the west side of the home. See Allan, *Life and Letters of Margaret J. Preston*, page 235, April 30, 1870: "Had the house photographed this morning" (author's collection, also Virginia Military Institute Archives, No. 0002286).

bought a large, beautiful home in the back lots of southwest Lexington. Contiguous with Woods Creek and accessed by an alley running up from Jefferson Street, it bordered Taylor's Grove. He and Sally had each spent their youth in the area or in the house. When still a lad, Preston had hunted squirrels and pigeons under the spreading oaks of Taylor's Grove with his teacher "Old Tidd" of Dame's School. And the house had been Sally's foster home for two years when she lived with Henry and Sally Ruffner. Ruffner had built it in 1821–24 after he came to teach at Washington College. When he moved into the President's House on campus in 1841, he sold his home to Alfred Leyburn, from whom Preston bought it in 1844.[20]

Needless to say, Sally was thrilled to escape the cramped quarters of their Main Street home and move into totally familiar accommodations. Libbie described their new home as "a large, three-story, double porticoed brick building, set in ten or twelve acres of land, at one end of the town, with fine trees about the house, a large garden on one side, a spacious lawn, a huge orchard on the other side, and a lot below the orchard for horses and cows."[21] Its wide windows featured a breathtaking view of the range that stretched from North and House mountains in the west across White Rock and Hogback to Jump Mountain in the north. The natural beauty of the setting was far preferable to downtown Lexington.

At the time of their move, Sally was pregnant with their sixth child. Born November 9, 1845, Edmund Randolph inherited the name of her father, but was called Ran. With a husband, five children, and servants living in larger quarters, Sally's housekeeping duties now demanded wise and ordered management of the home in all its details. In addition, she cooked for everyone, which the dictates of the time wouldn't allow a Virginia lady to delegate beyond herself. Her daughter Libbie recalled how she prepared dinners for family gatherings, often involving fifteen to twenty guests sitting at "a table stretched the entire length of the large dining room, loaded with such succulent dishes as you only read of in Miss Randolph's 'Old Virginia Cook-book.'"[22] She staged formal meals for members of the VMI Board of Visitors, the trustees of Washington College, and delegates to the Presbytery when it met in Lexington. The hospitality of the Preston house gained as wide a reputation as the gracious style of its hostess.

Preston too participated in the family's social gatherings as host, but less gregariously than his convivial wife. In his home he stood as "a model of civility," as William Ruffner described him, and supported the society of his friends with genuine hospitality. Even outside the home he was fully involved with the community and ever ready "to confer, to debate, to vote, to act, and to give" so that people turned to him in emergencies, for special occasions, or for his views on civic or religious issues. But popularity, whether at home or in public, was never his concern. Unlike his extraordinarily tactful wife, he "sometimes spoke his mind too plainly for the comfort of others." Always courteous, he was "more apt to criticize than to flatter."[23] As William Couper remarked, even his own family "at times found him almost blunt and aloof to routine."[24]

Not one to attend gatherings involving purely social gossip, he preferred as an alternative retiring alone to his farm or escaping on horseback to the countryside. He spent as much or more time on his own than in the casual company of others. This led some to conclude, as his close friend William Ruffner so memorably expressed it, that J.T.L. Preston was "generally unsocial, but spasmodically social."[25] Preston enjoyed joining in the company of others, but he was more effectively energized when he was alone. According to the prevailing view of an introvert, he might be called aloof, blunt, haughty, even arrogant, as some in Lexington considered him. But true to the actual nature of an introvert (a term that hadn't been coined in his time), his being "spasmodically social" meant that he fluctuated. VMI historiographer William Couper described his temperament as "changeable and robust."[26]

During his unsocial periods he would ride off on his horse to check on holdings in Kentucky and revel along the way in the restorative powers of nature. In his youth his favorite diversions had been walking in the woods, horseback riding over fresh and virgin fields, hunting in the countryside, and wading or swimming in the North river and nearby streams. When young, he had enjoyed fishing but found it "very dull" as he grew older.[27] As an adult, however, he still pursued shooting on the wing, chasing with hounds, and working in the harvest field. William Ruffner described him as "very strong, full of energy, and [valuing] physical achievement as much as he did intellectual."[28]

Preston loved nature for much the same reason as the Scottish naturalist Thomas Edward, whom nature had inspired to write a natural history of Britain and whom Preston greatly admired. Reflecting not only Edward's enthusiasm for nature, Preston also shared his attraction to ornithology, which he demonstrated in his review of Edward's biography. Preston's eloquent paean to birds would have made a proper introduction to any appeal for membership in the Audubon Society, if the society had existed in his time. He wrote,

> Birds delight all, and offend none. With a liberality as free as the air through which they glide, they bestow their attractions unbought and even unsought upon all. We need scarcely go abroad to search for them; they come to show themselves to us. In the

forests, in the fields, in the gardens, at our doors, under our eaves, even in the parks of crowded cities, we meet with them. They ask not at our hands food, shelter, or defence, never themselves annoying us, they are our efficient allies in the contest we wage with noxious insects, which, unchecked, would render the earth uninhabitable. To every sense they afford gratification. The artist cannot transfer to his canvas their grace of form, nor match the brilliancy nor variety of their coloring; nor can the musician emulate the exquisite tones of their song.[29]

Preston never considered his long journeys to inspect property that he owned in Kentucky, Illinois, Indiana, Missouri, or Ohio tedious or boring, for his love of nature energized him in a way that society never could motivate. In his youth nature had converted a total skeptic into a devoted believer. Ruffner, who knew him best, recalled that so complete was his religious skepticism in his adolescence that "it did not stop at theism" but rejected "any feature of even natural religion," which David Hume and Cicero before him had argued from design. But soon the young Preston's "mind became troubled," Ruffner related. "In this state he went alone to the Peaks of Otter [in the Blue Ridge Mountains], and whilst upon the pinnacle he knelt in great darkness of spirit, and rose a believer in God. This was the beginning of a long, consistent Christian life. He was a complete Christian; that is, there was no yielding anywhere to the world, the flesh, or the devil."[30] It was Preston's unwavering faith that had sustained him as much as Sally through the agonizing loss of little Edmonia, but it was nature that played a close second in refreshing his soul during his "unsocial" retreats from society.

The Preston family suffered a great loss in 1847 when Preston's mother, Edmonia, died on October 1. She had divided her time between the families of her son and daughter for the last twelve years of her life. Preston described her as born into the wealthy family of Edmund Randolph and "brought up under the influence of a unique circle of society in Richmond."[31] She had seen her father's political rise and fall cost him most of his property before his death. His downfall, along with the premature loss of her husband from which she never fully recovered, had led her to spare no pains in giving her children the same education of a high order that she had received in her childhood.

Both Preston and his sister Elizabeth had benefited enormously from what he described as "her acquaintance with history and polite literature, especially English, [which] was remarkable even for those days, when the culture of the privileged class was, in its way, superior to the general level now enjoyed by the many." He remembered her as "an elegant French scholar, a delightful musician, and her manners were of that style which Virginians of a certain age are prone to think belonged exclusively to the Virginia of a former day!"[32] Dr. William Ruffner would remember her as "one of the loveliest and most saintly of women—a beautiful old lady with a sweet voice and cordial manners; but as strong in character as she was abundant in good works."[33] In many ways she had been a model for Preston, who himself exhibited many of her strong traits of mind and character.

She was buried at the head of her husband's grave. On the large, raised, horizontal headstone, Preston had inscribed, "Sacred to the memory of our dear mother, Edmonia Madison Randolph, wife of Thomas L. Preston, daughter of Edmond Randolph, who was born April 17th, 1787, was married June 1806, and after a widowhood of 35 years' devotion to her children, died Oct. 1st, 1847, in the 61st year of her age." He added the heartfelt phrase, "A holier Christian mother never lived."

10

The Challenge of Discipline

This son of a Baptist minister was probably the institute's all-time "hell raiser."
—John Barrett and Richard McMurry

The birth of the Prestons' seventh child, Elizabeth Randolph, known as Libbie, on December 22, 1848, followed on the heels of a tumultuous year that staged one of the most bitterly memorable battles in town. Ranked second in infamy to Hunter's subsequent raid during the Civil War, it "stirred Lexington to its very depths, and not alone Lexington, but this whole section, Rockbridge county and surrounding counties, with repercussions extending to far distant localities."[1] The clash began rather innocuously with a private letter, dated August 12, 1847, suggesting that the Rev. Dr. John Skinner resign as minister of the Lexington Presbyterian Church.

A Scot from Edinburgh, Dr. Skinner was a fluent speaker, diligent worker, and very popular servant of the congregation. But after seven years, according to Dr. Alfred Leyburn, "an increasing number of people were dissatisfied with Dr. Skinner both as preacher and as pastor: his sermons were generally regarded as too coldly theological, and his dealing with people lacked human warmth and 'spirituality.'"[2] Royster Lyle, Jr., recorded that "Skinner was an intelligent preacher who at first held the great admiration of his congregation, but his rigid supervision of their lives and personal habits made him increasingly unpopular." The clear intent of the private letter, "which was couched in respectful and becoming language," was that Dr. Skinner would take the hint and "quietly seek other pastures."[3]

But when he refused to address the grievances in confidence and brought them openly to the Presbytery, Preston found himself called upon, as Lexington's delegate, "to amplify the charges in the letter."[4] While lamenting that Dr. Skinner had taken the matter this far, Preston listed the congregation's complaints, ending with what disturbed him most, as a teacher, that "there is such a tediousness about our public services, that our young people are complaining of it as a task to go to church."[5] According to William Bean, Dr. Skinner promptly singled out Preston as "the originator and instigator" of the entire affair, and "upon his [Preston's] head the irate doctor poured vials of wrath and bitterness: he accused the major of deceit, treachery, and hypocrisy; of being the father of the letter without daring to sign it."[6]

In truth, Preston was one of the eight gentlemen who had authored the letter, but Dr. Skinner expanded his attack and used what he had learned during his pastoral calls to sharply criticize and embarrass other members of the congregation. As Leyburn summarized,

> So began the epochal Skinner case (sometimes called the "Skinner War"), which resulted in a trial before Presbytery whose minutes cover three hundred thirty-two

pages, and which culminated in appeal to the General Assembly of the Presbyterian Church. During the months of the controversy Lexington hummed like a hive of angry bees; language became vituperative and tempers frayed. Lexington Presbyterians seemed to be reliving ancient Scottish history with its long record of feuding.[7]

On one occasion, on February 9, 1848, during the Presbytery's proposal to censure Dr. Skinner's conduct, Preston felt a line had been crossed when Skinner publicly slandered his wife. As reported in the *Record of the Presbytery*, Skinner, complaining of being snubbed by two members of the congregation, accused Sally Preston of putting her fan between her face and his because she was either "ashamed of her iniquity" or else "iniquity hideth her face and is ashamed." The *Record* relates that Preston reacted immediately, twice demanding he retract the remark, which Skinner ignored. Whereupon Preston, pointing his finger, angrily intoned "in a voice audible to only a few persons besides the parties;—'You hoary-headed slanderer, if you repeat that remark, I will slap you in the mouth.'"[8]

Later tellings of this incident embellish Preston's retort with language he never used, but even so, his actual words were surprisingly direct. Within a short time, when he had regained his composure, according to the *Record*, he "addressed the moderator, stating in substance, that he did not mediate any violence in the presence of the Presbytery, but there was a point beyond which there was no endurance; that no insulting language towards himself had provoked him;—but that his wife was entrusted to his protection, and he felt it to be an act, which he believed he could most honestly justify to his own conscience, to this judicatory, and to his God, to take her defence into his own hands." He then asked leave to resign as a member of the prosecuting committee because of the incident. The Presbytery admitted it could "by no means justify" Preston's conduct and felt "bound to record its solemn censure upon words spoken in its presence," but it reaffirmed its "high confidence in his piety and character as a gentleman," and the trial continued.[9]

By April 1, 1848, the charges against Skinner had grown to include libel, defamation, falsehood, and manifestation of an unchristian spirit. After a four-month trial the Presbytery ruled that he had defamed the president and professors of Washington College, the superintendent of VMI, and his brethren of the church, including Preston as delegate to the Presbytery, so it dissolved his relationship with the Lexington church.[10] When Skinner appealed to the Synod in Staunton, it upheld the Presbytery and suspended his ministry until he "makes suitably confession of his sins and gives satisfactory evidence of repentance."[11] Instead, he appealed to the General Assembly, which upheld his severance from the Lexington church but reversed his suspension from the ministry. Ultimately, his request that a grand jury indict the members of the session proved unsuccessful.[12]

In the end, Leyburn reported, "The irascible Scotsman forthwith shook the dust of Lexington from his feet."[13] He became a publisher of an agricultural journal in Philadelphia and later preached in Canada, where it was reported that his relationship with the congregation proved entirely satisfactory.[14] But the Skinner War had left in Lexington a battlefield of casualties. Too many in the congregation still suffered the wounds of having had their views of one another turned to slander and their innermost secrets unceremoniously revealed. On July 24, 1848, Preston was asked by Presbytery to invite the Rev. William Spottswood White to replace Skinner. As it happened, the Rev. White "had no desire to change either my home or my employment," and he knew about Skinner. But Preston recruited him as ardently and persuasively as he had enlisted Francis Smith for VMI and took him into his home until the manse was completed and his family could join him. Dr. Bean recalled it took nearly two decades for the Rev. White to heal the schism "which had shaken the church to its deepest foundations" and to restore the community's faith both in itself and in its church.[15]

Preston's devotion to religion, except for his flirting with atheism in his younger years, was as passionate and enduring as his wholehearted commitment to education. It led him and Francis Smith in 1848 to supplement their normal courses at VMI with Evidences of Christianity and the Bible, a course they taught every Sabbath.[16] Despite his being Presbyterian and Smith's being Episcopalian, each one was careful to foster a decent respect for "religion and morality, without any attempt at the dictation of a creed."[17] Both considered the school's original intent to promote not only the physical and intellectual but also the moral and spiritual development of its cadets. Even the class ring, which was first introduced in 1848 at a cost of $5, reinforced the religious argument.[18] Cut into the stone in old English script were the letters Mizpah, meaning "watchtower," the Hebrew benediction from Genesis 31:49: "The Lord watch between me and thee, when we are absent one from another."

In matters of education, as in religion, discipline for Preston was the indispensable lynchpin. Between 1845 and 1849 VMI faced one of its greatest challenges to a strict disciplinary system intended to inculcate moral and spiritual maturity. In July 1845, appearing in the deceptively innocuous form of a Baptist minister's son, a youth of seventeen from Albemarle County was admitted to VMI, and overnight Benjamin Franklin Ficklin strode into legend.[19] Unknown to the faculty and the institute's board of visitors, regulations to Cadet Ficklin were as red flags to a bull. Mischievous pranks were boundless fodder for his restless brain. Never mean or vicious, this bold and reckless youth with debonair indifference considered consequences distracting and disobedience laudable.

His pranks entailed burying Old Spex's (Colonel Smith's) boots in a snow bank during a winter storm. He set off fireworks beneath the reviewing stand during a 4th of July dress parade. He balanced buckets of water over a faculty member's door. Once when ordered by his room inspector to arrange his shoes symmetrically, he seized "the broom, his badge of office, and coming to carry saber, he marched to the left flank of the line of shoes, and without moving a muscle exclaimed in stentorian tones: 'Shoes! By pairs, left backward, dress!'"[20] His saving grace was his unvarnished sense of humor, which almost always exonerated him from serious consequences.

Ficklin overstepped his extended bounds, however, when he painted Old Spex's horse, Old Coley, "red with white zebra stripes."[21] The next morning he explained to an irate superintendent that Old Coley must have rubbed against his freshly painted red house and white paling fence. But his explanation failed to elicit even the slightest smile. He was promptly confined to his room under close arrest and was ipso facto dismissed on November 12, 1846, after only one year at the institute. Enlisting in the army, he served in Mexico, fighting in seven battles before he was severely wounded and left for dead. A year later he showed up again at VMI, seated on the doorstep of the superintendent's home and refusing day after day to leave until he was reinstated. Old Spex eventually relented upon Ficklin's solemn oath to tread the straight and narrow path.

Ficklin's path proved wider than most when he answered without consequence an absence from reveille with the excuse that he had fought through seven armed assaults in Mexico, was severely wounded and left for dead on the battlefield, and had just that morning dreamed he was officer of the day. Similarly, on July 3, 1848, by order of the board of visitors, he was publicly reprimanded for "permitting a cannon to be fired on the 12th of June while he the said Ficklin was on guard and the duty of guarding the said cannon particularly assigned to him."[22] He had fired a blank charge directly at Barracks so that the concussion broke all the windows and rattled half the china in Lexington.

It's astounding that Ficklin actually graduated. Finishing fourth from the bottom of his class, he left the school with a flourish, receiving his diploma on July 4, 1849, by skewering the parchment with his bayonet at the precise moment during the ceremony that he was declared free of the institute's regulations.[23] Perhaps it's a testimony to the military disciplinary system at VMI, which Ficklin continually tested, that in the end the system survived its greatest challenge.

It might also be said that Ficklin himself was molded by the same regulations he so vehemently opposed and under which he was determined to graduate. In the final analysis he became the ideal citizen-soldier. A confirmed bachelor, he landed a mail contract from Leavenworth to Pike's Peak and went on to co-found the famed Pony Express in California.[24] It was during the Civil War that his boat *Giraffe*, one of several he owned, successfully ran the Federal blockade from Nassau, bringing textbooks and supplies to his beloved alma mater.[25] In 1864 it was Lieutenant Colonel Ficklin who purchased Thomas Jefferson's Monticello and 600 surrounding acres for $80,500 and held it until its reclamation by the U.S. government after the war.

During the year that Ficklin was banished from the institute and fought in the Mexican War, VMI was experiencing a shift in its academic emphasis that filled Preston with alarm. In his report on the progress of his classes in 1847, he noted that William Gilham had joined the faculty as professor of physical sciences. At Gilham's request Preston suspended his recitations for two months so that Gilham might teach a course in astronomy. As a result, Preston felt the pressure on his First Class had fallen heaviest on the Classics Department "because of the prevailing sentiment in the institute, that the mathematical and scientific studies are more important than any others."[26] He would feel some relief in 1849 when Lieutenant Raleigh E. Colston, Class of 1846, took over as head of a new French Department.[27]

But in 1850, the year that Preston was commissioned a major at the rank of full professor, a search was launched for a professor of natural and experimental philosophy. The overworked

Ben Ficklin, 1827–71, Class of 1849. Photograph ca. 1860 (**Virginia Military Institute Archives, No. 0002341**).

Major Gilham needed relief in the Department of Physical Science and was transferred to the Department of Chemistry, Geology, and Mineralogy.[28] At the same time, Preston's uncle, Governor John B. Floyd, was lauding VMI's current status as "the only school in the whole South, in which the physical sciences are exclusively and to a large extent thoroughly taught."[29] As proud as Preston felt that the school was being recognized for its significant contributions to practical instruction, he feared an exclusive shift to the sciences. In 1851, Major Thomas J. Jackson was appointed the new professor of natural philosophy (physics) and artillery tactics.

The same year that Jackson joined the faculty, Preston was granted a sabbatical to spend the summer in Europe. His mind turned immediately toward London's Great Exhibition at the Crystal Palace. There 14,000 exhibitors from around the world would display the Industrial Revolution's astounding marvels of technology. He was granted leave of absence until September 1, which should have afforded him the leisure to close out the term. But fate proved not so kind. Within less than a month VMI would experience the first mutiny of its twelve-year existence. Since Colonel Smith was away on institute business and Preston was serving in his absence as acting superintendent, the first decisive test of VMI's ironclad system of discipline occurred on Preston's watch.

The town of Lexington was awash with excitement over a criminal trial involving the murder of a family near House Mountain. Knowing firsthand from his time spent in the courtroom the value of witnessing the American justice system at work, "Major Preston, acting superintendent, gave permission to cadets to attend the court" for three or four days.[30] It was presumed that Prosecuting Attorney for the Commonwealth Thomas J. Michie would present the jury with his closing argument on Saturday evening. As it progressed, the trial proved riveting. But Mr. Michie, a master of persuasion, had achieved the height of eloquence when court was forced to adjourn on Friday. He would have to complete his argument when court resumed on Monday.

VMI's First Class promptly requested extended leave for Monday, which Preston dutifully denied. When they disregarded his denial and attended the trial, they were accompanied by the remaining cadets. They assumed their requests would also be denied, so they asked no permission. Consequently, on Monday, April 21, Major Preston dismissed the entire senior class of twenty-four cadets under Articles 122 and 123 of the regulations. Some were dismissed for having left the institute without permission and others for having remained in barracks but refusing to do duty. When Smith return to post, he supported Preston's actions.

On May 3 the contrite cadets appealed to the board of visitors for clemency. Agonizing over the quandary confronting them, the board felt compelled to uphold Preston's dismissal. But it also felt obliged to state clearly and sympathetically both sides of its verdict:

> In coming to this painful decision, the board have acted under a profound sense of the mighty responsibility imposed on them, on the one side their feelings and sympathies are strongly excited and appealed to in behalf of the interest, character and destiny of the young gentlemen who have so unhappily involved themselves in difficulty, and on the other hand the board cannot forget, or fall short of their duty to the institute and to the state. In a military school discipline must be uniformly and strictly maintained, otherwise disorder and disorganization eventually result and as obedience is the first duty of a soldier, so insubordination and mutiny are the highest offences he can commit.

The board took "official leave of them with paternal sorrow rather than in anger."[31]

Within days the board was asked to reconsider the dismissal due to "the failure of the commandant of cadets" to stop the disobedience when he had been informed of their intention to commit it. Holding the commandant of cadets responsible, the board opted to reinstate the cadets, subject to faculty approval, punishment by demerits, and confinement to post until graduation.

But on May 15, the board heard from the commandant that he had indeed "ordered the 1st Class to duty." The board promptly admitted it would not have reinstated the cadets if it had known the commandant's side of the matter, so the board absolved him of culpability. However, still torn by the "severe conflict between duty and feeling" in considering "the application of the dismissed cadets for re-instatement," the board took into account "the uniform good character of the class, the absence of turbulent, notorious or immoral conduct, the deep sorrow they express, and above all, the hope & confident belief that they will show by their future career that they will uphold and sustain rightful authority." So the board let the reinstatement stand.

There is no record of Major Preston's reaction to the board's final decision, but he would face another mutiny, when Colonel Smith was again absent in 1858 on a fact-finding tour of schools in Europe. Hazing had reached its peak when an upperclassman was dismissed from summer camp for abusing a *rat* (the term that had recently replaced *plebe* in the institute's lexicon). The upperclassman's dismissal was followed by a second one for hazing three weeks later. This dismissal provoked fifteen cadets to refuse to attend parade. Preston dutifully dismissed all fifteen, expressing his regret that they had "manifested so inadequate sense of the evil resulting from the practice of maltreatment." But he also informed them of their "right of appeal to the board of visitors."

Henry Wise found it "interesting to speculate whether it was mere coincidence that these mutinies happened when Colonel Smith was absent on institute business."[32] Whatever their motives, the dismissals of the cadets on this occasion were upheld not only by the board of visitors but most emphatically by board member General Richardson. He was well known for speaking his mind. He wrote to Preston from Richmond, "I feel more gratification than it is in my power to express, that the unmanly and most cowardly and detestable practice of quizzing and maltreating the new cadets is at an end. This has brought more discredit and injury upon the institute than anything that has occurred since its foundation."[33]

Preston's devotion to discipline and duty was absolute but not simplistic. In the same way that his method of education respected a cadet's freedom to express his opinion in a colloquium rather than sit silent through a lecture, his method of discipline respected a cadet's freedom to disobey an order, his right "to refuse to obey the law." This respect stemmed from his recognition that freedom was God-given. No one, whether teacher, priest, or commander, could afford to ignore it. Preston considered that every individual must be regarded as free to make his own mistakes at his own peril—even if his "disobedience must work out ultimate destruction"—but he must also assume personal responsibility for his noncompliance.[34] One such situation he would record later in his journal while stationed at Craney Island. When a subordinate asked his permission to visit his wife in Portsmouth, Preston advised,

> "Get your permission first," said I.
> "But my captain will not come here with me."
> "Then I cannot grant you permission."
> "It's a hard case," said he.

> "Very," said I; and I might have added a case of labour as well as hardship, "but I will not grant the permit until you see your captain."

"He did not see his captain," Preston remarked, "and went to see his wife. Good luck to her."[35] The subordinate was left to face the consequences of his absence without leave on two fronts.

On another occasion, an officer approached Preston to report that prisoners being held at the island were disorderly and mutinous. He ordered that they be marched to the end of the wharf and kept there all night by three guards with loaded muskets. He instructed the guards to shoot any prisoner who might attempt to escape. "By morning they were cool enough," he observed.[36]

Preston's philosophy of discipline, including his allowance for disobedience with its consequences, was not unique. One of his closest friends and fellow teachers, Thomas Jackson, who would join the institute as professor in 1851, would share his religious devotion to duty and respect for individual freedom as though the two men were cut from the same cloth.

Part IV:
Morning and Evening Star

These are the two great days in the calendar of my life.
—J.T.L. Preston

11

A New Physics Professor

It is not my opinion that he would ever have become very distinguished as a professor.
—J.T.L. Preston

Harriet Beecher Stowe's *Uncle Tom's Cabin* appeared in 1851 as a serial in the *National Era*, an anti-slavery paper in Washington, D.C. Preston missed it because he was on sabbatical in Europe, visiting Italy, France, Switzerland, the Netherlands, and Prussia.[1] For Sally's entertainment but also as a useful resource for his teaching, he kept a journal and would mail home sections as he finished them, only the last section of which has survived. Despite his reluctance to leave Lexington, Sally had encouraged the trip so that he might attend the first World's Fair in London. His sister, Elizabeth, true to the tradition of Virginia hospitality, had invited Sally and all six children to spend the summer on her 3,000-acre plantation at Oakland.

At summer's end, when Preston returned home, he was greeted with the death of his cousin and close friend, James McDowell. Former governor of Virginia and strong supporter of Preston's struggle to help establish VMI, McDowell passed away at his home at Col Alto. A new professor at the institute, Thomas J. Jackson, ordered a twenty-one gun salute to honor McDowell. Brevet Major Jackson had been appointed to teach at VMI almost as a last resort. None of more than a dozen candidates recommended to the board of visitors had agreed or were available to serve.[2] In fact, Alexander P. Stewart of Tennessee was actually appointed but declined. It was only through the recommendation of Major Daniel H. Hill, the Cincinnati professor of mathematics at Washington College who taught military science at VMI and had fought with Jackson in the Mexican War, that Jackson was offered the position, which he readily accepted. In Mexico he had served with more than two dozen VMI alumni who had acquainted him with the institute.

During Preston's sabbatical, the institute had undergone significant changes. The familiar barracks were gone so that returning cadets occupied brand new quarters. Gas lighting stood in for old oil lamps and efficient steam heat replaced the cumbersome wood stoves. A variety of theoretical and practical courses were now offered within six academic departments: mathematics; English and Latin; engineering, drawing and geography; chemistry, mineralogy, and geology; French; and natural and experimental philosophy. Each department employed the proven method of recitation for effective teaching and learning, except for one: the newly created Department of Natural and Experimental Philosophy. It was established under Jackson's care.

As in the past, recitations were conducted daily by Smith, Preston, Williamson, Gilham, and Colston. Recitations encouraged more class participation by the cadets than by their professors, since student performance was considered so vital to the institute's philosophy of education. But the new professor of natural and experimental philosophy didn't teach by recitation; he only lectured. In addition, he expected his students to master all three volumes of *Bartlett's Course of Natural Philosophy* by rote learning, as he himself had done under Professor Bartlett at West Point. Recitation in his class, if it could be called such, involved no two-way interchange of questions and explanations or even general discussion but rather a strictly monitored regurgitation of what was presumed to have been precisely memorized.

It was customary at VMI for cadets to assign professors nicknames. Superintendent Smith was "Old Specs"; Williamson, "Old Tom"; and Gilham, "Old Gil." Colston was either "Old Parlez" or "Old Polly." Why Preston was called either "Old Ball" or "Old Bald" is unknown.[3] Ordinarily, professors received their christenings over time. But the new professor, Thomas Jackson, earned his epithet almost immediately. Dubbed "Old Jack," he was also called "Old Tom Fool," although not to his face. Old Jack's knowledge in the world of physics was remarkable, for he had a prodigious memory.

But as a professor of physics he proved less noteworthy. Just as Old Ball could recite long, metric passages and stanzas from Greek or Latin poetry, so also could Old Jack quote long, intricate equations and formulas from Bartlett's *Analytical Mechanics, Optics and Acoustics,* or *Spherical Astronomy.* But where Old Ball's students were led to an understanding of what he had to teach, Old Jack's students were left foundering in darkness. Indeed, one of his third classmen inscribed on the flyleaf of his copy of *Bartlett's Optics:*

> 'Tis said that Optics treats of light,
> But oh! believe it not, my lark;
> I've studied it with all my might,
> And still it's left me in the dark.[4]

What could be learned in Jackson's class, as opposed to Preston's or Williamson's, was restricted solely to the text. As a teacher, Jackson was singularly monotonous, showing little understanding of a student's needs, less tolerance for error, and almost no sense of humor. Less than six months after Jackson's arrival at VMI, Preston found himself presiding over the court martial of James A. Walker, a First Class cadet. Walker had followed a sequence of steps different from those dictated by Jackson to solve a problem. Faced with the demand that he solve it solely on Jackson's terms, Walker flew into an uncontrollable rage that led to his arrest and ultimate expulsion from the institute.[5]

As much as education was at issue in Jackson's class, discipline also suffered attack. Whereas Ficklin had challenged the despotism of the school, the school's cadets rebelled against the tyranny of Jackson's lectures. Testing Jackson's resolve, Abe Fulkerson fashioned a collar from nearly a yard of linen and convulsed the class at the ludicrous way he wore it. It was the only part of the cadet's uniform, as he well knew, that was not rigidly delineated under the Code of Regulations. Jackson was all too familiar with the code, so that his response was awkwardly passive. Davidson Penn evoked a similar reaction when he asked the major in feigned seriousness if a cannon could be bent so as to shoot around a corner. As professor of artillery and without the slightest acknowledgment of mischief or merriment, Jackson replied soberly, "Mr. Penn, I reckon hardly."[6] If he had a sense of humor, Jackson rarely revealed it during class, save for a subdued, embarrassed smile when cadets made serious attempts to break through his impenetrable armor and evoke chaos in class.

Only once did he retain the upper hand so as to best the class at its own game. Contrary to the prevailing notion that he lacked all humor, this incident stood out because of its singularity. It achieved fame as "Old Jack's conundrum." James Lane recalled that many members of the Class of 1853 were "called up" by Jackson to explain why a telegraphic message (today's telegram) could not be sent from Lexington to Staunton. Most probable among the many scientific reasons put forward was the enormous deposit of iron ore in the immediate vicinity. But Jackson dismissed that explanation along with all others with a faint smile. When he called up Gabriel Gray, Old Gabe confessed with trepidation that he didn't know why. Perhaps no telegraph line existed between the two towns! The class laughed, totally out of control, while he stood blushing before a stone-cold statue with eyes fixed on him immovably. Eventually order was restored, whereupon Jackson stiffly saluted Gray and, with a twinkle in his eye, replied, "Yes, sir! That is right; you can take your seat, Mr. Gray."

"Old Jack's conundrum" would be the subject of retellings for many years afterward. In Lane's retelling, he marveled, "Little did we 'young rascals'—embryo Southern soldiers—then dream that our plain, 'big-footed,' taciturn, fearless, prayerful, tender-hearted and punctiliously polite 'Professor of Natural History' was to flash so soon, meteor-like, before the world as one of its greatest military heroes, and that so many of us bright, ruddy faced boys, under his matchless leadership, were to go down to death with him under the 'Stars and Bars,' in defense of 'Dixie,' the land of fair women and brave men."[7]

Little did anyone at the institute, faculty and members of the ruling boards included, imagine that Jackson would ever master the art of teaching, for which he was hired. He had chosen to enter this untried and difficult profession because he famously believed, as his second wife would attest, that "one can always do what he wills to accomplish."[8] But Preston knew that Jackson could never become the teacher he willed himself to be, no matter how dutifully he tried. "It is not my opinion," he would later explain, "that he would ever have become very distinguished as a professor."[9]

In January 1853, the Prestons celebrated the birth of their fifth son. This brought the total number of children to seven, provoking a lively discussion over what to name him. Sally wanted him named for his father, which would have made Preston's youngest child a Junior. But Preston objected, considering that his oldest son already bore the name Thomas Lewis Preston, and he didn't want the repetition. Instead, he quietly asserted that "his name was to be John Lyle."[10] John Blair Lyle had been one of Preston's closest friends at Washington College. He most admired Lyle's spirit of self-sacrifice, even before knowing the extent to which it related to himself.

Thomas Jonathan Jackson, 1824–63, photograph by Mathew Brady. The uniform in this image, which was taken in 1851, was later "doctored" by Brady to show Jackson as a Civil War general (Virginia Military Institute Archives, No. 0003028_F02_04).

All the while that Preston had loved Sally, from his first encounter with her as his boyhood ideal at age eight, John Lyle had loved her just as intensely in the shadows of his own reticence to tell her. Preston would later learn from Lyle's nephew, William Ruffner, who was Preston's closest confidant, that Lyle hid his feelings from both Preston and Sally even after their marriage, which he dared not challenge. In Ruffner's words, since Lyle felt he "had no fortune, no special intellectual gifts, was plain even to homeliness, he never declared his love, but stood aside, that the rich, gifted, handsome young Preston might go in and win the prize."[11]

When Preston married Sally, Lyle left town for a while. Preston learned the cause from Ruffner and persuaded him to return. Feeling he could never adequately repay his friend, he took on his debts.[12] He knew that Lyle was too philanthropic an individual to care about money. Anna Jackson would describe Lyle as "one of those whole-souled, large-hearted Christians whose lives are full of love and sunshine. His genial face and ready sympathy made him a great favorite with young and old, and he was known as the comforter of the afflicted, the restorer of the wayward, and the counsellor of the doubting. Indeed his heart was big enough to take in all who sought a place there."[13]

When Preston set him up in a bookstore on Main Street, Lyle made it an "automatic bookstore," meaning he left it open so that anyone wishing anything in the store could sign a slate on the counter and take it. He lived in a room in the back of the store, which became a gathering place for students and faculty of Washington College and VMI. Old timers stood around a huge stove at the rear and talked about times gone by. Royster Lyle, Jr., described him as "a hopelessly confirmed bachelor, he was counted beyond the winning charms of any of the then reigning belles of Lexington."[14] Henry Boley, who took over the bookstore in later years, claimed that Lyle was happier to give than to take: "The size of his gifts was measured by his feelings rather than his ability. Upon a warm appeal, he would plunge his hand into his pantaloons pocket, which was his money-drawer, and bring out a handful of silver change and drop it in the collection basket. He died about the time he reached the bottom of his pocket."[15]

On November 2, 1856, Lyle suffered a stroke while attending Presbyterian services, and Preston took him into his home. Lyle's left side was paralyzed, but his mind remained alert. He remained with the Prestons for nineteen months until his death. Preston had him buried in the family plot rather than at Timber Ridge beside his parents. Inscribed on his friend's headstone was the tribute:

JOHN B. LYLE
DIED JULY 20, 1858
AGED 50 YEARS.

———

He was the truest friend,
the bravest man, and the
best Christian ever known
to him, who erects this stone
to his memory.

Preston's wish, at the birth of his and Sally's last son on January 17, 1853, had been to name him after Lyle, which he did. But providence had another more permanent name in store. When Sally's favorite uncle and close friend, John Alexander, died on November 10, the boy's name was changed from John Lyle to John Alexander. "I am quite sure it was with John Lyle's hearty consent," Libbie would later report, "for he was one of those rare human beings who never seemed to consider himself, but always somebody else first."[16]

12

Irreparable Loss

"I can say it, mother:—'The Will of the Lord be done!'"
—Willie Preston

January 4, 1856, should have been a glorious day for Sally Preston, who at the age of forty-four was giving birth to her ninth child. Certainly the whole family was expectant, and nothing in the process had given any hint that this delivery would differ in the slightest from eight successful deliveries in the past. Except for the loss of little Edmonia, the children were all healthy, ranging in age from twenty to two. But the child was stillborn, and after a few hours of illness, Sally succumbed. Of all the children it was eleven-year-old Willie who was able to grasp the moment of his dying mother's last breath. With childlike honesty and docility, he consoled, "I can say it, mother:—'The Will of the Lord be done!'"[1] Sally died, and the family's happiness was abruptly and unexpectedly ripped from its core as a heavy pall settled over any promised glory of the day.

Libbie was only seven but suffered "the stark realization of irreparable loss."[2] No matter how courageously or patiently those around her tried to bear their distress, their solemn faces betrayed their anguish. The one on whose bosom they would have sought comfort and solace, who could turn grief to joy and laughter and offer the only real security in moments of helpless vulnerability, was gone, permanently, on a day when falling snow darkened the sky. Preston was devastated. Five years later, writing in his journal on what would have been the anniversary of their marriage, he would recall with painful clarity, "An angel gave me her hand when hardly more than a boy. I stepped forth into the world, suddenly her hand slipped from mine and I was desolate."[3]

Sally was not solely his wife and the love of his life. She was also his best advisor and best friend. William Ruffner contended that "no wife was ever more highly valued, or more deservedly so." He remembered Preston's frequently saying "that he never departed from her advice without regretting it." She showed sound judgment and devotion to her family and friends "without ebbing or gushing." The quintessential altruist, she was herself always content and cheerful and "a perennial fountain of happiness" for others. Ruffner summarized her "as a lady, who, in mind and character, was one of those superior women of whom even such a community of Lexington can rarely boast more than two or three in a generation."[4]

Because of Preston's importance at VMI, academic duties were suspended during exams to allow the whole corps of cadets to attend "one of the largest funerals ever held in Lexington."[5] Libbie remembered "the ceaseless movement of hushed footsteps" and the "clear, solemn tones of the minister's voice, echoing in the thronged house" full of friends and family. In vain the minister tried to bestow peace and confidence, even to a little child, with the sacred words, "Father, ... be with Me, where I am."[6] A family burial site was created for Sally. A stone was also erected for little Edmonia, who was buried elsewhere in the graveyard. Preston had his wife's headstone carved with the words, "She was the joy of her husband's heart and the light of his household for more than 23 years."

For months during the first year following her death, Preston penned his most intimate memories of their life together and his passionate distress over her loss, trying to heal the grievous wound that made him loath to go home, even keen to join her. His granddaughter, Janet Allan Bryan, would later consider these memoirs too personal and emotional for publication, "or indeed, for reading, except among those of his inheritance, who see in it the beauty and fidelity of two highminded and devoted people."[7] Janet's reservations would not be the only restriction placed on Preston's most intimate thoughts. Presumably she was only following the precedent set by her mother, Elizabeth, who would actually destroy the letters that Sally and Preston exchanged during their courtship and marriage. They had caringly saved their letters, as Libbie acknowledged when she caught them on one occasion, during the autumn prior to Sally's death, reliving their past in the privacy of their home.

Libbie and a guest had entered the firelit library and discovered her mother seated in her chair by the hearth. Her father was "seated boyishly beside her on the floor." They had a bag of their letters, which they were reading aloud to each other. Despite the interruption, they greeted Libbie and her guest with a cheerful welcome. Her father confessed in a gay, confident tone, "Sally and I have been reading over our love letters, … don't you think that is a rash thing to do?"[8] Libbie heard them laugh and saw an exchanged look that even a seven-year-old could understand.

The parlor of the Preston home in 1870 (author's collection).

These were the letters that years later Libbie would systematically burn during the closing of their home. Her reasoning at the time was that "the dead lovers would themselves have withheld" them as not of general interest. "So there they lie, in ashes, on my hearth!" she would observe dispassionately. "One feels almost like a vandal in committing to the flames so much poetry and romance, so much merry wit and sparkle of gay words, so much sweet philosophy and heartfelt piety; but these things are inextricably interwoven with the love-making that should be, and must be held sacred."[9] As much as Libbie, the family chronicler, valued the exchange of personal letters, it's ironic that she would be the one in the family responsible for their destruction.

At the time of Sally's death, apart from Libbie's personal despair and concern for her father's severe loss, the child who drew closest to Preston in his anguish was Willie, who simultaneously served the needs of his two-year-old brother Johnny. Of all the children, Willie was the most loving and beloved. In appearance his face conveyed an indescribable sweetness. He would always be remembered for his smile, which his stepmother would later describe as having "that radiant, haunting charm about it which Rafaelle [sic] has made familiar to us in the countenance of his St. John; and the bright, winning, sympathetic face was but an index to those inner lineaments which so remarkable endeared him to all who knew him." He possessed a thoughtful tenderness, which he devoted at his mother's death "to the father whose every wish it was his study to anticipate, and to the little motherless brother who clung to him with peculiar fondness."[10]

Willie's kindhearted gentleness, again in the words of his stepmother, showed "all the delicate, inexpressible, suggestive considerateness and self-forgetfulness that one only looks for on the part of wife or mother. His looks, his words, his tones, his movements—how full of refined feeling and gentleness they were!" He also displayed a conscientiousness extraordinarily rare for his age, which had emerged very early in his development. Preston recalled that when he was about to correct Willie "for the first and almost only time in his life," Willie looked up into his face, and "with that beaming, truthful expression peculiar to him, the little fellow said,—'If you *think* I have done wrong, father, it is right for you to punish me.'"[11]

For a month after Sally's funeral Preston's sister Elizabeth remained in Lexington, helping to care for the grieving children. When she returned to her Oakland home in February 1856, she took the five younger children with her. The two older sons, Tom at twenty, as professor of Latin and modern languages at Washington College, and Frank at fourteen, just entering Washington College, remained with their father. Phoebe at sixteen lamented not being allowed to stay and care for the household. But Preston felt

Elizabeth "Libbie" Randolph Preston Allan, 1848–1933 (facing page 89 of Elizabeth Allan's *March Past*).

"the burden was too great for her young shoulders."[12] So at Aunt Lib's urging Phoebe accompanied twelve-year-old Willie, ten-year-old Ran, seven-year-old Libbie, and three-year-old Johnny to Oakland. Aunt Lib had lost her husband the previous summer, and three of her four sons were away at school. The oldest, William Armistead Cocke, had quit the University of Virginia to help her manage the plantation, and, as Libbie would later confirm, "the property in Kentucky yielded Aunt Lib $6,000 a year."[13] So she could afford to take on her brother's young children.

Meanwhile, in Lexington, Preston's desolation over the loss of his soulmate found a sympathetic ear in his VMI colleague Tom Jackson. He and Jackson now shared the same heartache, since hardly a year had passed since Jackson had lost his young wife, Ellie, under similar circumstances. Elinor Junkin Jackson had died in childbirth in October 1854. In his profound grief, he found solace in the Junkin household. There he was entreated to keep the room he and Ellie had shared during their marriage. In short time he discovered a confidante in Ellie's devoted and inseparable older sister Margaret, known as Maggie, for Maggie shared his intense loss. Both he and Maggie now consoled Preston in the throes of his present anguish.

Preston had known Jackson as a colleague and friend since his arrival at VMI. But during the months after Ellie's death it was Maggie who had come to appreciate Jackson's character for its hidden qualities that Preston had not discerned in the ordinarily stern and taciturn major. Her quick intellect didn't scruple to challenge "Jackson's idiosyncrasies" sportively, and he amiably welcomed her criticisms without objection as worthy of careful consideration. Maggie conveyed the impression that she understood him well enough to know, as she would later explain, that "much that passed under the name of eccentricity was the result of the deepest underlying principle, and compelled a respect" that she always gave him.[14]

Preston and Jackson were both essentially restrained, modest men, who normally concealed their emotions from public scrutiny. But Maggie was the catalyst that formed a bond between them, allowing free rein to all aspects of their personalities. She was even able to gain privileged access to Jackson's "sporting, rollicking side" with which few people, including Preston, were acquainted. In her relaxed presence, Jackson "would tell amusing stories, and be so carried away with them himself, as almost to roll from his chair in laughter. More contagious and hearty laughter I have never heard," she confessed. He told of hunger raids on Mexican gardens during the war. He recounted the festive life in Mexico City after the war when nobles, boasting of their Castilian blood, were oblivious of their having been conquered. And he described the beautiful Mexican women in the old palace of the Montezumas, who had inspired him to learn Spanish so well that it had become the language between himself and Ellie. "His natural temperament," Maggie would later contend, "was extremely buoyant, and his cheerfulness and *abandon* were beautiful to see, provided there were only one or two people to see it."[15]

To the casual observer, when Maggie stood between these two similar men, each six feet tall, dark complexioned, blue eyed, and reserved in demeanor, they must have seemed like stabilizing bookends on either side of a barely five-foot, fair-skinned, auburn-haired daughter of the Junkin clan. But her "dignity of carriage" gave her "the appearance of a greater height" than she really possessed.[16] Certainly, this tiny, slight woman, whose little feet, when she sat in an ordinary chair, hardly touched the floor, held her own in the presence of these two titans.

In addition, she was getting to know Preston as intimately as she had come to know Jackson in the comfortable environment of her own home. In the same way that she taunted Jackson, she challenged Preston, but on a wholly different plane. Preston possessed an intellect that was fully the equal of hers. Maggie had never attended school, but she had been reared by her father and mother to be a formidable scholar. Like Preston, she had mastered the Greek language, beginning with the alphabet at age six. In her home her father had tutored her in Latin, French, English literature, and theology, exposing her to Calvinism and giving her a thorough familiarity with the stories of the Bible. Like Preston, she had learned history, fiction, and poetry under the patient tutelage of her mother.[17]

Maggie shared Jackson's affliction of poor eyesight, attributed in her case, however, to too much study by candlelight in darkened rooms and not enough exercise due to delicate health. She didn't require Jackson's sheer determination to learn, for she shared Preston's natural love of learning that set no boundaries on extent or content. By the time she was fifteen she was reading Locke's *Human Understanding* and steeping herself in the works of Silvio, Pellico, Sheridan, Kant, Coleridge, Carlyle, Goethe, and Tacitus. She devoured Petrarch's biographies and the verses of many poets of her time. Not satisfied solely with reading, she had tried her hand early on at writing with considerable success. She published a number of serialized stories as well as dramatic and lyric poems. In 1856 she produced her first work of extended fiction, which she titled *Silverwood: A Book of Memories*. It was an autobiographical novel published anonymously, as was customary for a female author in her time to preserve her privacy.

The fact that it was not glowingly received did not detract in the slightest from her growing reputation as a highly accomplished poet. She had a prodigious memory, which she manifested in her writing and her conversation but was never seen to flaunt. She had the unusual ability to combine erudition with disarming humility. Like both Jackson and Preston, she was reserved in the presence of groups of people. Only in the innermost circle of home or of those who fully understood her would she drop her reserve and shine. This being true of all three companions, it made for a warm coterie of friends. Inspired by cheerful abandon, they found great comfort in one another and joy during those grievous months of shared bereavement.

As Preston frequented the Junkin home, he grew to know and admire the patriarch of the family, Maggie's father, the Reverend Dr. George Junkin. He quickly discovered that Dr. Junkin had "two absorbing passions" for "education and religion" that closely paralleled his own.[18] Twenty-one years Preston's senior, the elderly educator and preacher engaged Preston in discussions that were as animated as they were enlightening. Short, heavy set with deep black eyes that never required glasses and an ardent, quick temper, Junkin proved to be a man of intense convictions. He possessed all the force, power, and originality of a dedicated reformer. A staunch Scots-Irish defender of the Calvinist faith and former president of Miami University of Ohio, he had graduated from Jefferson College in Pennsylvania, where he was known, like Preston, as "the best debater in the college."[19] He evolved to become a dynamic preacher, teacher, and prolific author, especially of religious works.

Like Preston, Junkin was a confirmed advocate of physical labor, which he had sought to elevate in the public's esteem during his tenure as principal of the Pennsylvania Manual Labor Academy. It was one of the first institutions of its kind in America where students worked in the fields and shops to pay for their education. As a founder and first president of Lafayette College, also in Pennsylvania, he had brought with him to Lexington his manual labor system with its emphasis on both mathematics and the classics. He came at the instigation of Sally's uncle, Dr. Archibald Alexander, to assume the presidency of Washington College. He had survived three stormy years as president of Miami University, which couldn't adjust to the inflexibility of his monarchical style of administration. But Washington College, since his arrival to succeed Henry Ruffner as president in 1848, had thrived under his firm guidance.

Although his marriage to Julia Rush Miller had brought a generous dowry, he was an extraordinarily generous soul and essentially dispersed it, with her approval, to help young men prepare for the Presbyterian ministry. Money, in his Christian worldview, wasn't intended for "comfort and luxury" but for charity. In this sense he was much like Preston, but in his case he allowed his wife and eight children live a life of "rigid economy, feeling at every turn the limitations of a narrow income."[20] They lived in a plain, simple home on a small farm, where he had determined the whole family would develop a healthy work ethic. Enrolling his boys in school, he chose to home school his girls.

The Rev. Dr. George Junkin, 1790–1868. This carte de visite shows Dr. Junkin in 1861 just before he abandoned Virginia for Pennsylvania (Washington and Lee University, Leyburn Library Special Collections, RG41, Seth McCormick-Goodhart Collection).

During the months that Preston visited the family, Dr. Junkin grew to respect the young widower whose educational and religious views complemented his own and whose acute intellect and wide ranging erudition uniquely matched that of his daughter Maggie. As for Preston, it was obvious from whom Maggie had inherited her strong, acute intellect and independent, forthright character. As much as he still suffered unremittingly the loss of Sally, he found himself drawn to Maggie as a kindred spirit on a level of consciousness that he had neither known nor imagined. And just as Maggie's and Jackson's relationship had grown stronger over their common loss, so also her relationship with Preston evolved over his singular loss.

Why Maggie, at thirty-four and the oldest of the Junkin children, was not married had long been a question, not in her own mind, but often entertained by others. Both of her younger sisters, Ellie and Julia, and three of her four surviving brothers had all married by 1856. As Libbie would remark, "It goes without saying that lovers had not been wanting to one so gifted and attractive" as Maggie. But by her own admission she had loved but once in her early life and lost. It was not by choice but by "the disapproval of her parents," who autocratically dismissed her beau. And she "had closed her heart, during all those years of young womanhood, to any thought of love or marriage."[21]

Understandably, as Maggie's and Jackson's relationship had grown, there had been some speculation they might fall in love. But it was not to happen. As James Robertson has suggested in his biography of Jackson, their religious beliefs forbade marriage. "A canon in the Presbyterian Confession of Faith expressly prohibited a man's marrying his deceased wife's sister."[22] This had served to restrict their affection invariably to that of brother and sister. Certainly by the fall of 1856, after Jackson took his sabbatical in Europe and when his attention was turning to Anna Morrison, it was now Preston who was gaining Maggie's undivided attention. And his attention was focusing exclusively and irresistibly on her.

13

Venus

Which is dearest, the companion with whom we begin our pilgrimage or the one with whom we end it?
—J.T.L. Preston

At forty-five, Preston was nine years Maggie's senior but "still in the prime of a splendidly vigorous, active manhood." As Libbie would later remark, Maggie saw him as "the most attractive man" she had ever known. In appearance and manner he was typically Virginian: "graceful, courteous, dignified, cordial, quick-witted, fluent, masterful." He was well educated, well traveled, well read of books old and new, and of strong heritage and ample fortune. But what most attracted her to him was "his earnest, lofty Christian character. Not only was he a knight *sans peur et sans reproche*, but even from his youngest manhood he had 'walked with God,' in a spiritual communion that was as simple and sincere and unfaltering as a child's intercourse with a loving earthly father."[1]

Maggie had known his wife, Sally, as a close friend. Sally had admired Maggie's many talents and had often said to her, partly in play but partly in earnest, that "if she were called from earth she would like to have Miss Maggie Junkin for her children's stepmother." On the contrary, Maggie had more than once declared to her own family that "if I ever marry a widower, and especially a widower with children, you may put me in a straight jacket; for I will never do such a thing while I keep my mind."[2]

Perhaps it was Maggie's heart, more than her mind, that was attracted to this charming Christian widower with seven children ranging in age from twenty-two to three. Even though all but two of them were living with his sister in eastern Virginia, she knew they existed. This alone should have given sufficient pause to such a shy, sensitive nature. But even more daunting was the devotion they still held to the memory of their lovely, loving, and only recently departed mother. Moreover, it was their mother who "was the joy of her husband's heart and the light of his household for more than 23 years," as was carved on her gravestone, and she still lived as vividly in his aching memory as in theirs.

The following year Maggie expressed this last anxiety in a lyrical letter she sent Preston while she was visiting her brother George in Philadelphia. Diffident about her ability to follow Sally in her fiancé's affections, she frankly admitted,

> —I doubtingly question my spirit—have I
> Strength to summon the sunshine all back to his sky?
> Can I think to rekindle the warmth, or restore
> To his hearthstone the blaze of its home light once more?
> Can I hope to rebuild so the temple that falls,
> That no traces of ruins will cling to its walls?
> Have I skill for the tasks which her hands left undone?

> Dare I finish the picture that she had begun?
> —Dear Father in Heaven! Thou knowest alone
> How void is thy creature of strength of her own!
> Let me feel that thy Providence surely has set
> Me the work, and I'll trust to accomplish it yet;
> And then when called upward, what joy to say, "Here
> Lord, am I, and the children thou gavest me to rear!"[3]

Apart from this overpowering concern, there were other difficulties that love must conquer before Preston and Miss Junkin might marry. Their engagement in the spring of 1857 had first to face the impropriety of Preston's marrying again hardly a year after Sally's death. Custom required a two-year wait, which Preston considered a moot point. He loved Maggie and, according to his daughter Libbie, determined their marriage "should take place the next August."[4] Maggie favored waiting the extra five months, as custom required.

But what provoked her temper and quickly distinguished her from Preston's more demur and acquiescent former wife was her reaction to his particular insistence that they marry August 2, "his former wedding day!" If Preston was seeking to replace Sally with Maggie, he was suddenly and unmistakably made aware that Maggie was not the calm, well-poised, tactful, subservient woman he had married first. Quite the opposite! More like Preston himself, she was strong-willed and honest but also impulsive, rebellious, and quick-tempered.

Perhaps it's to Preston's credit that he could love so unreservedly such contrary temperaments as Sally and Maggie. But Maggie, her taste shocked at his choosing his former wedding day to be their own, informed him unambiguously that August 2 was out of the question. As Preston's daughter would later relate, "After trying to coax and persuade her, Father took the bit in his teeth, and said she would marry him on that date or not at all! And with proper spirit, the lady broke the engagement and dismissed her imperious suitor."[5]

Dr. Junkin, who had come to admire and appreciate Major Preston as a suitable match for his daughter, found himself allied with Preston in trying to convince his daughter that the difference of a few months, even the choice of the day, was "a matter of little consequence" in the decision of a lifetime of mutual love and happiness. Even Maggie's brother-in-law, Major Jackson, sided with her father in support of Preston. One argument in favor of August was the need for Preston's children to return to their home in Lexington without further delay. In the end it was Jackson who was able to reconcile the couple. Maggie conceded the five-month delay, but under no circumstances would she relent the day. When Preston compromised on August 3, the crisis subsided. Years later, we are told, Libbie would tease her stepmother unmercifully, "If you had only held your own, you would have kept the upper hand the rest of your life!"[6]

To satisfy Jackson as mediator, Maggie surrendered much in the compromise, but Preston considered his concession also significant. Notwithstanding the trivial motive that remembering one anniversary is easier than remembering two, he considered the day important symbolically for linking two halves of a single love. Four years later Preston would reflect in his journal on his love for both Sally and Maggie as so intricately entwined that each complemented the other. By then he was fully reconciled to separating "Augt 2 (1832) Augt 3 (1857): These are the two great days of the calendar of my life."[7] But he never separated Sally and Maggie as the two great loves of his life.

The French author Gérard de Nerval, whom Preston would have known for the two books he published in 1853 and 1855, depicted the two women of his life as "les deux moitiés d'un seul amour" (the two halves of a single love).[8] But Nerval's halves of his single love were the imagined and the real. Preston viewed each woman as wholly real. Employing Nerval's metaphors to describe his single love for Sally and Maggie, he regarded them as the two realities of his life. In his mind they were connected in a way that made their separation impossible. They existed, as he would later explain to Maggie, as a single entity in a time continuum: "Half the year Venus is the morning star and half the year the evening star, equally beautiful as either. Which is dearest, the companion with whom we begin our pilgrimage or the one with whom we end it? Very dear are both."[9]

Beneath Preston's dignified exterior was the heart of an incurable romantic. In the same year that he described in his journal the nature of his love for both Sally and Maggie, he would confess in a letter to Maggie his being essentially sentimental. "I claim not to be the equal of many men for military talents; I find and acknowledge many superior in business, in oratory, in scholarship, and many other things, but that man who knows better than I do how to appreciate and return the love of a noble woman, I never expect to see."[10]

Preston's romantic nature, apart from his highly cultivated mind and sincere, fervent Christian character, was a chief attraction to the women who knew him best. Libbie even speculated that her father might have benefited from being less attractive. "I used to tell him," she recalled, "when I was old enough for him to take my impertinence as a joke, that he would have been a much more agreeable person, if he had ever had the experience of being refused a time or two."[11] She attributed his imperious temper to his never having encountered such a catastrophe, such that only his genuine humility prevented his becoming vain or conceited.

Much later she would further confide in her nephew that his grandfather would have been a finer man but for this "most unusual and unique" misfortune. He would have been "much easier to live with, if he had ever in his life been crossed by any woman." She avowed that, as the only son of a widowed mother who adored him, "he lived and died in the fixed belief that it was a woman's duty to mind the men." She further confided that if Preston's "two wives, who were both women of education and culture and fine minds, had more rigorously asserted their own opinions in opposition to his, it would have been much better for him."

Her story had the opposite effect on her nephew than she intended, since he later declared, "Whoever heard of a man, living eighty years, having two wives and numerous daughters and never having had any trouble with any woman, not even an argument. We do not believe any man was ever so fortunate as you [Aunt E] represent old JTL to have been. Or was he so fortunate?"[12]

The marriage took place the evening of August 3, Dr. Junkin officiating. The next day Preston left Lexington with his bride to reunite with his children who had spent more than a year and a half at Oakland. Maggie's introduction to plantation life in eastern Virginia was daunting. The imposing mansion was set in a twelve-acre oak-strewn lawn surrounded by cultivated fields. It hosted informal breakfasts and luncheons and formal five- and six-course dinners. Conversations on topics ranged from politics and religion to literature and social life. "The new wife bore herself in this great household with shrinking diffidence, but with no awkwardness. She was so slight and fair and girlish-looking in her low cut blue silk gown." At thirty-seven she "looked twenty-five" from her "low voice and shy manner." But with ease she entered into any discussion, no matter what the topic, and quickly became, without fanfare, "the most interesting woman in the company."[13]

Preston's cousin, William Campbell Preston, former senator from South Carolina and one of the foremost orators and statesmen of the U.S., posed perhaps the greatest threat to her acceptance into the family. Sharing the prevailing prejudice against female authors, he remarked on "the little red-headed Yankee's want of style and presence." But the deeper he engaged her in talk about literary subjects, the more astounded he became at her profound knowledge of authors, both classic and modern. And in short order he was lauding her as "an encyclopaedia in small print!"[14]

On the return to Lexington, despite her status as stepmother, Maggie was warmly accepted at home by the two youngest children, Libbie and Johnny, and by Willie, who had been the only one of the children to return to Lexington for the wedding. She only gradually won the hearts of Phoebe, Frank, and Ran through her selfless devotion to making the family happy and comfortable without questioning the sainthood of their dear departed mother or showing resentment when she was unfavorably compared by the servants to Miss Sally. Instead, she graciously forgave the comparison as kindly intended.

Tom was away preparing for the ministry at Union Theological Seminary, Phoebe was still at seminary in Pennsylvania, and Frank was attending Washington College, leaving four children for Maggie to rear at home. But also living at home were Preston's nephews, William, Thomas, and Edmund Cocke, the latter two studying at Washington College. Preston's nephew Abbott Alexander, whom he was helping prepare for the ministry, brought the total number of children and boarders to eight. Then to these were added the following year Maggie's first child, George Junkin Preston, born on July 2, 1858, and named for his grandfather.

Margaret "Maggie" Junkin Preston, 1820–97, photograph ca. 1867 by Boude and Miley (author's collection).

14

A Grave Question of Educational Reform

Nor will truth be ever reached by ridicule.
—J.T.L. Preston

Between Preston's painful parting from Sally and his joyful marriage to Maggie, teaching at the institute had helped preserve some measure of continuity in his life. Two months before his marriage to Maggie he was heavily involved in making arrangements for delivery of a $10,000 bronze statue of George Washington to VMI.[1] A replica of Jean-Antoine Houdon's famed marble likeness in the rotunda of Richmond's Capitol, it was designed by William J. Hubbard and dedicated on July 3, 1856. Despite three initial failures, it was the first bronze statue successfully cast in the United States and the first statue erected at the institute. Union General Hunter would confiscate this masterwork eight years later as a trophy of war. But it would be returned in 1866 to stand above Preston's inscription on the parapet, where it remains today.

In March 1857, Superintendent Smith published his customary "Introductory

Hubbard's statue of Washington, photograph in 1866 by Boude and Miley. Cadets and townspeople gathered in front of the statue shortly after it was returned to Virginia Military Institute following the Civil War (Virginia Military Institute Archives, No. 0000221_026).

Address" to open the spring session of classes. After seventeen years as superintendent, he felt inspired to summarize VMI's accomplishments since its founding. In particular, he lauded its curriculum as having revolutionized "educational progress and prosperity" in the South. Almost a decade had passed since Washington College had launched its attacks against the institute in general and Smith personally. Any jealousies or resentments that were festering then had been mostly laid to rest in a community that now supported the institute with pride. So Smith was caught entirely off guard when his "Introductory Address" evoked a challenge from a source outside the confines of Lexington. As the public face and voice of VMI, he found himself again under personal and general attack.

Soon after he gave his address, an article entitled "Progress of Education in Virginia" appeared in *Southern Literary Messenger*. Since its founding, this periodical sought to encourage the pride and genius of the South. The author of the article chose to remain anonymous. He began, innocently enough, by congratulating the colleges and universities of the state for their extraordinary advances and prosperity. Then he launched into a personal diatribe against the superintendent of the Virginia Military Institute. Referring to his praise of VMI in a "very curious speech," he equated him with "the child who thought that the pendulum made the clock run."[2] He ridiculed Smith's implication that other colleges of the state, like "Rip Van Winkle," had been suddenly awakened and "in strict Indian file" had followed "in the broad foot-prints of their illustrious chief, the 'superintendent!!'"

He denounced Smith's exclusive focus on the "engineer or mere mathematician," which left out orators, statesmen, jurists, divines, professors, and professional men. Contending that it was as one-sided as the "badly balanced system of West Point," he gave greater credit to "the *classical* instruction of the University of Virginia" as the fountainhead of educational progress in the state. He depicted Smith as a pre–Copernican man, taking the earth "as his standpoint" and viewing the sun, moon, planets, and stars in their several orbits as if they were "moving around *him*." From Smith's narrow perspective, he argued, "the whole educational universe swings its tiny orbs around his little 'που στω.'"[3] This insertion of the Greek word for "perspective" clearly meant to emphasize VMI's lack of a "chair of Greek," which the University of Virginia had newly established.

He proceeded to compare Virginia's educational system to a mountain range, the summit of which represented the University of Virginia. The surrounding pinnacles were the state's colleges. The hills on the plain were the academies and high schools. And the plain was the primary schools. No part of the entire range, he argued, could "be dispensed with, without injury to the whole and to every part of that whole." (This phrase he had pointedly lifted from a baccalaureate speech that Dr. Junkin had given in 1853.) He then placed VMI in his geographic scheme as merely tangential. "As a valuable appendage, but outside of the system, stands the Military Institute—the best school of the kind in the South—not a college, but an institution *sui generis*—the institution to which we may safely look in the future for our engineers and state military officers." The article capitalized on VMI as the West Point of the South.

As in the past, Smith summoned Preston to his and the school's defense. The following month a sequel appeared under the same title, "Progress of Education in Virginia." The author of the sequel praised "the introductory lecture of the superintendent of the Virginia Military Institute" for having "received the distinction of the elaborate review which appeared as the leading article in the March number of this magazine."[4] But he suggested that the reviewer showed more fancy and wit than logic or truth, neither of which "could ever be reached by ridicule," while adding, "This is the argument of weakness, not of strength." Then followed a list of facts to show that the number of non-professional college students in Virginia when VMI was founded in 1839 "scarcely exceeded 500." Quoting from an 1844 convention of delegates from the leading colleges of Virginia, he added, this number was greatly reduced because of ineffective discipline, substandard scientific instruction, and the lack of well-qualified teachers in the state.

The sequel contended that VMI arose from the midst of this crisis as "a *normal school* for teachers." It offered high scientific instruction while modeling its military system of discipline on that of West Point. After 1839 its successful system of discipline and improved curriculum of scientific instruction was adopted by other schools, including Washington College, Randolph Macon, and Lynchburg College. In the meantime, the number of non-professional students enrolled in the six colleges of Virginia decreased from 500 to 450. The University of Virginia, after twenty years of existence, had no more than 41.

The sequel lamented the fact that Virginia in 1844, with a population of "700,000 white inhabitants," could send only 491 students to its colleges and University of Virginia. This could not be blamed on monetary pressures alone. In fact, an inquiry by the Virginia House of Delegates had recently concluded that the university itself suffered from "*defective discipline* and *inadequate preparatory training*" more than lack of funding. While the colleges and the university were shrinking, VMI "actually increased the number of its students to nearly double" and was turning away those it lacked the room to accommodate.

This, the sequel argued, was because VMI offered that which the university and other colleges needed and which parents and students alike appreciated. It provided "a demerit system and class standing," which encouraged better discipline and a more earnest desire for education. But it also offered "a better system of scientific instruction." Not only did it meet the practical demands of the state, it also prepared its students more completely for the professions. Since its establishment as Virginia's first normal school in 1842, it had "supplied the state with nearly 150 teachers and with 50 civil engineers." And it contributed to the professions of theology, medicine, and law "some of their most promising" candidates.

In conclusion, the sequel maintained that the institute stood in no rivalry to the esteemed university or other colleges of Virginia but rather in support of them all. VMI's distinctly different system of discipline and broad curriculum, which combined scientific studies with the classics, had increased the demand for education in the state's schools. The increase should be "a source of gratification" to all involved. "The colleges of Virginia need not fear the operations of the institute," the sequel reasoned. Its graduates would be judged "not by the name of the institute" that prepared them but by "the fruit" of their labor. In the meantime, "While they are gathering laurels in the various fields of science and literature and arts; their bountiful mother will steadily press onward in her work of USEFULNESS TO THE STATE, and like the rebel flower, flourish the more she is trampled upon."

In the June issue of the *Messenger*, Smith's nemesis launched a spirited counterattack.[5] He ridiculed his "*abnormal* institution" and his inflated claim to have caused the "Reformation of 1839." He admitted that he didn't know whether the superintendent's reply had been "sanctioned at 'head-quarters' or not," since the writer had claimed no rivalry to the university. "If he is a man-at-arms, he seems to have thought it quite within the sphere of his dignity to doff his military *chapeau* in the presence of that magnificent institution. Its pride of pre-eminence he would by no means wound. But the superintendent himself is not so entirely deferential."

The author accused the superintendent of having "a magnified view of things." Quoting from Smith's Report to the Board of Visitors, he asserted, "the Epic Muse seems to have infused into his brain an inspiration altogether too big for the event narrated, when she makes him say—'It was an eventful day—the *birth-day* of the Virginia Military Institute.'" He suggested "the superintendent's glasses may be concave" to have such a magnifying power. "It is this which enables him to see in one of *his graduates* the capacity to impart 'a better education than the colleges of Virginia supplied fifteen years ago.'"

Continuing the attack, he declared that in his first article he had shown every unprejudiced reader that the university was "the great central power" behind the educational progress in the state. He scoffed at the idea that VMI had "in *ten years, revolutionized*, in a great degree, the *systems of education* existing in Virginia." He considered his assault on VMI to be justified "when any institution puts on gaudy plumes, and assuming self-complacent airs, begins to tell us, that the educated men ... who were sent out by the colleges previous to the last fifteen years ... were not as well educated as boys *now* are in many of *our subordinate schools*." He accused VMI of having "a magnified conception of its own importance" so that no one should be surprised "if we take the liberty of plucking a feather or two out of its cocked-hat."

In conclusion, he cited the need to keep the institute within its proper bounds. "While we believe the *university* to be the *primum mobile* in the educational progress of our state, we believe that the military institute is the best school in the South for training *engineers* and *militia officers*. Let it keep itself within its appropriate sphere, ... and we shall have nothing to say against its course, and shall heartily rejoice in its prosperity."

Aware that silence condones but also gives consent, Preston would not allow VMI's adversary to rest on his self-conferred laurels. In the July issue of the *Messenger,* the sequel writer suggested that "the true questions at issue had been evaded by the reviewer." In addition, "*ad captandum* appeals to prejudice had been substituted for a calm discussion of a grave question of educational reform."[6] Reaffirming Smith's claims for the institute, the writer added that before VMI, "a want was seriously felt by large classes" of Virginians "with respect to the kind of education" that the colleges, including the university, did not supply. While the colleges and university catered to the professions, VMI gave instruction in all "branches of knowledge." This included practical courses for the agriculturist, the engineer, the merchant, the manufacturer, and the mechanic.

In support of the claim that VMI was the first to introduce the demerit system into collegiate discipline, he quoted letters from the presidents of Brown University in Rhode Island and the University of Alabama, among others. They all gave credit to VMI for their system of demerits, which they had copied to improve the government of their institutions. He cited Edmund Ruffin, the venerable patriarch of agriculture, who hailed Major Gilham's chemistry class at VMI as "the first, and so far, the only" scientific aid to agriculture in Virginia. It had steered farmers away from the frauds of spurious fertilizers that were being sold "under the name of *super-phosphates*." VMI was already being called "the best agricultural school in the South." But as the writer was quick to point out, it was also being praised for its classical courses in "Latin as well as French."

The author of the sequel asked the public to judge for itself the validity of the superintendent's claims. It warned the public against the wit of a "prejudiced and uncandid reviewer" who considered himself "the *champion* of the *University of Virginia*." The issue was not a dispute "between the *university* and the *military institute*" but rather about the "*defective discipline*" of the colleges, the "*insufficiency of their scientific course,*" and "*their* inefficiency as *normal* institutions for the supply of teachers to our elementary schools prior to 1839." The writer contended that these were the real achievements of the institute, which had helped supply the university itself with its best pupils. Many of these pupils had advanced from the high schools and academies directly to the university without having to attend college at all because they were so thoroughly prepared after 1839 by a "well qualified corps of *native* school teachers" from VMI.

In a final attempt to best the apologist for VMI, the University of Virginia spokesman ignored the sequel's factual arguments in favor of extending the *ad hominem* assault on the superintendent.[7] He claimed the superintendent was just angry "with bristling front and visage fierce." He accused him of giving vent to his wrath like a defeated child justifiably floored in argument. He compared him to Oliver Goldsmith's schoolmaster: "E'en though vanquished he could argue still." Claiming that "every military establishment is a despotism," he eulogized Washington College for holding "a position from which all the glittering bayonets and roaring artillery of its belligerent neighbour will not be able soon to drive it."

And with that, the series of articles ended. Defense rested its case. Preston's claim that VMI was the first school to aid the Virginia farmer scientifically would be further validated in 1859 when the board of visitors established a chair of agriculture for Major Gilham, endowed by Philip St. George Cocke with $20,000.[8] The previous year Colonel Smith had traveled to Paris to visit the *L'École Polytechnique*, and on his return he had enthusiastically recommended a full-fledged technical school of three parts: agriculture, engineering, and the fine arts.

His proposal, however, would be delayed by the onset of the Civil War. The passage in 1862 of the Morrill Act, which allowed for the creation of land-grant colleges, came at a time when the Southern states were excluded from receiving any benefits until after the war because of their rebellion against the U.S. When Virginia was readmitted to the Union in 1870, twenty-four colleges, including VMI, would fight for the land-grant. But the prize in 1872 would go instead to Preston and Olin Institute for the establishment of a new Virginia Agricultural and Mechanical College, today's Virginia Polytechnic Institute. The new VPI would be founded mostly on land that belonged originally to Preston's grandfather William Preston.[9]

VMI never established the three-fold technical school that Colonel Smith had envisioned. But in 1860 with a faculty of fourteen and a corps of cadets numbering 200, it already offered the necessary academic balance between the sciences and classics that Preston's Cives articles had originally advocated. A quarter century had honed the curriculum to an extraordinary variety of academically challenging courses.

The Fifth Class, which was added on a trial basis for cadets with poor educational backgrounds, took courses in arithmetic, algebra, geometry, geography, composition, declamation, and drawing. Fourth Class added trigonometry and descriptive geometry. Third Class took analytical geometry, shades and shadows, perspective, surveying, differential and integral calculus, mechanical drawing, composition, and declamation. Second Class studied mechanics, optics and acoustics, astronomy, chemistry, Latin, and infantry tactics. And First Class focused on civil engineering, architecture, military engineering, human physiology, military history and strategy, political economy, infantry tactics, artillery tactics, mineralogy, geology, rhetoric, moral philosophy, mental philosophy, constitutional law, and logic.[10] Despite the school's detractors, of which there were now very few, the future looked bright amid ominous rumors of war.

Part V:
Reluctant Confederates

Lincoln's proclamation came, which I then regarded, and now regard, as a declaration of war.

—The Rev. William S. White

15

Shades of Conflict

So perish all such enemies of Virginia! all such enemies of the Union! all such foes of the human race!
—J.T.L. Preston

For anyone living in America as slave, master, or neither during the first half of the nineteenth century, when the practice was legally sanctioned, it would have been impossible to escape the questions raised about its morality, if not also its legality, and its abuses in the South and the North. These questions provoked heated exchanges, even in communities as isolated and relatively free of slave owners as Lexington in the western part of Virginia, where livestock and small farming operations rather than plantations prevailed.

The issue of slavery was first considered by the Franklin Society in Lexington as early as 1816 when it debated, "Ought the Virginia legislature pass laws for gradual emancipation?" Recorded only as figures, the vote at the time was affirmative seven to one.[1] In August 1831, the well-educated and highly intelligent slave Nat Turner led a rebellion in Southampton County, Virginia, which left more than 50 European Americans and over 200 African Americans dead in its aftermath. It spawned new laws by the Virginia General Assembly. These laws prohibited the education of enslaved and free African Americans and restricted their civil and voting rights.

The Franklin Society, rephrasing its original question, proposed to debate the issue again on September 6, 1834. This time it asked more directly, "Is it consistent with Christianity to buy and sell slaves?" Apparently the society's members felt unprepared to discuss such a potentially explosive topic. They postponed the debate until September 13. They delayed it again to the 27th, and at that meeting all members present were "fined 12¢ for failing to discuss the question." So it was rescheduled for October 4. Finally debated on the 11th, a month after the question was first raised, the vote was ten to four in the negative. The members deemed the buying and selling of slaves to be incompatible with Christianity.[2]

In April of the following year the original question resurfaced in the society with the proposal, "Ought Virginia immediately to adopt some scheme for the gradual removal of her slave population?" This time the vote proved unanimous. The African nation of Liberia had been founded in 1821 by the African Colonization Society. It was the brainchild of Kentucky Senator Henry Clay, the Quaker Abolitionist Paul Cuffee, and John Randolph of Roanoke. For those who felt it wrong that Africans had been taken from their homes originally, this solution would return them "with their own consent" to "free citizenship" in what was perceived as their homeland.[3]

In November, at a subsequent debate, the society voted eight to two to abolish slavery in the District of Columbia. And in December it decided six to four that slavery was not justified by the Bible. The prevailing sentiment among the leading citizens of Lexington from 1816 until 1835 tended toward abolishing or reducing the institution of slavery.

By the end of 1835, however, political movements in the North in support of inflammatory abolitionists were producing adverse effects on sections of the South. On December 12 the Franklin Society proposed the question: "Are the Northern states bound through their legislatures to take measures to put a stop to the incendiary movements of the abolitionists?" In a split vote, seven to six, the verdict was "yes" to curb rabid abolitionists.

In April 1836, two years after the society had voted eight to two to support Congress's constitutional right to abolish slavery in the District of Columbia, it reversed its vote fifteen to five. It conceded Congress no such right to end slavery. Revisiting the issue in January 1837, it again denied Congress that right, twelve to six. By April 1 of that year, the same society that had originally voted ten to four to reject slavery's consistency with Christianity voted nine to five in defense of slavery as entirely consistent with God's law.

As Preston would later claim, this general reversal of the Franklin Society's position from seeking to abolish or reduce the institution of slavery to defending it reflected a general trend across the South in opposition to the inflammatory "abolition movement," rather than any assertion of virtues that the institution of slavery itself might have suddenly acquired. Moreover, in other areas of the state and in other states, southerners were similarly adopting a defensive rather than questioning stance on slavery. Preston partly blamed the abolitionists who were "exciting well-grounded fears of terrible disaster, enraging the South against fanatical intruders, and chilling the kindness and deadening the sensibilities of the masters."[4]

Where Preston himself stood on slavery cannot be discerned from simple tallies of the Franklin Society's votes on the issue. Neither the specific arguments nor the names of their proponents were ever recorded. It's certain that by December 1849, he was participating in a church service bidding farewell to thirty free Africans emigrating from Rockbridge to Liberia. Colonel Smith delivered an address, followed by a hymn, written by Miss Margaret Junkin. It hailed the voyage as a return to a home "where bondage cannot enter," fully "free from all oppression."[5] Preston delivered the farewell address.

In January 1850, Preston attended a colonization meeting at the Lexington Courthouse. The legislature had appropriated $30,000 a year for five years "for the removal to Liberia of the free people of color of this state with their own consent." On Preston's motion, everyone present voted to support the venture with a subscription of $160.[6] Six months later the *Liberia Packet* sailed from Baltimore with fifty-five free Africans, bringing the total to over 7,000 persons emigrating to Liberia since the founding of the Colonization Society. They were given provisions and a large quantity of goods for the purchase of territory.

Throughout the 1850s basic divisions were developing within Lexington's populace over the existence of slavery. Judge John Brockenbrough, the Rev. George Junkin, and Superintendent Smith contended that slavery was justified by the Bible and must be preserved as an institution at all costs. In his semi-annual report to the board in 1856, Smith recommended that students at VMI be taught to "understand and believe the foundation of that divine institution of *slavery* which is the basis of the happiness, prosperity and independence of our Southern people, and thoroughly fortified to advocate and defend it."[7] On the other hand, abolitionists, of whom there were hardly any in Lexington, considered slavery evil and called for its immediate eradication. Their most radical spokesman was William Lloyd Garrison, who had begun the abolitionist movement in Massachusetts.

Between these two extremes, Virginia Governor John Letcher, Samuel McDowell Moore, and Dr. Henry Ruffner agreed that slavery should be abolished but over time rather than precipitously. In 1847 Ruffner had proposed before the Franklin Society and then in his "Ruffner Pamphlet" the removal of slavery from Virginia west of the Blue Ridge Mountains. He rejected the extremes of both the abolitionists and pro-slavery extremists by claiming the "middle way." Although himself a slaveholder, he considered the institution not only "pernicious" but economically, socially, and politically bad.[8] And, according to Henry Boley, "most of the men of Rockbridge agreed.[9]

Ruffner's pamphlet was endorsed by many leading figures of the region. Unlike the abolitionists, who objected to slavery on moral grounds, Ruffner rejected it on economic grounds. He argued that most people in western Virginia worked on small farms where slavery was not economical. Not only was it not profitable, it took jobs from white laborers. Favoring gradual emancipation, he suggested that the only way the western part of Virginia could ever rid itself of slavery was by separating from eastern Virginia, which it eventually did on his terms. Only then could gradual emancipation proceed.

John Wise, in his *End of an Era*, reflected that many Southerners "were working earnestly and loyally towards the adoption of some plan of gradual emancipation which would not destroy the labor system of the South nor leave the slave-owner impoverished."[10] Dr. Junkin and even President Lincoln, as reflected in their correspondence before the war, felt that the sudden abolition of slavery "would throw unprepared slaves into a system requiring more educational and moral structure than they then possessed."[11] And Robert E. Lee decreed fifteen years before the war that his slaves should be "liberated as soon as it can be done to their advantage," meaning gradually.[12]

Slavery was becoming a volatile and in some cases violent matter of public concern. Ever since the passage of the Kansas-Nebraska Act with its nullification of the Missouri Compromise on the slavery issue, debate had raged over whether Kansas should be admitted as a slave or free state. In May 1856, pro-slavery advocates attacked and killed an anti-slavery settler in Kansas. A band of anti-slavery men led by the abolitionist John Brown retaliated by massacring five pro-slavery men. Fears of similar slave uprisings swept through Virginia, where Nat Turner's revolt twenty-five years earlier still haunted the memory of most Virginians. By December "rumors relative to insurrectionary designs among the slaves" had reached such a peak in Lexington that VMI was posting guards "with ball cartridges" in the Guard Room and in Major Jackson's classroom "all night after taps."[13]

By the end of the 1850s individuals, towns, counties, and states of the South that depended solely on slave labor in cotton and tobacco fields for their survival were feeling compelled to secede from the Union and fight for their right to own slaves. But most towns and counties in western Virginia, including Lexington, were composed of pro–Union anti-secessionists who relied on African Americans, both free and slave, solely as household servants, mill hands, artisans, tenant farmers, and some who tilled their own acres. These residents adamantly opposed any break up of the Union. In 1860, only 105, less than seven percent, of Lexington's 1,528 residents owned 601 slaves.[14]

Even those who owned slaves were advocating the adoption of some plan of gradual emancipation, such as Ruffner's, that would not destroy the labor system of the South or leave plantation owners bankrupt. A model of such a plan for gradual emancipation would be provided the following year in Russia, when Alexander II inaugurated the Peasant Reform of 1861. Twenty-three million Russian serfs would be freed over a two-year period. This allowed each peasant to earn land from his landlord, for which the landlord would be reimbursed in government bonds.

But America was headed down a different path that would ultimately end in violence. Even Lexington, with only seven percent of its population owning slaves, was not immune to slave revolt. Two of Dr. Junkin's slaves were arraigned in court in April 1859, for "the poisoning of Dr. Junkin, President of Washington College, and his entire family" with arsenic on the night of March 20. It was "put into cream used at supper," but the dose "was so large that it acted as an emetic, thus saving their lives."[15] The case was dismissed due to insufficient evidence, but the popular belief in slave loyalty to their masters that many in Lexington held, whether slave-owners or not, was shaken by the revolt of the Junkins' slaves, who claimed "Dr. Junkin was mean."[16]

Then on the heels of John Brown's vengeful slaughter in Kansas came the news on October 16 that he had led an even more violent Sunday massacre at Harpers Ferry. It was the largest arsenal in the South and on the very edge of Virginia. Killing five and wounding nine, he was seen by Virginians as a bloodthirsty murderer who showed no sympathy at all for peaceful emancipation, gradual or otherwise. He had opted instead for the uncompromising path of war. It took twelve marines under the command of Lieutenant Colonel Robert E. Lee to defeat Brown. He was tried for treason and murder on October 25 and sentenced to be hanged on December 2.

John Brown's attack had failed, but it served to electrify the nation, instilling fear in the South and exhilaration in the North. James Robertson makes the claim that "more than any other event which had up to this time happened, this intensified the bad feeling then existing between the two sections."[17] Brown was both vilified and glorified. He was a madman and terrorist or a saint and visionary. Amid rumors of infiltration by abolitionists and potential bloodshed, Virginia Governor Henry Wise called up 1,500 militia to safeguard Brown's execution at Charles Town. Included in the militia was an anti-abolitionist, John Wilkes Booth, who would electrify the nation with his own brand of violence at the end of the approaching war.[18] Also included were eighty-five cadets as guard militia from VMI. They were led by Majors William Gilham and Thomas Jackson and commanded by Colonel Smith with J.T.L. Preston serving as quartermaster.

The hanging took place on December 2, 1859. Although Jackson gave a long and detailed description of the event, it was Preston's report in his letter to Maggie that still stands as the classic account of John Brown's execution. VMI historiographer William Couper quoted the entire letter before concluding, "A thoughtful eye and judicious mind it was which watched the execution of John Brown and wrote this moving description. No blame did Preston, the factual reporter, lay at the swinging feet of John Brown. With pure, reportorial skill he presented the picture of the execution of this controversial figure and all sides were clearly evident."[19]

Preston described how Brown was taken from the jail to the gallows, seated on his coffin. He told how he ascended the steps to the platform with intrepid demeanor "without being braggart," how he made no speech, while his manner showed no fear. But his face "was not free from concern" and had "a little cast of wildness." After the white cap

Cadets at the execution of John Brown, December 3, 1859, drawing ca. 1880 by C. L. McClung (Virginia Military Institute Archives, No. 0003663_22).

was pulled over his eyes and the noose adjusted, "it was curious to note how the instincts of nature operated to make him careful in putting his feet as if afraid he would walk off the scaffold. The man who stood unblanched on the brink of eternity was afraid of falling a few feet to the ground."

Preston recalled that Brown stood for ten or fifteen minutes—blindfolded, the rope around his neck, expecting any moment the fatal act—like a soldier in upright position, motionless. "I was close to him, and watched him narrowly, to see if I could perceive any signs of shrinking or trembling in his person, but there was none. Once I thought I saw his knees trembling, but it was only the wind blowing his loose trousers." Still, he had to wait while Colonel Smith confirmed to the sheriff that all was ready. But the sheriff didn't hear, so it bore repeating louder.

With a hatchet the sheriff struck the rope that held the trap door, and Preston encapsulated the essence of John Brown's controversial life at the very moment that it ended. He described how the door "instantly sank beneath him, and he fell about three feet; and the man of strong and bloody hand, of fierce passions, of iron will, of wonderful vicissitudes, the terrible partisan of Kansas, the capturer of the United States Arsenal at Harpers Ferry, the would-be Catiline of the South, the demi-god of the abolitionists, the man execrated and lauded, damned and prayed for, the man who in his motives, his means, his plans, and his successes, must ever be a wonder, a puzzle, and a mystery—John Brown—was hanging between heaven and earth."

Preston noted the profound stillness that followed as Brown's struggles grew feebler and feebler without any writhing or violent heaving of the body or chest, "until at last, straight and lank he dangled, swayed to and fro by the wind." There was no expression of elation or triumph by the crowd of onlookers over the death of this butcher who had traveled a thousand miles to kill Virginians. Neither he nor the Virginians had known each other. Nor was there "one throb of sympathy for the offender. All felt in their hearts that it was right. On the other hand, there was not one single word or gesture of exultation or of insult. From the beginning to the end, all was marked by the most absolute decorum and solemnity. There was no military music, no saluting by troops as they passed one another, not anything done for show."

The only cry that broke the profound silence as Brown hung from the gallows was that of Preston, proclaiming to those around him, "So perish all such enemies of Virginia! all such enemies of the Union! all such foes of the human race!" Seventy years later Stephen Vincent Benét would memorialize Preston's proclamation in his epic American poem, *John Brown's Body*. He would quote it as the introduction to "John Brown's body lies a-mouldering in the grave," which in early 1861 became the marching song for the Union before evolving into the "Battle Hymn of the Republic."[20]

Ralph Waldo Emerson described Brown as "the new saint awaiting his martyrdom, and who, if he shall suffer, will make the gallows glorious like the cross."[21] But as Preston described the scene in his letter to Maggie, he believed the moral was that "a sovereign state had been assailed.... Law had been violated by actual murder and attempted treason.... But, greater still—God's Holy Law and righteous Providence was vindicated, 'Thou shalt not kill.'—Whoso sheddeth man's blood, by man shall his blood be shed." The man of violence had met his fate in the same way that his two sons were cut down pursuing the violent career into which he had led them. "So perish all such foes of the human race," Preston had concluded, while admitting, "the mystery was awful, to see the human form thus treated by men, to see life suddenly stopped in its current, and to ask one's self the question without answer—'And what then?'"

The execution of John Brown was a major catalyst in the polarization of North and South. The more praise Northerners heaped on Brown, the more suspect their motives became in the South. His ends were being used to justify his means. Northern poets like Whittier, Emerson, and Longfellow composed panegyrics about him. Wendell Phillips and William Lloyd Garrison counted him a martyr.[22] Southerners, especially Virginians, began to dread the influx of fanatical abolitionists intent on inciting bloodshed. The fear was that if the anti-slavery Republicans were to win the upcoming presidential election in 1860, they would replace James Buchanan's Democratic policy of suppressing violence and lawlessness. So in preparation for possible conflict, the Virginia General Assembly authorized John Letcher, the newly inaugurated governor from Lexington, to appoint a three-man commission to supervise the purchase and manufacture of "Arms and Munitions of War."[23] One member of the commission was VMI's Colonel Smith.

Virginia had no intention of seceding from the Union, which it had helped to create and maintain. Admittedly, since the mid 1840s, the question of secession had been a lively topic of debate in the attempt to find a fair, equitable, and just solution to the slavery issue. The Franklin Society confirmed Virginia's right to secede in 1851 when it asked, "Has any state of this Union a right to resort to the remedy of secession in any emergency?" It answered in the affirmative eight to three.[24] But it fiercely questioned whether a separation of the states would be preferable to a limited monarchy. This it decided in the negative, because the U.S. government might then be "divided into two or more distinct governments within the next two hundred years."[25]

On August 25, 1860, the society voted nine to three against Virginia's seceding.[26] The people of Lexington were opposed to secession even with Abraham Lincoln's election on November 6, 1860. With South Carolina now threatening to secede in protest and with enthusiasm for a confederacy of southern states growing among the young people in Lexington, the older residents were determined to preserve the Union. Preston, Jackson, Barclay, and Dorman invited Rockbridge County citizens to meet at the courthouse to discuss the issue.

On December 3, attendance was large at a public meeting that Major Preston opened to consider the alarming state of public affairs. In the opinion of the correspondent from the Richmond *Dispatch* who attended the meeting, "The able and eloquent speech of Major Preston came nearer expressing the sentiment of the people of this county than that of any other speaker. He rebuked the conduct of the extremists, North and South, in the severest terms; expressed his satisfaction with the Union as it is, and thought it best to wait further developments before taking any steps that we might hereafter regret. He distinctly stated that he would await the action of Virginia, and would, without hesitation, do whatever she thought best should be done in the premises."[27] He went on to denounce "the hot haste of South Carolina" and, considering the large number of Scots-Irish settlers, declared that western Virginia "sided with Pennsylvania and Ohio."[28] Although the Union, which he favored, stood on the cusp of disunion, Preston concluded his ultimate loyalties would rest with his native state.[29]

Col. Smith also attended the meeting and, as William Couper confirmed, "frankly admitted that his views were more extreme than those which generally prevailed in the locality." He acknowledged what Preston said in his opening statement was sound, firm, and Virginian, but he felt Preston went too far in denouncing South Carolina."[30] Speaking in defense of that state's right to secede, he favored a general convention of all the states to decide the issue.

Among the growing number of young supporters of secession in Lexington was Preston's daughter Libbie. She had learned to regard Lincoln as a monster and to sing "Dixie" and "The Bonnie Blue Flag." Preston caught her and a young friend wearing blue rosettes, the Confederate badge, which she promptly flaunted in his face. She was furious when he playfully jeered back, "Tut, tut! Tad Lincoln will be coming down here to marry one of you some day!"[31]

On December 20, 1860, four days after the Crittenden Compromise had tried to resolve the slavery issue and failed to pass Congress, South Carolina seceded. Major Robert A. Anderson moved his entire force to Fort Sumter. This was the fort that President Andrew Jackson had reinforced almost thirty years earlier when he proclaimed that no state could secede because each secession would destroy the unity of a nation. By the end of the month, spurred on by the inevitable chain of events, Preston was preparing to include Virginia's Constitution in his course list for First Class cadets.[32]

By the end of January, Mississippi, Florida, Alabama, Georgia, and Louisiana had followed South Carolina, as did Texas in February. A Washington peace convention, headed by former President John Tyler of Virginia, was called in a last ditch effort to compromise and save the Union. But no compromise was reached, and the Confederate States of America was formed on February 9, 1861. Jefferson Davis of Mississippi would serve as provisional president in Montgomery, Alabama.

For two months, from February to April, the Virginia State Convention broke into opposing factions. Secessionists were pitted against Unionists, with more than half the delegates lining up for the Union. On March 4, Lincoln was inaugurated as the sixteenth president of the United States. He vowed to hold the Union together but declared to Southerners, "In *your* hands, my dissatisfied fellow countrymen, and not in *mine*, is the momentous issue of civil war. The government will not assail you. You have no conflict without being yourselves the aggressors…. We are not enemies, but friends. We must not be enemies."[33]

But it was obvious to Virginians that if Federal troops tried to restore the seceding states to the Union by force, "Virginia would become the battleground of the war." Some Southern states were awaiting Virginia's lead. But Virginia tossed the question back into Lincoln's hands: "Virginia would not secede unless forced to by actions of the federal government."[34] On April 4, after the territory of Arizona seceded, the Virginia Convention voted 88 to 55 to support a joint resolution offered by Preston's conservative cousin, William Ballard Preston. He had served as secretary of the navy under President Zachary Taylor. His Preston Resolution declared that the federal government had no power to subjugate a Southern state. The convention sent three delegates to ask President Lincoln what policy he planned to pursue toward the seceded states.

While the legislature was grappling with the secession issue, Preston was acting superintendent during Smith's absence from VMI. In anticipation of impending hostilities, he began to assemble guns, rifles, caissons, and mortars and forty-seven cadets to instruct a company of volunteers.[35] Then on April 12, when Confederate soldiers took Fort Sumter in Charleston, the country plunged into war.

16

Virginia First and Last

> *Rockbridge was revolutionised at once: And now our secessionist friends say, they are the true conservatives now, and that we are the fire eaters.*
> —James Davidson

On April 13, the day after Fort Sumter fell, war on a small scale loomed over the little town of Lexington as well. At VMI barracks two cadets had replaced the American flag with a makeshift secession flag. It displayed the Goddess of Liberty standing between the Virginia state motto, *Sic Semper Tyrannis*, and the cry "Hurrah for South Carolina."[1] Major Jackson summarily removed it. Several cadets promptly raised another secession flag, this time on a flagpole near the courthouse in the center of town. It was quickly countered when several militiamen raised a Unionist flag. After an exchange of threats and several altercations bordering on violence, a cadet retaliated, and a fight ensued.

The cadet's comrades sent word to the institute for reinforcements. And 180 cadets, fearing their comrade was in mortal danger, marched toward town, muskets loaded, in battle array. Colonel Smith tried unsuccessfully to turn the tide back to barracks, as did Captain Massie. Moderates also tried to quell the passions of the Unionists farther up the street. One account claims that Jackson faced the battalion and, without words but sternly glaring, forced the cadets to retreat. But according to VMI historiographer William Couper, Benjamin Colonna gave the only "clear cut account of the episode." He claimed Major Colston "rode up to the marching cadets on his beautiful charger, 'Pompey,' and quietly turned them back to the barrack."[2]

Colonel Smith ordered the corps to assemble in Major Preston's section-room, since it held the most seats at the institute. Smith gave the cadets a tongue-lashing for insubordination, which was reinforced firmly but less vociferously by Massie and Preston. Then turning to Jackson, who was sitting quietly in a chair on the rostrum, Smith declared, "I have driven in the nail but, it needs clinching. Speak with them."[3] Jackson arose, stood erect, and, eyes flashing, encapsulated all that was necessary to say in a few clipped words: "Military men make short speeches, and as for myself I am no hand at speaking, anyhow. The time for war has not yet come, but it will come, and that soon; and when it does come, my advice is to draw the sword and throw away the scabbard." The electrified corps of cadets erupted in unrestrained applause.

Two days later, on April 15, the day that Preston turned fifty, Lincoln called for 75,000 troops, three regiments of which must come from Virginia, to crush the rebellion in the South.[4]

> Whereas, the laws of the United States have been for some time past and now are opposed, and the execution thereof obstructed, in the States of South Carolina, Geor-

gia, Alabama, Florida, Mississippi, Louisiana, and Texas, by combinations too powerful to be suppressed by the ordinary course of judicial proceedings, or by the powers vested in the marshals by law: now, therefore, I, Abraham Lincoln, President of the United States, in virtue of the power in me vested by the Constitution and the laws, have thought fit to call forth, and hereby do call forth, the militia of the several States of the Union to the aggregate number of 75,000, in order to suppress said combinations and to cause the laws to be duly executed.

Governor John Letcher promptly responded, "In reply to this communication I have only to say that militia of Virginia will not be furnished to the powers at Washington for any such use or purpose as they have in view. Your object is to subjugate the Southern States, and a requisition made upon me for such an object—an object, in my judgment, not within the purview of the Constitution, or the Act of 1795—will not be complied with. You have chosen to inaugurate civil war, and having done so, we will meet it in a spirit as determined as the Administration has exhibited toward the South."[5]

In Lexington, Dr. William White, pastor of the Presbyterian Church, reported a profound change that swept over his town and the state. It was a change so abrupt and so intense that on April 15 staunch Unionists suddenly became "reluctant Confederates."[6] The Rev. White had made a speech that morning to a crowd of Union sympathizers in support of their views. But he now voiced the shock that he and most Virginians felt when "Lincoln's proclamation came, which I then regarded, and now regard, as a declaration of war. Thus forced to fight, I claimed the poor right of choosing whom to fight. Necessity was laid upon me to *rebel* against *him* [Lincoln], or my native state. I chose the former, and became a rebel, but never a secessionist."[7]

James Davidson, a Lexington lawyer, later wrote to U.S. Senator Robert Hunter, "I have been a Union man of the strictest faith until the Proclamation. On the 16th of last month I gathered around me in my office, some thirty of our strongest Union men, and prepared a dispatch to our delegate Dorman, in which they all concurred: 'Vote an ordinance of Revolution *at once.*' Rockbridge was revolutionised at once: and now our secessionist friends say, they are the true conservatives now, and that we are the fire eaters."[8]

On April 17, Virginia became the eighth state to secede from the Union. But it took up arms with considerable regret, which more than 1,300 battles on Virginia soil and more than a million soldiers, dead and wounded, would subsequently justify. Colonel Robert E. Lee, whom Lincoln offered command of the entire Union army, declined because he could not draw his sword against his home state and his own people. Edward Echols, a Rockbridge County justice, declared, "I'm now for annihilating Lincoln's government and all the departments, putting all the states back where they were at the beginning of the Revolution."[9]

Like Lee, Preston had believed the South could maintain its freedoms within the Union. But this hope was dashed with Lincoln's call for Virginia's troops to coerce itself and its sister states. It was an act that he regarded as unconstitutional tyranny. He concluded, "The President has forced Virginia to secede."[10] His allegiance had been to Virginia *in* the Union, but if there was to be *no* Union, then to Virginia first and last. Virginia had existed well before the Union.

By contrast, Preston's father-in-law, Dr. Junkin, a Pennsylvanian, was adamant in his support of the Union at all costs. His allegiance was to that Union for which his father had shed his blood as a Revolutionary War officer. When he learned that Preston had given up on the Union, he denounced him. Preston, showing respect for seniority, weathered the attack without anger. But what infuriated his children was that Junkin had denounced their father in his own home. Maggie found herself torn between the divided loyalties of husband and father. Of the two men, it was Preston who remained calm and unbiased, showing no bitterness toward the North. "None of us ever heard a harsh utterance on this subject from his lips," his daughter Libbie would later confirm.[11]

Dr. Junkin's rage almost reached its peak when, the day after Lincoln's call for troops and before Virginia's Act of Secession, Washington College students hoisted the unofficial "Bonnie Blue Flag with a Single Star" over the official statue of "Old George" atop Washington Hall. This was not the bronze statue of Washington that crowns Washington and Lee University today but the wooden figure carved by cabinetmaker Matthew Kahle seventeen years earlier from a log floating in the North River. When Dr. Junkin learned of the travesty, he ordered that the flag be removed at once. Reminding the students gathering on the campus that Virginia was still a part of the Union, he reaffirmed as president of the College that he was still in charge.

But his order to strike the flag was met instead with shouts for the Confederacy and rousing renditions of "Dixie" and "The Bonnie Blue Flag." Almost at wits' end, Dr. Junkin escaped further insubordination and embarrassment when his grandson, Willie Preston, appeared on the roof of the colonnade. He declared that Virginia was indeed still in the Union and that Dr. Junkin was still president. "We must wait a few days," Willie called out, "and I am going to take the flag down." Knowing that it was Willie who had helped raise the flag originally, the students protested angrily. But he promptly climbed the ladder to the summit of the cupola, retrieved the flag, and, waiving it aloft, shouted, "Three cheers for the Confederacy."[12] Amid the tumult of applause the confrontation was resolved.

We don't know how Preston responded to the role his son played in the flag raising incident, but much had changed within two days. Lexington was now calling for volunteers to repel invaders from Virginia's soil. Four companies were formed: the Rockbridge Artillery, the Dragoons (Cavalry), the Rifles, and the Liberty Hall Volunteers, which Willie would join. At a second hoisting of a southern banner, Dr. Junkin resigned his position as president of the college, declaring that he would never teach under a rebel flag.[13] Bidding farewell to the members of his family and taking his recently widowed daughter Julia with him, he promptly returned to his native state of Pennsylvania.

The wooden statue of Old George above Washington Hall (Washington and Lee University, Leyburn Library Special Collections, RG41, Washington and Lee Architecture).

The same conscience that had led him to abandon his Northern home, because of his sympathy with the institution of slavery as sanctioned by the Bible, now compelled him to leave his Southern home, because of his sympathy with preserving the Union. A man of strong convictions and passionate expression, he was disgusted at the dreadful turn of events. Tradition has it that he stopped his carriage at the Mason-Dixon line near Williamsport, Maryland, just long enough "to shake the dust of Virginia forever from the hooves of his horses" before crossing the Potomac.[14]

Maggie would lose not only her father but her brothers Johnny and George to the North. Dr. John Miller Junkin served as surgeon for the Federal army, and George Junkin, Jr., became a Northern sympathizer. Her brother Eben, the Rev. Ebenezer Dickey Junkin, became a Southern sympathizer. And brother Willy, the Rev. William Finney Junkin, joined the Confederates. With her widowed father, two brothers and a sister in the North and two brothers and a sister in the South, Maggie's family was evenly split by the arbitrary whimsicality of war. It broke her heart as much as did the war itself. She became irrevocably torn between her homeland and home, her love for her father and husband, her ancestors in Pennsylvania and descendants in Virginia.

The day after Virginia seceded, Colonel Smith met with Governor Letcher in Richmond to form a military council of three. It comprised Commodore Matthew Maury, Chief Justice John Allen, and himself. As acting superintendent, Preston took command to put VMI on a war footing. He arranged for the casting of cannon balls and at the urgent request of Major Jackson requisitioned ammunition. All of Lexington, which five days earlier had been fiercely split between Unionists and Secessionists, was now united in defense of its native state. Preston found himself caught up in the patriotic fervor of the moment. "The just blood shed for the defense of our Mother will rise like incense to Heaven," he wrote to Colonel Smith amid a swarm of pressing responsibilities. "Let it be ours if such is God's will. If those who come after us owe their freedom to our fall it is gloriously enough—more than enough. But I have no time for feelings."[15]

On April 20, Robert E. Lee resigned from the Federal Army. Preston prepared the Corps of Cadets at Camp Lee in Richmond to serve under the command of Major Jackson as drill instructors for the new Confederacy. Whereas Jackson would inspire his listeners with few words, Preston now employed his well-honed power of elegance and thrilling oratory to instill in the assigned cadets a fervent commitment to their cause. His marching orders intoned, "When the muster is held for men who have souls to defend their native soil from violation, insult and subjugation, the heart of every Virginian responds to the voice as with stern delight he answers 'Here!'" And for the unassigned cadets, he consoled, "Those who remain are doing duty to Virginia as really, and it may be as efficiently, as those who are gone. It is not the service that any one of us would prefer. But the soldier who is prepared to do only such duty as pleases him is not to be trusted. The soldier that would desert a post would fly in battle."[16]

He concluded his call to arms with a stirring tribute to the corps, whose members "will prove their birth and breeding and exhibit to Virginia the worth of her favorite institute. The cadet will not fail to manifest the advantage which the military education gives to him over those not less brave than himself. The corps will go forth the pride of its friends, the hope of the state, and the terror of her foes. May the blessing of the God of Hosts rest upon every one who is battling in this holy cause."[17]

Preston's marching orders inspired such enthusiasm among the 176 cadets who heard his call, as he himself readily admitted, that those who had to remain behind were "in tears that they cannot share danger and glory."[18] But he was suffering the same despair, as he wrote to Smith in Richmond, "Oh how I wish I possessed the qualifications that would justify me in joining you. I feel mystified to be obliged to be shut up here in these safe mountains when others are offering an oblation of blood to Liberty and to Native Land."[19] Preston was left with forty-seven cadets, which quickly dwindled to thirty when more were called. But these thirty would train the 100 volunteers of Company H, the "Rockbridge Grays" of the famous First Stonewall Brigade.

The students from Washington College formed Company I, the "Liberty Hall Volunteers," captained initially by mathematics professor Alexander L. Nelson. He was followed by the Presbyterian minister's son, Greek professor James J. White; then the West-Point-trained rector of the Episcopal Church William Nelson Pendleton; and eventually VMI Cadet W. H. Morgan. Morgan put the volunteers in their final state of proficiency. At first the college students were denied recognition as a legitimate company by Governor Letcher because of their young ages. But they bypassed securing their equipment officially from the county by turning informally to "the ladies of Rockbridge County." Learning of their rejection by the governor, the women made uniforms for them with their own hands.

One of the students, valedictorian John Newton Lyle, recalled whimsically that the women "sent us word that they would equip and send us forth as their special knights to do battle for their dear old mother, Virginia. Here was glory without the smell of gunpowder. The fair sex had chosen us as their own champions, and our breasts puffed out with pride." Lyle described the fair ladies as the best recruiting agents that Virginia had. They loved their native state, and "if their reproving glances failed to make a swain enlist in her defense, they made life miserable for him. They would send him dolls and dollgags, refuse his escort, chide and rebuke him until, in sheer desperation over their cruel treatment, he joined the army."[20]

The cadets from VMI who went to Richmond would remain for eight months drilling 15,000 to 20,000 men for the Army of Northern Virginia.[21] This was what Preston had foreseen twenty-six years earlier. He had proposed in his Cives articles that VMI would remedy an inefficient militia organization by providing in times of dire necessity fully qualified military officers capable of defending their respective counties or the state. These well-trained cadets were now training Confederate recruits who would succeed beyond all expectations at First Manassas the following July. The training manual they used was authored by their own Professor William Gilham and would be the standard guide for both Southern and Northern armies during the war. On April 27 the *Richmond Daily Examiner* heaped praise on the cadets, claiming they were "progressing finely in their instructions to recruits and have vastly improved some of the previously organized companies of volunteers."[22]

Not all the volunteers, however, many of whom were considerably older than their youthful trainers, were convinced that things were progressing finely. One recruit, George Bagby, a thirty-three-year-old from Lynchburg, resented early reveille and the primitive indignity of having to wash his face in a tin basin. But the height of insult was "to be drilled by a fat little cadet, young enough to be my son, of the Virginia Military Institute, that, indeed, was misery. How I hated that little cadet! He was always so wide-awake, so clean, so interested in the drill; his coat-tails were so short and sharp, and his hands looked so big in white gloves. He made me sick."[23]

The cadets trained recruits from all the Southern states at Camp Lee. While the army was being prepared, the officers of the army were advancing swiftly in rank as specific needs developed. On April 23, Robert E. Lee, as major general, was given command of all the military forces in the state. Jackson swiftly ascended from major in the engineering corps on April 24 to Colonel in the Virginia Volunteers on the 25th. On the 25th, leaving Major Stapleton Crutchfield in command at Camp Lee, Preston departed for Richmond to discuss the continuation of VMI.

On May 1, when Maryland turned down secession, Lee ordered Colonel Jackson to relieve General Kenton Harper as commander at Harpers Ferry. Here, across from Maryland, was the South's largest arsenal. It stood where the Potomac and Shenandoah rivers joined and where eighteen months earlier John Brown had staged his notorious attack. Jackson was directed to organize the troops, send the arsenal's muskets and munitions to Richmond, and collect weapons from the populace. Major Preston was assigned as his assistant adjutant general or chief of staff. VMI would not resume until late May.

17

Jackson's Chief of Staff

I have been acting as chief aid to Jackson, settling questions for colonels, majors, captains, and sometimes when Jackson was absent looking after his fortifications, acting as commander-in-chief as well.
—J.T.L. Preston, May 12, 1861

The arrival of Jackson at Harpers Ferry, his first appearance on the theater of the war, had an immediate impact on the scene. As the commander of the Staunton Artillery observed,

> The commanding colonel and his adjutant had arrived, and were occupying a small room in the little wayside hotel near the railroad bridge. Knowing them both, I immediately sought an interview, and delivered a letter and some papers I had brought from General Lee. Jackson and his adjutant were at a little pine table figuring upon the rolls of the troops present. They were dressed in well-worn, dingy uniforms of professors in the Virginia Military Institute, where both had recently occupied chairs. Colonel Jackson had issued and sent to the camps a short, simple order assuming the command, but had had no intercourse with the troops. The deposed officers had nearly all left for home or for Richmond in a high state of indignation.[1]

Despite the unassuming appearance of the new commanding officers at Harpers Ferry, military discipline was established within two weeks. Preston would later ask Jackson how he established discipline in an army that had lost all semblance of order. Jackson responded that "he would take up a single point of discipline at a time, elevate and secure this, then turn his attention to others in succession." Preston concluded that "two truths must be borne in mind by every man who deals with masses of men." One was "that he cannot do everything that he aims at; the other, that he can do a great deal."[2] Patience and courage were required to teach the lesson that, although many things might need amending, it was a question for common sense to decide how fast to advance.

Under Jackson's command, constant drilling converted 4,500 volunteers into combat-ready soldiers. Preston wrote Maggie, "I have been acting as chief aid to Jackson, settling questions for colonels, majors, captains, and sometimes when Jackson was absent looking after his fortifications, acting as commander-in-chief as well. We have regular earnest war on hand—in all but the battle—and that has yet to come."[3]

Preston astonished himself with how quickly he adapted to new circumstances. Much of his flexibility he attributed to "the technical acquaintance with military matters" that he had absorbed during his twenty-two-year connection with VMI. It was indeed one of the unanticipated benefits of his original wish to prepare young cadets for the disciplined life of the soldier as much as the citizen. Later he would write, "It is aston-

17. *Jackson's Chief of Staff* 141

ishing to see how experience, such as the V. M. I. life gave, tells now. Every man from the oldest to the youngest, who has been connected with it, is looked to for extra service."[4]

On May 20, North Carolina became the tenth state to secede. The Confederate capital was moved from Montgomery, Alabama, to Richmond. Preston wrote to Colonel Smith that he had raised a company of volunteers, but it was disbanded to encourage other communities to meet their quota. So he had applied to command a regiment from the western part of the state and wanted to know the results of his application.[5]

Before any changes could affect his status, however, Colonel Jackson was transferred from Harpers Ferry when Union troops captured Alexandria, Virginia, and Preston returned to VMI. Now serving as Joseph E. Johnston's principal lieutenant, Jackson took command of the First Virginia Brigade. It consisted of four regiments from western Virginia, one of which was led by Preston's cousin, Colonel James Francis Preston. Included in the brigade was the Rockbridge Artillery, led by the Rev. Pendleton. The Rev. Pendleton's artillerists had christened the three small six-pounder and one twelve-pounder howitzers Matthew, Mark, Luke, and John out of respect for their priestly captain. They stand today on the VMI parade ground in front of Jackson Hall.[6]

Prior to Major Preston's return to VMI, his son Tom was commissioned the new chaplain of the 27th Virginia Regiment. He requested to serve west of the Blue Ridge Mountains near his home.[7] Almost a hundred new cadets had arrived under Preston's

Cadet Battery: Matthew, Mark, Luke, and John. The custom-designed Cadet Battery was cast at the Cyrus Alger Foundry in Boston and arrived at Virginia Military Institute on June 6, 1848. From 1851 until the beginning of the Civil War, the guns were commanded by Stonewall Jackson. During the war they were employed by several units, including the Rockbridge Artillery under Pendleton's command (photograph by Virginia Military Institute. Used by permission).

command to be drilled for service as the Class of 1864MS (Military Service). But as soon as they arrived, they began dropping out to serve. They wanted to serve despite the news that on June 4, Confederate Captain John Quincy Marr, a VMI graduate of 1846, became the "First Blood of the War," the first Civil War soldier and first Confederate officer to die in combat.[8] Three days later Governor Letcher issued a proclamation that all cadets must be drilled at least once a week. Preston knew this requirement would "serve no earthly good until they were drafted." They would be eager to learn when they knew they were being trained to serve. In fact, "the rules require they be drafted before preliminary steps can be taken."[9]

On June 8, Tennessee became the eleventh and last state to secede. By the 18th, Preston was already questioning his role at the institute as useless at a crucial time when Virginia was most in need of its staunchest disciples. He wrote Colonel Smith to offer again his services: "I am not in the least ambitious, and would as soon do humble work as great work ... provided I can really serve the state, and share the dangers of those who are defending her from her invaders."[10] By the 20th seven officers had been called up, leaving Preston "without a single officer," some seventy new cadets, only thirty old cadets, and "little or nothing left to guard."[11] The future of the institute was in dire jeopardy with no more need now for a guard than a mere watch. When Captain John McCausland asked for fifteen cadets as drill masters near Charleston, Preston felt the rest of the corps should be furloughed if they weren't willing to volunteer for a battalion.[12]

Yet nothing could convince Preston to put an end to twenty-two years of determined effort to keep the dream of VMI alive. Colonel Smith was "anxious to place the battalion of cadets into the field at as early a day as possible," rather than have them function only as drillmasters. He even proposed to Colonel Gilham that he himself command the battalion. He argued, "While students of the other university and colleges are taking the field as private soldiers, I do not wish the cadets to be in the background."[13] But the cadets opposed serving as privates when they felt they could better serve the state as drillmasters and officers. Even as Smith was making his proposal to place them in the field, Preston wrote to implore him to reopen the school for their training in the fall: "I have no hesitation in saying that it is your duty not to allow the work of 20 years to be destroyed, and that the only way to prevent this is to come to the rescue, and rally around you as many of the old corps of officers as you can get."[14]

On July 1, Preston wrote to Smith his intense disappointment that fellow Lexingtonian Frank "Bull" Paxton had declined any commission that would require him to leave Jackson's brigade.[15] Preston was thus denied the opportunity to serve with Jackson at Manassas. Instead he was offered a promotion to lieutenant colonel in the artillery. But he wrote Smith on July 6, "I cannot accept an appointment which I cannot meet with some degree of efficiency. I went as far as I could with a good conscience in being willing to accept a Lt. Col. role in an infantry regiment. In one of artillery where the officers must necessarily be detached, my want of knowledge might be of serious detriment."

He went on to add that he had asked the governor "to change it to an infantry commission and order me to report to Jackson—or to send me there on my institute commission as major," to which he characteristically added, "the rank is nothing to me."[16] But the next day, having declined to serve in the artillery, he was commissioned instead lieutenant colonel in field and staff of the newly formed 9th Virginia Infantry

Regiment to serve at Craney Island.[17] His assignment under Colonel Smith would be to defend Norfolk and Portsmouth against Federal invasion from the north.

Apparently Providence appeared to prefer that Preston be stationed, instead of Manassas, near where his father had been assigned at the beginning of the War of 1812, when young Preston was not yet two. During Preston's service at Craney Island, academic work at VMI ceased and would not resume again until the end of the year. Few of the cadets who had recently matriculated as the Class of 1864MS would return to graduate, although all would be listed later in the alumni records. But as enthusiastic as the cadets were about volunteering to actively defend the Confederacy, not all of Virginia concurred. In fact, the western part of Virginia beyond the Allegheny Mountains, where many residents had opposed secession, was sliced away to become a new state.

Many Virginians begrudged West Virginia's separation, as Preston's daughter Libbie would testify, especially its retention of Virginia in its name. Libbie would later recall thinking, "Let them go, they never really belonged."[18] Like the Pyrenees between France and Spain, the Alleghenies formed as much a political as geographical, though not linguistic, division between two sections of the state. On June 20, West Virginia—although not officially a state until two years later—formed a rival government and elected two U.S. senators, becoming the first state to secede from a Confederate state.

By July 15, with the superintendent and most of the principal professors absent from VMI, the board of visitors suspended the salaries of all in service.[19] Preston's salary at Craney Island dropped immediately from $183 to $170 for the months of July through October.[20] Major Crutchfield was left in charge of 100 cadets at the institute, where he supervised the manufacture of 60,000 musket cartridges and 1,000 rounds of ammunition for field artillery. Two days later Jefferson Davis ordered General Joseph E. Johnston to Manassas Junction. It was the site of the only railroad entering the Shenandoah Valley in northern Virginia. General Lee correctly reasoned that any attempt to take Harpers Ferry would originate at Manassas in a march toward Richmond. And as expected, on July 21, two Confederate columns of Johnston at Manassas and General P.G.T. Beauregard at Winchester clashed with Union General Irvin McDowell at Bull Run, the dominant stream in the area. The first major battle of the Civil War was underway. "All day long," wrote Mrs. Moore in Lexington, "we could hear the guns at Manassas. I think it was one hundred and fifty miles away."[21]

Considering that the Blue Ridge Mountains lay between Lexington and the battlefield, Libbie would recall how difficult it might have been to believe that the reverberations of cannon firing could be heard at such a distance, "if the testimony were not abundantly confirmed by those who heard this sound" that July Sunday.[22] Two of her brothers (Tom, as chaplain, and Frank) and four of her cousins (James Francis Preston and William, Randolph, and Preston Cocke) along with many VMI cadets fought at First Manassas. The people of Lexington "walked the moonlit floor most of the night, expecting and dreading the news of battle." Many of them had been students at the college, cadets at the institute, and their own sons and brothers. According to cadet drillmaster Junius Hempstead, Class of 1864, his fellow warriors were remembered at Manassas as "those little soldiers with buttons all over their coats."[23]

Despite the presence of so many close relatives at Manassas, Preston was absent from the battlefield that fateful Sunday. He was traveling to Augusta, Georgia, on Saturday to help set up the autonomy of the Southern Presbyterian Church during its first

General Assembly. But he had detoured to visit his two sons and four nephews in Jackson's army. While there he had asked if a battle was imminent, in which case he wanted to be present. As Libbie recalled, "It was the only time I ever knew Father to be willing to put anything before the interests of his church."[24] But the staff officers assured him there was no sign of an impending fight. He would later rue the fact that Jackson withheld his plans from even the most trusted of his officers, himself included as a close friend. By sundown on the day he arrived in Augusta the victory at Manassas had already been won and largely by Jackson's brigade.

18

Craney Island

I am ready to march into the heart of the mountains and struggle there by the side of my highlanders.
—J.T.L. Preston

On July 24, 1861, Lieutenant Colonel Preston accompanied Colonel Smith and Major Crutchfield to the confluence of the James and Elizabeth rivers at Craney Island.[1] In the newly formed 9th Virginia Infantry Regiment, Preston would serve as Smith's aid. But as it turned out, Smith's frequent absences from the island left Preston in full command of the twenty-one guns of the infantry unit manning coastal batteries. Moreover, during his assignment on the island all his field officers were lost to other assignments.[2]

Embracing only twenty acres, as Preston would write in his journal, Craney Island was vital "as a defence against the landing of Federal troops from Newport News just across the mouth of the James River."[3] Strategically it had proven significant in the defeat of the British during the American Revolution and again during the War of 1812. Preston noted that there had been severe illness among the soldiers stationed at Craney Island in 1812, without betraying any awareness on his part that the same illness had proven fatal to his father in the initial year of that war.

On July 26, Preston took charge of the island in Smith's absence. His journal recorded many of his thoughts and feelings during the two months he served there. Among his entries Preston lamented keenly that the only obstacle to his entering the service was his age: "My chief feeling in desiring to enter the service, was not that my aid would be important, but that I might share the hazards of the campaign with my countrymen. And here [at Craney Island] we find ourselves comparatively secure ... while the battle of Manassas has been fought and while in the west our fellow soldiers are beset by foes.... I would have been with Jackson at Manassas.... I am ready to march into the heart of the mountains and struggle there by the side of my highlanders."[4]

By his own admission, Preston the teacher could not become the soldier, which better characterized Jackson. Preston had no illusions of heroism or leading charges that younger men would more readily accept. In his journal he expressed to Maggie the emotions he felt he could confide only to her, for he viewed war as repressing much that he himself might have to offer. In times of war, he wrote, "everything is so intensely physical, the ultimate to which war is reduced is the application of physical force—as the olden times men of gigantic preposterous strength were the only great men. Then came archers and slingers of stones and then the mail-clad warriors, and now the men who can make and get together and use great guns and ships, and build fortified towns defying assault. A man dares not show a love for beauty or admiration of the sublime or enjoyment in the picturesque, or to snatch a kiss from the muse of poetry, or to be

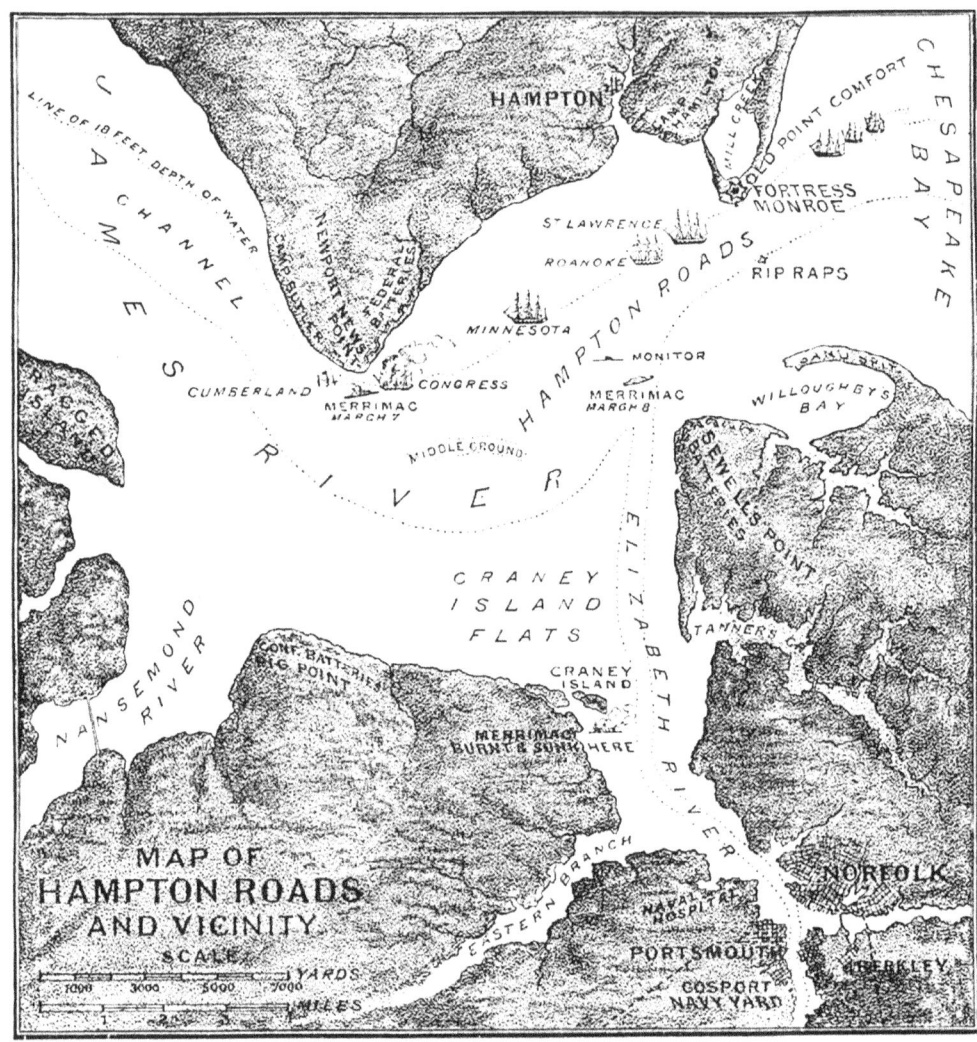

Map of Craney Island during the Civil War. A vital Confederate defense against Federal invasion, Craney Island witnessed the first clash between ironclad warships, the CSS *Virginia* and the USS *Monitor*, during the famous Battle of Hampton Roads on March 9, 1862 (courtesy Norfolk Public Library, Sargeant Memorial Collection as displayed online by Norfolk Navy Yard History website, http://www.usgwarchives.net/va/portsmouth/shipyard/nnytoc.html).

kindled with a thought of Romance. These things and such like would be ridiculed as unreal."[5]

Yet he questioned, "Are they unreal therefore? Then why does my heart respond to them? Are the good waters around me, merely the highways for those Yankee vessels that vex my soul as they pass up and down, and have they nothing on their face to gladden, nothing in their depths to inspire? Are my mountains only bulwarks for defense, alas, that they are not more efficacious, or are they also the heaven aspiring homes of high thoughts?"[6]

By September 1861, the war had entered its fourth month, and Craney Island had seen no action. A feeling of restlessness was settling over the men who remained entirely ignorant of the enemy's intent. They watched frigates evacuating—or were they reinforcing?—Newport News. Despite a great victory for the South in August at Wilson's Creek in Missouri, General Lee's defeat at Cheat Mountain on September 11 secured West Virginia for the North. Virginia was becoming acutely aware of the evils of war. On September 17, Preston received a copy of the *New York Tribune*, in which he learned that a peace party had been formed in Connecticut.[7] The majority of the Connecticut populace stood for war. But with the Union defeat at Bull Run, a determined minority had opted for peace in the indecisive aftermath. The article revealed a division of sentiment, but there was no mention that people there felt any of the ill effects of the war.

Noting this discrepancy, Preston complained, "Our best men are imperiling their lives. Their armies are composed mainly of those who can be spared." He recalled that Maggie's sister Julia, writing from Pennsylvania, had described how "peacefully they were enjoying themselves in some summer retreat that except for the newspapers, they would hardly know of the existence of war." He noted how Maggie, deprived of husband, two sons, and a brother in the service, was preparing food and clothing for the army. His own life was curtailed to the bare minimum. His property confiscated, his horses impressed, and his business in doubt, led him to conclude, "All these evils are sent upon us by those who are living in comparative ease." If Rockbridge County were asked to raise 200 more men "to give rest to our soldiers war-worn and wearied … we have not at home those who can take their places even temporarily." Yet even as these dark thoughts threatened to depress his spirit, Preston refused to let them daunt his courage: "I resist and will resist to death and am ready to see property perish, and myself and family beggared and exiled, rather than submit. If hope ever departs, the obstinacy and recklessness of despair will take its place."[8]

It was not that the North alone was spared the suffering of war. There was also little suffering in the deeper South, since the battles were mainly fought on Virginian soil. Preston found it offensive "to hear men from other states talk about coming to fight the battle of Virginia. She has in fact offered herself as the champion of the cause. Her territory is invaded, her society is convulsed and her means are exhausted to supply the defense of those farther South who are in comparative quiet."[9]

On a visit to the Navy Yard in Norfolk on September 21 he found it nearly stripped of all its guns. "From the Chesapeake to New Orleans all the coast defense is with Virginia guns," he observed, "and so also up the Mississippi, and this too when we actually need more guns for the further armament of our own state. Here at Craney Island we cannot get any of the guns that are being rifled, because the secretary of war has sent down an order for all to go to New Orleans and even to Galveston. Virginia is a generous old mother. She gave away all her public lands to the new one and in both cases, as far as I can learn, without any thanks. The public lands she gave away made up Ohio, Indiana, and Illinois, that now are seeking her ruin. The guns she sends to the cotton states will never, it is hoped, be turned against her."[10]

Preston witnessed firsthand at Craney Island the successful embodiment of what he had hoped for at VMI. Even the most hopeless cadet had within him the potential for a mature awakening. Cadet John Robinson, Class of 1855, stopped at the island on his way back from a clandestine visit with his parents in Philadelphia, and Preston was amazed at what he saw. "The development of his mind and character is beyond degree surprising. He is well informed, cultivated, mature, clear in his news of things and with an unusual power of expression. When he was a cadet he was the full reverse of anything promising such results."[11]

Preston could watch and appreciate the development of former cadets on Craney Island. But his real concern was for his sons serving in the 27th Virginia Regiment, the Stonewall Brigade. He was not anxious that Tom should act as chaplain on the staff of General Jubal Early. It was a post that placed him beside the wounded and dying on the battlefield or in the camp hospital. Even though he didn't bear arms, he was not immune to danger. Preston wanted him settled elsewhere with Lucy, his bride of four months, already pregnant with their first child.[12]

He saw in Frank a certain similarity to Cadet Robinson. "He is a curious fellow," Preston mused. He seemed "the least calculated for a soldier than any of my boys, and the most likely to become disgusted with the hardship of the life, and yet he has been pretty well [adjusted] in service and yet not a word of misery in his letter."[13] Frank had mustered into 1st Company, Virginia Rockbridge 1st Light Artillery, and was almost immediately promoted to 5th sergeant. But he requested in August a rank reduction to private, which is what he would remain until his discharge for wounds the following year.

As September drew to a close, Preston was given fifteen days' furlough. The first week he traveled to Manassas to join the command there. But he spent the rest of furlough with Maggie and the two children, George at three and Bert at eight months, neither of whom he had seen during the last three months in service.

19

He Cannot Be Spared

His services are so valuable to me, that I regret to say he cannot be spared.
—Thomas J. Jackson, Nov. 11, 1861

On October 21, 1861—three months after the Union's surprise defeat at First Bull Run, six weeks after its unexpected loss at Wilson's Creek, and in the second largest battle of the Eastern Theater—General-in-Chief George McClellan's Union forces were yet again routed by General Nathan Evans' Confederates at the Battle of Leesburg, Virginia. The indignant dismay in the North would soon force Congress to establish the Joint Committee on the Conduct of the War. In a shakeup of the chain of command, General Winfield Scott, under whom Jackson had served in the Mexican War, retired as general-in-chief of the U.S. Army. He was succeeded by General McClellan, at the young age of thirty-four and despite his recent defeat. General David Hunter relieved General John Frémont as commander of Western troops. And Union forces began to amass in the Eastern Theater on the banks of the Potomac River.

On October 22, Preston was transferred to General Jackson's staff as adjutant general, a position he would hold until February the following year.[1] Jackson wrote to his wife, "I have written to Colonel Preston, of Lexington, to join me. My desire is to get a staff specially qualified for their duties, and that will render the greatest possible amount of service to their country."[2] The next day he wrote to Maggie, "I am anxiously expecting his arrival, but fear he will not reach us for another week or two."[3] He also wrote requesting leave of absence from VMI for as long as the war would continue.[4] The following day he learned from Acting Secretary of War Judah P. Benjamin that he would command the Valley of Virginia District between the Blue Ridge and Allegheny mountains. On October 28, knowing that he would have to headquarter at Winchester, he took leave of his much beloved Stonewall Brigade. In five months he had transformed the five regiments of Valley Infantry from raw recruits into battle-hardened veterans. In the short time he had known them, their deep love of their commander had grown to match his own genuine affection and respect for them.

In one of his rare public displays of emotion, he addressed them in briefest terms from horseback, "Officers and men of the First Brigade! You do not expect a speech from me. I come to bid you a heartfelt goodbye. This brigade was formed at Harpers Ferry and the command of it assigned to me. You have endured hard marches, the exposure and privations of the bivouac, like men and patriots. You are the brigade which turned the tide of battle on Manassas Plains and there gained for yourself imperishable honor, and your names will be handed down with honor attached in future history." Then rising in the stirrups, raising his arms, and exclaiming in a loud voice, he chanted,

"You were the First Brigade in the Army of the Shenandoah, the First Brigade in the Army of the Potomac, the First Brigade in the Second Corps, and are the First Brigade in the hearts of your generals. I hope that you will be the First Brigade in this, our second struggle for independence, and in the future, on the fields on which the Stonewall Brigade are engaged. I expect to hear of crowning deeds of valor and of victories gloriously achieved! May God bless you all! Farewell!"[5]

Jackson always contended that his brigade, not he, had earned the name that made it famous. His separation from them was one of his most difficult trials, as he accompanied Preston and aide "Sandie" Pendleton to the depot at Manassas Junction. On November 4, still accompanied by Preston, he departed for Winchester, where they found the valley utterly defenseless except for a very small militia.[6] Jackson dispatched Preston to Richmond on November 5 to request reinforcements for his new command from Secretary of War Benjamin.[7] One result of Preston's mission to Richmond was the promised return to Jackson of his Stonewall Brigade. In it Jackson had all the confidence he needed to defend the valley from invasion. He headquartered at first at a hotel in Winchester but soon moved to a quieter home for privacy. He invited Preston to share his sleeping quarters. But, familiar with Jackson's private ritual of praying daily in his bedroom, Preston bedded instead with the aides on a military cot across the hall.[8]

A month had passed since Preston had seen Maggie and the children, and now a hundred miles from Lexington, he wished to visit them. But Jackson wrote to Maggie on November 11, "Your dear husband has gone to Richmond for a few days. I have received a letter from him in which he speaks of a desire to spend one day with you, but his services are so valuable to me, that I regret to say he cannot be spared."[9]

In mid November he sent Preston to consult with General William "Old Blizzards" Loring in Huntersville about concentrating all his troops with Jackson's at Winchester. The plan was to consolidate and recapture the outpost of Romney, which the Federal army was rapidly reinforcing. The Union hoped to gain a stronghold in the Potomac River Valley.[10] But Loring was not a fan of Jackson, whose aggressive style of leadership he considered rash and irresponsible. He resented strengthening Jackson's troops with his own. Procrastinating, he argued the impossibility of such a daring campaign and allowed his command to straggle into Winchester during the entire month of December.

Meanwhile, the Stonewall Brigade was assigned to General Richard Garnett. Although Preston considered him a good soldier and a pleasant individual, he was opposed to his serving as the brigade's commander. He strongly felt the brigade "ought to be commanded by one of its own colonels; they have made their own glory, and a stranger should not have been made to share it."[11] But it was his office to introduce Garnett to the men, which he dutifully did. As it turned out, his reservations proved prophetic when Garnett, like Loring, began sanctioning costly delays.

One delay involved Jackson himself. It stemmed from a religious conviction that his wife Ellie had instilled in him long before to keep the Sabbath. A prime objective of the Romney Campaign was to destroy two of the Union's most vital arteries: the Baltimore and Ohio Railroad line and the dams along the Chesapeake and Ohio Canal. But on Saturday, December 7, Major Frank Paxton's detachment was unable to demolish Dam No. 5 on the Potomac, which provided water to the C&O Canal leading to Washington. Jackson blamed Paxton for extending his failed attempt into Sunday in violation of the Sabbath. A week later he instructed Preston to use only the powder procured on Saturday and Monday to destroy the Winchester canal. "Colonel," he ordered, "I desire that you will see that the powder which is used for this expedition *is not the powder that was procured on Sunday.*"[12] As though validating Jackson's belief, the delayed attempt successfully breached the dam and dried up the canal.

Not everyone approved of Jackson's rationale, which spawned unfavorable rumors. On December 27, Preston wrote Maggie that he was leaving Governor Letcher's office in Richmond. He had been unsuccessful in his attempt to secure more troops for Jackson's Romney campaign. The Confederate government was responding to fabricated rumors about Jackson, some of which were launched by Loring concerning the rashness of his plan. Despite the cordiality with which Secretary of War Benjamin and President Davis received Preston, his mission became "a forlorn hope" to "accomplish what could not be done." He teased Maggie that when he was introduced to Davis, the Confederate President confessed "he had expected to see a Col. Preston that he had met before, but so many of your name have entered the service, that it is no wonder I was mistaken." The remark spurred Preston to caution Maggie, "So much for your name, Mrs. Preston!"[13]

As long as Preston was needed for Jackson's Romney campaign, the governor granted him, at Jackson's request, "leave of absence from the institute."[14] The march to retake Romney consumed two weeks through freezing cold and snow. In his report of operations, Jackson praised Preston for having "rendered very valuable service, not only during the expedition, but preparatory to it."[15] But he was frustrated by the continual delays of the disgruntled Loring. He was also concerned, as Preston wrote to Confederate legislator Colonel Boteler in Richmond, by "the practice of the enemy to burn every house into which any of our troops have at any time been received." Preston reported, "The object of this barbarity is to dismay our loyal citizens, and in this letter you have proof that the policy is not without its effect."[16] In mid January, Jackson left Loring and his division to guard the lonely Romney outpost and retired with the rest of the army to winter in hospitable Winchester.

Preston returned to VMI on February 1, 1862, when some 268 cadets reported for classes without books.[17] There was no First Class with its much needed age and experience. Its members had graduated in December, and discipline was lax. Several cadets were the first to be dismissed for dueling. Maggie's journal gave a detailed description of the hardships "this horrid and senseless war" was inflicting on the people of Virginia. For her it had meant the sudden break up of her family, her father's and sister's departure for Philadelphia, her husband's year-long absence, and "days and nights of torturing apprehension while he was campaigning with General Jackson."[18]

Asking herself where it would all end, she protested, "My very soul is sick of carnage. I loathe the word—*War.* It is destroying and paralyzing all before it. Our schools are closed—all the able-bodied men gone—stores shut up, or only here and there one open; goods not to be bought, or so exorbitant that we are obliged to do without. I actually dress my baby all winter in calico dresses made out of the lining of an old dressing-gown; and G. [George] in clothes concocted out of old castaways. As for myself, I rigidly abstained from getting a single article of dress in the entire past year, except shoes and stockings."[19] Preston was fifteen years over conscript age and was one of only a few men in Lexington. All except the old men were in the army, Maggie lamented. "No boy over seventeen could be restrained; our world was a world of femininity with a thin line of boys and octogenarians."[20] As if to compound her concern, Frank, who was on furlough, re-enlisted in the Rockbridge Artillery in February.

Apart from Jackson's abortive Romney Campaign, the South now found itself plagued with defeats. Union forces had occupied Mills Springs in Kentucky, Forts Henry and Donelson in Tennessee, Roanoke Island in North Carolina, and Harpers Ferry and Charleston in Virginia. In March, Jackson experienced at Kernstown the only defeat he would ever suffer. Preston was already considering returning to service since the cadets might disperse at any time if called. Then in April he was ordered by Jackson to return to active duty at his camp at Mt. Jackson beyond Staunton. Maggie made several futile attempts to dissuade Mr. P., as she called him in her journal, from rejoining Jackson. George Junkin, her first cousin and one of Jackson's aides, had been captured at Kernstown.[21] She feared for her husband, but she was left to mourn, "Oh! if we might only be permitted to withdraw ourselves from this turmoil of horrid strife—if it were only to a log cabin on some mountain side!"[22]

A week later she was inexpressibly relieved by Preston's return. Considering his legal proficiency, Jackson had offered him the post of inspector-general. But he felt the position didn't suit him at all. He considered investigating complaints less vitally important than training soldiers and officers at the institute.[23] So he declined Jackson's offer and returned to Lexington.

His choice to help prepare young men for combat would prove significant both for him and for the institute. By the end of the war VMI would contribute almost 1,800 cadets and graduates, or ninety-four percent of its living alumni, to the service of the Confederacy and seventeen graduates to the Union. It would provide the South with 3 major generals, 15 brigadier generals, 95 colonels, 65 lieutenant colonels, 110 majors, 310 captains, and countless lieutenants. It would supply the North with 1 brigadier general, 3 colonels, 1 lieutenant colonel, 3 majors, 3 captains, and 1 lieutenant.[24] At the time, in early 1862, a saying was already circulating, which some would attribute to Lincoln but which Maggie had heard originated with a Union general. It claimed that the South would have been defeated much earlier if it had not been for "that pesky little military school in Virginia, which kept turning out officers and fighters as fast we could kill them off!"[25]

No sooner had Preston resolved to devote his talents to training soldiers than he was summoned on May 1 to march with the entire corps of 200 cadets as backup for Jackson's McDowell Campaign. Jackson intended to stop Generals Nathaniel Banks and Frémont from reinforcing the Union's offensive against Richmond. He needed the corps as reserve, since the "safety of this section of the valley" made their presence greatly important.[26] It took three days, through cold rain and mud, to reach Staunton on foot. And the cadets were equipped with small smooth-bore guns "quite unsuited for war."[27]

Hearing no news for ten days apart from unsupported rumors from the battle scene, Maggie experienced "heart-crushing suspense!"[28] By May 9, Preston had marched with the corps for thirty-four miles in one day to arrive at the Battle of McDowell just as it had ended. He and the cadets were left in charge of guarding the prisoners and stores at McDowell, bearing the wounded off the field, and burying the dead.[29] But for the cadets who had seen no fighting, he remarked that this was "their first actual look upon the horrid visage of war."[30]

Preston's unannounced return with the corps on May 17 thrilled Maggie. Jackson was acting out of respect for the board of visitors' disapproval of his subjecting any portion of the corps to the risk of battle "unless in the immediate defense of the institution *at Lexington.*" The board considered it "a breach of good faith on the part of the institution towards parents and guardians."[31] So the corps was ordered to return, but not before it helped save Staunton from Union occupation.

If Maggie believed the corps' return to Lexington would assuage her fears for her husband's welfare, she had only to wait another week for a personal tragedy that would demand he travel immediately to Jackson's camp in Winchester. General McClellan, whom Lincoln had removed as general-in-chief of the Union Armies, had amassed 100,000 troops of his Army of the Potomac eight miles from Richmond and was awaiting reinforcements from General Banks. But on May 23 at the Battle of Front Royal, Jackson's defeat of Colonel John R. Kenly forced Banks to retreat toward Winchester. Then on May 25, Jackson and General Richard S. Ewell attacked Banks directly and drove his army back to Harpers Ferry across the Potomac. Preston's son Frank was a sergeant in Captain Archibald Graham's Rockbridge Artillery. It was during a deadly enfilade fire in a fierce artillery duel early in this Battle of Winchester that he was severely wounded.

When word reached Preston two days later in Lexington, he headed northward without delay. Frank had been struck by a Minie ball in his arm and sustained "a great gash in his side from a bit of shell."[32] An army surgeon had amputated his left arm at the elbow.[33] But when one of Frank's comrades leaned over him to convey his sorrow at the loss, "Frank looked up with that radiant smile which was one of his attractions, and answered, '*Loss?* I *give* it cheerfully for such a cause.'"[34] Preston was able to stay with his wounded son only a day and a half. On May 31, Jackson had to abandon Winchester with only hours to spare, barely escaping a pincer movement by Generals Frémont and James Shields. Preston was forced to abandon his son among strangers behind enemy lines. He walked the eighteen miles to Strasburg, sleeping at night on the ground, before securing a ride to Harrisonburg and notifying the family in Lexington.

One of Frank's friends in the Rockbridge Artillery, John Williams, had him transported to his parents' home in Winchester. There other wounded Confederates were being housed. Two of the injured men were soon taken as prisoners of war. But Mrs. Williams engineered Frank's escape by having him ferreted beyond the pickets, from where an ambulance took him to Staunton. His arrival on July 21 at his home in Lexington, unannounced during dinner, caught his distraught family totally off guard. "We sprang up and rushed toward him," Maggie recalled, "forgetting to lay down our knives and forks, and he laughingly declared that this was more dangerous than a battle!"[35] Inspiring laughter without tears or pity was Frank's nature. He related how the amputation at the elbow had been insufficient. While he was a prisoner in Winchester, Federal surgeons skillfully removed the rest of his arm at the shoulder. Since his taking chloroform during the first amputation had caused such a terrible sense of suffocation, he'd begged the surgeon to perform the second operation without an anesthetic. But in their kindness they could not allow it.

One of Frank's unspoken sorrows would be his laying aside forever his beloved violin. But since his military service had given him the rank of lieutenant, he was permitted to train officers as professor of tactics at VMI. Maggie claimed that each time Lieutenant Preston took charge of the dress parade, her heart "swelled with pride at the sight of his tall, well knit figure with the red sash and sword, and the empty sleeve pinned across his breast! I thought all the girls grouped under the trees at the edge of the parade ground, were in love with him," she remarked. "I think so still!"[36] At the time neither she nor they nor Frank himself had any inkling of the laudable role he would play in two years' time as captain on VMI's celebrated Field of Honor.

Part VI: The Gloom and the Glory

Civilization ceases in war, barbarism comes back, and religion stands aghast at the spectacle of God's creatures, arrayed against each other for mutual destruction.

—J.T.L. Preston

20

Slain in Battle

*Dead—my loving, gentle heart,
Noblest, bravest of the brave,
Fallen amidst the rush of battle
Lying in a nameless grave.*
—Margaret J. Preston, "W.C.P."

While Frank was teaching at VMI, his brother Willie, too young at seventeen to enlist for duty, was enrolled for classes. Having spent a year at Washington College, he had wanted to serve under Jackson because others his age had already mustered. After some of his classmates fell on that fatal 21st day of the previous July at Manassas, including his best friend, Willie Page, he often expressed his only regret, "I shall never get over not being at Manassas!"[1] But his father and Jackson urged him instead to enter a session of VMI to better fit himself for service, which he promptly accepted.

As a new cadet, Willie was immediately exposed to "bucking," the euphemistic term for hazing, which was strictly forbidden by the institute. It was customary for an upperclassman to order a plebe to hold up his hand, subject to twisting until the arm was almost out of joint. If the plebe resisted, he was called impudent. His hands were then bound together and placed over his knees and legs, and a stick was thrust between his thighs like a pig on a spit. He was then bucked from behind with a bayonet scabbard, each letter of his name spelled with a separate lick, including "Constantinople" for a middle name and "Rockbridge County, Virginia Military Institute," and the class he was entering.[2] For the most part new cadets weathered the entrance ordeal. But coming from a year at Washington College, Willie opposed the practice on principle. His friends advised him not to resist so as to avoid harsher punishment.

Their advice, however, went unheeded. Regarding pain as a temporary discomfort, Willie refused "in perfect good humor" to submit to what he considered "tyranny on the part of the older classmen and degrading to the younger." When the upperclassmen invaded his room, he seized a heavy wooden chair by the back. Then warning them that he would hate to hurt anyone, he announced he "would certainly strike out if attacked." The challenge issued, he placed himself in a corner of the room. As his sister reported, "The four stout legs of the chair furnished a pretty formidable weapon in his resolute hands, and at first the attackers were somewhat daunted."[3]

Not to be intimidated, however, the upperclassmen assailed him. He was able to knock down some, but the rest overwhelmed him. In the ensuing brawl he was rendered unconscious by a serious blow over his right eye, causing his scalp to bleed profusely. When the surgeon arrived, Willie had regained consciousness and, keeping "his good temper," took full responsibility for the incident. He spent a week at home before the swelling and pain subsided enough to return for classes. But he had made his point. A classmate confided to his sister that it was fully understood that Willie hadn't risked injury "from any desire to protect *himself* but to establish a better principle in the corps. It was a brutal and degrading custom, and none of us ever forgot Willie's resolute protest against it."[4]

On June 6, Willie mustered into "I" Company Virginia 4th Infantry, the Liberty Hall Volunteers.[5] As a result of General Joseph Johnston's having been wounded at the Battle of Fair Oaks and Seven Pines, Robert E. Lee now commanded the Army of Northern Virginia. In three days Jackson would end his Valley Campaign, sending the Union army retreating across the Potomac from Cross Keys and Port Republic. His army had marched 400 miles in forty days, fought four pitched battles, defeated four separate armies, taken 3,500 prisoners, neutralized forces three times its own size, held McDowell's corps idle at Fredericksburg, and captured vast stores sorely needed by the Confederacy.[6] The success of his Valley Campaign had freed him to reinforce Lee in the Peninsula Campaign to defend Richmond.

This is the campaign that Willie joined, still only seventeen, a buoyant, loving, merry kid with a proven record of independence and courage without having fought in a real war. The South was attempting to deflect a crippling blow against its capital. Beginning on June 25, the North fought for seven days to take Richmond. If it had succeeded, the war might have ended there. Union deaths during those seven days were 16,000 to the South's 20,000, a horrific prelude to the Campaign of Second Manassas.

Willie didn't enter the conflict until the Battle of Cedar Mountain. On August 9, Jackson and A. P. Hill were attacked by Pope and Banks but rallied to halt their advance into central Virginia. The next day Willie wrote his father that he had survived a battle in which 3,000 soldiers had perished.[7] In the late afternoon, he wrote, his battery had been ordered to charge Federal troops retreating across a cornfield into the woods. But they were forced to fall back when supporting regiments failed to advance.

A second charge succeeded, but suddenly in the confusion Willie found himself "with some of Hill's Brigade in the woods" and "no general officer present." He and a lieutenant were able to round up a regiment from different

A fellow Liberty Hall Volunteer and Willie Preston (right), 1844–62. Photograph probably taken April–June 1862, found in the belongings of Fanny Randolph Page (Meredith), who was reportedly engaged, or about to be engaged, to Willie Preston when he died (Washington and Lee University, Leyburn Library Special Collections, Coupland Page File, courtesy of Tucker Shields and Page McLemore).

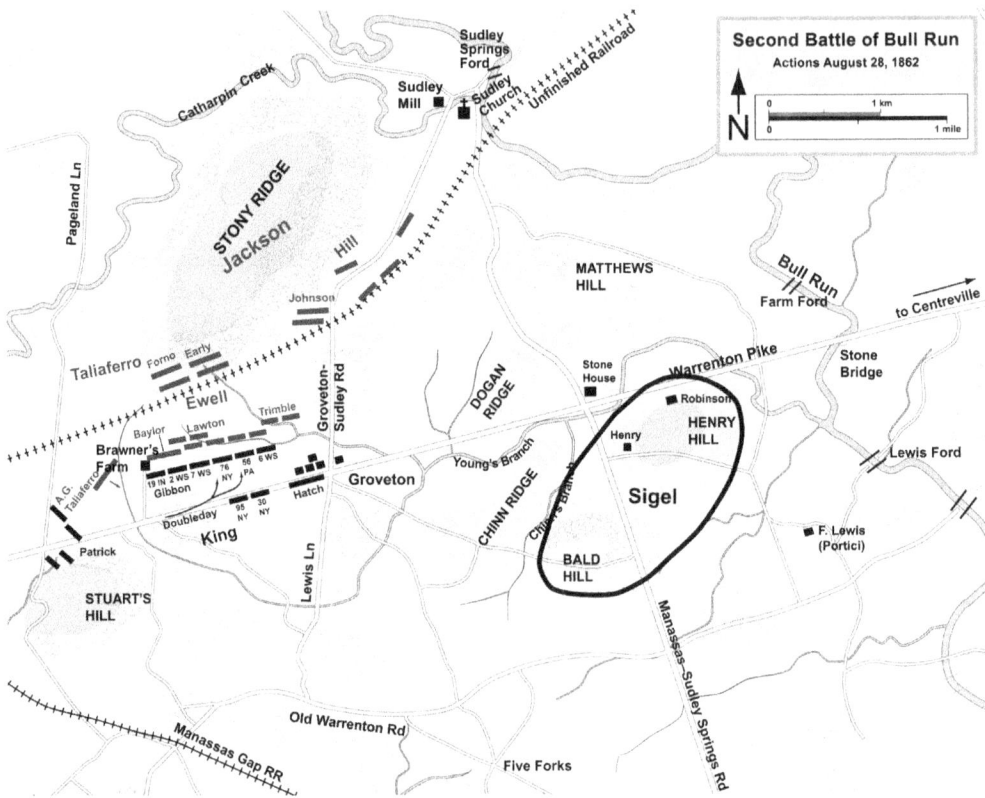

Map of Second Manassas battlefield, August 30, 1862 (map by Hal Jespersen, www.cwmaps.com).

commands and lead them back into the field. There they opened fire on the fleeing Federals, forcing them to surrender. It was growing dark when they stumbled upon a colonel ordering his forces to advance down the hill. But his men were so tired they held back. Willie reported, "I stepped forward and offered myself—put my hand in my cartridge box, and found that I was without a single cartridge. Without comrades or cartridges, it did not look as if I could accomplish much."[8] So he returned behind the lines to locate recruits and cartridges and chanced upon General Jackson.

"I was so excited when I went up to General Jackson," Willie exclaimed, "that I believe I slapped him on the leg, and I know I slapped his horse so hard that he came near jumping from under the rider."[9] Willie excused himself in his letter to his father since he reasoned, "It was the first time I had ever been under fire." When he announced his need for weapons and volunteers, Jackson chose to accompany him back to the crest of the hill. Willie was so energized that he called out to the waiting soldiers, "General Jackson is coming! General Jackson is coming!" and was greeted by thundering cheers.

In the subsequent charge the brigade lost only two or three killed, a dozen or so wounded, and took 300 prisoners. Characteristically modest, Willie wrote, "I have described only what happened under my own eyes, and have consequently mentioned myself more perhaps than was becoming, but I hope you will not think that I am trying to make myself out a hero."[10] The letter didn't reach Lexington for two weeks, for it was on August 23, when Maggie wrote in her diary, "Willy Preston has been in a battle

(Cedar Run) and we hear he behaved with remarkable gallantry, rallied a disorganized regiment, or rather parts of several companies, and with a lieutenant, led them to a charge."[11]

A few days before the actual Battle of Second Manassas began, Jackson invited Willie to stay at headquarters before joining his company. He had loved Willie as a little boy in his first Sunday school class. Dr. Hunter McGuire, his medical director, recalled that Willie slept and messed with the officers, who "all became much attached to the young fellow." Jackson himself endeavored to make "the gentle, kindly, and diffident" boy, with his "beardless, blue-eyed, boyish face so manly and so handsome," feel welcome and at ease.[12]

On the morning of August 27, Willie returned for duty with his company. During the next three days Jackson's 20,000 troops would mystify, mislead, and surprise the 62,000 troops of General John Pope. On the first day Pope and Jackson each lost 1,100 to 1,200 killed. By the second day Pope's attack had been repulsed, some 30,000 of his troops beaten back again and again by the Light Division of A. P. Hill. At one point, when Hill's division had driven the Federals back, the general officers in Willie's company had all been killed, including the flag bearer. Willie grasped the Confederate banner and, hoisting it high, rallied his company. But in the midst of leading the charge, he was shot down on the Plains of Manassas. Some two and a half years earlier it was Willie who had raised the same Confederate flag over Washington College.

On August 29, 1862, the surgeon informed Willie he would not survive. But Willie reassured his comrades, "Don't distress yourselves about me, boys; I'm not afraid to die."[13] He then asked his Captain Hugh White if he could get a letter to his father. But quickly realizing the difficulty, he delivered his message orally instead. Soon afterward he died. The message never reached Preston and will never be known because the young messenger himself expired a few hours later, just as he too had seized the fallen colors to lead a charge. But a message expressing Willie's filial love would reach his home from the field hospital where he breathed his last with tranquil resignation: "Tell my father that I am not afraid to die. I am at peace with God, and at peace with all the world."[14]

By the night of August 29, Jackson and General James Longstreet had driven the Federals in full retreat over Bull Run. Dr. McGuire reported to Jackson the casualty lists from this particularly bloody day. Jackson betrayed no uncommon emotion until he heard among the mortally wounded of the 4th Virginia Infantry the name of Pvt. William C. Preston. McGuire was astonished at the general's unrestrained reaction to the news: "The muscles in his face were twitching convulsively, and his eyes were all aglow. He gripped me by the shoulder till it hurt me, and in a savage, threatening manner asked why I had left the boy. In a few seconds he had recovered himself, and turned and walked off into the woods alone. He soon came back, however, and I continued my report of the wounded and dead."[15] Jackson's attachment to Willie had been profound. In his letter of sympathy to Maggie he confessed, "I had expected to have him as one of my aides-de-camp, but God in His providence has ordered otherwise."[16]

News that Willie had been mortally wounded didn't reach Lexington until the afternoon of September 3. Preston left immediately for Staunton. Willie's death was confirmed the next day. Maggie wrote in her diary, "This has been a day of weeping and of woe to this household. I did not know how I loved the dear boy. My heart is wrung with grief to think that his sweet face, his genial smile, his sympathetic heart are gone. My eyes ache with weeping. But what is the loss to me, compared to the loss to his Father, his sisters, his brothers! Oh, his precious stricken Father! God support him to bear the blow!" Not only Willie, but many other sons of Lexington families perished at Manassas, including the Rev. William White's son Hugh, Dr. Paine's son Henry, young Will Baylor, a colonel at twenty-one, and Major Patrick. "It is like the death of the first born in Egypt," Maggie cried out. "Who thinks of or cares for victory now!"[17] All told, 805 men died under Jackson's command in one of the bloodiest three days of the war. Second Manassas saved Richmond again from having to surrender and placed Washington in line for possible attack, but at a horrific loss of 3,000 dead and 15,000 wounded.[18]

Preston returned to Lexington on September 11 without Willie's remains. "Slain in battle—Slain in battle," he kept reiterating, as though unaware that he was even repeating it. "Valr—Valr" he knew as the Norse cry for those whose souls the Valkyries escort to Valhalla, the hall of the slain, having earned their immortality. As Maggie related, Preston had searched for Willie's grave but could not be certain which was his. "He had the one he supposed to be, opened."[19] He unwrapped the blanket from one decomposed body "on the northern side of seven who [lay] side by side in one pit."[20]

"Alas! for our poor humanity!" Maggie cried out in her journal. "He could not distinguish a feature of his boy on the despoiled face—he tore open the shirt, and there where *I* had written it was W. C. Preston! He thought to bring a lock of his hair,—it crumbled to the touch! It was impossible to have him removed, so he carefully marked the spot, and left the removal to be accomplished another time."[21] He would later erect in the family plot in Lexington a stone, on which he had engraved, "He was a private in the College Company of the 4th Virginia Regt, Stonewall Brigade, and fell at Manassas August 28th 1862, in the 19th [actually 17th] year of his age. The young patriot lost his mortal life in defense of his native state. The young Christian found his nobler life in Christ who died for him." The stone referenced his mortal remains still interred on the battlefield.

The actual burial site on Sudley Plantation near Centreville remained undisturbed almost a hundred years before it gave way to a golf course in 1959. The head and foot stones are protected today by the Fairfax County Cemetery Preservation Association. They stand at the former site of the 18th hole of the Fairfax National Golf Club. It was said that a golfer landing a ball in the fenced enclosure was subject to a one-stoke penalty.[22]

Charles Walker, a New Market cadet who would join the faculty at VMI as professor of chemistry and

Willie Preston's gravestone in Lexington (photograph by the author, April 10, 2010).

math after the war, wrote a memorial to Willie. It's one of the 170 biographical sketches he later composed for VMI cadets who lost their lives during the war. He dedicated a copy of the memorial to Preston, who passed it on to Maggie, who passed it eventually to her stepson John. In 1890 John penciled into the margins of his copy, now in the rare books collection of the Virginia Historical Society, his own poignant recollection of his brother Willie's death. "The loss of this brother was to me," he wrote, "like being a second time bereaved by loss of a mother; for he had taken the place of a mother: always carried me up stairs when I fell asleep at night, undressed and dressed me too. The news of Willie's death was so great, that although I have seen *many* such trials since, *this* one seems to be far darker than all others; the family were *stunned*—sat in the *Library* with scarcely a word, broken only by an occasional sob from some one, which would become universal, and then again, the awful quiet would follow. I slept with brother Ran, the night we heard the news, in the room on 3rd story, S. E. corner, and probably cried myself to sleep."[23]

Willie's eldest brother Tom, in his sorrow, accepted his wife's suggestion that they change the name of their six-month-old son—previously named for her father, Livingstone Waddell—to William Caruthers Preston. The name change was intended to help soften this terrible blow to the family. A few hours after the news of Willie's death, Maggie penned a poem that captured the abject despair expressed by Preston in the oft repeated cry from his heart: "Slain in Battle." She sent it to Willie's sister Phoebe, to console her, titling it "W.C.P." Her poem cried out,

> Dead! Poor lips repeat, repeat it,
> Wrench from out that word of dread
> All the sharpest sting of meaning
> Shut within it—He is dead!
>
> Dead, my Willy—in his beauty,
> Ere the morning flush of joy
> Yet had caught the chastening shades
> Mankind flings above the boy.
>
> Dead—my loving, gentle heart,
> Noblest, bravest of the brave,
> Fallen amidst the rush of battle
> Lying in a nameless grave.
> ....
> All love's sweetest ministrations—
> All its needs for him—arc o'cr;
> Never will he cross the threshold
> Of the old familiar door;
>
> Never will his ringing laughter
> Pass joyous through the Hall,
> Never will I answer gaily
> To his fond caressing call.
>
> Never press his smooth white forehead
> Never stroke his shining hair,
> Never feel his arm about me
> Never greet his smile so rare—
> ....
> Dead! Oh grief hath drowned my vision
> Blotted all the gladness o'er,
> Made me half forget he liveth
> As he never lived before![24]

21

The Shuddering Horror of Death

It's well that war is so terrible—else we should grow too fond of it.
—Robert E. Lee

On September 4, 1862, after having defeated the North's armies on the Virginia peninsula and at Second Manassas, General Lee decided to invade the North. He crossed the Potomac River into Maryland. The ensuing battle at Antietam (Sharpsburg) on September 17 was the bloodiest single battle in U.S. history. The Union had 12,400 casualties, including 2,100 killed. The Confederate casualties were 10,320, of which 2,700 were killed. The day ended in a stalemate. Lee retreated the following day to Virginia. And when McClellan failed to pursue, Lincoln replaced him with Ambrose Burnside. He remarked, as only Lincoln would phrase it, that "sending reinforcements to McClellan is like shoveling flies across a barn."

Confident of having halted the South's invasion, Lincoln issued on September 22 his Emancipation Proclamation to take effect January 1. Outlawing slavery in all states that continued to rebel against the Federal government, it effectively gave a cause to the war that many in the South, particularly in western Virginia, refuted as their motive for fighting. The defense of homeland, their beloved Virginia, and the right to determine their own future remained the only causes worth their dying.

Despite the wounding of Frank and death of Willie, Preston's son Ran was already training at VMI for the same service his brothers had entered. Now barely seventeen, he had marched with the cadets in May when Jackson requested reserve forces for the McDowell Campaign. But he was still too young to muster when he returned home in November, wild and incoherent with a critical illness that confined him to bed. Throughout his month-long illness, Preston, Maggie, Frank, Phoebe, Libbie, and Cousin Betty Alexander, a trained nurse, all shared vigils by his bedside until December 18, when the ravages of typhoid fever finally consumed him. The family was doubly bereaved of two sons in three and a half months.

Ran's passing was Libbie's and John's first experience of death personally. They hadn't seen their mother die, nor Willie's corpse in far-off Manassas. Libbie would later describe the "shuddering horror of death" that came over her when Preston took her and John "into the icy chamber to take a last look at the dear brother." She never recovered from the immutable influence it had on her. "Death often has a beauty and majesty of its own, but it was not so here," she would recall. "I would never have recognized the changed and wasted countenance. Nor had anything prepared me, when Father bade us kiss the white brow, for the unforgettable chill that is like nothing else on earth."[1]

Maggie recorded in her journal the effect this loss of still another son had on Preston. As she observed, "Few parents have as noble boys to lose; and yet their father bows to the stroke with entireness of Christian resignation. May God sustain his bruised heart!"[2] But she was careful not to dwell on the family's personal distress, which she recognized as common to all in these terrible times of anguish and loss. Brief periods of triumph and hope occasionally offset the ever-increasing episodes of defeat and dejection that crashed unexpectedly into the daily lives of the community.

Maggie found herself uniquely burdened with a twofold sadness. As Libbie would later interpolate between the lines of Maggie's journal, it was not possible for her to "feel the same intense love and loyalty to Virginia and the Confederacy that we did. She was true to the South, believed in the justness of our cause, and prayed for the overthrow of our enemies; but it must not be forgotten—for she did not forget—that those enemies were her own people, her blood kin, whom she loved and honored through all, whom she knew to be honest and true also."[3] With her loyalties torn between Virginia and Pennsylvania, her heart was filled at every turn with despair.

On the other hand, her husband suffered a more pervasive sorrow. After Ran's death, she saw etched on his face the graven lines "of grief for his sons and kinsmen and neighbors."[4] These lines would never be effaced. She knew—which the other members of the family hadn't yet discerned—that "her husband had not from the first had much expectation of success in the struggle." Despite the illusive hope that occasional brilliant victories "might wrest independence from the so much stronger nation," there was always his calm, judicial awareness of "the hopeless inequality of the contending powers." There were "few months when he did not fear the worst."[5]

In addition, as if to reinforce his apprehension in a tangible, physical way, the gaunt specter of hunger haunted the land. Maggie listed a pound of tea for $20, a pair of coarse shoes for $11, and a plain calico dress for $110. Her husband helped support the Confederate government with "every pound of bacon he could spare, and put us on a ration of a quarter of a pound of meat a day—half a pound for the colored people."[6] And Maggie made petticoats for herself and Libbie from a window curtain.

It wasn't until December 22, with the Battle of Fredericksburg behind him, that Jackson received news of Ran's death. He wrote Preston of his great "desire to see *peace, blessed peace*."[7] He was beginning to divest himself of his belongings and asked Preston to hire out his slaves to anyone with whom they might desire to live. He wished to sell his eighteen-acre farm, which he had bought from Jacob Fuller for $500 before the war and on which he was still making payments. "I do not desire to keep it any longer. You need not consult me about the price, but take what you can get." Preston sold it the following month at a profit, for $620.

Christmas of 1862 stood in stark contrast to the previous Christmas. A year earlier, except for Frank who was away and Preston who was serving Jackson, all the children had enjoyed a beautifully decorated tree, presents for everyone, and a gay and hilarious air of relaxation. There had been no victims of the war who were absent from their happy family. But now, Maggie observed, "The sadness of the household forbids any recognition of Christmas; we are scattered to our own separate rooms to mourn over the contrast, and the library is in darkness. Willy, whose genial face rises so brightly before me, lies in a distant grave—cut off by a violent death. Randolph's coffin has been carried out of the house so recently that no sunshine has yet come back. Frank is here with his one arm, making me feel perpetually grieved for him."

Despite good reason to mourn, Maggie continually asked herself what right she had to complain. "My husband and children are spared to me, so that I have peculiar cause for gratitude. I have been permitted to hear of my father's and sisters' and brothers' welfare too."[8] Jackson had just sent word that he met her brother John, a surgeon for the Union, on the battlefield. He sent word that her family and friends were well.[9]

What Jackson did not tell her was that brother John had brought with him a package, which her father had mailed to General Hooker. It contained an autographed book and a request that it be forwarded under a flag of truce to "General T. J. Jackson." Inscribed on the flyleaf were the words, "My Dear Son and Brother in Christ: Read this, and send it to my deeply afflicted son, Colonel J.T.L. Preston. I will send you a thousand for distribution if you desire it, and express that desire to me in any way."[10] It was signed by George Junkin.

Junkin's new book would enjoy wide circulation in the North. It was titled *Political Fallacies: An Examination of the False Assumptions and Refutation of the Sophistical Reasonings, Which Have Brought On this Civil War*. It was a refutation of John Calhoun's doctrines of secession and the notion that national sovereignty belonged to any one state of the Union. A review in Boston's *Christian Examiner* lauded the book as based on the personal experience of "the president of a Virginia College, who maintained an intrepid resistance to the prevailing madness till absolutely driven from his post." The review credited Dr. Junkin with having controverted "the wretched fallacies that have wrought so much misery and ruin."[11]

The North's *Continental Monthly* described Dr. Junkin, "the father-in-law of 'Stonewall' Jackson," as "one of the noble band of patriots who have preferred leaving friends, comfortable homes, and honorable positions, to ceding self-respect, and polluting conscience by yielding to the tyrannical requisitions of local prejudice or usurped authority."[12] But when Jackson was handed Dr. Junkin's book and saw its title, *Political Fallacies*, he responded it was well named. He quipped, "That's just what the book contains, 'political [fallacies].'"[13] Understandably he didn't tell either Maggie or Preston about it, because he knew how much Maggie revered her father. He also understood her pain of separation. His own sister, Laura, was a strong Unionist, nursing Federal soldiers wounded by Confederate troops.

The war was having a profound effect on Maggie, even on her young children. In early January she noted how George and Bert had adopted the language and operations of war in their games. She wrote in her journal, "George cuts lines of soldiers every day; marches them about; has battles; beats 'the Yankees,' and carries off prisoners.... He gets sticks and hobbles about, saying that he lost a leg at the Second battle of Manassas; tells wonderful stories of how he cut off Yankees' heads, bayoneted them, etc." And while George marched about with a stick for a sword and a "pistol" in his belt, little Bert "also kills 'Lankees,' as he calls them, and can talk war lingo almost as well as George."[14] She was amazed and saddened that, at four and not quite two, her children knew the lingo of pickets, cartridges, cavalry, ambulances, cannon, and infantry better than she ever did in her infancy.

It was almost two weeks after this entry in Maggie's journal and a full month after Ran's death at Fredericksburg that a letter from Jackson finally reached Preston in Lexington. "You have tasted deep of the cup of domestic affliction," he consoled his friend.[15] He admitted that all he could offer by way of help was to pray for the family. Delivered with the letter for safekeeping was his sword, which would play a very dangerous role at a future time when the Preston home would be threatened with destruction and she would be hard pressed to hide it.

By the beginning of February the Confederate dollar had deflated to a buying power of only twenty cents. Unable to afford shoes for little Herbert, Maggie was overjoyed when her sister-in-law Agnes Junkin sent her a coarse pair. By April, bread riots were breaking out in Richmond, and already meat was scarce in Lexington. The town was crowded with refugees from Fredericksburg and Winchester. Jefferson Davis was advising the Confederacy to concentrate less on tobacco and cotton than on cash crops, especially corn, oats, peas, and potatoes for daily food. The cost of feeding a family in the South had risen from $6.65 per week in 1861 to $68.25 in 1863.

For Maggie, who received word only occasionally from her family in Pennsylvania, all these hardships led her to conclude, just as Preston had observed, "Northern people can't *conceive* the horrors of this war. It is far away from them; their private soldiers are all from the lower classes—persons with whom the masses of Christian and cultivated people feel no tie in common; while the mass of Southern private soldiers are from the educated classes; this makes a woeful difference in the suffering a battle entails ... oh! the sickness of soul with which almost every household in this town awaits the tidings to-morrow may bring!"[16]

Just before Christmas 1862, Preston began to invest heavily in land as a hedge against inflation and general loss. He partnered with William Gilham, George Shields, and Jacob Fuller in purchasing 289 acres of the Mayberry Tract on Guy's Run near Goshen.[17] In January 1863, he partnered with Gilham, Fuller, and Jackson to buy a 320-acre farm, part of the Hart's Bottom (now Buena Vista) estate in the Blue Ridge Mountains.[18] They leased the banks of the canal for the deposit of tan bark from their tannery, which they had bought at auction in 1860 from the estate of Andrew Withrow. Known as the Lexington Tannery, it was located at the southwest corner of Henry and Randolph streets below Preston's former home (later Blandome), where Fuller now lived.[19] Managed first by George Shields and then by Fuller, the tannery would prosper greatly, providing additional income for all four investors during the early years of the war.

Since Preston's, Jackson's, and Gilham's salaries at the time were only $1,800 with a $100 annual increase, these investments provided highly valued income.[20] Indeed, the tannery was the only source of gainful earnings for them in Lexington. In a letter to Jackson on April 28, 1863, Preston reported that it had earned "from ten to fifteen thousand dollars" in profits. He added that he had "purchased for you $2,700 of 8 percent Confed. Bonds" from the proceeds. He also advised that "we have on hand a contract for tanning from the government which will not be as profitable as our operations heretofore have been, but it will be remunerative and at the same time safe."[21]

In the same letter Preston announced he had been elected a delegate to the General Assembly, the Presbyterian Church's highest court. He would leave on April 30 for Columbia, South Carolina, to argue that "the real battle of the church will begin when the national struggle is closed, and peace opens the floodgates through which will flow upon society the stream of evils generated by the war." He reasoned that "Profanity, Sabbathbreaking, intemperance, idleness, lawlessness and general looseness of morals may be expected partly as the direct result, and partly as the reactive influence of the scenes through which the entire youthful population of the land have been called to pass."[22]

As if in response to Preston's concerns, Jackson had written one of his last letters the day before to ask him, as a delegate to the assembly, to have the church request the Confederate Congress to repeal the law requiring that mail be carried on the Christian

Sabbath. His reasoning was that "divine laws can be violated with impunity neither by governments nor individuals," and this was "an auspicious time for action, as our people are looking to God for assistance."[23] It was during this hopeful exchange of letters between Preston and Jackson that General Joseph "Fighting Joe" Hooker, who had relieved Burnside as commander of the Union's Army of the Potomac, crossed the Rappahannock River to clash with Lee and Jackson at the Battle of Chancellorsville.

22

This Savage and Ferocious War

My heart overflows with sorrow. The grief in this community is intense; everybody is in tears.
—Margaret J. Preston

Chancellorsville was where Jackson would meet his God. The campaign lasted five days, commencing on April 30, 1863. It ended when Lee's force of 47,000 men split Hooker's 70,000 troops, driving them back across the Rappahannock in defeat. Jackson's devastating attack on Hooker's unprotected right flank, caught in a twelve-mile stretch of tangled Virginia Wilderness, turned the tide of battle. Just before the assault, Jackson had noticed how many soldiers and officers in his corps were former VMI pupils and associates. As many as twenty of them stood in positions of high command. He turned to his cavalry leader Colonel Thomas Munford, Class of 1852, and fellow VMI officers—artillery chief Colonel Stapleton Crutchfield, Class of 1855, and generals Raleigh Colston, Class of 1846, and Robert Rodes, Class of 1848—and prophesied aloud what Preston had foreseen thirty years earlier, "The institute will be heard from today!"[1]

On Tuesday, May 5, news reached Lexington of the terrible battle that led to the death of General Frank Paxton, commander of the Stonewall Brigade, and the wounding of Jackson, A. P. Hill, and Colonel Crutchfield. Maggie recorded,

> Of the mothers in this town, almost all of them have sons in this battle; not one lays her head on her pillow this night, sure that her sons are not slain. This suspense must be awful. Mrs. Estill has four sons there; Mrs. Moore two; Mrs. Graham three, and so on. Yet not a word of special news, except that a copy of General Lee's telegram came, saying, a decided victory, but at great cost. God pity the tortured hearts that will pant through this night! And the agony of the poor wife who has heard that her husband is really killed![2]

Maggie also feared for her surgeon brother John Junkin in Hooker's army, which she'd heard Jackson had routed. She agonized, "Oh, the sickness of soul with which almost every household in this town awaits the tidings to-morrow may bring!"[3]

News that Jackson's arm had been amputated didn't reach Lexington until Friday, May 8. Unaware of his death on Sunday, May 10, Maggie composed a letter to Jackson the following evening, urging him "to come to stay with us" as soon as the wound would permit him to be moved. But the morning of the 12th brought the rumor of his death. It was not confirmed until that evening. In her journal she cried out, "My heart overflows with sorrow. The grief in this community is intense; everybody is in tears."[4] Maggie wondered with amazement, Jackson's death from pleura-pneumonia at thirty-nine, just two years into the war, was "the first time it had dawned on us that God could let us be defeated." She greatly feared his loss for the Confederacy but also for herself. "The people made an idol of him, and God has rebuked them. No more ready soul has ascended to the throne than was his. Never have I known a holier man."[5]

Jackson was buried in Lexington on Friday, May 15, his coffin draped in the first Confederate flag ever made. Maggie described his solemn military funeral. It was escorted by the VMI Corps of Cadets and attended by a throng of "heart-broken mourners, a clan bereft of its chieftain: a country in peril, from whom its defender had been snatched." In a poem she composed after his death, she speculated on what mystical vision he had seen that would provoke his remarkable last words, "Let us pass over the river, and rest under the shade of the trees."[6] It was not that he was retreating from the toils and tasks of war, she contended, but rather yearning for union with God on another far more substantial shore. Jackson's widow, Anna, with her six-month-old daughter Julia, spent several weeks with the Prestons recovering from her painful loss before leaving for her family home in North Carolina.

On June 3, 1863, during General Grant's protracted siege of Vicksburg in the far South, General Lee decided once more to invade the North. This time he headed for Gettysburg. While Maggie could share the anxiety in Lexington over the fate of the Confederates in Mississippi, she remained alone in her anxiety about the army's advance into her native Pennsylvania. Her worries about her father and sister and friends were hers alone, as they had always been. "When I am compelled to hear scorn and loathing predicated of everything *Northern* (as must continually be the case), my heart boils up, and sobs to itself," she lamented. "But I must be silent."[7]

On the other hand, two years of suffering the ravages of war firsthand had given her an increasingly detached perspective. "Hear that Lee's army is invading my native state. Well! Virginia has endured it for more than two years! So I must not think it hard that another state whose troops have been helping to ravage her all the time, should take its turn." She hoped the Confederates would not be guilty "of the outrages which have everywhere characterized the Federal armies in Virginia. It is perhaps well that those who still keep up this terrible war should have some short experience of what war is. But this will not give it to them. The country would have to be overrun for two years before the Pennsylvanians could know what the Virginians know of war."[8]

The casualty list for VMI graduates in the war had grown fearsome. In his June 26 annual report to the board of visitors, General Smith noted that of the 460 graduates of the institute, averaging twenty-two a year, ninety had been wounded and ninety-five killed. That was nearly forty percent at the hands of "our vandal foes in this savage and ferocious war."[9] Not counting reports from the Army of the Mississippi, VMI's 185 casualties included 4 generals, 40 colonels, 25 lieutenant colonels, 16 majors, 44 captains, 43 lieutenants, and 13 privates. Yet the institute still continued to prepare cadets for service. Despite the loss and wounding of his own sons, Preston would recommend his sister's son J. Preston Cocke, not yet eighteen, for admission in the fall "to fit himself for service in the spring."[10] As a consequence, Cocke would become one of the wounded cadets that spring during the celebrated Battle of New Market.

For the South, Lee's drive into Pennsylvania would prove disastrous. Coupled with the simultaneous loss of Vicksburg, it would mark an irreversible turning point in the war. It wasn't until the evening of July 7 that Lexington learned there had been a great battle fought at Gettysburg, involving thousands of casualties. General Longstreet's division sustained heavy losses. This increased Maggie's anxiety because two of Preston's sister's sons were serving under Longstreet. News arrived on July 11 that Elizabeth's second son, Edmund, had been wounded during Pickett's notorious charge up Cemetery Ridge across a mile of open field. And her oldest son, William, was missing. "The household is wrapped in gloom," wrote Maggie. "Mr. P. thinks from what he heard of the fearful loss in Pickett's Division, that William is most probably killed."[11]

The family was doubly concerned, because William was fiancé to Preston's daughter Phoebe. Both Preston's sister and his daughter would endure five months of suspense before William's death was positively confirmed on December 11. A returning prisoner had seen him fall on the field.[12] Phoebe had loved William since childhood. She had lost not only him but her brothers Willie and Ran and seen her brother Frank maimed in this terrible war. Under the accumulated weight of such sorrows, hers was a hard burden to bear.

The ill-fated Pickett-Pettigrew assault cost the combined Confederate and Union forces 10,000 casualties in only fifty minutes of fierce fighting. Pickett's division alone sustained 500 killed and 2,007 wounded, more than half its number. All but two of its fifteen regiments were commanded by VMI officers.[13] Indeed, the regiment that suffered the most severely of any regiment on either side of the conflict was the 26th North Carolina, commanded by twenty-one-year-old VMI graduate Colonel Harry Burgwyn, Class of 1861. It lost 708, or 88 percent, of its 800 men killed or wounded.

Apart from the dismal failure of Pickett's charge, Preston's assessment of Gettysburg was that Longstreet's delay in obeying Lee's orders to launch an attack as early as possible, at a time when the issue was still doubtful, "cost Lee the victory."[14] Preston held the opinion, which he expressed more than once, that "if Jackson had been in command, Longstreet would have been up within the expected time, or Jackson would have known the reason why with lightning speed."

By August, General Henry Halleck had replaced McClellan as general-in-chief of the Federal Army. He hatched a plan to sever the railways that the South used for communications and supplies between its Eastern and Western theaters. He sent General William Averell and his 8th Army Corps on a series of raids not far from Lexington. This meant the VMI Corps of Cadets would be dispatched on three separate occasions within the next four months to help defend their homeland.

On August 25, Averell launched his first raid to destroy the saltpeter works and iron furnaces that supplied munitions for the Confederacy. The corps arrived in Goshen on orders from Colonel William L. Jackson. Colonel Jackson was a former lieutenant governor of Virginia. His men had nicknamed him "Mudwall" Jackson to distinguish him from his cousin Stonewall.[15] The mission of the cadets was to guard state property, rather than engage in any military operation.

A question arose, however, during the mission about the need of more effective arms for support. General Smith requested from Adjutant General Richardson some rifled guns, because all the institute had were smooth bore guns, a howitzer 12-pounder with no ammunition, and worn-out cadet muskets with few cartridges. They were no match for the Parrott guns and Enfield rifles of the enemy. What the institute received, however, were "two three-inch rifled field pieces, which had been captured from the Union forces," and "200 Austrian muskets" and ammunition. These became their artillery equipment for the rest of the war.[16] Even while such a modest request for rifled guns was being only partially fulfilled for Smith, the Union was dispensing a new Spencer Repeating Carbine, which would give its army considerable advantage over the muzzle-loaders of the Confederates.

Throughout the rest of 1863, VMI would function intermittently between responses to Averell's raids and the demands of the curriculum for its 300 cadets, the largest corps in the history of the institute.[17] Preston found himself overwhelmed with eighty students in his Latin classes. Moreover, the board wanted to increase the number of cadets in each section from sixteen to twenty, which he considered "impossible" to properly instruct. The class size alone would "reduce recitations from currently three to two per week."[18] During the 1863–64 school year there would be a total of 129 new arrivals, resignations, dismissals, and other casualties.

In addition, Averell's raids were disrupting not only the task of teaching but also the life of the town. His second raid en route to destroy the New River bridge on the Virginia and Tennessee Railroad required immediate action by Colonel Jackson and General John D. Imboden. It resulted in another abrupt call for the Cadet Corps, accompanied by Preston, to proceed to Covington. A courier brought the alarm late on November 6.

On the morning of the 7th Maggie recorded, "The cadets have gone, and the Home Guard from the various parts of the country. Mr. P. gone too ... the whole town is in commotion; no men left in it; even those over sixty-five have gone." Late that night Preston returned: "Yes! to my joy—but he had hardly drawn off his gloves, had certainly not been one minute in the house, before he was sent for to receive a dispatch brought by a courier, summoning the cadets to Covington."[19] Imboden had cancelled and then renewed his request for auxiliary support. Preston wouldn't return again home until November 12.

On December 16 the corps of 180 cadets, serving under Colonel Scott Ship (later Shipp),[20] departed Lexington yet again to oppose Averell's third raid at Rockbridge Baths. Maggie wailed, "When will these alarms cease? I am in despair about the war." This raid, Averell's last, successfully destroyed the Virginia and Tennessee Railroad at Salem before his men escaped, contrary to Lee's order that they be captured. Two days later Imboden's dispirited cavalry passed through Lexington. Maggie described them in alarming detail. "It is the first time I have seen an army. Poor fellows? With their broken down horses, muddy up to the eyes, and their muddy wallets and blankets, they looked like an army of tatterdemalions; the horses looked starved.... At night my husband came; the cadets were water bound; some of them waded to their waists in water, building bridges for artillery. Mr. P. says he saw one marching along in his *naked* feet. This is 'glorious war!'"[21]

Two days more, and the cadets were marching to Buchanan, having traversed muddy roads in torrential freezing rain. Although a year had passed since Ran had died, Maggie remembered it as "Pain in the heart—pain in the head—Grief for the living—grief for the dead!" She had just received a flag-of-truce letter of sympathy from her sister Julia in Pennsylvania. "It doesn't matter how soon all of us go," Julia had written philosophically. "She would feel so indeed," Maggie mused, "if she were in the midst of such war scenes as now surround us."[22] The only significant Confederate victory in the last seven months since Chancellorsville had been at Chickamauga in mid–September. Furthermore, an impending currency bill would soon deflate Confederate money to two-thirds its present value. Everyone was trying to dispose of it. The *Richmond Examiner* headlined its December 31 issue of 1863 the "gloomiest year of our struggle" from defeat at Gettysburg to the loss of the Mississippi and the fall of Chattanooga.

23

It Made Our Hearts Leap

> *They never faltered, but went into the "harvest of death" as though they had been accustomed to such bloody work.*
> —J. H. Wartmann,
> Rockingham Register

Because General Grant had succeeded General Halleck as commander-in-chief in February, the Union's grand strategy changed. The plan now was to strike at the heart of the Confederacy simultaneously from multiple directions. In the Western Theater the armies of Generals Sherman and Banks had begun their marches through the south. In the Eastern Theater the armies of Generals Meade and Butler were threatening Lee's Army of Northern Virginia from the north and the southeast. Generals George Crook and Averell and German-born General Franz Sigel were advancing on Virginia's Kanawha and Shenandoah valleys in the west.

At the beginning of May 1864, Grant attacked Lee in the Wilderness Campaign. The battle cost the Union 17,500 casualties to the Confederates' 7,000. Grant knew the Union had greater resources than the Confederacy to replace lost soldiers and equipment. He would win the war, not by battles for towns or cities such as Spotsylvania or Richmond, but by eating away at Lee's Army until there was nothing left for Lee but to surrender. In the "Bloody Angle" at Spotsylvania, Grant suffered 6,800 casualties to the Confederacy's 5,000, but the loss still fell within his overall strategy.

During the Spotsylvania Campaign on May 10, Confederate General John D. Imboden sent an urgent dispatch to General Smith at VMI that the Corps of Cadets might be required again for support. They would be needed to help defend the Shenandoah Valley against Sigel's advance up from Winchester. Sigel was determined to win control of the valley "before the wheat in its fields was ripe for grinding into flour to feed Lee's army."[1] The corps was ordered to join General John C. Breckinridge's forces at Staunton on their way to reinforcing Imboden's cavalry at New Market. The goal was to protect Lee's left flank. General Breckinridge had served as America's youngest vice president under James Buchanan in the 1850s and suffered expulsion from the U.S. Senate at the end of 1861 for having joined the rebel army as brigadier general. He now commanded Confederate forces in western Virginia.[2]

The Preston family was awakened at 5 o'clock in the morning by an order to requisition Maggie's carriage horses. They were needed to pull the two three-inch rifled field pieces, which the cadets had captured during the first of Averell's raids in the valley.[3] At the time that the corps was called to action, Preston was attending a Presbyterian General Assembly meeting in North Carolina. Two-thirds of the corps' members were new cadets averaging eighteen years of age and led by twenty-four-year-old

Lieutenant Colonel Scott Ship.[4] In four days they marched seventy miles north, down the valley through drenching rain and mud. They met Breckinridge in Staunton, arriving in the evening within seven miles of New Market.

Shortly after midnight they began preparation for the last leg of their trek to the battlefield. As reported by Cadet Corporal John Wise of D Company, it was then that "a thing occurred which made a deep impression upon us all,—a thing which even now may be a solace to those whose boys died so gloriously that day."[5] Colonel Ship asked Colonel Gilham, as acting superintendent, to deliver a prayer. But Gilham declined, deferring instead to the popular one-armed tactical officer of B Company, Captain Frank Preston. A typical valley Presbyterian, Frank was neither reticent nor embarrassed to pray. Instead, he offered a sincere "appeal to God for his protection of our little band."

John Wise, himself just seventeen, described Frank's prayer as

> a humble, earnest petition, that sunk into the heart of every hearer. Few were the dry eyes, little the frivolity, when he had ceased to speak of home, father, mother, country, victory and defeat, life, death, and eternity. Having served as an officer in Jackson's command when he lost his arm at Winchester, Captain Preston was no stranger to the perilous edge of battle. Now on the retired list and a sub-professor of Latin, he was nonetheless prepared to command his company in the thickest of the fight. In a few hours those who heard his heartfelt prayer would fully realize the beauty of the lines that declare "the bravest are the tenderest, the loving are the daring."[6]

Breckinridge's mission at New Market was to stop Sigel from cutting Confederate supply lines between the fertile Shenandoah Valley and Lee's army in the Virginia Wilderness. If Sigel could capture Staunton and destroy Lee's supply line—the Virginia Central Railroad—before Lee could send reinforcements, then the fall of Lynchburg and ultimately Richmond would appear inevitable. "Sigel had about 6,000 men," and "Breckinridge about 4,500," but success for Breckinridge was mandatory.[7]

Arriving within a mile of New Market after daybreak on Sunday, May 15, it was Breckinridge himself who inspired his army. Cadet Wise depicted his passing through the ranks, magnificently mounted, uncovered, "bowing and riding like a Cid." Wise claimed it was "impossible to exaggerate the gallant appearance of General Breckinridge. In stature he was considerably over six feet high. He sat his blood-bay thoroughbred as if he had been born on horseback; his head was of noble mould, and a piercing eye and a long, dark, drooping mustache completed a faultless military presence."[8]

Cheering the soldierly Breckinridge, the cadet corps formed in the left line of battle a mile from town. A sudden turn in the road displayed a full view of the day's battlefield. A deep ravine extended between two large hills with the Shenandoah River on the left and the Massanutten Mountains and Smith's Creek on the right. Beyond the town lay meadows and orchards where the Union had posted its infantry and artillery. It was eleven o'clock on Sunday morning as they faced their first action under fire.

Cadet Wise, who was corporal of the guard in charge of the baggage wagon with a detail of three cadets, described the looming pressures of battle. As the son of General Henry A. Wise, who even now was fighting on the eve of saving Petersburg from a Federal assault, he suffered under the frightening vision of his father, "the grim old fighter," judging him from afar. John had badgered his father for permission to leave VMI and join the army, and now that the corps stood on the verge of its first and perhaps only opportunity for combat, he knew what was in store for him if he failed to fight. General Wise "had a tongue of satire and ridicule like a lash of scorpions." John feared his father's reproach more dreadfully than he feared the enemy. He recalled from his class in military history that Napoleon in Egypt had pointed to the towering Pyramids and informed his soldiers that "from their heights forty centuries looked down upon them."[9]

From the tailgate of his baggage wagon, Cadet Wise issued his Napoleonic call to action: "Boys, the enemy is in our front. The corps is going into action. I like fighting no better than anybody else. But I have an enemy in my rear as dreadful as any before us. If I should return home and tell my father that I was on the baggage guard when the cadets were in battle, I know what my fate would be. He would kill me with ridicule, which is worse than bullets. I intend to join the command at once. Any of you who think your duty requires you to remain may do so."[10]

Moving at double-quick, his detail quickly overtook the cadet corps and in an instant was in the line of battle. But hardly had Cadet Wise entered the fray, pressing down Shirley's Hill, than he was struck by a six-pound shell exploding directly in his face. The last thing he saw as he lost consciousness was his fellow cadets closing the gap that his absence left open as they pushed forward. His first thought, when he regained consciousness in torrents of rain, was how far ahead the battalion had advanced.

Discovering that he was bleeding from a gash in the head and that four other cadets had been felled by the same blast, his next thought, recalling his father, was "Hurrah! Youth's dream is realized at last. I've got a wound, and am not dead yet." Leaping to his feet, he trudged triumphantly to the hospital, "almost whistling at [the] thought that the next mail would carry the news to the folks at home, with a taunting suggestion that, after all the pains they had taken, they had been unable to keep me out of my share in the fun."[11] His wounding, however, ruled out his further participation in their glory.

It was Frank Preston in a letter to his family who wrote the first eyewitness account of the Battle of New Market only four days after its occurrence. A week later his father would have it published in the *Lexington Gazette and General Advocate*.[12] His report, according to Frank's cousin Preston Cocke, served as the basis for Cocke's own memoirs of the battle on its fiftieth anniversary. Frank's version, Cocke reported, was generally considered the "much more reliable authority for what the cadets actually did, than the 'recollections' of participants on either side, written many years after the event."[13]

As Captain of B Company, Frank narrated from a fresh memory how the cadets marched down Shirley's Hill behind the 26th Virginia Battalion commanded by Colonel George Edgar, Class of 1856. "Fully exposed to the enemy's batteries," they were still "too far to reply with small arms." He told how they waited a half hour in the ravine at the hill's base, "shot and shell flying and bursting" high over their heads. They lingered in anxious anticipation of "charging the infantry, whose dark lines" they saw outlined in the woods. He vividly remembered "what resolutions and vows were made then. What thoughts passed through each mind, as everyone nerved himself for the struggle, resolutions heard by God alone—vows recorded only in Heaven."

When Edgar's line began to advance, the cadets followed. "Our nerves were strung and our lips firmly closed," Frank continued, "our breath coming short and quick, waiting for the crash of musketry." But the Federals retreated, training their batteries instead on General Imboden's men who were struggling to advance through ankle deep mud, many dying in an open plateau. Then the enemy retired again to "some woods, extending along the crest of a wheat field."

From the woods the Federals "made their stand," subjecting us, Frank reported, to "a terrible fire of artillery" that brought down three cadets of D Company. Sergeant

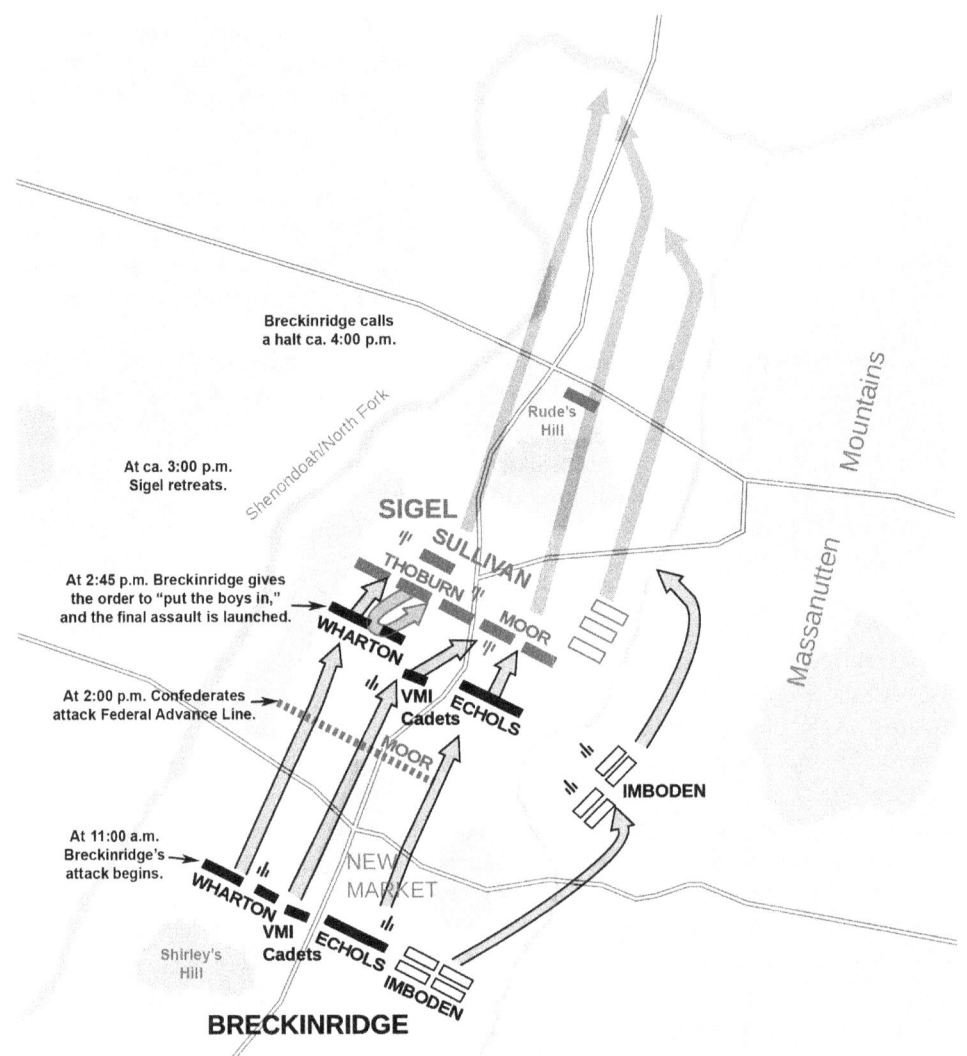

Map of New Market Battlefield, April 15, 1864 (adapted from Wikimedia Commons).

William Cabel and Privates Henry Jones and Charles Crockett "fell dead from the explosion of one shell." Private William McDowell, cousin to Stonewall Jackson's second wife and a member of Frank's Company B, promptly fell, "pierced through the heart with a bullet." Frank detailed the advance as it continued to the orchard south of the Bushong House. Here, "in this fatal orchard," two more cadets from his B Company, Privates Jack Stanard and Tom Jefferson, "fell mortally wounded."[14]

For a brief moment, Frank recalled, the cadet line faltered as its commander "Col. Ship was knocked down, and we thought mortally wounded." This would be "the first and only time" that the cadet line was broken. But, even then, the cadets "did not retreat, but ran forward 30 yards where in confusion, yet still together," they crouched and lay down "behind a fence and began for the first time to fire upon the enemy." Frank stressed that "this was far the most trying time in the whole day." The Virginia regiment in front had fallen back in some disorder, and the regiment behind had not arrived, "except for the Cadet Battalion, which had advanced too rapidly," colliding with the regiment in front. "Someone shouted out that the whole line was giving way, and for a moment," Frank confessed, "I thought that all was lost. The enemy's battery at a distance of 160 yards poured incessant volleys of canister and grapeshot into us. We still fired, however, and soon the fire became too hot." The Federal battery "limbered up and moved off, and the line of infantry began to retreat.

"Almost at the same time," Frank vowed, "Wise and myself (I am telling only what I saw) rose up and called the cadets to push on." The color bearer "advanced to the front with the colors," and "though the company organizations were gone," the whole battalion rushed forward and "rallied round the colors," forming "some sort of a line as we advanced."[15] The corps charged up Bushong's Hill through the celebrated "field of lost shoes," where the shoes and stockings of many cadets were sucked from their feet in the quagmire of the rain-soaked and recently plowed wheat field over which they advanced.

Frank Preston, 1841–69, photograph by C. R. Rees and Bro. Captain Frank Preston of B Company wrote the first eyewitness account of the Battle of New Market only four days after its occurrence (Virginia Historical Society, Acc 1/7/80).

A *Rockingham Register* journalist from behind the lines reported later, "It made our hearts leap to see the cadets from the V.M.I. move forward in the charge upon the enemy's battery. Their step was as steady as the tread of veteran soldiers. They never faltered, but went into the 'harvest of death'

A view of New Market Battlefield, photograph taken ca. 1920, showing Bushong's Hill on the right and the Field of Lost Shoes (Virginia Military Institute Archives, No. 0001953).

as though they had been accustomed to such bloody work."[16] As the Federal line gave way, Frank reported, "Everything was forgotten but the excitement of pursuit. We ran after them in not much better order, but in far better spirits and firing as we ran."

A matter of considerable debate has centered on whether it was actually the Corps of Cadets that turned the tide in the Confederate rout of Sigel's forces. Fifty years would pass before Professor Edward Turner published his *New Market Campaign*, a defense of the other soldiers who had also fought so courageously on that day.[17] These veterans "protested indignantly against the growing myth that it was the cadets alone who had saved the day and won the battle." Turner argued that "the Cadets made up about one-sixteenth of the Confederate army, so that it would have been physically impossible for them to have turned the tide of battle."[18]

Instead, he claimed, the battle was decided by the veterans. It was won "by the stubborn resistance of Derrick and the wondrous handling of the artillery on the right." They had given the Confederates full access to the Federals' rear and Sigel no choice but to withdraw. It was won by "Edgar's movement on the extreme left," for his battalion had silenced the Federals' relentless bombardment of the 51st and 62nd Virginia regiments and the cadets pinned between them. It was won by "the steady advance and desperate rushes of the Confederate center," for the 51st and 62nd had recovered from the full force of Sigel's fire and already resumed their advance.[19]

Turner defined the actual "turning-point in the engagement" as occurring before the famous charge of the cadets. During "one of the most critical moments in the battle," the cadets, acting as a reserve, had rushed forward to fill a gap in the front line. And it was here, Turner acknowledged, that, crouching behind a fence, "the cadets did their best service." Despite a withering barrage of artillery fire, during which they sustained their heaviest losses, "they held their place with stubborn resolution." And when they "rose as a man, got over the fence, and moved forward across the field straight for the enemy's guns," they were not leading the charge. Instead, they "stirred to enthusiasm the adjacent commands" that were already advancing, with the end result that "the whole Confederate line rushed forward."[20]

Turner quoted Cadet Capt. Benjamin Colonna of D Company, who witnessed the critical role the cadets actually played in inspiring the veterans on their flanks. The reinvigorated veterans called out, "'Look at the Seed Corn Battalion, look! look!' And they in turn were inspired and sprang to the front ... they yelled, we yelled with them, the onrush was irresistible. The Federal line wavered, fell slowly back to the battery, and broke into full retreat."[21]

Turner's efforts to demythologize the role played by the cadets at New Market gave well-deserved credit to the veterans from the other commands. But in the end he confessed, "The charge of the cadets upon the Federal position at New Market is one of the most remarkable episodes of the Civil War, or, indeed, of any war. That a body of youths ranging in age from fourteen to twenty should conduct themselves well in battle would in itself have been sufficiently creditable. But in the first battle in which they had ever served they should do what they did is almost beyond belief."[22]

The battle proper, lasting five hours, ended when General Breckinridge called a halt around 4 o'clock in the afternoon. Frank's letter reported 600 Confederate casualties compared to 700 to 1,200 among the Federals, including prisoners. Losses among the 257 cadets engaged in the battle were five killed (later revised to ten killed to include mortally wounded) and forty-five wounded, fully a fifth of their battalion.[23] Frank's sister Libbie asked him later what he felt as he charged with the cadets into the hail of bullets from the Federals. "Why—I believe," he replied, "my only coherent thought was the hope that if hit, I might fall on my good arm, to protect it from injury, in case the wound was not mortal."[24]

For General Breckinridge the performance of the corps was as much a great relief as it was a source of genuine pride. From the start he had refused to engage them at all, other than as reserves to bolster a small army. At one point, when his adjutant general entreated him to launch the cadets on the guns of the enemy, he had objected to "the sacrifice of these children." But when his other regiments were disrupted, necessity dictated that he close the gap. His hands trembling, he signed the order to put the boys in, exclaiming, "God forgive me for the execution of this order."[25] He would later both regret and honor that decision for the wounded and killed and for the courage and discipline displayed. Cadet Captain Colonna of D Company said the cadets took to heart Breckinridge's commendation and thanks to them for "the result of today's operations."[26] They revered the general as though he were a reincarnated Jackson.

The New Market battle was memorialized at VMI in a 1914 mural by Benjamin Clinedinst, Class of 1880. It graces today's Jackson Memorial Hall. But it doesn't convey the glory of war so much as what a visiting Englishman described as the dreadfulness and realities of war. "What horror!" he exclaimed, very much moved when he stood before it. "This is the greatest argument against war that I have ever seen."[27]

Sir Moses Ezekiel, Class of 1866, himself a New Market private in C Company, further celebrated the battle with his 1912 statue of *Virginia Mourning Her Dead*. It stands on the parade ground over the graves of the cadets killed and mortally wounded on that fateful day. Indeed, every year since 1887, the Corps of Cadets has honored those ten youths. In a beautifully inspired ceremony on May 15, the anniversary of the battle, ten cadets from the appropriate companies answer the roll with "died on the field of honor" when the names of the deceased are called.[28]

On May 22, before the euphoria and anguish of battle at New Market could even begin to abate, the VMI cadets were dispatched on General Lee's order to Richmond to help guard the city and relieve veterans at the front. The news of their gallant conduct at New Market had preceded them. It prompted a formal resolution of appreciation by the Confederate House of Representatives and meetings with Governor William Smith and President Davis. Frank Preston was with the corps in Richmond when his letter describing the New Market battle reached his father a week after he sent it. Preston arrived in Lexington to receive it on May 23, having walked twenty miles because of a Union break in the canal.[29]

Seven years would pass before Preston would give his own assessment of the role the VMI Corps of Cadets had played at New Market. In 1871 he was asked to address the corps on the seventh anniversary of the battle.[30] He began generally by crediting the institute with having contributed "between six and eight hundred officers from lieutenants to lieutenant general" for service in the current war. He added, "'Slain in battle' is the epitaph that consecrates no fewer than 125 names." He explained that the "old corps" at VMI had been expected to serve militarily during the war. But the governor of Virginia had reorganized a new corps in January 1862, to be exempt from military service. "The corps was new," he admitted,

> but the spirit was the old spirit of those who vowed and kept their vow, never to forget the Virginia Military Institute. When the new corps was reorganized it was hardly

anticipated that they would see active service. The authorities of the land deemed it unwise that the education of the youth should be altogether suspended; and the military ardour of many a lad, too young to bear arms, could only be restrained by placing him where he would be in training for war, and whence (for the corps was at all times on a war footing) there might be a call into active service.

Preston acknowledged that despite the reluctance of the authorities to enlist the services of the new corps, during the war the call "occurred oftener than once. The cadets were in the trenches at Richmond, and were twice called out with the Home Guards of this county." They were honored by demands from General Jackson for their aid in defending the valley. "But the engagement in which they bore the most conspicuous part," he contended, "was that of which we today commemorate the anniversary."

Charge of the VMI Cadets. **Mural by Benjamin West Clinedinst, Class of 1880. The painting, measuring 18 by 23 feet, is in Virginia Military Institute's Jackson Hall (Virginia Military Institute Museum, No. 0004629).**

> On that day the *new* corps proved that they were the worthy successors of the old. The same spirit actuated them. They did not forget the Virginia Military Institute. And will the institute ever forget that day, or its actors? Never! As long as any of us live who have known the institute from its cradle, we will point to that day as a proof that our labours, if humble, have not been in vain. Virginia entrusted to us the training of a portion of her youth. Here was seen the character of the patriotism that fired their bosoms. So far as the inspiration was due to the institution from which they went forth, it is for it a crown of glory, and for all connected with its management, a source of thankfulness, and (may we not say) of allowable pride.

However, not content to let success on the battlefield rest solely with the institute Preston went on to conclude,

> And when, as the years roll on and bear away the actors in the scene and those who can give living testimony about it, its record will be in history, and tradition will add to the wonders of truth the halo of romance. And those that fell, the early dead! the bright eyes closed in sleep while their morning sun had hardly risen! Had they been spared, what might they have accomplished! Vain such regrets, and unwise! How could they have achieved in a long life a fame more noble and more pure than that which now glorifies their names? Proud as the crown of laurel or bay around the head of the warrior or the poet, but amaranthine, like that of God's martyrs, is the crown that liberty places upon the brows, flushed with immortal youth, of those, her boy defenders who offered their virgin lives upon her altar.

The lesson that Preston drew from the example of the gallant Corps of Cadets representing VMI on its day of glory was probably not what his youthful audience was expecting. "Cadets of the V.M.I.," he intoned, "May you never be summoned to war. Perhaps secretly you envy the experience of those whom you have heard recounting the scenes of the camp, the march, the fight. It is the noble impulse of generous youth; but it is also the mistake of inexperience." He advised,

> Be ready ever to risk your life for your country, but pray that your country may never again confront the horrors of war. All the best interests of mankind are imperiled by war. Sometimes Liberty has been vindicated by arms, but alas, full often has it been crushed by the superior power of despotism. Civilization ceases in war, barbarism comes back, and religion stands aghast at the spectacle of God's creatures, arrayed against each other for mutual destruction. You have seen our land conquered, subjected, despoiled, our government subverted, and our social system confounded. You have seen with your own eyes, these fair walls, dedicated to science and literature, a burned and blasted trophy of desolation.

Fully conscious of the age of his audience, Preston acknowledged, "You have not known, you are too young to have known the anguish beyond remedy of fathers, mothers, brothers, sisters and maidens, when the bloody, remorseless hand of war tore from their hearts, what to them individually, was more precious than liberty, government, home, or anything in Heaven." His plea to the cadets was not that they would shun the call to battle in their country's time of need. "Believe me, you will every one have full scope to prove your courage." His plea instead was to eschew praise when it is fairly won. Quoting a proverb from Horace, *sine pulvere, nulla palma* (no palm of victory without the dust of effort), he accepted their envy of the New Market cadets. "Do you desire praise? You are ignoble if you do not. He who despises true fame despises the virtues by which it is won." Preston warned, however,

> I know not but that in the years to come, when the voices of those who now address you shall be silent, some one may stand here to recount the deeds, glorious to them-

Replica of the Virginia Military Institute cadet flag at New Market. The flag was made of white silk. One side depicted the seal of Virginia; the other included a likeness of George Washington. Before leaving Lexington, in advance of Gen. Hunter's raid and destruction of Virginia Military Institute, the Cadet Corps tore their New Market flag into pieces to distribute so that their beloved ensign wouldn't fall into enemy hands (Virginia Military Institute Museum, No. 0003391).

selves, and fruitful to their country, of the young men before me. Breathes there one with soul so dead as not to cherish the resolve that he will strive to have his name among those who will make up the Roll of Honour for the next generation of alumni for the Virginia Military Institute.

This distinction is not to be won by wishing for it—it would be worthless if it could be.

Preston concluded by holding up for his audience "one single clear example" of someone who, like the cadets of New Market, had taken from the VMI parade ground the "first step in the pathway of glory." But, unlike the cadets, he was not so young to have shed his "light beyond the mere opening of life." The example of General Jackson, he contended, was the model to emulate. "Learn that it was not his military genius alone, surpassingly great as that was, to which he owed his success, nor yet to his almost superhuman force of will. See his indefatigable industry, his self-control and self-denial, his conscientiousness, his truth, his purity, and, above all, his piety." Preston considered the New Market cadets at the beginning of life and Stonewall Jackson at the end of it as singularly clear examples of admirable achievement. They owed their valor to the history of an institute that claimed as her children both the past and the current generation of young men, who would one day serve as models for future cadets.

Part VII: Twilight

Life still has joys that do not pall,
* Love still has hours serene and tender*
'Tis afternoon, dear! ... that is all!
* And this is afternoon's calm splendor*
        —Margaret J. Preston

24

Like a Bolt of Lightning

News has come that Lee's army has surrendered! We are struck dumb with astonishment! Why then all these four years of suffering—of separations—of horror—of blood—of havoc—of awful bereavement!
—Margaret J. Preston

Hardly a month had passed before the glorious victory at New Market was eclipsed by Hunter's vengeful raid on Lexington. In the afternoon of June 12, 1864, VMI lay in ruins. What had taken twenty-five years to create took only one day to destroy. The corps, having no home to occupy, returned to help defend the Confederate capital. By December, they had resumed academic work at the state almshouse, a former hospital in Richmond. Sherman had completed his march from Atlanta to the sea, having sent Lincoln the city of Savannah as "a Christmas present."[1] Union forces under General Sheridan were ravaging the crops and livestock of the vast Shenandoah Valley. The Confederacy was in the throes of gloom and hopelessness, its subsistence becoming narrower and narrower with threats of starvation.

The Preston household now contained six youngsters, ranging in age from twenty-five to three. It included John Williams, who had rescued Frank on the battlefield at Winchester but lost his home to enemy hands. He had arrived as an invalid to live with the Prestons until cured of his wounds after war's end.[2] How Maggie found time to write with so much turmoil and so many demands on her time might be a mystery, were it not that she had ceased recording the anguish and excitement of war in her diary and begun to create the singular work for which she would become best known and revered throughout the South, even in some far corners of the North. The impulse to write a ballad of the war, in whose throes she was still very much enmeshed, sprang from a letter she received from Preston in Richmond. It accompanied a booklet, which he admitted was "a pathetic little story, told in very ordinary rhyme, and having no merit as a work of art." He challenged her to "do something much better in the same line."[3]

In total secrecy, Maggie took up the gauntlet and in three weeks produced her first great success. It set forth an impassioned record of two frightful years of the Civil War extending from the McDowell and Shenandoah Valley campaigns to Chancellorsville. She wrote by firelight with a poor pencil on rough paper made in the Confederacy. This was necessitated in part by the high price of tallow candles and by the pain that bright light inflicted on her weakened eyes. She either composed without looking at the page or dictated in the shadows to sixteen-year-old Libbie, the only literary child whom she trusted to share her secret as her amanuensis. The lines flowed swiftly and easily, because since early childhood she had habitually thought in verse. She was also drawing closely from recent vivid experience.

24. Like a Bolt of Lightning   183

The story was personal in the sense that it told of a Colonel Douglas Dunbar's having to leave his wife, Alice, and their three children in 1861 to go to war. But it was also "the story of thousands in the Confederacy," Libbie remarked." Its depiction of "the scenes, emotions and sorrows of the war was so true to life, that not many of us who experienced them can bear to read it today."[4] Maggie completed the ballad and sent it off to Preston in Richmond, fearful how it might be received. He responded that he'd read it to numerous groups of officers, the sternest of whom had reacted with tears of endorsement, even demanding that Douglas not be allowed to die. While appreciative of their approval, she concluded, "It delights *him* [Preston], and that is enough for *me*."[5]

Preston had the ballad printed in late March 1865, by his distant cousin Joseph W. Randolph, Richmond's leading publisher. He paid 2,600 Confederate dollars for 2,000 copies.[6] Fifty of these were mailed from Richmond, as Maggie would later report, before "the end of the world—*our* world—came." The publishing house, along with Richmond, would be burned when the capital fell, so the rest of the first edition perished.

A second edition in 1866 by Kelly and Piet, a Baltimore publisher, would sell 7,000 to 8,000 copies, and within two years the book would go through eight printings. This ballad, more than any other of Maggie's works, earned her the accolade "Poetess of the

Beechenbrook, **published 1865, photograph of a surviving copy from the burning of Richmond in 1865 (photograph facing p. 160 of Elizabeth Allan's *March Past*).**

Confederacy." She dedicated it "to every Southern woman, who has been widowed by the war." But it was equally felt by many widows of the North, who read it with tears as genuine as her own. It was a springboard for a literary career of poetry, stories, reviews, essays, reminiscences, and volumes of correspondence with the literary men and women of her time.

In mid–March 1865, Preston left Richmond on furlough with a severe lung infection that would require rehabilitation at home.[7] Before he departed, he received a request from Governor William Smith for 100 young men from the Corps of Cadets for service on horseback. General Lee was determined to stop Sheridan's Union cavalry from entering Richmond. The governor even offered to provide mounts donated by Richmond citizens if Preston would only "provide the cadets."[8] Such a request had been made twenty years earlier to the state from VMI, when it was just getting established. The institute had made the appeal repeatedly until 1858, but the state had consistently refused to fund a horsemanship program for drills.[9] Preston responded to the governor that unfortunately a cavalry wasn't part of the bill that had established VMI. The cadets were trained only as infantrymen and artillerymen but never drilled as cavalry. He informed him he could provide the cadets but "could not promise any special efficiency from them on horseback," whereupon the request was duly rescinded.[10]

On April 2, 1865, the eve of the fall of Richmond, the Corps of Cadets evacuated the capital. The city was aflame as Confederate soldiers burned stockpiled supplies, and chaos ruled. Before the Union army arrived to occupy the city, the corps had disbanded, each cadet left to find his way home as best he could. A week passed, and Preston was still languishing at home on furlough when "news of Appomattox fell like a thunderbolt upon the little town of Lexington." Maggie noted in her journal on April 10,

> News has come that Lee's army has surrendered! We are struck dumb with astonishment! Why then all these four years of suffering—of separations—of horror—of blood—of havoc—of awful bereavement! Why these ruined homes—these broken family circles—these scenes of terror that must scathe the brain of those who witnessed them till their dying day! Why is our dear Willy in his uncoffined grave? Why poor Frank to go through life with one arm? Is it wholly and forever in vain? God only knows![11]

In years to come, Preston would look back on the fall of Richmond as one of the three "most interesting events of the war" that he had missed. According to Libbie, it was "without any carelessness on his part" but as if fate had intended he miss them. The first had been Manassas in July 1861, when he was told "there was no immediate prospect of battle" and had left for Georgia to help set up the Southern Presbyterian Church. He had missed Jackson's victory by hardly twenty-four hours. The second was when he had left in May 1864, for a Presbyterian General Assembly Meeting in North Carolina while the cadets, including his son Frank and nephew Preston Cocke, had "covered themselves with glory at New Market." And the third was this illness, "as unusual a thing as an eclipse of the sun," that had necessitated a home furlough in April 1865, when Richmond fell and Lee surrendered. But what Libbie described as fate, she admitted, Maggie would call "special providences" in that her husband had missed all three events without harm.[12]

The returning soldiers, including Preston, had no time for despair. Indeed, on one occasion, when his nephew Preston Cocke, the first cadet to return from Richmond, appeared in the yard, weary, exhausted, and broken, the family burst into tears. Preston scolded sternly, "If you cannot show the boy a decent courage and cheerfulness, leave the room."[13] Self-preservation drove all returning soldiers to care for their families by restoring devastated and long neglected fields. Many found a measure of solace in their work.

Libbie would later credit in part the magnanimous gesture of their conqueror, General Grant, for the renewal of hope and courage from the anguish of defeat. She imagined the poignant moment when "the silent victor looked out over the Virginia hills, showing faintly green in the spring promise," and said to Lee, "Let your men keep their horses, General; they will need them for the spring plowing."[14] Lee in turn informed his men, "Go to your homes and resume your occupations. Obey the laws and become as good citizens as you were soldiers." Libbie thanked God for work, which served to restore a defeated army's spirits. Of course, the companionship of girls contributed, she confessed, as she spoke of the walks, the rides, the musical evenings, "and all the witching ways of men and maids!"

Maggie kept up her journal only fragmentarily for three months after the surrender. In it she made no mention of Lincoln's assassination on April 14. On July 4, with the onset of reconstruction, she remarked that "the Confederacy disowns forever as sacred the Fourth of July. I never saw a quieter day as martial law was proclaimed.[15] But Preston expressed no bitterness toward the North either during or after the war. "Angry he often was," she conceded, "at outrages committed during the war, and especially at the indignities suffered during Reconstruction days. But while many devout ministers of the Gospel and good people on both sides of the line allowed themselves to revile their enemies, Major—now Colonel—Preston followed the noble examples of Lee and Jackson, of Lincoln and Grant, in giving the enemy credit for honesty of purpose, and for patriotism as they interpreted it."[16]

Maggie's last entry in her journal on July 10, 1865, confirmed that Preston "dismissed four of our servants" since he "thought it best to change."[17] She noted that Anakee's having lived with him for twenty-five years, "he was grieved to give her up, and she wanted to stay." Old Uncle Young, who "manifested no pleasure at the idea of freedom," went to live with Maggie's cousin in Pennsylvania.[18] Her final thought wondered at their reactions: "It is astonishing how little it seems to affect them; they seem depressed rather than elated."[19] But Preston could no longer keep them as hired servants. There being no money for the first six months in the ex–Confederacy of 1865, he had not a dollar to pay them.

In the wake of the war's end, according to Libbie, Maggie noticed a disturbing change in Preston. Her husband had "lost the buoyancy of youth" and appeared aged. Weighing heavily on him was the outcome of the war. He had lost two splendid sons, Ran and Willie, his nephew William Cocke, and his close friend Jackson. His dream of a Virginia Military Institute lay in ruins. And land, horses, and livestock were gone. "The old Confederate uttered no complaint, no moan, no word of unavailing regret; but his head grew white, his brow furrowed, his eye sad." He concealed what anguish he might have felt with "long silences" but for the most part maintained a social demeanor.[20]

In the fall of 1865, with the war over, Maggie left for her first reunion with her family in Philadelphia, while Preston remained in Lexington. The institute lay in ruins with virtually no financial support. It might very well have remained a scarred shell with little hope of a future were it not for Superintendent Smith, who returned to Lexington from Richmond determined to raise the Phoenix from its ashes. He convened the faculty and board on September 25, 1865, to consider plans for rebuilding. When the faculty agreed to reduce their salary by one-third, the school was able to secure a loan and to market bonds. VMI reopened in mid October with scarcely sixty cadets attending classes in the superintendent's undamaged quarters. They boarded with private families and in hotels.[21]

New faculty members were appointed as replacements for those who didn't return from the war. General Custis Lee, eldest son of Robert E. Lee, accepted the position of professor of engineering, and Navy Commander John Mercer Brooke arrived to fill the new chair of practical astronomy, geodesy, physical geography, and meteorology. During the war Brooke had helped redesign the frigate USS *Merrimack* into the ironclad CSS *Virginia* for the Confederates. He had also helped develop the torpedo and invented what Preston called "a new and formidable species of gun," known as the Brooke rifle, which the Confederate Navy employed as counterpart to the Federal Parrott.[22] It was his invention in the mid–1850s of a deep sea sounding and core sampling device which

Superintendent Smith Convenes a Meeting of the Faculty to Rebuild the Institute. Study for uncompleted painting by William D. Washington, 1865. Numbers 1–15: General Francis H. Smith, Colonel James W. Massie, Colonel J.T.L. Preston, General Thomas H. Williamson, Commodore Matthew Fontaine Maury, Governor John Letcher, General William H. Richardson, Dr. R. L. Madison, Colonel Scott Shipp, Captain John M. Brooke, Colonel William B. Blair, Colonel Thomas M. Semmes, Colonel Mark B. Hardin, General George Washington Custis Lee, and Colonel Marshall McDonald. Although Commodore Maury (#5) appears in Colonel Washington's drawing of the faculty and board in 1865, he was never a member of the board and did not come to Virginia Military Institute until the fall of 1868 to become Brooke's colleague in the newly established Department of Physics (Virginia Military Institute Archives, No. 0003161).

proved a major contribution to Matthew Maury's charting the floors of the world's oceans in 1855.

The year after VMI's reopening in 1866, class enrollment had increased to 150 cadets. The rebuilding of Barracks was completed in January. But just as progress appeared well on track, Congress passed the first Reconstruction Act of 1867, placing Virginia under a military governor. A year later the Virginia Legislature remodeled its Constitution. In a resolution hostile to VMI, it demanded "that the superintendent of the Virginia Military Institute be required to show cause why the property known as the Virginia Military Institute should not be obliterated." Smith adroitly persuaded the lawmakers that the institute, with its practical and scientific training, "might be made an agent to the state" in its recovery from the devastation of the war. But equally important for the state, he argued, would be the availability of the school's newest faculty member, the celebrated scientist "Commodore Matthew Fontaine Maury."[23]

Maury enjoyed world-wide fame as geographer of the seas. As the father of modern oceanography and naval meteorology, he had served as the first superintendent of the U.S. Naval Observatory. As Preston noted, Maury's "undisputed supremacy in nautical physics" had led him to produce "the wind and current charts by which modern navigation is directed."[24] His charts were helping sailors navigate the North Atlantic, and they had drastically reduced the length of ocean voyages. Smith contended that Maury's presence at VMI would allow him to conduct "a physical survey of Virginia," including its transportation routes, soils, and minerals. The legislature's resolution to obliterate VMI "was laid upon the table, and there it still lies."[25] All rebuilding was completed by 1869.

At the same time that VMI was fighting for its continued existence, Washington College was teetering on the verge of bankruptcy. In 1865 it desperately needed a new president. A few weeks after the war ended, the U.S. government confiscated the ancestral home of General Robert E. Lee's wife at Arlington. Lee received offers to live with his kindred in England, but he turned them down with the gracious reply, "No; I will not leave my own people in their extremity: what they endure, I will endure, and I am ready to share with them their last crust."

Many Virginians made extravagant offers to Lee, but when Preston's sister, Elizabeth Cocke, proposed Derwent house, a plain but comfortable dwelling on her estate near Richmond, he accepted the offer as "the most unpretending of them all."[26] He spent the summer and part of the fall sequestered among the splendid oaks that overshadowed the cottage, pondering what to do with the rest of his life. What saved Washington College from financial collapse was his deciding at the request of the trustees to invest his future in education at an annual salary of $1,500. He found a ready welcome in August of 1865 by the people of Lexington.

Maggie would later describe the veneration and love that citizens and soldiers alike felt for this unassuming hero after his demoralizing surrender. Contrasting the affection that Lee inspired in his men with the devotion great leaders of history commanded in their soldiery, she observed,

> Cromwell's Ironsides would march into the breach, and die at his bidding. Washington's Continentals were content to starve and perish, inspired by the unselfish patriotism of their chief. Napoleon's Grenadiers never ceased to feel the electric power of his name. Wellington's troops rushed upon death, proud to be the sharers of their leader's glory. But none of these great commanders captivated and held the hearts of their men,

Last photograph of Robert E. Lee, 1807–70, taken by Michael Miley, October 2, 1870 (photograph facing p. 198 of Elizabeth Allan's *March Past*, also available from Virginia Military Institute Archives, No. 0001314).

as did the grand soldier who, possessing the calm dignity of Washington, united with a warmer heart and a far more gracious manner, was able to impress himself personally upon every one under him.[27]

One of Preston's first contacts with President Lee at Washington College was in the early morning as Preston rode his horse across the campus to classes at the institute. His daily routine entailed a morning shower from a bucket suspended in the stable, a milk punch before breakfast, and a customary horseback ride across Washington College's lawn. He initiated this shortcut when his father-in-law Dr. Junkin was president. But on this occasion the new president had ordered that an improved roadway of broken stone be laid to facilitate passage through the grounds. The stones were new and rough, so Preston rode alongside on the grass. When he saw General Lee, they halted for a short talk. At one point during the conversation, Lee reached up and put his arm affectionately around the neck of Preston's horse. Then patting him, he said to Preston, "Colonel, this is a beautiful horse; I am sorry he is so tenderfooted that he avoids our new road."[28] The hint taken, Preston thereafter rode on the stone way.

25

God and Slavery

> *Col. Preston's experience on the slavery question was peculiar. He had always refused to own slaves until he read* Uncle Tom's Cabin.
> —William H. Ruffner

In retrospect, seventy-four years after the end of the Civil War, VMI historiographer William Couper declared he personally found it peculiar "that Preston refused to own slaves during a period in our southern history when a man of means was expected to own them."[1] And if that weren't remarkable enough, Dr. William Ruffner found it even more peculiar that Preston had refused to own slaves "until he read *Uncle Tom's Cabin;* which led him to think better of the institution than he had ever done before. He afterward bought a few slaves, in time to lose them in a body."[2]

What provoked Harriet Beecher Stowe to write *Uncle Tom's Cabin*, which burst onto the political and literary scene in 1852, was the controversial Fugitive Slave Act that the U.S. Congress passed in 1850, also known as the "Bloodhound Law." It legalized tracking down runaway slaves to return them to their masters. Living in Maine at the time, Mrs. Stowe was shocked by the prevailing attitude that had facilitated passage of the act. The South had endorsed it, and the North had "defended, encouraged, and participated" in what she considered an unwarranted compromise.

It appalled her, she confessed, "when she heard, with perfect surprise and consternation, Christian and humane people actually recommending the remanding [of] escaped fugitives into slavery, as a duty binding on good citizens."[3] She added, "These men and Christians cannot know what slavery is." Motivated by their apparent ignorance of "the woes and evils" of slavery, she set out "to exhibit it in a *living dramatic reality.*"

In the spring of 1852 her book appeared in two volumes, selling 5,000 copies in two days, 50,000 in two months, and 300,000 in the first year. It had already been introduced by forty installments in the *National Era*, chiefly in Washington, D.C., beginning in June of 1851. This fueled its meteoric popularity at a time when Preston was touring Europe.

Whatever possessed Preston to favor slavery after reading Mrs. Stowe's powerful anti-slavery polemic isn't obvious. No records exist of any statements Preston might have made on the issue of slavery before the war. His motives for thinking "better of the institution than he had ever done before" after reading her book can only be inferred from articles he wrote on reflection after the war.

In 1877 he expressed his views on slavery in an article he published in the *Presbyterian Review* entitled, "The Colored Man in the South." Without benefit of modern sociology but with a thorough grounding in contemporary anthropology, he claimed he had come to view the Negro as caught between two cultures.

He had never been to Africa, but he had read extensively about Africa. Avoiding hearsay as unacceptable, he had looked for reliable firsthand accounts from writers who had lived and traveled there. Based on testimony from missionaries, travelers, and explorers, he formed his understanding of what life was like for the African in his homeland. He studied the journals of the Rev. Thomas Jefferson Bowen, the first Baptist missionary to Africa; Bayard Taylor, the American explorer of Central Africa and the White Nile; and Sir Samuel Baker, the British explorer and abolitionist who described and photographically illustrated in many volumes the conditions on the continent.

These eyewitness reports described an Africa that lacked the virtues and benefits of civilization as Preston knew it. They documented the native African as steeped in a heathen environment, where "the king was surrounded by sorcerers, both men and women," and the people were superstitious, believing implicitly in "witches and wizards … their faith resting upon a simple belief in magic." His sources described "the actual, degraded, hideous condition of the negro as at present found in Africa, with strong doubt expressed as to his capability of improvement." Preston admitted he could not refute these negative encounters with Africans in Africa by witnesses living in and traveling around the continent. He could only confirm his own positive encounters with "this same race" in America.[4]

He described, for instance, attending a meeting of the Colored Baptist Association of Virginia. In his estimation of its delegates, he saw them as "spirited, sensible, and practical." They debated "in an orderly manner" under a Negro moderator who was "more efficient than many a presiding officer that I have seen in the chair at conventions of whites." The topics, he remarked, "were identical with those met with in a Presbytery—reports from individual churches, ministerial support, foreign and domestic missions, education, and temperance." They thoroughly discussed how their young men must educate themselves in a systematic way for the ministry of their ninety-six churches across the state. Preston acknowledged that many of the prominent speakers at the gathering "had white blood in their veins," but he noted that "the most impressive was a pure African."[5]

Preston deduced that the difference between the eyewitness reports of the Negro in Africa and his personal familiarity with the Negro in the southern states was a "question of comparative civilization." He proposed that slavery in America had become "the civiliser, the great benefactor, of the negro." It had "made for the negro the difference between civilisation and barbarism." And expanding this negatively, as "a bare assertion, for which we offer no proof," he added, "Nothing else could have effected it."[6]

"Not all slavery," he argued, was beneficial. "In every part of Africa, slavery has always existed. Where master and slave were alike uncivilised, in the nature of the case no good could be germinated." Egypt, he claimed, "has ever been slave holding. But Egyptian slavery had in it nothing beneficent." He considered Oriental slavery and slavery in Spanish Cuba, the West Indies, and English Jamaica and concluded, "Only in the United States … did the negro enjoy under the most favorable conditions, the slavery which was his only hope." But even in the United States, he believed, there was a regional difference. "In Africa, in the West Indies, and in New England, the negro slave was regarded as stock. Society had not taken him under its protection, and as yet the conscience of the master had not been awakened in his behalf. Owing to the character of the Puritans and the climate of New England, he was worse off in Massachusetts than he was in Africa or in the West Indies." Preston contended, "Slavery can never develop its beneficent influences until the slave becomes a *quasi* member of the family."[7]

And this, he claimed, "never came to pass in New England." He believed that in the southern states, "the negro found his predestined home." From the Biblical perspective, he was cast there like Joseph in Egypt, under the all-seeing eye of a beneficent Providence, "to progress from African barbarism to Christian civilisation." Preston acknowledged that, even in the South, slavery "had its serious drawbacks and positive evils to both races." He further argued that he was "not claiming for the South the merit of having foreseen and intended this beneficence, any more than we suppose the slave trade of the North had its origin in love of righteousness. Slavery, in its results, has proved itself too large for human foresight."[8]

Instead, he credited the results to "the great Ruler of the universe." He was persuaded that God had prepared "four millions of human beings" for their ultimate assimilation into Christian civilization. It was this difference between what eyewitnesses claimed the slave had left behind in his old home in Africa and what Preston had witnessed himself of the slave's new home in the United States that convinced him to approve of slavery in the American South, "with God's providence," as "humane, equitable, and beneficent."[9]

Preston was speaking for slavery only as he knew it in western Virginia and Kentucky. The author of *Uncle Tom's Cabin* also acknowledged that in western Virginia as in Kentucky, "the mildest form of the system of slavery is to be seen."[10] There, unlike in "the more southern districts," she conceded, "the general prevalence of agricultural pursuits of a quiet and gradual nature" made "the task of the Negro a more healthful and reasonable one, while the master, content with a more gradual style of acquisition, has not those temptations to hard-heartedness" that accompany the desire for rapid gain. Slavery, as Preston claimed to know it firsthand in Kentucky and western Virginia, was more protective and caring.

He himself extended to his servants and slaves, as *quasi* members of the family, the same courtesy and respect he gave to all the members of his household, whether black or white, young or old. It wasn't often that he was called upon to defend their honor. But on one occasion, when he was engaged in private devotionals in his study as he was wont to do in the mornings, he overheard a youth outside say something offensive to his black maid, who was sweeping the front porch.

He arose from his Bible and strode out the front door. Ripping a picket from his fence, he caught up to the young man and whacked him over the head, admonishing him angrily, "I will teach you to speak respectfully to the women of my household."[11]

He then returned to his devotionals and calmed himself. He had recognized the youth as a carpenter in town, so on his way to teach his Latin class, he entered the carpenter's shop, removed his hat, and sincerely apologized to him. He confessed that, although he felt he was right to be angry, he had acted wrongly to attack an unarmed man who had doubtlessly refrained from striking back at an elder.

In a broad sense, Preston saw the institution of slavery in the American South as "humane, equitable, and beneficent," whereas Mrs. Stowe saw "the thing itself as the essence of all abuse."[12] What he considered "the hand of God,"[13] she regarded as deserving "the wrath of God." They differed in their teleology. The last lines in Stowe's "Concluding Remarks" charged, "Both North and South have been guilty before God; and the Christian Church has a heavy account to answer. Not by combining together to protect injustice and cruelty, and making a common capital of sin, is this Union to be saved,—but by repentance, justice and mercy; for, no surer is the eternal law by which the millstone sinks in the ocean, than that stronger law by which injustice and cruelty shall bring on nations the wrath of Almighty God!"

With these lines she ended her book, dashing all hope of America's saving itself from the "accursed system" it had created. But where she saw despair, Preston saw hope. Where she saw God's vengeance, he saw God's beneficence. Preston had concluded that slavery was the only redeeming force in America that could have possibly prepared the African for his eventual emancipation and successful assimilation into American society. And as a system of discipline, labor, and religion, it "had done all for the negro race it could do."[14] He believed "the time for emancipation had come."

Like Stowe, he was sympathetic to the plight of the African slave, but ontologically rather than existentially. He had not seen slavery in America as "the essence of all abuse," as she had her chief spokesman, Augustine St. Clare, describe it.[15] In her book St. Clare faulted slavery for inflicting a "state of sin and misery" on "a whole class,—debased, uneducated, indolent, provoking—put, without any sort of terms or conditions, entirely into the hands of such people as the majority in our world are, people who have neither self-consideration or self-control, who haven't even an enlightened regard to their own interests."[16]

Preston held no such view of the majority of mankind, especially mankind in the South. As his daughter Libbie would later remark, in her own account of having read Stowe's book, "our Northern reformers refused to recognize the devotion of the slaves to kind masters, or the fact that kind masters were the rule, in the South."[17] Whether myth or reality, this view of slave holders as kind in the South was rooted in the indispensable notion of character. Preston held that "beneficent" slavery depended entirely on "the conscience of the master."[18] Stowe herself had acknowledged in her book that "the character of the master" was the only safeguard "to protect the slave's life."[19] In his article Preston laid down a condition of slavery—a prerequisite—that the master "must be of a character at once strong and generous."[20]

It's ironic that in a particularly cruel scene in *Uncle Tom's Cabin,* Stowe actually stated a motive for buying a slave. When the slave Prue was whipped to death, she had her spokesman, Augustine St. Clare, lament, "What can a man of honorable and humane feelings do, but shut his eyes all he can, and harden his heart? I can't buy every poor wretch I see. I can't turn knight-errant, and undertake to redress every individual case of wrong in such a city as this."[21] It's true that not every case of wrong could be individually redressed. But rectifying one case of wrong in a system of slavery that Preston believed had been beneficial and "had done all for the negro race that it could do" would be motive enough for a man of strong and generous character to buy a slave as part member of his family or in order to free him.[22]

It's true, as both William Couper and William Ruffner have attested, that Preston hadn't bought a slave before reading *Uncle Tom's Cabin.* The census of 1840 lists in Preston's household one slave and three free colored males. But the slave was twenty-seven-year-old Anakee, a mulatto whom Preston had held in trust for his wife's eldest brother John Caruthers until he died in August 1840.[23] Preston's daughter would later confirm, "Father did not buy and sell slaves; those he inherited, he of course worked and took care of. When additional servants were needed for extra help, they were hired from their owners. This was the case of Sylvia, Preston's mother's hired maid, and Isaac, her hired coachman."[24]

The Slave Schedule of 1850 lists five slaves in Preston's family. But two of these were hired slaves Sylvia and Isaac; and the third, Anakee. The fourth was Jane, a sixteen-year-old, whom Preston had raised from a child. She was the daughter of a slave whose master died in 1849, so Preston was made her legal guardian until her majority at twenty-one.[25] The fifth slave was a sixteen-year-old mulatto, presumably Anakee's daughter.

By the 1860 Slave Schedule, Sylvia and Isaac had been returned to their owners, and Jane had reached her majority. Anakee was the only slave remaining under Preston's care, apart from a fifty-year-old female, Coralie, and a twenty-six-year-old male, Phil, both of whom had been hired to help in Lexington after the children returned from Preston's sister's home at Oakland.[26]

So Libbie's assertion that her father didn't buy or sell slaves would appear to be valid, and Couper's claim that Preston refused to own slaves is technically correct in that he took care of "the coloreds" as trustee, guardian, or employer. But contrary to Libbie's assertion, Ruffner's contention that he bought slaves after reading *Uncle Tom's Cabin* turns out to be partly true.

On December 12, 1864, he purchased one slave named John in Richmond, for whom a receipt exists for the sum of $5,500.[27] Hardly had he bought him than he freed him, as Ruffner confirmed, since he isn't named among the servants or slaves he released on July 10, 1865, or included in the census of 1870. Preston's motive for buying John is nowhere stated, and John is not listed in the *Database of Virginia Slave Names* recently issued by the Virginia Historical Society, so his subsequent life is unknown. But if Preston's motive is not suggested by his personal view of slavery as expressed in the articles he wrote defending it, then his intent must remain a mystery.

As much as Preston placed his faith in the institution of slavery as "humane, equitable, and beneficent" and under "the hand of God," he differed from many of his compatriots after the war who objected that emancipation was premature. They still believed that for emancipation to be successful it had to be gradual. Indeed, at the war's end, as historiographer Henry Boley would observe, many Lexingtonians thought "the manner in which the enfranchisement of the blacks was accomplished was a political blunder" because it was so precipitous.[28]

In an article Preston published in 1878, entitled, "Religious Education of the Colored People of the South," he conceded that during post-bellum emancipation of the slaves the burden of slavery had been "suddenly lifted off them, without any gradual approach to liberty, and without preparation for it."[29] But he rejected the notion that their liberation was premature.

His basic argument was that "the colored people are neither barbarians nor semi-barbarians, neither heathen nor semi-heathen. They are in full possession of American civilization, and of Protestant Christianity, though not fully appropriating the benefits of either."[30] After 200 years of slavery they had earned those benefits, and all that was lacking after emancipation was the granting of them.

Indeed, he felt that further delay of emancipation would have been debilitating. He cited Tuckahoe, the plantation founded by his Randolph ancestors near Richmond, as a prime example of the general trend toward the reliance on slavery. It had threatened to make western Virginia as dependent on slaves as eastern Virginia. As historian Oren Morton observed, there were few slaves in Rockbridge County before the Revolution. But the iron industry in the west had led to the hiring of slaves from masters in the east. So Preston concluded that "by 1861 we were quite a slaveholding people; a few more years, and we would have had to undergo much that Tuckahoe did on that score. It was well the unpleasantness came as soon as it did."[31] Writing after the war, he would ask rhetorically,

> Is it either fanatical, superstitious, or presumptuous, to hold that it was God who brought this people from the arid land of their nativity, to a land of Christian light and privilege? ... Is it fanatical to see the hand of God in connecting emancipation with the issue of a war belonging to a wide destiny of a mighty nation? If not, then it is reasonable to entertain the hope, that all this progressive providential work is not to come now to an abrupt and fruitless end; but that it all is preliminary to something further, equally beneficent and of enlarged proportions.[32]

Preston believed that, if slavery's purpose under God's hand had been to civilize a previously uncivilized race, it had achieved its predestined aim to the extent that "every particular of American civilization possessed by the white man is shared by the black. He uses the same speech, dresses after the same fashion, lives under the same laws, and accepts the same religion, the same code of morals, and the same organization of domestic and social life."[33] Furthermore, "there is no crime nor immorality peculiar to the colored race, and only two found among the whites, from which they are exempt—they never commit suicide, and they never fight duels."

The blacks were no more fanatical or superstitious now than their white counterparts. And they were free of what Preston regarded as "the great threatening evil of modern times—Scepticism," considering their devotion to God.[34] Their religion was refreshingly simple and based on the obvious interpretation of the Bible.

In their loyalty to America, African immigrants were not hampered in the way that most European immigrants retained allegiances to the lands of their forefathers. Irish, German, Scot, and even English descendants still celebrated their homes of origin. But the African, no longer African, was an American, "nothing but an American."[35]

Preston offered statistical support that in 1863 there were 84,000 Negroes who had not owned—indeed could not own—anything in Georgia. But in fifteen short years through their own ingenuity they now owned in 1878 half a million acres of land.[36] It was valued for taxes at $1.2 million with city property worth $1.8 million. The aggregate total—including horses, mules, hogs, cattle, and other property not enumerated—was almost $6 million.

In Preston's own county of Rockbridge, he reported that one-third of its 6,000 inhabitants were blacks, who owned "$50,000 of real estate, and $10,000 of personal property."[37] They paid their assessed taxes, only 16 percent of which was returned insolvent. Among many of the Negro's advances overall in the country, these typical examples in Georgia and Rockbridge County led Preston to conclude that, as bona fide property owners, the blacks had a real and well-earned stake in society.

Preston's article was written more than a decade after the Civil War by a Southerner intended for Northern readers. Published in the *New Englander and Yale Review*, it was hailed by the editor of the *Review* as a "trustworthy account of the condition of the colored population of the South."[38] Henry Fairchild, the distinguished president of Berea College in Kentucky, the first interracial college in the South, fully supported Preston's assessment. He was quoted in the *Review* as agreeing, "It gives me pleasure to express my accord with almost the whole of this article."

One proof that the slaves of Rockbridge County were prepared both educationally and spiritually for their immediate emancipation was the Sunday school that Jackson and Preston had supervised in Lexington. Slave Sunday schools had existed in Virginia since 1750. In 1845 William Ruffner had established the first colored Sabbath school in Lexington at the Presbyterian Church.[39] His Sunday school served about 100 slaves but languished after he left in 1848. It was reestablished in 1856 when Maggie suggested the idea to Jackson.[40] Instead of missionary efforts overseas, Jackson preferred evangelizing slaves in America, despite the Fugitive Slave Law that made it illegal to educate them.

Jackson began with fifty slaves on his roll. He was aided by Preston, Maggie, and his wife Anna. They focused initially on oral instruction, since only a few of the older slaves had been taught to read. Many of their pupils, aided by their mistresses at home, learned by heart *Brown's Child's Catechism* and eventually were accepted into church membership. When Major Jackson was called into service at the outbreak of war in April 1861, Preston was also conscripted. But much of Preston's service involved preparing cadets at VMI, which allowed him to cover in Lexington as superintendent of the Sabbath school.[41]

Despite the fact that attendance at the school was now voluntary rather than mandatory, the turnout actually increased to around 150. Preston's primary emphasis was on teaching the children to read. He expanded the lessons to include the life of Christ, Old Testament history and the commandments, the New Testament parables and miracles, the Lord's Prayer, and the Creed.

Preston and the teachers he recruited sustained the school for more than twenty-five years. By then it had achieved its purpose and was no longer needed. Maggie would remark, "When the sessions of the school came to a final close, it would not have been easy to find anywhere a white Sunday school in which the pupils gave greater evidence of comprehensive biblical knowledge."[42]

Many visitors to the school were amazed at the depth of understanding the children showed of systematic theology. The success of the school served to confirm Preston's favorite axiom of education that "there is scarcely any height to which you cannot conduct your pupils, if you will only make the step short enough."[43] He believed in making the lessons as thorough as the minds of his pupils could handle, and their hunger for education generally matched the challenge.

When the school closed in 1887, three African American churches were created in Lexington, two of which still exist today.[44] Many pupils from the Sabbath school became members, including young men who went abroad for further instruction and became ministers to their own people. In 1895, Lylburn Liggin Downing became pastor of a small congregation, a post he would hold successfully for forty-two years.[45] Remembering his childhood in Lexington, he began raising funds for memorial windows "as a tribute to the memory of Stonewall Jackson and Col. J.T.L. Preston" in what would become the Fifth Avenue Presbyterian Church of Roanoke.[46]

Although born the day after Jackson's wounding at Chancellorsville, Downing had heard his parents speak often of their conversion to Christ in the Sabbath school and Jackson's "efforts to teach Christianity to the slaves and free blacks."[47] And after the war, Downing himself had attended the school where for years Col. Preston was his superintendent. So in 1906, the 50th anniversary of the beginning of the Sabbath school in Lexington, and on May 10, the anniversary of Stonewall's death, three stained-glass windows, which he himself had designed, were finally installed.

Downing dedicated the central window to his parents' teacher, displaying a view

Stained-glass commemorative windows at the 5th Avenue Presbyterian Church in Roanoke, Virginia, before it burned. The window in the center memorialized Stonewall Jackson, and the window to the left honored Col. J.T.L. Preston (courtesy of the Rev. Russ Merritt).

of the Shenandoah River and Valley above Jackson's last words inscribed on a scroll. He devoted the smaller window on the right to Preston and the window on the left to Dr. and Mrs. James I. Brownson, who had assisted him through college. Unfortunately, the wooden church burned in 1959, and the windows honoring Preston and Brownson were lost. But the window commemorating Jackson remains in the rebuilt brick church as a testament to the man Downing credited for his family's Christian heritage. Correspondingly, the Preston window was a memorial to the man who had taught him to read and from whom he "received the inspiration to become a minister of the Gospel."[48]

26

Beyond the Sunset

If individuals die, the race survives. Look at the forest ... the generations of vernal leaves and summer bloom and autumn wealth, is gone; but the trees abide.
—J.T.L. Preston

In the months subsequent to the war Preston spent as much time as he could afford indulging in his love of nature. He and Maggie would take "delightful rambles" to Cave Spring, stopping by the ruins of old Liberty Hall. At 5:30 in the morning they would gallop on horseback "over the misty hills and down into the little green shaded glens, under overhanging branches, all sparkling with silvery dew." And after dinner they would walk to the cliffs on the North River, serenaded by grasshoppers and katydids, to watch the sun set behind the mountains, then "saunter home just in time to have coffee" in the library.[1]

To satisfy his love of the chase, Preston borrowed books on hunting from the Franklin Society's library. He read *Hunter's Feast* by the naturalist Mayne Reid, describing camping and tracking on the prairie. He learned from Colonel William Hutchinson's *Dog Breaking* about breeding, rearing, and training dogs and identifying different breeds for hunting. He had always kept dogs around the house not only for his own but for his children's enjoyment. "Nothing is so companionable on a walk as a dog," he admitted, "and nothing half so acceptable" to children.[2] He knew enough about dogs to recommend a Newfoundland or Scotch collie as better for a child than a hunter's pointer and would not endorse a terrier.

Preston's dogs, according to one observer, "were among the best trained in the community and he even experimented with cross breeding to the extent that some of his animals were savage watch dogs which served as ample protection around his home."[3] He relished the works of Henry William Herbert, one of the best sports writers of the day, whose books under the pseudonym *Frank Forester* linked hunting with horsemanship. And for recreation he and son John, now twelve, would join parties of hunters with their hounds, driving foxes from the coverts in the woods and fields.

The year 1866 found Preston on the lecture circuit. At the reopening of the Franklin Society, which had been closed during the war, he gave a speech before a large audience at the Presbyterian Church, in which he recounted the history of "Lexington Fifty Years Ago."[4] He began by transporting his listeners—beyond "memory's horizon" for most of them—back to 1816, the year that the arsenal was built. At that time he himself was scarcely five, and the town's population was hardly more than 600 inhabitants.

He spoke of the layout of Lexington when it was a charming hamlet of twenty-seven acres, clustered beyond the spire of a single Presbyterian church set in a large oak-shaded cemetery. The entire hill east of Ann Smith Academy and south to the

"The Hunter is Home from the Hill." This rare photograph of the old Colonel, dressed in his Confederate uniform and sporting a full white beard, was discovered, after years of searching, in 1948 in a citizen's home in Lexington. Taken in 1865, it shows John T. L. Preston (seated) and surrounded by other members of a hunting party. Standing, left to right, are Walsh Shields, Matt Pettigrew, Barton McCrum, and Dudley McDowell. Seated left to right are Joe White, Mayor J. W. Houghawout, and twelve-year-old John A. Preston. Dr. Leslie Lyle Campbell, one of Preston's pupils at Washington and Lee, found the photograph in the home of Margaret Bledsoe, daughter of Barton McCrum, and had it published in the *Rockingham County News*. See "Picture of Col. J.T.L. Preston Is Found After Long Search," *Rockbridge County News*, March 18, 1948 (Virginia Military Institute Archives, No. 0000237).

Grove was nothing more than "a corn-field." There was perhaps no safer environment for young children and caring parents than this small town. The farthest any member of a family had to travel for water for drinking, cooking, and washing was a short walk pulling "barrels on low sleds" to "the back spring and the pump." For the young men and girls, he described the schools that he and his friends attended, the sports they played, clothes they wore, and parties, dances, and balls they frequented. And for the elders he related the history of the Franklin Society and its library, what its members read and debated, and who they were.

He ended his historical tour of the town with the nostalgic thought that fifty years is "a long, long while," during which entire generations pass away. Being units in a long series, generations allow for individuals to die while the race survives. "Look at the forest," he gave as evidence. "See the trees clothe themselves with greenness, bloom in beauty—hang rich with fruit, then grow pale, and presently stand leafless and drear. The generations of vernal leaves and summer bloom and autumn wealth, is gone; but the trees abide. So we are passing away, and soon will be no more; but the community of which we now constitute the strength, will rejoice in the new strength of those who take our places."

Following so soon on the heels of defeat in a great civil war, his lecture acknowledged the desolation and ruin that still surrounded the older and younger members of his audience after a terrible storm. But he urged them, like their ancestors who had built Lexington from scant means, to live not for themselves but for "those who are to come after us." Quoting Tennyson's recently published "Ulysses" and speaking directly to "our great sorrow," he offered his audience enduring hope in the midst of their abject despair:

> Come, my friends!
> 'Tis not too late to seek a newer world,
> Push off—and sitting well in order—smite
> The sounding billows....

In May 1866, a year after the war's end and three years after Jackson's death, the Graham Philanthropic Society invited Preston to lecture at Washington College on General Jackson. As a professional colleague and personal friend of Jackson, Preston had often been asked since his death what sort of teacher he was, so he spoke to the college on "General Jackson as a Professor."[5] There was a longstanding debate over whether Jackson was "a man of only moderate ability" or "a man of first-rate mind."

Focusing on Jackson's intellect, Preston admitted that "a moderate man may be raised to the head of an army, and may be in command when a great victory is achieved." But "a moderate man cannot plan and accomplish, unbroken by a single failure, a series of successes so grand as to command the admiration of the world." Having served as Jackson's chief of staff, Preston knew from personal observation that "in governing men, whether individuals or masses, General Jackson was supreme." His career left no longer open the question of his genius as a commanding general. "He governed by personal authority—by the gift of government bestowed on him by God."

So what sort of teacher was he? Preston recalled that on Jackson's arrival at VMI, he was assigned "the most difficult department of instruction in the whole college, natural philosophy." Here were taught mechanics, optics, acoustics, and astronomy. In this department, the two complements of knowledge—the practical and the theoretical—stood in starker contrast than in any other department of the curriculum. The practical dealt with mechanical instruments and the manual dexterity to handle them, and the theoretical concerned higher mathematics. Preston contended that where Jackson was deficient was in the practical branch of knowledge. This was the experimental part of his course, which most college students considered understandable and interesting and for which they had a certain aptitude. But he lacked the practical eye "for minute mechanics, and was inept, nay clumsy, in handling instruments."

On the other hand, where he excelled was in theory, because it required nothing more than "conscientious labor." In this branch of knowledge college students were weak. Even in a good class of students, "some never get a just idea of the calculus—more are superficial in their knowledge of it." Indeed, only a few acquired enough proficiency in calculus, as a result of hard labor and a natural aptitude for mathematics, that they could even apply it. So in every class of natural philosophy, Preston concluded, "some fail outright, all sweat over their work, and almost all are disposed to grumble at once at the subject and the professor, if he is faithful in his exactions." Jackson was a master of the theoretical: "In those larger mechanics upon which depends the movement of troops, and ordnance, and the transportation of supplies, his promptness and fertility of resource was amazing." Preston quoted an experienced railroad employee who said of Jackson he was "the only general he had met with who understood how to make full use of railroads in transporting troops."

Preston defined Jackson's relation to his students: "Where he was strong his class was weak, and he was not excellent, where some of them were very clever. They were disinclined for substantial reasons to his unmitigated mathematics, and many of them could beat him in experimenting. Nor was he a professor to make a hard subject easy." He was inflexible to the extent that "if a pupil did not apprehend a question, and asked to have it repeated, he gave it to him the second time in the precise words in which he had propounded it at first." He lacked the "ornate diction or sparkle of fancy" that attracted the young.

This was not to say that Jackson couldn't be really eloquent on great occasions when a few words instilled with power "are more impressive than a basket-full of tropes." But these occasions did not belong to the classroom. Preston reminded his audience of the instance "when a few sentences uttered by him to the Corps of Cadets, just at the period of Lincoln's Proclamation, made the hall in which they were assembled ring to its rafters with enthusiastic acclamations. And again, a few words spoken from horseback, when taking what he supposed was a final leave of the First Brigade, at Centreville, produced the electric effect of heaven-born fire."

Jackson had fully expected to return to teaching at VMI and was actually preparing some new textbooks for his courses. But Preston concluded, "It is not my opinion that he would ever have become very distinguished as a professor." The mark of a first-rate teacher is his ability to impart practical knowledge through the medium of books. The aim is not that students accumulate knowledge for its own sake but that their minds be trained and their whole characters be developed and invigorated. The best teacher, he insisted, is the "instructor who imparts in a permanent way, the greatest amount of useful knowledge." He must be a master of his subject but ought also to have a wide range of associated learning for use as illustration.

He doesn't have to be original, Preston remarked, "in fact the best teachers are the eclectics." Instead, he exists as a transferor, not a creator: "a sort of merchant, who moves literary commodities from marts where they have accumulated, to points where they are needed. In one particular the business of teaching has a dwarfing effect. The teacher is always dealing with minds, for the time being, inferior to his own, and thus never puts out the maximum of his powers. Doubtless with every one who has taught, the most constant feeling is regret that his pupils are not sufficiently mature for the full range of his subject."

"Mere teaching," Preston concluded, "is a secondrate profession. It has always been considered so, and must be acknowledged to be so, by all who have the candour to admit, that to prepare others to act, is inferior in dignity to acting oneself." Jackson was a master in first-class work, as all the world knew, but in second-class work he was "excelled by some fitted by nature in an eminent degree for the professor's chair, but for nothing beyond." It was true that Jackson faithfully fulfilled "the intermediate work assigned to him by Providence." But Providence didn't prepare him "for the ultimate purpose of teaching mechanics and optics, or even of training the choicest youth of the Old Dominion" to become future soldiers in her hour of need. He himself was destined instead to become "a leader, a defender—the pride of the Confederacy, the terror of our foes, the admiration of Europe."

In 1869, toward the end of a period of numb relief and slow healing from the intense life of wartime, the Prestons were struck yet again with loss and sorrow. Frank, at twenty-eight was arguably the most highly gifted of Preston's sons. His sister Libbie claimed, "Of all father's children he was the most fascinating to all sorts and conditions of people, 'grave and gay, lively and serene.' He danced, played cards, gave wine parties (though not the least dissipated), but loved his kind so truly, and had such a sweet seriousness underlying it all, was so cultivated, so witty, so tactful, so unselfish, that he was irresistible, and alas ! very susceptible."[6]

Much like his father, he was the intellectual who benefited less in college from the instruction of his professors than from the experiences he had outside school. William Ruffner claimed he "spent his college term in boyish fun" rather than the pursuit of learning and "graduated low in his class." But after serving on the faculty of VMI, he "bent all the energies of his mind to the study of languages," English, Greek, and Latin at the University of Virginia and German at Berlin University, preparing himself for his father's profession in teaching. He returned to his alma mater Washington College as assistant professor of Greek. In nine years he distinguished himself as "the best linguistic scholar of his age in Virginia."[7] He had just been appointed to the chair of Greek and German at William and Mary College for the fall of 1869.[8] But he contracted a sudden cold, coupled with a persistent cough that he had lived with since before the war, and was unexpectedly diagnosed with an incurable tubercular infection. After a few weeks he died on November 19.

Frank's death was the crowning blow that plunged Preston into a great sadness, having now lost three sons in the prime of their youth and manhood. He wrote his close friend Francis Smith, "Dear General, Sorrow with me. I have lost my son. A telegram from Richmond last night brought the intelligence. Please send word to Barracks, why I do not meet my Bible Class. JTLP."[9] Robert E. Lee suspended all classes at Washington College, where Frank had taught as associate professor of Greek. He praised Frank as a "brilliant scholar, trained in the best German universities, and a gentleman in the highest sense of the word." He had "served his state in the late war, and had left an arm on the heights of Winchester." Lee announced the institution's "deepest sorrow" and his own high esteem for Frank: "Endowed with a mind of rare capacity, which had been enriched by diligent study and careful cultivation, he stood among the first in the state in his pursuit in life."[10]

For Maggie, coming off the death of her father the year before, 1869 was fraught with sorrow. Her father had lived a complete life at seventy-seven, but Frank was snatched away at the very beginning of a bright career. It took a "year of tears," she would confess in the poem she wrote to come to terms with Frank's premature death. Only at the end of a prolonged period of grieving could she begin to picture with certainty his

> Year of progress in the lore
> That is not learned on earth.

She took solace in the realization that now his questioning mind,

> Unclogged of clay, and free to soar,
> Hath left the realms of doubt behind.
> And mysteries which thy finite thought
> In vain essayed to solve, appear
> To thine untasked inquiries fraught
> With explanation strangely clear.[11]

Not until the waning days of 1870 would Maggie thank God for "a year of mercies." During that year there were no serious sicknesses, no death, and no calamities with which to contend. By 1870, Tom, for reasons of health, had left his role as chaplain in the military and begun fourteen years of service as pastor of the First Presbyterian Church in Richmond. John was just entering Washington College. The youngest boys, George and Bert, had reached school age, leaving Maggie time enough to review books and to publish her first collection of 100 poems, *Old Song and New*, at her own expense on August 27, 1870. It became for her the "event of the day," since she had doubted in all modesty the worth of her poetry to a general public, calling it her "waifs and estrays of the past years."[12] She and Preston spent the year selecting and rejecting which poems she would include from among her many sonnets, ballads, poems from Hebrew and Greek stories, and war lyrics.

But the respite of mercies would have its inevitable end. As if a parent's loss of four of his eight natural children were not enough for Preston, 1873 witnessed the death of a fifth. Phoebe was the child that Maggie had described in her poetry as "rare-ripe, with rich, concentrate sweetness, all girlish crudities subdued." She stood at thirty-one "in the completeness of [her] consummate womanhood." She was the child who had matured through a combination of fierce heats, slant rains, and rude buffets of the wind that fill "bounteous grapes with wine." Sustained and strengthened in turn by joy and sorrow, she had "found the perfect poise of woman, the pivot balance of her soul!" Maggie had foreseen that she would face with "inviolable calm" whatever balm or bitterness the future might bring.[13] Indeed, Phoebe had lost her first love, McDowell Reid, to typhoid fever. She lost her fiancé, Lieutenant William Cocke, when he perished at Gettysburg. She married his brother Edmund Randolph Cocke in 1871, but two years later, standing at thirty-three on the cusp of motherhood, she herself died. The sole bright hope in her passing lived in the birth of her child, for Sally Lyle Preston Cocke survived.[14]

Preston found Phoebe's death particularly hard to face alone. Vividly reviving painful memories of his wife Sally's identical death fifteen years earlier, the loss of

Phoebe left him emotionally dependent on Maggie to lighten his depression. She understood and empathized with his melancholia. She had composed a poem in *Old Song and New* that spoke directly to his struggle against the mounting burdens of aging and despondency. In "Afternoon" she had voiced his gravest concerns at threescore years in the twilight of his life:

> You say the years have sadder grown
>   Beneath their weight of care and duty,—
> That all the festive grace has flown
>   That garlanded their earlier beauty.
>
> You tell me Hope no more can daze
>   Your vision with her bland delusions;
> Nor Fancy, versed in subtle ways,
>   Seduce you to her gay conclusions.

But holding up to him his inviolate past, she pronounced it clear of false glitter and bitterness. He had tasted the best that life could offer, aware all along that the blissful hours of youth were transitory. Advising him with as much encouragement as her heart could muster, she concluded,

> The sun slopes slowly westering still,
>   Behind you now your shadow lengthens,
> And in the vale beneath the hill
>   The evening's growing purple strengthens.
>
> The morning mists that swam your eye,
>   Too vaguely wrapped your young ideal:
> Now,—cut against your clearer sky,
>   You comprehend the true—the real.
>
> Life still has joys that do not pall,
>   Love still has hours serene and tender
> 'Tis afternoon, dear! ... that is all!
>   And this is afternoon's calm splendor.[15]

27

Brigadier General and Doctor of Laws

While deeply appreciating the honor thus tendered him, he returned the commission ... stating that he did not feel worthy of the honor proffered him.
—J.T.L Preston's grandson,
Edmund Randolph Preston

Libbie's marriage to Colonel William Allan in 1874 marked a turning point in Preston's hopes for the future. A close family friend and eleven years Libbie's senior, Colonel Allan had served as Jackson's chief ordnance officer and then under General Ewell before joining Washington College as professor of applied mathematics.[1] He left Lexington for Baltimore in 1873 to found the McDonogh School for poor boys of good character. He named the school after New Orleans millionaire John McDonogh, who endowed it. Libbie's marriage was the beginning of Preston's and Maggie's spending the next fifteen summers in Colonel Allan's home on the McDonogh campus. Preston was thoroughly impressed with the school, where fifty to 150 boys thrived in a healthy, upright, and happy environment that served many of the same goals as VMI.

"I have been a schoolmaster for almost half a century," he confided to Libbie, "but I have never seen such splendid management and training and teaching in my life, as your boys get here from Colonel Allan." The school was located on 800 acres of fields, woods, and streams that were intended for the agricultural training of the boys. Here could be found the peace and happiness that left all worries behind. Frequently the McDonogh boys would see Colonel Preston's "erect figure, dressed in the Confederate gray he always wore, striding over the McDonogh hills at daylight, his trousers stuffed in his boots cavalry fashion, and in his hand a posy of wild flowers for the old sweetheart's breakfast plate."[2]

He and Maggie devoted much of their time throughout 1873–74 to a project very close to heart: the construction of a Presbyterian outpost chapel. They had it built for the dock workers of East Lexington. Designed by Preston in the Gothic board-and-batten style, it was named after Maggie's *Beechenbrook,* the sales of which actually funded its construction.[3] Preston's son Tom preached the dedication service on May 17, 1874.

At sixty-three Preston was growing more and more dependent on Maggie for his happiness, just as she was drawing closer to him. During these elder years they were rarely seen apart. In fact, when a Lexington woman suggested to Maggie that she couldn't be happy in Heaven without Colonel Preston, she readily agreed and wrote a sonnet, "We Two," which confirmed in her own mind their inseparability and echoed Preston's enduring conviction that the two of them were actually one.

Beechenbrook Chapel in 1969. It was designed and built by J.T.L. and Maggie Preston in 1874 (Washington and Lee University, Leyburn Library Special Collections, Rockbridge Historical Society MSS, Royster Lyle Papers).

> Ah, painful sweet! how can I take it in!
>   That somewhere in the illimitable blue
>   Of God's pure space, which men call heaven, we two
> Again shall find each other, and begin
> The infinite life of love, a life akin
>   To angels,—only angels never knew
>   The ecstasy of blessedness that drew
> Us to each other, even in this world of sin.
>
> Yea, find each other! The remotest star
>   Of all the galaxies would hold in vain
> Our souls apart, that have been heretofore
>   As closely interchangeable as are
> One mind and spirit: oh, joy that aches to pain,
>   To be together we two—forever more![4]

The publication in 1875 of Maggie's most successful poetry, *Cartoons: Little Pictures or Imaginary Conversations,* received fan letters from such highly respected authors and critics as Henry Wadsworth Longfellow, John Greenleaf Whittier, and Professors James A. Harrison of the University of Virginia and H. C. Alexander of Union Theological Seminary. Ever since her husband's support of *Beechenbrook* in 1866, her poetry "had approached rapidly its floodtide: the last twenty years of her life [were] marked nearly every lustrum with a golden milestone,—a volume of collected verse, into which she has gathered the sheaves of miscellaneous poems that had accumulated in the interval."[5] Her art was receiving accolades even abroad. England's Prime Minister William Gladstone applauded "on the floor of Parliament" her poem "Sandringham," which touched on the illness and recovery of the Prince of Wales. The Princess of Wales "had written a letter to the editor" of the London *Cosmopolitan* thanking him for her poem.⁶

Maggie filled her days with writing letters, book reviews, poems, and stories as well as verse for children—all this while also preserving jellies, jams, pickles, and sausage. Her friend Paul Hayne, the poet and literary critic, was astonished that she could find time for writing at all, considering the immense difficulties under which it was accomplished. He had to admit that he would have given up the pen long ago in disgust over the daily tasks that challenged her brain: "puddings and poesy, household pother and divine propulsion, pickles and pathos, preserves and passion, the peace of creative art (like an ocean of surface calm, with infinite action beneath) and the due care of potatoes and packthread, in a word, those 'prune and prism' ordinances attached to 'the domesticities,' what a tremendous aspect of hostility they necessarily maintain towards each other, and who—short of a miracle—can reconcile their conflicting claims? And yet, in a measure, you really do seem to have performed this very marvel, this apparent impossibility!"⁷

As if this weren't admiration enough, he added, "One might fancy from the numbers of your published poems—despite the manifold difficulties of publication too—that you were a lady of leisure, free as any summer 'butterfly in a bower,' instead of being, probably, the most industrious, indefatigable, accomplished housekeeper in Lexington, or even in broad Virginia!"⁸

While Maggie composed her poems between household demands, Preston taught, wrote, and lectured. Having given two speeches on Jackson, his role as professor and his Christian character, Preston was requested by the board of visitors to write a biography of Jackson. But John Moncure Daniel, editor of the Richmond *Examiner* and a relative of Preston, had already published a biography of Jackson in London in 1863, the year of his death.⁹ Even so, the Massachusetts Historical Society invited Preston during the 1880s to lecture in Boston "on the subject of Jackson's military strategy." Libbie recalled that at first he doubted the wisdom of accepting the invitation "when the ashes of the conflict were by no means cold." But he went regardless and was amazed and gratified "at the spirit of fairness and courtesy shown." His audience responded, "We never dreamed of such conditions—we discounted entirely the alleged discrepancy in numbers reported by the Confederate recorders." Each of his subsequent speeches in the North were similarly well received "with benefit both to speakers and hearers."¹⁰

One of Preston's last lectures at VMI was his address welcoming the cadets in 1876. It followed by several months his decision on June 26 to retire from teaching and as head of the Latin and English departments. At first the board of visitors sought to ascertain if, in his resigning, there was any "shade of discontent or dissatisfaction with the management of the institute." But when he assured them he was resigning at sixty-five for private reasons and had always given and would continue to give the institute his full support, the board reluctantly accepted his resignation. It expressed regret for the loss "of one who has been prominently connected with [VMI] from its establishment, who by his ability as an instructor, and by his purity and dignity of character has reflected honor upon the institute, and greatly contributed in elevating it to its present commanding position among the colleges of the country." In consideration of Preston's thirty-seven years of service, he was "unanimously appointed emeritus professor of Latin language and English literature for life."¹¹

The following year, twelve years after the war, the Virginia Legislature restored commissions to all the officers of VMI, including Preston. On June 30, 1877, the board of visitors ordered that Superintendent Smith be continued in grade of major general and that all professors in charge of independent departments would remain colonels "with the exception of Colonel Preston and Colonel Williamson," who had been "in the service of the state as professors of the Virginia Military Institute, since the foundation of the school." The board ruled that "the rank of brigadier general" be conferred upon Preston and Williamson.[12] Williamson was at once commissioned a general officer and served as such until his death. But characteristic of Preston, he declined the rank. His grandson would later explain, "While deeply appreciating the honor thus tendered him, he returned the commission with an appropriate letter [to Governor James L. Kemper] stating that he did not feel worthy of the honor proffered him."[13]

More important to Preston than a promotion in rank in the military was his election by the church as a delegate to the first world-wide Presbyterian Council.[14] It was set to convene in Edinburgh, Scotland, in July. The council furnished an opportunity for the Northern and Southern assemblies to form an alliance, based on fundamental principles of the sovereignty of God, the authority of the Scriptures, and the necessity of grace through faith in Christ.[15] At the gathering they would be encouraged to discuss all matters of common interest while preserving their independence and their separate creeds.

The format fully reflected Preston's philosophy of reconciliation and communication. He would spend the next seven years following his retirement in 1877 writing articles and book reviews for the *Southern Presbyterian Review.* His perspectives on religion, morality, and education had evolved over so many years that he was eminently capable of defending them as effectively to a trusting as to a skeptical audience. "He had an infinite knowledge of the Bible," as his grandchildren recalled. "His prodigious memory served him well," for he "could quote at any length from the Bible" and "pages of Latin and Greek poets" in their original languages.[16]

Preston must have suspected, however, even when he retired, that he could not totally abandon his first love of teaching. When he was asked, as emeritus, to return to part-time teaching at VMI on July 1, 1879, he offered to instruct three sections for half the annual pay of $1,000. And by 1881 he was teaching three daily recitations of Latin five days a week to First, Second, and Third Class sections of eight to nine members each. At the time, other professors of Latin at VMI were facing disappointing results. Colonel Scott Ship reported that he had "never taught a section in which attendance was so irregular and progress so unsatisfactory." Absences from his recitations were thirty percent, some calling in sick but most away without leave. Similarly, Colonel John Patton reported that, with one exception, progress had been "very slow in every respect."[17]

It would have been hard for anyone, no matter how proficient, to compete with Preston at this stage in his teaching career. Self-confidence colored his manner with an imperious cast that would inspire awe in younger and less experienced members of the faculty. In addition, students often judge their mentors as much by appearance as by intellect. Appearance alone, apart from Preston's other qualities as a teacher, would have given him a decided advantage in the classroom, as expressed by one of his favorite Latin authors:

> *Ellum, confidence, catus,*
> *Cum faciem videas, videtur esse quantivis preti,*
> *Tristis serveritas inest in voltu, atque in verbis fides.*[18]
> [To look at him, you would take him for a man of consequence.
> For he looks as grave as any alderman and talks like a judge.]
> —Terence

Preston's success as a professor was recognized in 1881 when he was honored by what was then known as Washington and Lee University. His alma mater awarded him the honorary doctor of laws degree.[19]

28

Finis Opus Coronat

I have fought a good fight, I have finished my course, I have kept the faith.
—2 Timothy 4:7

Preston would teach only one more year, having reached what he called "the birthday of limitation, the threescore years and ten."[1] He had come to view the seventies as the "sunset limit" of life.[2] Physically he was still "in full possession of his faculties of mind and body, having almost the sight and hearing of a young man, will and memory strong, perception keen, the whole man practically intact."[3] He still showed, what Paul Hayne considered, many of the qualities of "the human oak."[4] But at seventy-one he was determined to resign his place, "rather than leave it to others to find him less efficient than a younger man!"[5]

A further consideration, his own good health notwithstanding, was his wife's poor health. She was failing, particularly her eyesight and hearing. More and more she needed his constant companionship and care. Their marriage had thrived for a quarter century, and for their silver wedding anniversary, he gave her a silver box containing twenty-five silver dollars and a sonnet he'd composed:

> Five lustrums passed, of which each year
> Hath been a circlet pure and clear,
> Of steady splendor mildly bright,
> Stamped with the die of Love's delight,
> Full weight and standard, through & through,
> However tested, ringing true,
> No counterfeit, bearing assay,
> Serving the wants of every day.
> And Pleasure's handmaid when to rest,
> We add enjoyment's lawful zest,
> And ever something more beside,
> With those who need it to divide—
> So be the future, day by day,
> With thankful hearts, dear wife, we pray,
> On this our *Silver Wedding Day*.
> Augt. 3, 1882.[6]

At sixty-two, Maggie had begun to admit, as she confessed in a letter to her friend Paul Hayne, that she was "well nigh done out." She found herself resenting the flood of letters she was receiving from "every literary fledgling who writes a poem or a book" with the request that she "put it in shape for the press." She felt tormented by these intrusions on her time and energy, which her conscience wouldn't permit her to dismiss without a proper response. Then one man, whom she'd never met and never expected to meet, actually sent her a voluminous translation, asking that "she revise it for the press," as he wanted it handsomely illustrated. "I haven't read a page of it yet," she protested, "and if I don't do this, he will be offended. Invariably I find this is the case." A lady from Kentucky sent her "the merest doggerel" and asked her "to sell it for her." Accompanying it with seven photographs she'd taken, she asked Maggie to "send all to her." In addition, a Virginia woman wanted a glowing review of the book she sent, which she said would assure its sale in Maryland.[7]

Both Maggie and Preston were in desperate need of a break, which Preston had been proposing since 1877 as a trip to Europe. As early as 1861 he had voiced his promise to take her over the sea.[8] Now in 1884 the time had come when he at seventy-three and she at sixty-four—in the autumn of their lives—needed the rejuvenation of an "Indian summer" before winter set in. Too old together to make the trip alone, Preston arranged for their eldest son, George, now a young doctor at twenty-six, and Maggie's widowed youngest sister and confidante Julia to accompany them, along with the families of her brothers George and William Junkin.

For Maggie this would be the rarest and purest pleasure she had ever known. She called it her "golden summer" from mid–June to mid–October, when she would visit all the places she knew from her reading far better than many a traveler who went abroad and stood where she would stand without understanding or appreciating what he actually saw. "Don't show me," she would caution her guide, "let me find that grave— or bust—or picture—myself." Then replacing the guide, she'd straightway lead the group to the intended spot. As Libbie recalled, "Her whole life seemed to have been a preparation for that one golden summer, and she enjoyed it to the full."[9]

Maggie's letters to the Hayne abounded with unqualified joy at seeing firsthand the heavenly beauty of England's Lake Country, the grand ruin of Furness Abbey, Wordsworth's and Southey's hilly green Ambleside, the lovely little gem of Grasmere Lake, Wordsworth's and Coleridge's graves, Shakespeare's home, the grand Christ College, the galleries of the Bodleian Library at Oxford, the recesses in Westminster Abbey, and the immortal collections in the National Gallery. The party entered Switzerland via Schaffhausen at the fall of the Rhine and visited enchanting Lucerne, climbed Alps upon Alps up to Hospenthal, St. Gothard Pass, and then through the most dangerous pass at Tête Noir to Chamonix at the foot of Mt. Blanc. There she recited Coleridge's hymn to "thy bald, awful head, oh sovran Blanc!" The group toured Calvin's haunts, his cathedral and home in Geneva, and then to Paris, which she appreciated less than London, not being enthused "by French emotions."[10]

On their return to Lexington in October, Maggie declared her golden summer "over and gone." But she conceded, "my picture gallery of memory is hung henceforth with glorious frescoes which blindness cannot blot or cause to fade."[11] Both she and Preston were aglow with all the excitement that four months abroad had contributed to reinvigorate their lives. In fact, no sooner was Preston back in Lexington than he was teaching again, this time as professor of belles lettres ad interim at his alma mater.[12] The Rev. Dr. John L. Kirkpatrick, former president of Davidson College in North Carolina, who taught the literature course at Washington and Lee, was suffering from what turned out to be a terminal illness. So Preston agreed to take his class.

One member of the class, who considered himself fortunate to study under Preston, was twenty-year-old Leslie Lyle Campbell. Although the book for the course was Hippolyte Taine's *History of English Literature*, "Colonel Preston did not lecture," Campbell declared. "He held a colloquium. He quietly drew the circle of students around him as he did the circle of hunters years ago. The quiet, reverent circle of boys were held bound together by the immortal spirits in English literature."[13] Years later, at age eighty four, it was Dr. Leslie Campbell who would discover in a Lexington home one of the rare photographs of his teacher on a fox hunt.

At the end of the academic year, Campbell attended Washington and Lee's commencement, where Preston was asked to read his wife's *Centennial Poem for Washington and Lee: 1775–1885*.[14] Campbell recalled how Preston read it with the same "quiet dignity of body and voice" that he'd shown in class. Maggie had closed her poem with a passionate expression of former President Lee's command to his troops, which was no longer directed to soldiers in surrender but to students expected to honor it:

> Ye will not walk ignoble ways;
> Ye dare not seek unworthy aims;
> Ye cannot do a deed that shames
> These heroes of our holiest days!
> Your oath a Roman oath must be,
> Sworn with a faith that will not yield;
> Sworn on the doubly sacred shield
> of WASHINGTON AND LEE![15]

"Ever since that poem was heard," Campbell recalled from Preston's reading, "there have re-echoed in the depths of our soul, the sacred words: 'Ye will not walk ignoble ways.'"[16] It was the last year that Preston would teach in an academic setting.

The year 1885 found Preston enjoying retirement. Content to remain at home, he was often seen sitting on his front porch, especially when the warm summer months arrived. His friend William Ruffner described this period of his stationary life. Preston's mind "was too full of resources, and his home too happy for him to have any craving for travel. He looked at the Tower of London, and at Mont Blanc once or twice, but in general he would rather go with Huck and the hounds for a week's hunt in the mountains, than visit objects far away." Ruffner added, "I once found him sitting on his shady front porch in his summer vacation, and asked him if he were not going to take a trip somewhere. 'Why should I take a trip?' he replied. 'There is not another place in the world as pleasant to me as just where I am sitting.'"[17]

In 1889 Preston spent his last summer at the McDonogh School in Baltimore. He knew that on the 4th of July his friend Francis Smith would be announcing his retirement after fifty years as superintendent of VMI, effective at year's end. So he carefully composed a letter to "my dear General and old-time comrade." He began it by saying, "*Finis opus coronat*: the crown of a worthy work is its successful completion. How unspeakably precious is this crown when the work is one's life work!" He praised Smith's work as twofold: "first in rearing a noble structure upon its foundation and then in raising it from its ruins." The state of Virginia, successive boards of visitors, and hundreds of alumni would confirm his indispensable worth, including Preston himself, "who is the sole surviving sharer of your labors from the founding of the V.M.I. to its semi-centennial Jubilee."[18]

Preston placed above all Smith's many accomplishments the testimony of Smith's "own conscience." He declared, "You have never swerved from your purpose, nor spared yourself in your devotion to the object you had set before you." For that adherence to conscience, Preston envisioned for Smith a greater crown, "a crown not for the closing of this mortal life, but a crown for the opening of an immortal life, a crown to be worn forever." He closed affectionately, "May this crown, my old friend, be yours and mine! And for this hope let us unite in saying—Laus Deo!"[19]

While Preston was lauding his comrade's career, he was also fulfilling a formal request from the board of visitors. He was invited as the "only survivor of the original board" to render a "Historical Sketch of the Establishment and Organization of the VMI."[20] He had known the institute's history from the first inklings that the dream might become reality. Since Preston was in Baltimore, the board requested that his son, the Rev. Thomas Preston, read his father's sketch to celebrate the school's jubilee at its graduation exercises. Historiographer William Couper described the address as "one of the highlights in all institute history" by the man "who had more to do with advocating the establishment of the institute than any other man."[21] Preston prepared it on a typewriter which was first used at VMI in 1887, adding his corrections in ink.

It was in this sketch of VMI's history that Preston disclaimed "being the first to suggest the idea" of converting the arsenal, and he credited "the friends of the measure" for supporting its conversion to "a literary institution for the education of youths."[22] Summarizing the steps that were taken to create the school, he praised the first board of visitors for resisting the temptation "to take West Point as a model" and for adopting instead the goal of furnishing its "graduates for their personal benefit, and for the advantage of Virginia, an education" that was both classical and practical under a system of military discipline. He summarized that "the institute had prospered" wherever it adhered to these "fundamental principles" with the ultimate aim of graduating the ideal citizen-soldier.[23]

Then to demonstrate the extent to which the institute had succeeded or failed in its mission, he quoted from a special report that General Smith had given to Virginia Governor Frederick Holliday in 1881. "In the forty-two years just closed, forty classes embracing 3,470 cadets, have been admitted and of these 1,241 have graduated. The record shows 200 killed in battle, 175 professors and teachers, 135 civil and military engineers, 120 merchants, 94 farmers and planters, 59 physicians, 30 clergymen, and 19 bankers." Smith had added that after Virginia became "the first to establish a state military school, her example has since been followed by many of her Southern sisters."[24]

Preston credited the first board with having organized "a school for which they had but a partial model" and given it "staunch firmness with flexibility" that had allowed it "to meet conditions that could not be anticipated and which were, when they actually occurred, so critical that had the foundation been less broad and

General Francis H. Smith at retirement, photograph in 1889 by Michael Miley. Smith served as superintendent of Virginia Military Institute for fifty years (Virginia Military Institute Archives, No. 0000388).

strong the whole structure would have fallen in ruins." He concluded by praising the board's fortunate decision to place Francis Smith, "an earnest Christian man," at the helm of the institute.[25]

VMI historiographer William Couper then updated Smith's report of 1881 to 1889. He showed that in the fifty years since its founding, the institute had grown from a corps of thirty to over 200; from two professors to eight plus one emeritus, one adjunct, and six assistants; and from an annuity of $6,000 to $30,000.[26] Attending the jubilee were 500 "Old Boys," including Governors Fitzhugh Lee of Virginia and Simon Buckner of Kentucky. But also present were several of the seventeen alumni who had fought for the Union during the Civil War, one being Colonel John F. Tyler, Class of 1859.

To close the jubilee, the oldest living graduate of VMI, Colonel Edmund Pendleton from the first graduating Class of 1842, read Maggie's *Semi-centennial Ode for the Virginia Military Institute*.[27] She, like Preston, was in Baltimore, but Couper reported that Pendleton's reading of her stirring ode produced a powerful effect on those gathered to celebrate the day.[28] It commemorated the inspiring sight of battalions of cadets clad in gray uniforms and gleaming buttons, who performed each day like clock-work on the parade grounds, flanked by the castellated grace and strength of the Barracks' towers. It evoked the rousing notes of "Reveille" and the peaceful strain of "Taps," the rolling drums and lively fifes. It recalled Stonewall's victories and woeful death, the throb of New Market, Hunter's ploughing raid, and the return of "o'ermastered, beaten, ruined, lost" soldiers to a wrecked past but dauntless future. Describing the evening gun, the gaily lit Crozet Hall, and newly built structures memorializing Jackson and Smith, it recapped with nostalgic emotion all that had come to be associated with VMI during the fifty years since its inception.

For the institute, Maggie's ode presaged the end of an era, an era that would close with the passing of the two men who had nurtured it for half a century from its infancy to maturity. They would depart this life within four months of each other the following year. In their late seventies, both Preston and Smith were suffering bouts of poor health. Preston's body was failing, but his mind was still quite fertile. He composed his last two works while he was still physically able in 1889.

Published by the Presbyterian Committee in Richmond, they appeared under the instructional titles *Pulpit Manner, as Seen from the Pew* and *Removing to a New Charge: Letters to a Young Minister*. They offered practical advice to young ministers, whom he was always grooming for service to the church. The first offered suggestions that most authors of ministerial guide books would not even think to discuss, such as how a minister should dress and act before giving his sermon. But the second gave broader advice from the accumulated wisdom of a lifetime of experience on how to live a good and successful life. These two books, although written in 1888, would not appear until after Preston's death, as though spoken from the grave.

He and Francis Smith both died in 1890. Smith laid up his crown of glory at the age of seventy-seven on March 21, 1890, three months after his official retirement as superintendent. In declining health, Preston was unable to attend his friend's memorial service. Maggie, whose life was about to change drastically, was struggling to publish her last two books. But her husband fell into the last of several severe illnesses in January, which caused her considerable anxiety and focused all her efforts on nursing him.

After six months, as Libbie would write about her father, it was already apparent to the family during his final weeks that he was "leaving forever the beloved hills of his boyhood's and manhood's home." He lay on a couch on the covered upper porch, too weak for conversation, wishing to be alone, and "gazing in silence—a serene and radiant silence—at the beauty of earth and sky." When he did speak, Libbie remarked, "his manner was not only cheerful, it was often merry; and many a smile kept company with our restrained tears, at his witty speech."[29] By his couch lay his Bible and a biography of Sally's devout Calvinist uncle, *The Life of Archibald Alexander*, first professor and principal of Princeton Theological Seminary.

One morning near the middle of July he called his children and grandchildren together at breakfast and *"himself conducted family worship."* At his side were Tom, Libbie, George, and Bert, four of his five surviving children. His great-grandchild, Elizabeth Randolph Preston, was not yet six months old, but he insisted she be present. "Never mind if the darling is restless," he said. "I want her to share the blessing I am going to ask from our covenant-keeping God upon me and mine." In his capacity as a minister, Tom read a chapter from the Bible; Preston made his confession of faith, thanked God for "the goodness and mercy that had crowned his days," humbly acknowledged his sins, and voiced "his gratitude for God's goodness in saving such a worthless sinner." The family sang from the Scottish Psalter, "O God of Bethel, by whose hand thy people still are fed," shedding tears over the lines: "O spread thy cov'ring wings around, till all our wand'rings cease, And at our Father's loved abode our souls arrive in peace." The old patriarch made a final prayer, kissed each one of his family, including little Elizabeth, and returned to his couch on the porch "hardly to speak again on earth."[30]

A few days and nights later he expired at midnight, on Tuesday, July 15, 1890.[31] He was buried the following day in the family plot near the headstones of his Sally and five of their eight children, Edmonia, Phoebe, Frank, Willie, and Ran, who had all preceded him.[32] The hymn chosen for his funeral in the graveyard was George Frederick Root's "Shining Shore." The *Lexington Gazette* reported that the funeral "was largely attended by all classes of our citizens who in life loved and honored the man, and in death showed their love for him by following his silent bier to the grave."[33]

His gravestone bears the inscription:

AN OFFICER OF THE COMMONWEALTH,
OF THE CONFEDERATE STATES,
AND OF THE CHURCH OF CHRIST.

including the line from 2nd Timothy:

HE FOUGHT A GOOD FIGHT,
HE FINISHED HIS COURSE,
HE KEPT THE FAITH.[34]

And at the base of the stone is engraved what Preston always considered as "the signet legend on my heart,"

LAUS DEO.[35]

Epilogue

> *He possessed a tender, noble nature that enwrapped his rugged qualities as the Tuscan grape entwines and festoons the towering elm.*
> —Dr. James Harrison,
> University of Virginia

At seventy, Maggie was devastated by the loss of the husband of almost half her life. She wrote a friend in Maine, "To us who mourn our departed, and our lost treasures, earth seems a sad and dreary place; but then how many happy homes and happy hearts there are left in it for all!"[1] Maggie was never one to dwell long on what she had lost at the expense of what she still had.

For the town of Lexington, Preston's death was the close of an epoch. His life had spanned four-fifths of the nineteenth century, making him a figure familiar to all classes of the entire community, whose population now topped 3,000.[2] The *Roanoke Times* called him "one of the oldest, most influential and highly respected citizens of the community."[3] He would be remembered as "a man of iron will, strong personality, high character and lofty purposes."[4] His grandchildren would remember him as "a gaunt old man with piercing blue eyes, white of hair, almost stern of mien who could quote at any length from the Bible."[5] The *Lexington Gazette* honored their "oldest native born citizen" with the encomium, "Like a shock of corn, fully ripe, he has gone to his reward to receive a crown of glory from the Master's hand, with the plaudit: Well done, good and faithful servant, enter into the joy of your Lord."[6]

Dr. James Harrison of the University of Virginia assessed his qualities as those of

> a typical Virginia gentleman of the olden times: urbane, cultured, affable, aristocratic, straight as an arrow, passionately fond of dogs and horses and hunting, a great reader, stern and unyielding to wrong, proud as Lucifer in matters of personal honor, a genealogist of the first water, with a pedigree stretching far into Merrie England, every leaf and branch of which he had at his fingerends; he possessed a tender, noble nature that enwrapped his rugged qualities as the Tuscan grape entwines and festoons the towering elm.[7]

Harrison credited Preston for the streams of southern youth who had crowded the classrooms of VMI and for forty years had their edges "emeried and polished against this courteous, steadfast, virile incarnation of manly manhood, to their infinite benefit and enrichment." He described Preston's pervasive influence as "a power in the town, a power in the church, a power in the lecture-room, a power in his home."[8]

The Lexington Presbyterian Church, of which Preston was the oldest member and ruling elder for more than forty-seven years, issued a memorial that eulogized his character as unique: "His manners were dignified and somewhat reserved, but frank as his nature, which was candid and sincere. A man of decided convictions, strong will and inflexible integrity, he was indifferent to praise or censure in the maintenance of what he thought right, and his steadfast and manly profession and practice of the principles of the Gospel of Christ were notable. Intrepid by nature and conscious of right as a Christian, he was not timid in counsel and was decided in action."[9]

In recognition of Preston's reticence to seek fame in public office, the memorial observed, "Though descended from a race, many of whom held conspicuous public positions, and eminently qualified by natural gifts and classical culture to take rank in public station, he preferred the charms of home and the attractions of a scholastic life, in which he spent nearly half a century as a Professor in the Virginia Military Institute, meanwhile contributing valuable literary and religious essays to the press, under the well-known signature J.T.L."[10]

Ten days after Preston's death, the VMI Board of Visitors passed a resolution: "Resolved that this board laments the death of Colonel Preston as an irreparable loss to the institute and a calamity to the state, but the example of his heroic devotion to duty added to his ripe scholarship and Christian purity is a rich inheritance to the institution his wisdom and foresight founded and his life work aided in bringing to the high position it has attained in the rank of schools." It concluded, "Resolved that we commend the life and character of Colonel Preston to the cadets of this institute as one which may well be followed; for as an officer he was impartial and firm; as a professor he was able and just, as a Christian he was pure and gentle, and as a gentleman he was generous and true."[11]

Under Preston's will his estate was estimated not to exceed $27,700. It gave Maggie "for her sole use during her life his lots of land adjoining the fair grounds near Lexington," which amounted to almost nine acres.[12] It gave her all the household and kitchen property except for any silver, books, or pictures that weren't her private property, which were to be distributed evenly to her and the children. In addition, she was allotted annual dispersals of $1,300 for her support.

In terms of today's dollars the economic value of the estate would equal $5,150,000. Maggie's annual income of $1,300 would approach $242,000, and would appear ample and fair.[13] But the problem facing Maggie, as she described it, was the loss of her lovely home of thirty years, which was to be sold and developed into building lots. As she wrote a friend in Maine, this tearing up of such sacred ties "proved too much of an added sorrow, and resulted in a spell of nervous illness, which has laid me on my back ever since; even now I cannot walk."[14]

Why Preston didn't leave Maggie the family home is not stated, except that the will stipulated that his real and personal property was to be divided equally among his heirs. This meant that sons Tom and Herbert, as executors, had to sell the house along with the real estate. So on February 19, 1891, Henry H. Myers bought the Preston home for $6,860.[15] He tore it down, claiming the yellow brick walls had structural weaknesses, and he constructed on the original foundation the current red brick residence with Victorian features.[16]

Considering Maggie's severe loss of sight and hearing, the question arises whether she could have maintained such a large house, even with servants. Her health would have compelled her as an invalid to live under the care of her stepdaughter. She had planned to move to Baltimore to live with her physician son George and be near Herbert. But having suffered a stroke that paralyzed her on one side, she was confined to a wheelchair and couldn't risk the trip. So she moved in with Libbie and her children on Main

The J.T.L. Preston Family in 1890. Photograph in John A. Preston's yard at 208 West Washington Street (Virginia Military Institute Archives, No. 0002364).

Main Street, Lexington, looking south in 1890, photograph by Michael Miley (Washington and Lee University, Leyburn Library Special Collections).

The Preston family plot in Lexington's Stonewall Jackson Memorial Cemetery (photograph October 2, 2011, by the author).

Street. Rolled out daily to the large porch by her grandchildren, she was read to by ear trumpet and visited by neighbors and friends. She soon became the lively "center of this household," where she would remain for two years until strong enough to endure the long journey to Maryland.[17]

Despite the turmoil that accompanied the painful loss of her home, Maggie was asked to write an ode to celebrate the unveiling of Edward V. Valentine's bronze statue of Jackson, which now stands at the center of the Stonewall Jackson Memorial Cemetery. Her recent bereavement and precarious health precluded her composing a poem about her closest friend, but she offered instead the poem she'd written in her despair over Willie's death. "Slain in Battle" was read as she sat on her stepdaughter Libbie's front porch across the street from the graveyard.[18] Jackson's grandchildren, Julia and Jack Christian, pulled the cord on July 21, 1891, unveiling the figure of the man she so highly revered. It was five-year-old Julia who, sixteen years later, would marry Preston's grandson, Edmund Randolph Preston, uniting in blood what the Jacksons and Prestons had previously shared only in friendship.

In December 1892, George and Herbert arrived at last to escort Maggie on her dreaded journey to Baltimore. She would reside in George's country cottage with his charming German wife Emma and their young children George and Margaret. They were "cherubs beautiful enough," she bragged, "to have been models for Raphael—a constant source of enjoyment to me." She missed the beautiful mountains of Lexington, the forests, and the green pastures, for her room faced brick walls and housetops, and the streets were filled with throngs of strangers. But the children kept her occupied, when she wasn't dictating four or five letters a day. "They are very merry little things," she wrote to a Baltimore friend, "and it is not easy to be low-spirited or morose or despairing in their presence."[19]

The following year found her trying to reconcile herself to her physical sufferings. Still clinging to life, she feared dying. Death, she admitted, had always held her in bondage. But more significantly she feared paralysis, which hung, she wrote, like "the sword of Damocles suspended by a hair" over her head.[20] Although Maggie would live for three more years, her fear of becoming paralyzed would prove prophetic.

On March 24, 1897, she was indeed stricken with paralysis. But at the same moment that she lost consciousness, it was as though the blessed ending, for which she had always prayed but doubted as her fortune, were truly granted. A week later, on Sunday, March 29, seven years after her husband's passing, she breathed her last and sprang into the mysterious paradox of life and death that she had once described in a sonnet:

> But the day comes, when some mysterious power
> Dissolves imprisoning circumstance, and lo!
> The soul springs upward, an embodied breath,
> Exultant; and in that supremest hour,
> When earth's last filament is snapped, we know
> That what we heretofore called Life, was Death![21]

Professor James Harrison had known Maggie for almost a generation. In a passionate tribute written shortly after her death, he called her "the Poet-Laureate of Virginia." He compared her powerful personality and radiant optimism to that of Elizabeth Barrett Browning.

> No one could come in contact with this bright, spiritual creature without feeling a benign influence streaming out of her brilliant talk, coruscating as it did with humor and pleasant jest and witty anecdote. Slightly deaf as she appeared to be in her latter years, she heard everything that was essential: her intuition was perfect and her tact most delicate. Richly stored as her mind was with every sort of reading, familiar as it was with many European literatures, she never allowed these learned incrustations to overlay the sprightliness of her vivacious intellect and make a précieuse or a pedant of her.

Professor Harrison recognized her salient genius as "a writer of religious verse." Her scriptural poems had "given comfort to thousands" who benefited from her passionate faith in God and immortality, clad in melodious poetic form.[22]

Maggie was buried nearest one of the last great forest oaks that rises today after two centuries over the Preston family plot. In her honor it's known in *Notable Trees of Virginia* as the Margaret Preston Oak.[23] Preceded in death by both her stepsons Tom and John, she was survived only by her stepdaughter Libbie and sons George and Herbert. The *Lexington Gazette* reported that her funeral service at the Lexington Presbyterian Church was attended by the entire Corps of Cadets "as a mark of respect for the memory of her husband, whose whole life was spent as an honored professor at that institution."[24]

Inscribed on her gravestone were the words by which she would be remembered:

> HER SONG CHEERED THE HEARTS
> OF THE SOUTHERN PEOPLE IN THE
> HOUR OF THEIR DEEPEST DISTRESS.
> And they sing a new song
> Before the throne.
> Rev. 14:3[25]

The Preston Library in 1939. Exterior view taken after the building was completed but before the dedication on November 11 (Virginia Military Institute Archives, No. 0003172).

Virginia Military Institute cadets on parade (photograph September 30, 2011, by the author).

Maggie's poetry would honor her long after her passing. Preston too would be honored in 1901, when the VMI Board of Visitors directed then–Superintendent Scott Shipp "to have painted for the library portraits of the late Col. J.T.L. Preston, and General Thos. H. Williamson."[26] Preston's portrait would eventually hang in the new $300,000 library that was dedicated at VMI's centennial on November 11, 1939. Colonel William Couper, Class of 1904, suggested that the building bear Preston's name and that it be called the Preston Library instead of Preston Hall. He reasoned, "Thousands of people will see this building, the first which they pass on entering the grounds, and it would be of great value to a military institution to have the word LIBRARY prominently placed on such an impressive building."[27]

At the dedication of the library, Virginia Governor James H. Price stood in for President Franklin Roosevelt, who was prevented from attending by Germany's invasion of Poland. In his address, Governor Price cited "the unfolding of the Virginia Military Institute as a pathfinding experiment in education."[28] While admitting that "a great many people are fond of thinking about V.M.I. as the 'West Point of the South,'" he credited Preston for having foreseen "very real differences from those of West Point."

He praised the original board of visitors for recognizing those differences and establishing "three major objectives" that defined the school. "First, the educational content of its curriculum, while not discarding entirely the value of purely classical education, sought also to relate itself to the practical needs of the student in the course of his civil occupations." Second was "the thorough mastery of this purposely limited course" through a "tutorial system of instruction." And third was its system of "military discipline ... which teaches self-control, co-operation, regularity of habits, democracy of outlook, and which produces a sound mind and body."

He urged the school to "hold fast to its belief that the teachings of the institute should be closely and practically related to the business of life itself." And he concluded, "as Virginia's chief executive," by expressing "on this centennial day" his own appreciation of the institute for having "enriched and ennobled the lives of thousands of our young men" and having "rendered a service to the state and nation that has immortalized its name."

Despite the unavoidable absence of President Roosevelt from the ceremonies, Governor Price's remarks were supplemented with a congratulatory address from Roosevelt by telephone through the public address system. He declared what is now inscribed on the Citizen-Soldier Cincinnatus Monument, which has stood since 1983 in front of the Preston Library. It reads, "The whole history of VMI is a triumphant chronicle of the part which the citizen-soldier can play in a democracy." Also inscribed on that monument, however, is the warning that VMI's General George C. Marshall, Class of 1901, issued at the close of World War II: "The citizen-soldier is the guarantee against a misuse of power."

It was entirely appropriate that the citizen-soldier be championed in front of the Preston Library. Preston's words that defined the vision, mission, and goals of the institute have changed only by the substitution of "youths" for "men" after the 1996 Supreme Court order to admit women. In the estimation of current Superintendent J. H. Binford Peay, his words remain "as inspiring and as valid as they were when Preston wrote them in 1837 in defense of establishing VMI."[29]

During the 1980s the Board of Visitors formulated the current mission of VMI to reaffirm the historic mission of J.T.L. Preston:

> It is the mission of the Virginia Military Institute to produce educated and honorable youths, prepared for the varied work of civil life, imbued with love of learning, confident in the functions and attitudes of leadership, possessing a high sense of public service, advocates of the American democracy and free enterprise system, and ready as citizen-soldiers to defend their country in time of national peril.

Chapter Notes

Preface

1. Thucydides, *Pericles' Funeral Oration*, 430 BC.

Prologue

1. James Davidson, letter dated June 1864, in Bruce S. Greenawalt, "Life Behind Confederate Lines in Virginia: The Correspondence of James D. Davidson," *Civil War History* 16 (September 1970): 224.
2. Elizabeth Preston Allan, *Life and Letters of Margaret Junkin Preston* (Boston: Riverside Press, 1903), 183, June 7, 1864.
3. J.T.L. Preston, "An address delivered to the Corps of Cadets on the 7th anniversary of the Battle of New Market and the 10th anniversary of VMI's entry into the war," Lexington, Va., VMI Archives, Box: VMI Faculty and Staff, 19th Cent., Preston, John T. L., Folder 2.
4. After Hunter's invasion of Lexington, these canal boats were soon discovered and pillaged or destroyed by Union forces. See "Blue Tide Engulfed Lexington," *Withrow Scrapbook* 7: 74, Washington and Lee Special Collections.
5. Rose Page Pendleton, "General David Hunter's Sack of Lexington, Virginia, June 10–14, 1864: An Account by Rose Page Pendleton," ed. Charles W. Turner, *Virginia Magazine of History and Biography* 83, No. 2 (April 1975): 173–83. See also Cecil D. Eby, Jr., "David Hunter, Villain of the Valley: The Sack of the Virginia Military Institute," *Iron Worker* 28, No. 2 (Spring 1964): 1–9; *The War of the Rebellion: A Compilation of the Official Records of the Union and Confederate Armies* (Washington, D.C.: Government Printing Office, 1897), Ser. 1, 37, Pt. 1: 96–97; and William Couper, *One Hundred Years at V.M.I.* (Richmond: Garrett and Massie, 1939), 4: 22–42.
6. Allan, *Life and Letters*, 186 (June 8, 1864), 353. Like Edgar Allan Poe and Commodore Matthew Maury, Cadet John R. Thompson was later editor of *Southern Literary Magazine*.
7. Ibid., 189, Evening, June 11, 1864.
8. Ibid., 189–90, Sunday Morning, June 12, 1864.
9. Ibid., 191.
10. Pendleton, "General David Hunter's Sack of Lexington," 178.
11. Allan, *Life and Letters*, 191, Morning, June 12, 1864. The illness of Superintendent Smith's daughter, Frances Henderson Smith Morrison (wife of Capt. James H. Morrison) with two-day-old Francis was reported in letter of June 17, 1864, from Francis Smith to Gen. Richardson, VMI Archives, Superintendent's Outgoing Correspondence, transcribed by Diane Jacob.
12. Cornelia McDonald, *A Diary with Reminiscences of the War and Refugee Life in the Shenandoah Valley, 1860–1865* (Nashville: Cullom and Ghertner, 1934), 207. "Gen. Crook had his headquarters on a hill near me, in a large handsome house belonging to Mr. Fuller." See also 207 n. 39: "Mr. Jacob Fuller. After the war this house (Blandome) was the residence of Hon. John Randolph Tucker, professor of law at Washington College." Rose Page Pendleton claimed Gen. Jeremiah Sullivan headquartered here.
13. Rutherford B. Hayes, *Diary and Letters of Rutherford Birchard Hayes, Nineteenth President of the United States: 1834–1860*, ed. C. R. Williams (Columbus: Ohio State Archeological and Historical Society, 1922–26), 4: 473–74. Also quoted by John G. Barrett and Richard M. McMurry, "VMI in the Civil War," in Thomas W. Davis, ed., *A Crowd of Honorable Youths: Historical Essays on the First 150 Years of the Virginia Military Institute* (Lexington, Va.: Virginia Military Institute Sesquicentennial Committee, 1988), 41.
14. James Schoonmaker, as quoted in Thomas J. Arnold, *Early Life and Letters of General Thomas J. Jackson ("Stonewall") by His Nephew, Thomas Jackson Arnold*, 363–64. Otherwise, see "Col. S.[J.]M. Schoonmaker, A Union Officer and Gentleman," *Withrow Scrapbook* 7: 86, Washington and Lee Special Collections.
15. Schoonmaker, as quoted by John Follet, see "Alumnus Explains Old Shot in East Wall of Barracks: John D. Follet, '22, Adds to Story of Colonel Schoonmaker, Says Orders Were Not Disobeyed," *The Cadet*, April 25, 1932.
16. Ibid., 2. A plaque honoring Henry Algernon duPont hangs near the entrance of Jackson Memorial Hall. See also T. H. Harrel and L. M. Caperton, *Fragments of V.M.I. History* (Lexington, Va.: Virginia Military Institute, 1933), 9, and Couper, *One Hundred Years at V.M.I.* 1: 298–99.
17. Rose Page Pendleton, "The Yankees in Lexington," in Charles W. Turner, *Stories of Ole Lexington: A Sequel to Mrs. McCulloch's Stories* (Verona, Va.: McClure Press, 1977), 88.
18. Allan, *Life and Letters*, 191, June 12, 1864.
19. Ibid., 196, June 14, 1864.
20. Ibid., 192, June 13, 1864.
21. Ibid., 197, June 16, 1864.
22. Jubal Anderson Early, *Lieutenant General Jubal Anderson Early, C.S.A., Autobiographical Sketch and Narrative of the War Between the States* (Philadelphia: J. B. Lippincott, 1912), 401.
23. Gen. John McCausland, "The Burning of Chambersburg, Penn.: Ordered by General Early in Retaliation or the Wanton Destruction of the Private Property of Citizens of Virginia," repr. from New Orleans, La., *Picayune*, August 2, 1908, in Southern Historical Society Papers 31: 266–70.
24. For the full extent of the destruction, see Ben-

jamin Schroder Schneck, *The Burning of Chambersburg, Pennsylvania* (Philadelphia: Lindsay and Blackiston, 1865).

25. Camp Lee was named after Robert E. Lee's father, Gen. Henry "Light Horse Harry" Lee, and was located at the Fair Grounds, a mile and a half north of Richmond, subsequently the site of the Broad Street Railroad terminal.

26. General Grant, as quoted in letter of July 17, 1864, from General H. W. Halleck to Major General Hunter, in Couper, *One Hundred Years at V.M.I.* 2: 302–03.

27. Allan, *Life and Letters*, 197, June 17, 1864.

28. "Minutes of the Board of Visitors" 3: 38, April 2, 1866, VMI Archives. The statue was eventually transported to Wheeling, West Virginia. It would not be restored to Virginia Military Institute until the year after the war ended, when the Governor of West Virginia authorized its return, and it was rededicated on September 10, 1866.

Chapter 1

1. Dr. William Ruffner, commenting about Col. William Preston's descendants, as quoted in Edmund Randolph Preston, "The Name William Preston," written for his grandson, William Edmund Preston, ca. 1955, an unpublished paper.

2. William Cabell Bruce, *John Randolph of Roanoke, 1773–1833: A Biography Based Largely on New Material*, 2 vols. (New York: Putnam's, 1922), 1: 10.

3. For the birth of Elizabeth Preston in Richmond, see Elizabeth Preston Allan, "Reminiscences of an Ordinary Life," original manuscript of *A March Past*, which includes information omitted from the book, Collection 2764: William Allan Papers, Box 2, Folder 12, Pt. 1: 2, Southern Historical Collection, University of North Carolina, Chapel Hill.

4. See Edmund Randolph Preston, "The Name Thomas Lewis Preston and some of those who have borne it," Chicago, June 24, 1945.

5. It was in Dorman's boarding house that Thomas Preston's son, J.T.L. Preston, was born, as William Couper concluded in his letter of August 28, 1939, to Major James W. McClung, Box: VMI Faculty and Staff, 19th Cent., Folder 1: Preston, John T. L.: General Correspondence, VMI Archives. For Dorman's building of the stone house after 1791 when he bought the property (lot 13), see Mrs. Charles McCulloch, "Rockbridge and Its County Seat," *Proceedings of the Rockbridge Historical Society* 1 (1939–41): 74.

6. Obituary by Thomas Ritchie, "Death of Thomas L. Preston, Esq.," *Richmond Enquirer*, August 18, 1812, and Preston, "Reminiscences of an Ordinary Life," Pt. 1: 3. "Thomas Lewis Preston was born August 19, 1781, and died of typhoid fever on August 11, 1812."

7. Edmonia Madison Randolph Preston, "Music Album, ca. 1805–1808, hand-copied piano music for two and four hands, and piano and voice, as well as exercises and scales," 48pp., MSS5:5 P9267:1, Virginia Historical Society.

8. Letter of December 19, 1812, from E. M. Preston in Smithfield to John Preston in Richmond, "Preston Family of Virginia," reel 11, #2812

9. Letter of February 19, 1814, from E. M. Preston at Avon Hill to John Preston, treasurer of Virginia, "Preston Family of Virginia," reel 11, #2907.

10. Letter of July 2, 1814, from E. M. Preston at Avon Hill to Mrs. Elizabeth Madison, "Preston Family of Virginia," reel 11, #2926.

11. Thomas Preston's twenty-one-acre lot was just outside of Lexington near Matthew Hanna's tan yard and northeast of where Randolph and Henry streets converged. He purchased it for ten pounds per acre from John Galbraith on September 5, 1808, see Deed Book F, 354, Rockbridge County Courthouse, Lexington, Va. This deed would be delivered to J.T.L. Preston on March 23, 1836. Matthew Hanna's tan yard was Lot #14 of the original plan of Lexington, at the northeast corner of Main and Henry streets. See J.T.L. Preston, "Address Delivered Before the Franklin Society of Lexington, at Its Semi-centenary Anniversary, February 1866, Lexington, Virginia," Collection 103: Franklin Society Library Book Collection (FSL/F/234/.LS/P74/1866), 568, Washington and Lee Special Collections. See also Map of Thomas Lewis Preston's twenty-one acres he bought from John Galbraith in 1808, in Preston Collection, Folder 1980.23.0019, Stonewall Jackson House, now stored at VMI Archives. On today's map of Lexington, Preston's 21-acre lot (known successively as Shields' Hill, Freedman's Hill, and Diamond Hill) would be bounded by Tucker Street, Hanna Lane, Peyton Street, and Marble Lane and include lots along Massie and Fuller streets. The annual rent on this property in 1916 was $40. See Deed Book K, 10, dated January 1, 1816.

12. Letter of February 16, 1818, from Eliza Madison to Maj. William Preston, "Preston Family of Virginia," reel 12, #3184, AC 6288a, Manuscript Division, Library of Congress, Washington, D.C.

13. J.T.L. Preston, "Address Delivered Before the Franklin Society of Lexington, at Its Semi-centenary Anniversary, February 1866, Lexington, Virginia," Collection 103: Franklin Society Library Book Collection (FSL/F/234/.LS/P74/1866), 569–70, Washington and Lee Special Collections.

14. Ibid., 570.

15. Ibid.

16. Elizabeth Randolph Preston Allan, *A March Past: Reminiscences of Elizabeth Randolph Preston Allan*, ed. Janet Allan Bryan (Richmond: Dietz Press, 1938), 87, and George West Diehl, "The Preston Saga: Chapter V," Rockbridge County, Virginia Notebook (Utica, Ky.: McDowell, 1982), 71. See also "The Caruthers Clan: Chapter IV," 18.

17. J.T.L. Preston, inscription on Sally Caruthers Preston's gravestone.

18. Preston, "Address Delivered Before the Franklin Society," 569. See also letter of April 13, 1820, from Edmonia Preston to Susanna Preston about preparing John for "Latin in the fall" at Washington College. The Filson Club, Louisville, Ky.

19. John H. Ingram, *Edgar Allan Poe: His Life, Letters, and Opinions* (New York: AMS Press, 1965), 16. See also Mary Newton Stanard, *The Dreamer: A Romantic Rendering of the Life Story of Edgar Allan Poe* (Richmond: Bell Book and Stationery, 1909), 62–66.

20. Edgar Allan Poe's natural parents were David Poe and Elizabeth Arnold.

21. Ingram, *Edgar Allan Poe*, 17.

22. From Virgil's 8th Eclogue.

23. Ingram, *Edgar Allan Poe*, 18.

24. Horace, *The Odes and Carmen Saeculare of Horace*, trans. John Conington (London: George Bell and Sons, 1882), 1: 2; 2: 18; and 4: 6.

25. Ingram, *Edgar Allan Poe*, 20.

26. Stanard, *The Dreamer*, 154–55.

27. See references to Jack Preston in Edgar Allan Poe, "William Wilson," in *Prose Tales of Edgar Allan Poe*, Second Series (Boston: Dana Estes, 1876), 64–69.

Chapter 2

1. For a description of Washington College in the 1820s, see J.T.L. Preston, "Alumni Address [June 25, 1878]," *Southern Collegian* (Washington and Lee University) 10, No. 18 (July 6, 1878): 3, 6.
2. For Preston's courses and achievements in 1823–28, see "Examination List for John T. L. Preston, October 1823–March 1818, Washington College," VMI Archives.
3. Preston graduated from Washington College in 1828 with an A.B. (bachelor's) degree. See *Catalogue of Officers and Alumni of Washington and Lee* (Baltimore, 1888), 81, #827.
4. Letter of June 17, 1823, from Edmonia Preston to Sarah Preston McDowell, Smithfield-Preston Foundation MS 97-002, Box 1, Folder 11, VPI Special Collections.
5. For Sarah "Sally" Lyle Caruthers's namesake, see Curtis Carroll Davis, *Chronicler of the Cavaliers: A Life of William A. Caruthers* (Richmond: Dietz Press, 1953), 42.
6. "Caruthers Clan," in George West Diehl, comp., *Rockbridge County, Virginia Notebook* (Utica, Ky.: McDowell, 1982), Chap. 4. Diehl claims that Mrs. Blain was sister of Sally's aunt, Mrs. Samuel R. Wilson. It's true that Sally's brother John would marry Mrs. Wilson's daughter, Mary Blain Wilson, shortly before 1830 and that Sally's sister Phoebe would marry Mrs. Wilson's son, John Mark Wilson, shortly before 1841. So Mrs. Blain would ultimately become sister of Sally's aunt twice, but not when Sally boarded with her in 1825. For the dates of John's and Phoebe's marriages to Wilson siblings, see Davis, *Chronicler of the Cavaliers*, 384, 391.
7. Elizabeth Preston Allan, "Reminiscences of an Ordinary Life," original manuscript of *A March Past*, which includes information omitted from the book, Collection 2764: William Allan Papers, Box 2, Folder 12, Pt. 1: 16–17, Southern Historical Collection, University of North Carolina, Chapel Hill.
8. Letter of April 29, 1822, from Archibald Alexander at Princeton to Margaret Graham in Lexington devotes a paragraph to the good qualities of Sarah Caruthers, as mentioned in Davis, *Chronicler of the Cavaliers*, 517 n. 35.
9. Preston, "Address Delivered Before the Franklin Society of Lexington, at Its Semi centenary Anniversary, February 1866, Lexington, Virginia," Collection 103: Franklin Society Library Book Collection (FSL/F/234/.LS/P74/1866), 574, Washington and Lee Special Collections.
10. *Students of the University of Virginia* (Baltimore, 1878), no pagination but listed alphabetically.
11. *Catalogue of the Officers and Students in Yale College, 1829–1830*, 7: "J.T.L. Preston, A.B. Va. Univ." For Preston's study under Prof. Silliman at Yale, see Davis, *Chronicler of the Cavaliers*, 389. Note also the authorship of "Sketch of John Howe Peyton," by "Col. John T. L. Preston, A. M., of Yale, Professor of Modern Languages etc., in the V. M. Institute," in Memoir of John Howe Peyton, *Sketches by His Contemporaries* (Staunton, Va.: A. B. Blackburn, 1894).
12. Letter of May 6, 1936, from George Derby to Col. William Couper. See Couper's reply of June 11, 1936, Box: VMI Faculty and Staff, 19th Cent. Folder 1: Preston, John T. L.: General correspondence, VMI Archives. For Preston's biography, see "Preston, John Thomas Lewis," in *National Cyclopedia of American Biography* (New York: James T. White, 1940), 28: 245.
13. In 1992 Mary Coulling, the biographer of Margaret Junkin Preston, confirmed that Preston attended Yale as a resident graduate. See letter of August 19, 1992, from Mary P. Coulling to Yale University Archivist Susan Brady in Mary Coulling Collection, Box 6, Folder 77, Washington and Lee Special Collections. Officially, Preston is listed in the *Catalogue of the Officers and Students in Yale College, 1829–1830*, even though not under a specific degree.
14. For Preston's first of three trips to Europe, see Janet Allan Bryan's introduction to Preston's unpublished "London Journal," 2.
15. Preston, "London Journal," 66–67, August 25, 1851, annotation by Bryan.
16. The Title Line for Blandome:
Summary:
(1) 1820 April 5 Cornelius Dorman to John Agnew Cumings, (2) 1822 April 24 John Cumings to Andrew Davidson, (3) 1823 April 17 sold by Davidson to William Caruthers, (4) 1835 August 17 sold by Caruthers to J.T.L. Preston, (5) 1844 November 24 transferred from Preston to William Taylor, (6) 1853 sold by Taylor's estate to John Wilson, (7) 1854 January 28 sold by Wilson to Jacob Fuller, (8) 1870 transferred from Preston via Wilson to Jacob Fuller, (9) 1872 September 14 sold to John Randolph Tucker.
Details:
(1) Deed from Cornelius and Nancy Dorman to John Agnew Cumings on April 5, 1820, for $228 for one acre and fourteen poles bordering lands of Daniel Blain's heirs, James Gold, Alexander Shields, and Thomas Preston's heirs [Deed Bk. M, 218]. Also deed from James and Elizabeth Gold to John A. Cumings on March 9, 1822, for $675 for a lot bordering Blain's heirs, Col. Shields, former property of Cornelius Dorman, end of Henry Street, Randolph Street, and the Spring lot [Deed Bk. N, 148]. Also deed from Alexander Shields to John A. Cumings on April 21, 1822, for $1 one acre and two roods and twenty-one poles bordering Lot 10 of the original town plat, Thomas Preston's heirs, former property of Cornelius Dorman, and former property of James Gold for half of a street or road in common between Shields and Cumings [Deed Bk. N, 191]. The house that Cumings built on the first lot ca. 1820 is mentioned on p. 51 of *Chronicler of the Cavaliers*, which describes how William Caruthers made "great improvements" to the house that Cumings had built on his lot, which is also mentioned in footnote 17, p. 421, and in Deed Bk. N, 270, in number (3) below.
(2) Deed from John A. and Ann C. Cumings to Andrew B. Davidson on April 24, 1822, for $5,000 for 3 lots of 6 acres bordering Preston heirs, as described in number (1) above. [Deed Bk. N, 192]. The first lot was conveyed to John Cumings from James Gold from the corner of Henry and Randolph south to spring lot to Daniel Blain's heirs to Cornelius Dorman (later the Jackson House) and Alexander Shields; and second lot borders Thomas L. Preston's heirs; and 3rd lot also borders Preston's heirs and Dorman. Note that Cumings's deed to Davidson [N, 192] states the wrong year of 1802, which is correctly noted at the end as "April 24, 1822," since in both deeds the adjoining property belonged to "Thomas Preston's heirs," Thomas having died in 1812.

Note: The Virginia W. P. A. Historical Inventory Project, sponsored by the Virginia Conservation Commission under the direction of its Division of History, claimed that there was a "first home" and a "second home" located "east of Randolph Street and the Catholic Church," which it called "Blandome." In a survey on June 10, 1936, James W. McClung set the building date for the first home at 1775 and the date of the second home at 1872. McClung claimed that the first home was "a small log structure," which was torn down and replaced by "the present two-story brick house," known as Blandome. Unfortunately, McClung confused Blandome with "Little House at Blandome." The house that Preston bought from William Caruthers in 1835, today's Blandome, was not a small log cabin but rather a mansion. The small log cabin that Prof. Tucker tore down in 1872 to build Little Blandome became his law office and classroom. It later became a cottage. The Little Blandome house can be traced back to the first owner of record, William Brown, who bought it on August 4, 1782 [see Deed Bk. A, 352], followed by Jacob Fuller on March 6, 1813 [see Deed Bk. Z, 443]. But the first owner of record of the Blandome house was John Cumings, who sold it to Andrew Davidson on April 24, 1822 [see Deed Bk. N, 192], followed by William A. Caruthers on April 17, 1823 [see Deed Bk. N, 470].

(3) Deed from Andrew B. and Susan Davidson to William A. Caruthers on April 17, 1823, for 6 acres on a hill 1/8 mile east of courthouse for $4,500. Deed Bk. N, 470. See also Davis, *Chronicler of the Cavaliers*, 51.

(4) For J.T.L. Preston's purchase of Dr. William A. Caruthers' house and lot east of Randolph Street on August 17, 1835, to retire Caruthers' debts, see deed of Sidney S. Baxter, trustee, and John T. Caruthers at auction for $4,000 in three installments to John T. L. Preston for house and lot where William A. and Louisa Caruthers resided on 15 October 1829, bounded by land of Thomas L. Preston heirs, Cornelius Dorman's and Daniel Blain's Heirs, which Baxter was to sell at auction after 1 July 1830, and by another deed of 17 October 1829 conveyed to Baxter for 2 lots, one adjoining the back spring with stone spring house and the other adjoining the lands of Thomas L. Preston's heirs with a small brick tenement thereon, all published in Union newspaper and which John T. L. Preston bought for another $150 [Deed Bk. T, 40]. Preston paid $4,150 for the combined purchase.

(5) On November 24, 1844, Preston bought the house on Main Street from his first cousin Susan Preston McDowell Taylor and her husband, Capt. William Taylor, for $2,000 [Deed Bk. Y, 226] and transferred the house above Randolph Street to the Taylors. He then moved to Main Street, and William and Susan Taylor occupied the former Caruthers house east of Randolph Street. (There is no deed for the transfer of the house to William Taylor other than an 1854 reference to its being in Taylor's estate after he died on January 17, 1846, in Deed Bk. KK, 179, in number [6] below.) See also William Henry Ruffner, *Washington and Lee Historical Studies*, 4 (1893): 126: Hon. William Taylor "lived in the house now owned by J. Randolph Tucker."

(6) Sometime after Capt. Taylor died, the house was transferred from Taylor's estate to Sally Preston's sister Phebe Shields Caruthers Wilson and her husband John. (There is no deed for this transfer other than an 1853 notice in Landbk. 13, Town Lots 1853 for Shaw district, p. 3, under John T. L. Preston that it was "transferred to M. Willson" and a reference in Deed Bk. KK, 179, to the house and lot as "being the same lot purchased by said Wilson of the estate of Wm. Taylor.")

(7) The Willsons sold it to Jacob Fuller for $5,000 on January 28, 1854 [Deed Bk. KK, 179]: John M. and Phebe S. (Shields Caruthers) Willson of Washington, D.C., to Jacob Fuller for $5,000 for house and lot adjoining J.T.L. Preston, C. A. (George A.) Baker, S. H. (Samuel M.) Dold, L. S. Palmer, et al., being the same lot purchased by Willson from the estate of Wm. Taylor dec'd, containing 5 1/4 acres and also another adjoining lot purchased by Wilson from Gen. C. P. Dorman, deceased, beginning at L. S. Palmer's corner on Washington St., then SE to corner of Dr. A. Graham, then NE to C. A. Baker's line, then NW to former Taylor lot, then along the new line between L. S. Palmer and M. Willson, then SW to a stone 17 feet from Dr. Graham's line, then SW to a new line between Preston and Willson, admitted to record March 16, 1869, in Rockbridge County. See deed correction of October 30, 1857, relating to Gen. Dorman's lot being a portion of Lot 1 that Archibald Graham had sold to Fuller on September 19, 1857, in Deed Bk. KK, 180.

(8) Although Fuller occupied the house during the Civil War, it was transferred to him from Preston in 1870, becoming his official residence in 1872. (Landbook 17, Town Lots 1870, John A. Shaw district, p. 2: house and lot of Jacob Fuller "transferred from J.T.L. Preston" and then in 1871, John Varner district, p. 3: house and lot of Jacob Fuller "transferred from J.T.L. Preston by J. M. Wilson," and finally in 1872, p. 4: house and lot are listed as Jacob Fuller's residence.)

(9) Deed from Jacob and Rachel Fuller to Preston's cousin, the renowned jurist John Randolph Tucker, and his wife, Laura, on September 14, 1872, for $6,500 [Deed Bk. MM, 391–92]. The house was named "Blandome" when the Tuckers bought and remodeled it in the Italianate style, adding a distinctive rectangular belvedere and two sawnwork porches. For the origin of the name "Blandome," see John Earle Perkins IV, "Documented History of 'Blandome,'" December 10, 1989, in Architecture Papers: Pam Simpson's Class, Washington and Lee Special Collections. Perkins refers to two legends concerning why the J. Randolph Tuckers named the home "Blandome": one being that the term connoted restful, peaceful, quiet; and the other, that it was named for the Blands, who were joyful, happy friends of the family.

(10) Deed from Laura Tucker through St. George Tucker to W. N. Key on October 27, 1904 [Deed Book 97, 133].

(11) Deed from W. N. Key to R. A. DePriest on November 7, 1910 [Deed Bk. 109, 324].

(12) Deed from R.A. DePriest via Paul M. Penick and D. C. Humphreys, trustees of Phi Gamma Delta on March 22, 1912 [Deed Bk. 112, 415], mortgaged to Washington and Lee University for $3,000 and failed to pay off the mortgage.

(13) Sold at public auction by Washington and Lee University through Paul M. Penick to Harry Lee Walker on April 28, 1917, for $4,000 [Deed Bk. 112, 449], inherited by Walker's daughter, Mrs. C. M. Wood. Lexington businessman Harry Lee Walker was an African American who began his life poor and ended as the proprietor of one of Lexington's leading sanitary meat markets that distributed hickory smoke–cured Virginia hams nationally and internationally, as well as locally to Washington and Lee College, Virginia Military Institute, and Lexington's fraternity houses. In the words of his admiring daughter, Walker was born in a cabin

"on the bottom of Henry Street and died at the top" in a stately home, namely Blandome. John Earle Perkins notes, incidentally, that after Walker's death, this daughter in 1947 won the sweepstakes. Walker's wife, Eliza Bannister Walker, championed the improvement of Lexington's black schools and the founding of an Old Folks Home and Orphanage.

NRHP: Blandome is listed at 101 Tucker Street on the National Register of Historic Places, Record No. 348532, NRIS No. 011001520, VDHR File No. 117–8027–0127, Washington, D.C.: National Park Service, January 24, 2002.

17. Davis, *Chronicler of the Cavaliers*, 51.

18. Allan, "Reminiscences of Elizabeth Preston Allan," Pt. 1: 3: "When my father was married, in 1832, at 21 years of age, he and my mother lived with Grandmother and "Aunt Lib…. Grandmother was mistress of the house, which my children remember as the one Mr. J. Randolph Tucker bought about 40 years later, and called "Blandome." See also J.T.L. Preston remark in his "Alumni Address: June 25, 1878," *Southern Collegian* (Washington and Lee University) 10, No. 18 (July 6, 1878): 3: "About forty years ago the distinguished senator from South Carolina, Wm. C. Preston, was standing with me at the door of my house on yonder hill, now the residence of Hon. J. R. Tucker."

19. Letter of January 12, 1832, from Edmonia Preston to Susan Preston McDowell, Smithfield-Preston Foundation MS 97–002, Box 1, Folder 11, VPI Special Collections.

20. Letter written in 1840 from Sally Preston to J.T.L. Preston, as quoted in Elizabeth Randolph Preston Allan, *A March Past: Reminiscences of Elizabeth Randolph Preston Allan*, ed. Janet Allan Bryan (Richmond: Dietz Press, 1938), 30. *The Knights of the Golden Horseshoe* first appeared serially from January through October 1841, in *Magnolia*: or, *Southern Monthly*.

21. For measures taken against a conspiracy, Col. William Preston received from Jefferson 1,000 acres in Fincastle, Virginia. They comprise today's Audubon Park, Camp Zachary Taylor, and the Belmar neighborhoods of Louisville, Kentucky. See patent dated July 17, 1780, and recorded in Book 6, page 50, in the Land Office at Frankfort, Ky., in "Preston Family of Virginia," reel 5, Folder #1080, AC 6288a. Manuscript Division, Library of Congress, Washington, D.C. See also Thomas Jefferson, "Survey Report No. 00308," 5, regarding suppression of a "horrid conspiracy," and "Survey Report No. 11416," 4, congratulating Col. Preston "on the measures taken against the conspiracy," in the Archives Division, Library of Virginia.

22. Letter dated June 1832, from Sally Caruthers to John T. L. Preston, as quoted in Allan, *A March Past*, 25.

23. For Preston's description of Sally, see "John T. L. Preston Diary, 1861 July 24–September 22," MSS 17,264, p. 5, Manuscript Division, Library of Congress, Washington, D.C.

24. William Caruthers left $70,000 at his death for the care and education of his seven children, $10,000 of which he turned over to Sally when she married Preston at twenty-one. See Allan, "Remembrances of an Ordinary Life," Pt. 7: 3.

25. Quoted from Margaret Junkin's unpublished letter before August 3, 1857, to her cousin Helen Dickey, in Mary Price Coulling, *Margaret Junkin Preston: A Biography* (Winston-Salem, N.C.: John F. Blair, 1993), 63.

26. William Ruffner, "Col. J.T.L. Preston," *Washington and Lee University Historical Papers* 4 (1893): 141.

27. Henry Ruffner, as quoted in ibid.

28. Curtis Davis, quoting an unknown gentleman in his *Chronicler of the Cavaliers*, 389, 517 n. 41. See also 27: Caruthers genealogy, "From an Old Scottish Paper."

29. Letter of October 1834, from Sally Preston to J.T.L. Preston, in *March Past*, 25–26.

30. Ibid., 26.

31. Ibid., 27.

32. Mrs. John H. Moore, *Memories of a Long Life in Virginia* (Staunton, Va.: McClure, 1920), 32.

33. The Franklin Society was founded in 1800 as the Belles Lettres Society. In 1804 it became the Union Society, in 1807 the Republican Society, 1808 the Literary Society, and in August 1811, the Franklin Society. In 1816 it incorporated as The Franklin Society and Library Company of Lexington, having begun its library in 1813. For a history of its origins, see J.T.L. Preston, "Address Delivered Before the Franklin Society of Lexington, at Its Semi-Centenary Anniversary, February 1866, Lexington, Virginia," Collection 103: Franklin Society Library Book Collection (FSL/F/234/.LS/P74/1866), 576–81, Washington and Lee Special Collections; repr. in *Lexington Gazette*, February 21 and 28, 1873. Its ten founders were John Caruthers, Layman Wayt, John Alexander, Andrew Alexander, Thomas L. Preston, Cornelius Dorman, John Leyburn, Alexander Shields, Dr. Samuel Campbell, and James Caruthers. For a succinct history of the organization in Lexington, see Charles W. Turner, "The Franklin Society, 1800–1891," *Virginia Magazine of History and Biography* 66, No. 4 (October 1958): 432–47.

34. Eugene P. Link, *Democratic-Republican Societies, 1790–1800* (New York: Columbia University Press, 1942), 1.

35. "Secretary's Books, 1830–45," November 15, 1811, Collection 103: Franklin Society, Box 40, Washington and Lee Special Collections.

Chapter 3

1. Oren F. Morton, *A History of Rockbridge County* (Baltimore: Regional Publishing, 1980), 199.

2. Francis H. Smith, *History of the Virginia Military Institute: Its Building and Rebuilding*, ed. F. H. Smith, Jr. (Lynchburg, Va.: J. P. Bell, 1912), 52.

3. Thomas Massie Boyd, "General Stonewall Jackson," *Southern Bivouac* 5 (1885–86): 355.

4. "Lexington: Thursday Morning," *The* (Lexington) *Intelligencer*, May 11, 1826.

5. "Secretary's Books, 1830–45," December 5, 12, 20, and 27, 1834, Collection 103: Franklin Society, Box 40, Washington and Lee Special Collections.

6. Matthew Paxton, ed., "When the Virginia Military Institute was Founded," *Rockbridge County News*, October 14, 1926.

7. Col. John Thomas Lewis Preston, "Historical Sketch of the Establishment and Organization of the Virginia Military Institute, prepared, at the request of the Board of Visitors, by Col. John Thomas Lewis Preston, Professor Emeritus V.M.I., July 4, 1889" (VMI Archives, Box: Preston, John T. L., Folder MS 0240), 1. Also quoted in Chap. 1 of Francis H. Smith, *History of the Virginia Military Institute: Its Building and Rebuilding*, ed. F. H. Smith, Jr. (Lynchburg, Va.: J. P. Bell, 1912).

8. For Preston's titles as "town speaker" and "Lexington's Demosthenes," see Henry Boley, *Lexington in Old Virginia* (Richmond: Garrett and Massie, 1936), 179.

9. J.T.L. Preston, "Sketch of John Howe Peyton," *Memoir of John Howe Peyton in Sketches by his Contemporaries* (Staunton, Va.: A. B. Blackburn, 1894), 163.

10. Ibid., 164.

11. Preston, as quoted by Elizabeth Randolph Preston Allan, *A March Past: Reminiscences of Elizabeth Randolph Preston Allan*, ed. Janet Allan Bryan (Richmond: Dietz Press, 1938), 100.

12. Not until fifty years later does Preston openly state that he was the author of the Cives articles, when he admits in his "Historical Sketch" during VMI's jubilee in 1889 that "the three articles" were "written by myself." See J.T.L. Preston, "Historical Sketch of the Establishment and Organization of the Virginia Military Institute, prepared, at the request of the Board of Visitors, by Col. John Thomas Lewis Preston, Professor Emeritus V.M.I., July 4, 1889" (VMI Archives, Box: Preston, John T. L., Folder MS 0240), 2. But from the outset, the Lexington community knew Preston to be the author, as confirmed in "Early History of the Virginia Military Institute" in *The Cadet* 1, No. 1 (March 1871): 26; by Morton, *A History of Rockbridge County*, 200; by Col. James A. Anderson, "The Founding of V.M.I. and Its Early Years, in J. Eston Johnston, ed., *Echoes of VMI* (Lexington, Va.: VMI, 1937), 2; by Col. William Couper, *One Hundred Years at V.M.I.* (Richmond: Garrett and Massie, 1939), 1: 15–16; by VMI Public Relations Director Robert W. Jeffrey in "Virginia Military Institute," *Iron Worker* 16 (Summer 1952): 3; by William Couper again in his "Remarks at the Preston Library Dedication, November 4, 1939," Box: Faculty and Staff; Folder: Preston Clippings and Articles, 2–3, Archives.

13. Cives, "The Lexington Arsenal," *Lexington Gazette*, August 28, 1835. All quotes from the first letter are from this issue of the *Gazette*.

14. Cives, "Lexington Arsenal—No. II," *Lexington Gazette*, September 4, 1835. All quotes from the second letter are from this issue of the *Gazette*.

15. Cf. Thomas Gray's *Elegy Written in a Country Churchyard*, 1751.

16. Cives, "Lexington Arsenal—No. III," *Lexington Gazette*, September 11, 1835. All the quotes from the third letter are from this issue of the *Gazette*.

17. The phrase "healthy and pleasant abode," which is how it was originally worded in the Cives article in the *Gazette* and on the single sheet that Preston would later give to the delegates, was subsequently corrected to read "healthful and pleasant abode," which is how it appears on the Parapet and how cadets today have memorized it.

Chapter 4

1. *Lexington Gazette*, December 11, 1835.

2. A Citizen of Lexington [pseud.], "Lexington Arsenal," *Lexington Gazette*, December 18, 1835.

3. Ibid.

4. Cornelius C. Baldwin, "Lexington Arsenal," *Lexington Gazette*, December 25, 1835.

5. A Citizen of Lexington [pseud.], "Lexington Arsenal," *Lexington Gazette*, January 1, 1836. All quotes from Citizen's reply are from this article in the *Gazette*.

6. A Citizen of Lexington [pseud.], "Communication," *Lexington Gazette*, January 8, 1836. All quotes from Citizen's communication are from this article in the *Gazette*.

7. *Virginia General Assembly Legislative Petitions*, Rockbridge County, 1834–1864, Box 222, Folder 63, Archives Division, Library of Virginia. See also *Journal of the House of Delegates*, in Records of the States of the United States, Cabinet: Virginia General Assembly. House Journals, etc., 1835–39, film 331, reel 15: 79, Archives Division, Library of Virginia.

8. Ibid., Folder 64.

9. Charles Dorman's Bill 279, Journal of the House of Delegates, film 331, reel 15: 82, January 16, 1836.

10. Petition of January 19, 1836, *Virginia General Assembly Legislative Petitions*, Box 222, Folder 82, Archives Division, Library of Virginia.

11. *Buchanan Advocate*, January 20, 1836.

12. For Capt. Alden Partridge's letter, which was actually written on December 31, 1835, see A. Partridge, "Military Academy," *Lexington Gazette*, January 22, 1836. See also "Virginia Legislature" in the same issue for notice of the petition introduced by Dorman.

13. Rockbridge, "Lexington Arsenal," *Richmond Whig and Public Advertiser*, January 26, 1836, film 144, Archives Division, Library of Virginia.

14. Baldwin, "Lexington Arsenal."

15. "Mr. Partridge's Letter to Col. Dorman, January 6, 1836," *Lexington Gazette*, February 12, 1836.

16. Citizen of Lexington [pseud.], "Lexington Arsenal," *Lexington Gazette*, February 26, 1836.

17. Journal of the House of Delegates, reel 15: 176, March 3, 1836. For the second and third reading, see 211 on March 11 and 227 on March 17. Oscar Minor Crutchfield would later become speaker of the House; and his son Stapleton, VMI professor mathematics after his graduation in 1855.

18. *Journal of the House of Delegates*, reel 15: 199, March 9, 1836.

19. Ibid., 261, March 22, 1836, and *Acts of the General Assembly of the Commonwealth of Virginia*, 1835–36 (Richmond, 1836), 12–14. See also Edgar W. Knight, ed., *A Documentary History of Education in the South Before 1860* (Chapel Hill: University of North Carolina Press, 1949), 4: 164–67.

20. "The Arsenal," *Lexington Gazette*, January 13, 1837, film 203, Archives Division, Library of Virginia.

21. C [pseud.], "The Arsenal," *Lexington Gazette*, January 13, 1837.

22. *Journal of the House of Delegates*, reel 16:103, January 13, 1837.

23. Ibid., 313, March 21 and 22, 1837.

24. Couper, *One Hundred Years at V.M.I.* (Richmond: Garrett and Massie, 1939), 1: 26.

25. Ollinger Crenshaw, *General Lee's College: The Rise and Growth of Washington and Lee College* (New York: Random House, 1969), 50–54.

26. Letter of August 9, 1837, from John Caruthers to the first board of visitors, Virginia Military Institute Records, 1837–1850, Accession 36739, State Government Records Collection, Archives Division, Library of Virginia, Richmond. See also William Couper, *Claudius Crozet: Soldier-Scholar-Educator-Engineer, 1789–1964* (Charlottesville: Historical Publishing, 1936), 95–96. See also the first report of the newly established board of visitors, dated 8 August 1837, to Gov. Campbell from Gen. Bernard Peyton, Col. C. Crozet, Gen. Wm. Ligon, Gen. Peter C. Johnston, and Gen. George Rust, Jr.

27. J.T.L. Preston, "Historical Sketch of the Establishment and Organization of the Virginia Military Institute, prepared, at the request of the Board of Visitors, by Col. John Thomas Lewis Preston, Professor Emeritus V.M.I., July 4, 1889" (VMI Archives, Box: Preston, John T. L., Folder MS 0240), 3.

28. Letter of August 9, 1837, from the board of visi-

tors to James McDowell, in Robert F. Hunter and Edwin L. Dooley, Jr. *Claudius Crozet: French Engineer in America, 1790–1864* (Charlottesville: University Press of Virginia, 1989), 126. See *Journal of the House of Delegates of the Commonwealth of Virginia* (Richmond, 1937), 13, for Gov. Campbell's agreement in his annual message to the General Assembly. James McDowell's bill was introduced on February 24, 1838.

29. *Acts of the General Assembly of Virginia*, 1838–1839 (Richmond, 1839), April 10, 1839.

30. Letter of April 5, 1838, from J.T.L. Preston to Gov. James McDowell, Smithfield-Preston Foundation, MS 97–002, Box 1, Folder 20, VPI Special Collections.

31. Preston, "Historical Sketch," 3.

32. *Journal of the House of Delegates*, film 331, reel 18: 41;

33. Ibid., reel 18: 17–19, March 29, 1839. See also Charles P. Dorman Papers, MS#066, Folder 3, VMI Archives, for the handwritten bill "amending and reducing into one the several acts concerning the reorganization of the Lexington Arsenal, and the establishment therewith of a military school at Washington College" and appropriating $6,000 annually to establish VMI, dated April 3, 1839. Or see a facsimile of the bill in Diane B. Jacob and Judith M. Arnold, *A Virginia Military Institute Album, 1839–1910* (Charlottesville: University Press of Virginia, 1982), 1.

34. For the members of the third and final board of visitors, see the Lexington *Valley Star* in one of its first issues, June 6, 1839. The ten members were Col. Crozet, Gen. Peter C. Johnston, Capt. John F. Wiley (replaced Gen. William Ligon?), Gen. Thomas H. Botts, Gen. Charles P. Dorman, James McDowell, Dr. Alfred Leyburn, Hugh Barclay, and Col. J.T.L. Preston with Adj. Gen. Bernard Peyton ex officio.

35. "Governor David Campbell Tells the Legislature of Virginia About the Importance of Free Schools in That State, 1839," in Edgar W. Knight, ed. *A Documentary History of Education in the South Before 1860* (Chapel Hill: University of North Carolina Press, 1949), 5: 85–86. See also *Journal of the House of Delegates of the Commonwealth of Virginia*, 1839, 7.

36. "Governor David Campbell," 86.

37. Ibid., 86–87.

38. Virginius Dabney, "Education in the Antebellum Era," *Virginia: The New Dominion* (Garden City, N.Y.: Doubleday, 1971), 248.

39. Ibid., 249.

40. "Governor David Campbell," 87.

41. William Couper, *One Hundred Years at V.M.I.*, I, 37.

42. Letter of April 29, 1839, from J.T.L. Preston to Francis H. Smith, Box: Preston-Smith Letters, 1839, BDVIS, Folder 2, VMI Archives.

43. Letter of May 6, 1839, from Francis H. Smith to friend William (M. Adkinson), ibid., Folder 1.

44. Francis H. Smith, *History of the Virginia Military Institute: Its Building and Rebuilding*, ed. F. H. Smith, Jr. (Lynchburg, Va.: J. P. Bell, 1912), 32.

45. Letter of May 17, 1839, from J.T.L. Preston to Francis Smith, Box: Preston-Smith Letters, 1839, BDVIS, Folder 3.

46. Letter of June 8, 1839, from J.T.L. Preston to Francis Smith, ibid., Folder 4.

47. Letter of July 1, 1839, from Francis Smith to J.T.L. Preston, ibid., Folder 5: Smith to Preston.

48. Jennings Wise, *Military History of the Virginia Military Institute From 1839 to 1865* (Lynchburg, Va.: J. P. Bell, 1915), 39. See also William Couper, *Claudius Crozet: Soldier-Scholar-Educator-Engineer (1789–1964)* (Charlottesville, Va.: Historical Publishing, 1936), 102.

49. Preston, "Historical Sketch," 5.

50. For the variety of textbooks adopted in the board's first reports, see letter of September 12, 1839, from Claudius Crozet to Major Smith, in Couper, *Claudius Crozet*, 105.

51. Preston, "Historical Sketch," 5.

52. Ibid., 6.

53. Letter of November 2, 1839, from J.T.L. Preston, Alfred Leyburn, Hugh Barclay, and Charles Dorman to Gov. David Campbell, in Virginia Military Institute Records, 1837–1850, Accession 36739, State Government Records Collection, Archives Division, Library of Virginia, Richmond. For the board's election of Preston as professor of modern languages, see "Minutes of the Board of Visitors, 1839–53" 1: 15, November 12, 1839, VMI Archives.

54. William Couper claims twenty-three of twenty-eight cadets actually showed up on November 11 and five more on the November 13. See Couper, *One Hundred Years at V.M.I.* 2: 52, 54. The cadets ranged in age from sixteen to twenty-two. The board of visitors had accepted thirty-three cadets on September 10.

55. For the founding of Albemarle Military Institute in Charlottesville, Virginia, in 1855, see Richard M. McMurry, *Virginia Military Institute Alumni in the Civil War*, 55. See also Charles Duy Walker, *Memorial, Virginia Military Institute: Biographical Sketches of the Graduates and Élèves of the Virginia Military Institute Who Fell During the War Between the States* (Philadelphia: J. B. Lippincott, 1875), 498. The Albermarle Military Institute closed with the onset of the Civil War in 1861, and Col. Strange died serving the 19th Virginia Infantry at the Battle of South Mountain in 1862.

56. Knox, writing pseudonymously, claims he witnessed the dismissal of the old guard and saw the new guard enter upon their untried duties. See Knox (pseud.), "Beginnings of V.M.I., Report by Eye Witness of First Commencement Held and the Honor Graduates," *Lexington Gazette*, June 3, 1841, in *Withrow Scrapbook* 7: 14, Washington and Lee Special Collections.

57. For the list of military programs by 1861 in the South, see Bradford A. Wineman, "J.T.L. Preston and the Origins of the Virginia Military Institute, 1834–42," *Virginia Magazine of History and Biography* 114, No. 2 (2006): 254–55. Wineman's list includes the South Carolina Military Academy with campuses at The Arsenal in Columbia and the Citadel in Charleston, the Kentucky Military Institute in Lyndon, the Hillsborough Military Academy in North Carolina, the Western Military Institute in Nashville, Tenn., the Georgia Military Institute in Marietta, and the Maryland Military Academy in Oxford. As reported by Edwin Dooley, two other military colleges and schools founded on the pattern of VMI were the University of the South in Sewanee, Tenn., and the Louisiana Military Academy in Pineville, founded in 1859 by William Tecumseh Sherman and described by Col. Crozet as "an exact counterpart" of VMI. See also Wineman, "Military Schools," in Maggi M. Morehouse and Zoe Trod, eds., *Civil War America: A Social and Cultural History* (New York: Routledge, 2012), 121–30; and Edwin L. Dooley, Jr., "Francis H. Smith and VMI On the Eve of the Civil War," in Thomas W. Davis, ed., *A Crowd of Honorable Youths: Historical Essays on the First 150 Years of the Virginia Military Institute* (Lexington, Va.: VMI Sesquicentennial Com-

mittee, 1988), 17–18. Currently there are six senior military colleges (VMI, VPI, Texas A&M, North Georgia, Citadel, and Norwich University), five junior military colleges (Wentworth, Valley Forge, New Mexico, Marion, and Georgia), thirty-five private college-prep military schools, twenty-one public military academies, and seven state-supported maritime colleges.

58. See Johnson W. Miller, "Citizen Soldiers and Professional Engineers: The Antebellum Engineering Culture of the Virginia Military Institute," dissertation (Blacksburg, Va.: Virginia Polytechnic Institute and State University, 2008), 23.

59. John S. Wise, "Battle of New Market, Va., May 15th, 1864: An Address, Repeated Before the Virginia Military Institute, May 13th, 1882," Speeches, Box 1: New Market Speeches, VMI Archives. Also quoted in Gov. James H. Price, "Remarks of the Governor at the Exercises Commemorating the Centennial of the V.M.I. and the Twenty-first Armistice of the First World War, Lexington, Va., November 11, 1939," Price Speeches: July-December 1939, Washington and Lee Special Collections.

60. Cives, "Lexington Arsenal—No. II," *Lexington Gazette*, September 4, 1835.

Chapter 5

1. James A. Anderson, "The Founding of VMI and Its Early Years," in J. Eston Johnston, ed., *Echoes of VMI* (Lexington: Virginia Military Institute, 1937), 1.

2. James Irvin Robertson, Jr., *Stonewall Jackson: The Man, the Soldier, The Legend* (New York: Macmillan, 1997), 167.

3. Knox [pseud.], "The Virginia Military Institute," *Lexington Gazette*, May 20, 1841. All quotes from Knox are from this article in the *Gazette*.

4. John Franklin Caruthers died on August 24, 1840. He was the eldest brother of J.T.L. Preston's first wife, Sally.

5. Letter of August 9, 1837, from John F. Caruthers, representing Washington College, to Col. Claudius Crozet, representing a proposed military school in Lexington, as quoted in William Couper, *Claudius Crozet: Soldier-Scholar-Educator-Engineer, 1789–1864, Southern Sketches*, Ser. 1, No. 8 (Charlottesville: Historical Publishing, 1936): 95–96.

6. Letter of December 27, 1861, from J.T.L. Preston to Margaret J. Preston, in Elizabeth Randolph Preston Allan, *A March Past: Reminiscences of Elizabeth Randolph Preston Allan*, ed. Janet Allan Bryan (Richmond: Dietz Press, 1938), 136.

7. J.T.L. Preston, "Historical Sketch of the Establishment and Organization of the Virginia Military Institute, prepared, at the request of the Board of Visitors, by Col. John Thomas Lewis Preston, Professor Emeritus V.M.I., July 4, 1889," Box: Preston, John T. L., Folder MS 0240), 1, VMI Archives. Also quoted by Francis Smith, *History of the Virginia Military Institute: Its Building and Rebuilding*, ed. F. H. Smith, Jr. (Lynchburg, Va.: J. P. Bell, 1912), Chap. 1.

8. Ibid.

9. Ibid., 2.

10. William Couper, *One Hundred Years at V.M.I.* (Richmond: Garrett and Massie, 1939), 1: 15.

11. William Couper, "Remarks at the Preston Library Dedication, November 4, 1939" (the week before the Dedication), Box: Faculty and Staff; Folder: Preston clippings and articles, 2, VMI Archives.

12. *In Memoriam: Francis H. Smith, Father and Founder of the Virginia Military Institute* (New York: Knickerbocker Press, 1890), 8–9.

13. *In Memoriam*, 11.

14. "Minutes of the Board of Visitors" 2: 54, June 22, 1854, VMI Archives. The superintendent's "15th Annual Report," 52–63, gives a "History of the origin and progress of the Virginia Military Institute."

15. Francis H. Smith, "Dedication to Colonel John T. L. Preston, Professor of Latin Language and English Literature, Virginia Military Institute, November 11, 1867 (28th Anniversary of the Virginia Military Institute)," in *Elements of Descriptive Geometry with its Applications to Shades, Shadows, and Perspective and to Topography* (Baltimore: Kelly, Piet, 1868), v–vi.

16. Francis H. Smith, *History of the Virginia Military Institute: Its Building and Rebuilding*, ed. F. H. Smith, Jr. (Lynchburg, Va.: J. P. Bell, 1912), 11–39.

17. Ibid., 54.

18. Henry Boley, *Lexington in Old Virginia* (Richmond: Garrett and Massie, 1936), 190.

19. Jennings Cropper Wise, *Military History of the Virginia Military Institute from 1839 to 1865* (Lynchburg, Va.: J. P. Bell, 1915), 31–33.

20. Ibid., 41. See also Crozet's photograph on p. 65 where he's captioned as "Founder."

21. Ibid. Crozet's letter of September 12, 1829, from Lexington to Francis Smith begins, "Dear Sir—You will receive by mail a printed copy of the Regulations adopted by the Board of Visitors for the government of the Virginia Military Institute."

Crozet was not, as Wise claimed, the originator of the name of the school, but to give credit where credit might be due, he may have been, as James Lee Conrad recently claimed, the first to call the school by its initials. Conrad contends that VMI was the first American college to become know by its initials and credits Crozet with the first use of "The V.M.I." See James Lee Conrad, *The Young Lions: Confederate Cadets at War* (Mechanicsburg, Pa.: Stackpole Books, 1997), 169 n. 12.

22. Smith, *History of the Virginia Military Institute*, 46–49.

23. Oren F. Morton, *A History of Rockbridge County, Virginia* (Baltimore: Regional Publishing, 1980), 200.

24. Boley, 71.

25. James G. Leyburn, "Dr. Alfred Leyburn (1803–1878), A Lexington Whig, Legislator, and Man of Affairs," *Proceedings of the Rockbridge Historical Society* 6 (1961–65): 26. J.T.L. Preston's wife, Sally, was younger sister to Ann Eliza Caruthers Leyburn.

26. *Virginia Military Institute Historic District*, Final Nomination to the National Register of Historic Places, Record No. 431843, NHLS No. 74002219 (Washington, D.C.: National Park Service, May 30, 1974).

27. E. W. Nichols, *Fifty Years of Service and Other Papers* (Lexington, Va.: Rockbridge County News Print, 1926), 27.

28. Ibid., 68.

29. Ibid., 21.

30. Ibid., 74.

31. Mrs. John H. Moore, *Memories of a Long Life in Virginia* (Staunton, Va.: McClure, 1920), 20. See also Oren F. Morton, *A History of Rockbridge County, Virginia* (Baltimore: Regional Publishing, 1980), 199.

32. Couper, *One Hundred Years at V.M.I.* 1: 31.

33. [Paxton, Matthew, ed.], "When the Virginia Military Institute Was Founded," *Rockbridge County News*, October 14, 1926. Paxton suggests Hugh Barclay as the

originator of VMI. All quotes from Paxton are in this issue of the *Rockbridge County News*.

34. "West Point Academy," *Lexington Gazette*, August 7, 1835.

35. Couper, *One Hundred Years at V.M.I.* 1: 18, 20, 324; 2: 57.

36. Couper. "Remarks at the Preston Library Dedication," 1.

37. Col. James Morgan, Jr., "Changing Face of the VMI," *Proceedings of the Rockbridge Historical Society* 7 (1966–69): 142.

38. Bradford Wineman's "J.T.L. Preston, VMI and the Revolution in Virginia Education, 1834–1839" was on file but is now missing from the archives at Appalachian State University in Boone, North Carolina.

39. Bradford Wineman, "J.T.L. Preston and the Origins of the Virginia Military Institute, 1834–42," *Virginia Magazine of History and Biography* 114, No. 2 (2006): 247.

40. Ibid., 228. For a list of the military schools modeled on VMI, see 254–55.

41. Ibid.

42. Ibid., 255.

43. Alden Partridge, "Plan of Establishing Additional Military Academies," April 1915, Alden Partridge Records, Box 3: Papers and Financial Records; Writings, Bound Manuscripts 1810–1817, Norwich University Archives, Kreitzberg Library, Northfield, VT., microfilmed by the Library of Congress in 1969 as Alden Partridge Records, 1807–1950 (MS 68–2061).

44. Gary Thomas Lord, "Alden Partridge's Proposal for a National System of Education: A Model for the Morrill Land-Grant Act," in Roger Geiger, ed., *History of Higher Education Annual* 18 (1998): 17.

45. Ibid., 12.

46. Ibid., 13.

47. Capt. Alden Partridge, *Discourse on Education* (Middletown, Conn.: E.&H. Clark, 1926), Pt. 2: 216–80. For Partridge's educational theory, see "Captain Partridge's Lecture on Education," 263–80, and for its practical application, see "Correspondence Between a Cadet and His Father," 216–62.

48. "History of Military Schools Founded by Captain Partridge and Norwich Men," in William Arba Ellis and Grenville M. Dodge, *Norwich University, 1819–1911: Her History, Her Graduates, Her Roll of Honor* (Montpelier, Vt.: Capital City Press, 1911), 1: 395–402. See also Lord, "Alden Partridge's Proposal," 13–14. Partridge's other literary, scientific, and military academies were established at Portsmouth, Virginia (1839–56); Bristol, Pennsylvania (1842–45); Harrisburg, Pennsylvania (1845–48); Wilmington, Delaware (1846–48); Reading, Pennsylvania (1850–54); and Pembroke, New Hampshire (1850–53). His National Scientific and Military Academy (1853) was at Brandywine Springs, Delaware. Several other short-lived imitators were Western Literary and Scientific Academy (1829–46) in Buffalo, New York; the New Jersey Institution in Orange, New Jersey (1828–30); the Literary, Scientific, and Military Academy in Fayetteville (1830–31) and Oxford (1830), North Carolina; Jefferson Military College (1828–34) in Mississippi, and Richland School in South Carolina (1830–35).

49. Alden Partridge, "Military Academy," *Lexington Gazette*, January 22, 1836.

50. For Thomas Jefferson's ideas on education, see Cornelius J. Heatwole, *A History of Education in Virginia* (New York: Macmillan, 1916), 199.

51. Letter of February 15, 1810, from Thomas Preston to James McDowell in Dumfries, Va., James D. Davidson Collection, McCormick Historical Association Library, Chicago. See also "Petition to the Congress of the United States by the Rector and Trustees of Washington Academy," n.d., in Washington and Lee Trustees Papers, Cabinet C, Drawer 4, Washington and Lee University Scrapbook, "Original Papers Relating to Early History of Washington and Lee College and Society of the Cincinnati," No. 7, Washington and Lee Special Collections. The petition to Congress was to endow the military school with the $15,000 of the Cincinnati Fund.

52. For the decision of the Washington Academy trustees "not to petition Congress at present on the subject of a military school," see Washington Academy Records of Board of Trustees: January 15, 1811–October 1844, Washington and Lee Trustees Papers, Cabinet B, Drawer 1, 1, January 15, 1811, Washington and Lee Special Collections. See also "Address of the President and Trustees of Washington College to the Cincinnati Society of Virginia," Washington and Lee Trustees Papers, Cabinet C, Drawer 4, Washington and Lee University Scrapbook, "Original Papers Relating to Early History of Washington and Lee College and Society of the Cincinnati," No. 11 1/2, Washington and Lee Special Collections.

53. Robert W. Jeffrey, "Virginia Military Institute," *Iron Worker* (Lynchburg, Va.), 16, No. 3 (Summer 1952): 3.

54. Couper, "Remarks at the Preston Library Dedication," 12.

55. Preston, "Historical Sketch," 3.

Chapter 6

1. According to Preston's grandson, Edmund Randolph Preston, Preston's son George claimed "he never in his life heard his father [J.T.L. Preston] ever mention his father's [T. L. Preston's] name or refer to him in any way." See Edmund Randolph Preston, "The Name Thomas Lewis Preston and Some of Those Who Have Borne It" (Chicago, June 24, 1945), 3.

2. Letter of July 16, 1945, from Assistant General Counsel Thomas L. Preston in Washington, D.C., to Edmund Randolph Preston.

3. For Preston's view of "Uncle McDowell" as "the only father he ever knew," see letter of August 28, 1939, from William Couper to Maj. J. W. McClung, in Box: VMI Faculty and Staff, 19th Cent., Folder 1: Preston, John T. L., VMI Archives.

4. Letter of September 10, 1835, from J.T.L. Preston at Cherry Grove to James McDowell, Jr., in Warm Springs, Smithfield-Preston Foundation, MS 97–002, Box 1, Folder 20, VPI Special Collections.

5. Deed of September 22, 1835, from Elizabeth R. Preston to J.T.L. Preston for her interest in Thomas L. Preston's lot, bounded by John Parry, Jacob Clyce, Wm. H. Letcher, Matthew White, John L. Caruthers, Robert White, Cornelius Dorman, and said John Preston for $1 in Deed Bk. T, 67.

6. Elizabeth Preston Allan, "Reminiscences of an Ordinary Life," original manuscript of *A March Past*, which includes information omitted from the book, Collection 2764: William Allan Papers, Box 2, Folder 12, Pt. 1: 3, Southern Historical Collection, University of North Carolina, Chapel Hill.

7. Letter of May 28, 1836, from J.T.L. Preston to James McDowell, Jr., Smithfield-Preston Foundation, MS 97–002, Box 1, Folder 20, VPI Special Collections.

8. Deed of December 14, 1837, to J.T.L. Preston from Hugh and Mary Barclay for $2,425 for 78 1/2 acres adjoining John Bowyers, Edward Browns, John Ruff, in Preston Collection. Folder 80.23.8, Stonewall Jackson House (now stored at VMI Archives). See also Elizabeth Randolph Preston Allan, *A March Past: Reminiscences of Elizabeth Randolph Preston Allan*, ed. Janet Allan Bryan (Richmond: Dietz Press, 1938), 29; William Ruffner, "Col. J.T.L. Preston," *Washington and Lee University Historical Papers* 4 (1893): 140, and William Couper, "Remarks at the Preston Library Dedication, November 4, 1939," Box: Faculty and Staff; Folder: Preston Clippings and Articles, 9, VMI Archives, for Preston's use of the farm. For Preston's purchase of an additional 124 acres at auction, see deed of January 1, 1863, to J.T.L. Preston and Robert McDowell from William White, commissioner, during suit between Bowyer heirs, for Lot 1 of 124 acres and 74 poles for $3,376.04, with 56 acres going to Preston in Deed Book II, page 42; and 69 105/160 acres to Robert McDowell, which McDowell is conveying to Preston, about 2 1/2 miles south of Lexington on the Plank Road, bordering Brockenbrough, in Deed Book II, 249, plat attached. Both deeds also in, Preston Collection, Folder 80.23.10, Stonewall Jackson House. For his naming it Foxwood, see J.T. L. Preston, *Removing to a New Charge: Letters to a Young Minister* (Richmond: Presbyterian Committee of Publication, 1890), 4.

9. Ruffner, "Col. J.T.L. Preston," 140.

10. Preston, *Removing to a New Charge*, 4.

11. For some of Preston's land holdings, sales, and purchases, see the 21-acre town lot that Thomas Lewis Preston bought on September 5, 1808 [Deed Book F, 354] and was delivered to J.T.L. Preston on March 23, 1836; 1,000 acres in Shelby County on the Ohio River, 300 acres on the Kentucky River, and 700 acres near Poplar Level as of June 1836 [Jackson House, Folder 80.23.64]; 78 1/2 acres from Hugh Barclay on the James River two miles southwest of Lexington and bounded by John Bowyers' Thornhill Estate [Deed Bk. U, 151; also Jackson House, Folder 80.23.8]; twelve acres east of Lexington from Matthew Kahle at public auction on October 3, 1838, adjoining his hilltop property [Deed Bk. V, 189], etc. See also six certificates for sales of Lexington property from 1834–35 on Randolph Street [Preston Collection, Folder 80.23.6, Stonewall Jackson House] and lots on six certificates for sales of Lexington property in 1834–35 on Randolph Street [Preston Collection, Folder 80.23.6, Stonewall Jackson House] and lots on Randolph Street and its extension in the 1850s–80s from J.T.L. Preston to Thomas Caffrey on April 18, 1857 [Deed Bk. FF, 234], to Lucretia Marks (wife of a shoemaker) on October 1, 1864 [Deed Bk. JJ, 75], to John C. Middleton (mayor of Lexington) on April 28, 1866 [Deed Bk. JJ, 166], to George F. Pulse (a carpenter) on February 29, 1868 [Deed Bk. JJ, 589], to Edward Hefrin (a stonemason) on May 29, 1868 [Deed Bk. JJ, 687] and on December 24, 1875 [Deed Bk. OO, 507], to John S. Sam on July 8, 1873 [Deed Bk. NN, 190], to D. C. Masters on December 11, 1877, across from G. W. Pulse near the school lot. The side and back alleys had now been dedicated to the public, the street being 40 feet, side alley 12 feet, and back alley 20 feet. [Deed Bk. QQ, 126], to Lucretia Hook (wife of a brick mason) on March 13, 1878, for part of the "School House Lot" and bordering Union Baptist Church lot [Deed Bk. UU, 77], to Susan Roberts nee Wallace on November 7, 1888, for part of school house lot on Shield's Hill near the second colored Baptist Church [Deed Bk. 72, 6], to Susan Jane Adams on January 4, 1890, bordering the street in front of J. R. Tucker and John Carmichael and alley from Massie Street [Deed Bk. 70, 304], and to Mary Susan Hildegrand through Herbert and Thomas Preston, his executors, on January 29, 1891 [Deed Bk. 68, 493]. The lot that Preston sold to Edward Hefrin, now numbered 207 North Randolph Street, is where the William Alexander house was rebuilt when it was moved from the site of the house built for Gen. R. E. Lee in 1868–69 on the Washington College campus. See Leslie L. Campbell, "House at 207 North Randolph St.," Rockbridge County, Virginia, Rockbridge Historical Society Manuscripts, Washington and Lee Special Collections. See also Amanda Askew, "207 North Randolph Street, Lexington, Virginia: A Study of Vernacular Architecture," a paper written for Prof. Pamela Simpson's class in American Architecture, Washington and Lee Architectural Papers, April 2007, Washington and Lee Special Collections.

12. Before the war the area was known as Shields' Hill, named for Alexander Shields.

13. "Preston Street," in Winifred Hadsel, The Streets of Lexington (Lexington: Rockbridge Historical Society, 1895), 113.

14. See the six houses in Preston Row on *Gray's New Map of Lexington, Rockingham* [sic] *County, Virginia*, published in 1877.

15. For Preston's distaste for the law, see his daughter Elizabeth Preston Allan's remembrance in Janet Allan Bryan's introduction to J.T.L. Preston, "London Journal," 2.

Chapter 7

1. Hugh Blair, *Lectures on Rhetoric and Belles Lettres* (London: T. Cadell and W. Davies, 1812), 1, 6.

2. Ibid., 15.

3. Francis Smith, as quoted in William Couper, *One Hundred Years at V.M.I.* (Richmond: Garrett and Massie, 1939), 1: 69.

4. See Edmund Pendleton, "Early Days at the V.M.I." *The Bomb: The Virginia Military Institute, Lexington, Virginia* (Philadelphia: Huston, Ashmead, Wilson, 1896), 15.

5. Bradford Wineman, "J.T.L. Preston and the Origins of the Virginia Military Institute, 1834–42," *Virginia Magazine of History and Biography* 114, No. 2 (2006): 252.

6. "Minutes of the Board of Visitors" 1: April 15, 1840, VMI Archives.

7. Ibid., April 20, 1840. Commissions of the officers at VMI—Major for Francis Smith and Captain for J.T.L. Preston—were confined entirely to the institute "as a separate military post independent of any organization with the residue of the militia." See also Couper, *One Hundred Years at V.M.I.* 1: 159.

8. Preston, "London Journal," 33.

9. Quoted by Edwin L. Dooley, "A New Look at the Old Guard," *VMI Alumni Review* 48 (Winter 1972): 10.

10. Francis H. Smith, A.M., *College Reform* (Philadelphia: Thomas, Cowperthwait, 1851), "Preface."

11. Ibid., 27–28

12. See the Cincinnati Monument erected in front of the Preston Library.

13. "Minutes of the Society of Cincinnati of Virginia," Richmond, Washington and Lee University Scrapbook, "Original Papers Relating to Early History of Washington and Lee College and Society of the

Cincinnati," No. 5, December 13, 1802, Washington and Lee Special Collections.

14. "Resolution of the Society of Cincinnati of Virginia," Richmond, Washington and Lee University Scrapbook, "Original Papers Relating to Early History of Washington and Lee College and Society of the Cincinnati," No. 8, December 16, 1807, Washington and Lee Special Collections.

15. "Petition to the Congress of the United States by the Rector and Trustees of Washington Academy," n.d., Washington and Lee Trustees Papers, Cabinet C, Drawer 4, Washington and Lee University Scrapbook, "Original Papers Relating to Early History of Washington and Lee College and Society of the Cincinnati," No. 7, Washington and Lee Special Collections.

16. When the Virginia Society disbanded in 1824, the fund was worth $15,000, and by 1848 it had accrued to $25,000. See Henry Boley, *Lexington in Old Virginia* (Richmond: Garrett and Massie, 1936), 63. Washington College began drawing from the fund in 1840. See Couper, *One Hundred Years at V.M.I.* 1: 71.

17. For the origin of the term "rats" as it applied to VMI cadets "sometime in the 1850s," see Henry Alexander Wise, Jr., *Drawing Out the Man: The VMI Story* (Charlottesville: University Press of Virginia, 1978), 17.

18. See William Couper, *One Hundred Years at V.M.I.* 1: 311, where the Hon. Peter J. Otey, Class of 1860, recalls that in 1856 "I came here a 'Rat.'" See also Beverly Stanard, *Letters of a New Market Cadet*, eds. John G. Barrett and Robert K. Turner, Jr. (Chapel Hill: University of North Carolina Press, 1961), 9. Cadet Stanard, who was killed at New Market, referred to himself and his fourth class as "Rats" on page two of a letter dated August 28, 1863.

19. "The Cadets of Lexington," *Richmond Enquirer*, January 11, 1842.

20. *Acts of the General Assembly of Virginia, Passed at the Session Commencing 6th December 1841, and Ending 26th March 1842, in the Sixty-Sixth Year of the Commonwealth* (Richmond: Samuel Shepherd, 1842), 21, Chap. 24.

21. William Arthur Maddox, *The Free School Idea in Virginia Before the Civil War* (New York: Teachers College, Columbia University, 1918), 122–23. See also Jennings C. Wise, *Military History of the Virginia Military Institute from 1839 to 1865* (Lynchburg, Va.: J. P. Bell, 1915), 52. The University of Virginia became a normal school by the act of March 12, 1856.

22. Edwin L. Dooley, Jr., "Francis H. Smith and VMI on the Eve of the Civil War," in Thomas W. Davis, ed., *A Crowd of Honorable Youths*, 19.

23. "Annual Report, Superintendent, V.M.I., 1843," *Richmond Enquirer*, February 1, 1844.

24. For the names of the first 16 cadets to graduate from VMI, see Jennings C. Wise, *Military History of the Virginia Military Institute from 1839 to 1865* (Lynchburg, Va.: J. P. Bell, 1915), 52–53.

25. Superintendent Francis Smith, "Report to the Board of Visitors, June 22, 1848," in "Minutes of the Board of Visitors" 1: 222. See also Francis Smith, "Report of June 28, 1850," in ibid., 307–10.

26. Col. Joseph R. Anderson, "Col. Preston as Teacher," a one-page remembrance written ca. 1891, Box: VMI Faculty and Staff, 19th Century, Preston, John T. L., Folder 5: Miscellaneous, VMI Archives.

27. "Report of the Professor of Languages on the Progress of His Classes," Box: Superintendent 19th Century Subject Files, Annual Reports, Departments, June 13, 1844, VMI Archives.

28. Francis Smith, "Annual Report, June 13, 1844," VMI Archives, Box: Superintendent 19th Century Subject Files, Departments Annual Reports.

29. Ibid.

30. Francis Smith, Annual Reports, 1845 and 1846, VMI Archives, Box: Superintendent 19th Century Subject Files, Departments Annual Reports.

31. Letter of April 16, 1846, from John T. L. Preston to Prof. George Frederick Holmes, Richmond College, Johnson Family Papers, 1821–85, Section 3, MSS1 J6496 d 19, Virginia Historical Society.

32. J.T.L. Preston, "Historical Sketch of the Establishment and Organization of the Virginia Military Institute, prepared at the request of the Board of Visitors, by Col. John Thomas Lewis Preston, Professor Emeritus V.M.I., July 4, 1889" (VMI Archives, Box: Preston, John T. L., Folder MS 0240), 5.

Chapter 8

1. "Minutes of the Board of Visitors" 1: 105, June 30, 1845, VMI Archives.

2. Letter of August 28, 1844, from F. H. Smith to J.T.L. Preston, Superintendent Francis H. Smith, Outgoing Correspondence Letter Book 1844–48, VMI Archives.

3. Letter of June 25, 1844, from J.T.L. Preston to Gov. James McDowell, Smithfield-Preston Foundation, MS 97–002, Box 1, Folder 20, VPI Special Collections.

4. For the charges leveled against Smith and Preston's defense, see "Minutes of the Board of Visitors" 1: 80–81, June 24, 1844, and letter of August 29, 1844, from J.T.L. Preston to Francis Smith, Superintendent's Incoming Correspondence, #0042, VMI Archives.

5. "Minutes of the Board of Visitors" 1: 74, July 3, 1844.

6. Ibid., 109–10.

7. Ollinger Crenshaw, "General Lee's College: Rise and Growth of Washington and Lee," unpublished typescript in two volumes (Lexington, Va.: Washington and Lee University, 1973), 1: 265.

8. For Speaker V. W. Southall's consideration of moving VMI elsewhere, see Superintendent's Incoming Correspondence, March 24, 1846.

9. *Acts of the Virginia General Assembly, Session Laws 1848–49* (Richmond, 1849), film 358a/reel 2:16, March 16, 1849, Archives Division, Library of Virginia. For a detailed summary of the Legislative Act of March 16, 1849, and the town's response, *see* William Couper, *One Hundred Years at V.M.I.* 1:196–206.

10. Francis H. Smith, *History of the Virginia Military Institute: Its Building and Rebuilding*, ed. F. H. Smith, Jr. (Lynchburg, Va.: J. P. Bell, 1912), 119.

11. *Lexington Gazette*, June 5 and 12, 1849.

12. Resolution of the Trustees of Washington College, June 21, 1849, in William Couper, *One Hundred Years at V.M.I.* (Richmond: Garrett and Massie, 1939), 1: 205.

13. VMI Board of Visitors, "Report to Governor John B. Floyd, September 15, 1849," in Francis Smith, *History of the Virginia Military Institute: Its Building and Rebuilding*, ed. F. H. Smith, Jr. (Lynchburg, Va.: J. P. Bell, 1912), Chap. 7: 5. See also *Lexington Gazette*, September 18, 1849.

14. William Couper, *One Hundred Years at V.M.I.* (Richmond: Garrett and Massie, 1939), 1: 223.

15. Royster Lyle, Jr., and Pamela Hemenway Simpson. *The Architecture of Historic Lexington* (Charlottesville: University Press of Virginia, 1977), 27.

16. "Deaths," *Richmond Enquirer*, April 27, 1849, 1, col. 7.

17. J.T.L. Preston's father, Thomas Lewis Preston, had been joint editor with Thomas Ritchie of the *Richmond Enquirer*. See Dr. William Henry Ruffner, "Capt. Thomas L. Preston," *Washington and Lee University Historical Papers* 4 (1893): 137, and "Sketches of Trustees," *Washington and Lee University Historical Papers* 5 (1895): 49. See also William Bowker Preston, *Preston Genealogy*, 180. But Thomas Preston is not listed in Lester J. Cappon, *Virginia Newspapers 1821–1935: A Bibliography with Historical Introduction and Notes* (New York: D. Appleton-Century, 1936) 171, #1262 *Richmond Enquirer*. Nor is he mentioned in Charles Henry Ambler, *Thomas Ritchie: A Study in Virginia Politics* (Richmond: Bell Book and Stationery, 1913).

18. "Gross and Malicious Imposition," *Richmond Enquirer*, April 27, 1849, 2, col. 3.

Chapter 9

1. Hardly ever is Franklin Preston mentioned with a middle name, but if he had one, it would have been Caruthers. He is listed in *Virginia Regimental Histories Series* as "Franklin C. Preston," when he mustered for service on April 29, 1861. See R. J. Driver, Jr., *The 1st and 2nd Rockbridge Artillery*, 2nd ed. (Lynchburg, Va.: H. E. Howard, 1987). See also Virginia Regimental Histories Series (Duxbury, Mass.: Historical Data Systems), www.civilwardata.com.

2. Edmonia Madison Randolph Preston died on August 7, 1842.

3. "Minutes of the Board of Visitors" 1: 57, VMI Archives.

4. Elizabeth Preston Allan, "Reminiscences of an Ordinary Life," original manuscript of *A March Past*, which includes information omitted from the book, Collection 2764: William Allan Papers, Box 2, Folder 12, pt 4: 2, Southern Historical Collection, University of North Carolina, Chapel Hill.

5. Ibid.

6. Elizabeth Randolph Preston Allan, *A March Past: Reminiscences of Elizabeth Randolph Preston Allan*, ed. Janet Allan Bryan (Richmond: Dietz Press), 1938, 32.

7. Willie's name is spelled as such in every source consulted, except in the two books by Elizabeth Preston Allan, who favored the spelling "Willy." Quotes from Allan's books will retain her spelling. Otherwise, "Willie" will be the spelling of choice.

8. For the move from Preston's home on the hilltop to their second home on Main Street, see Allan, "Reminiscences of an Ordinary Life," Pt. 1: 4. For Taylor's move to the hill top, see "The Prestons," *Washington and Lee Historical Papers* 4 (1893): 126. According to Preston's daughter Elizabeth, "Five of my Father's children were born either in the hill-top house, or the Main Street one; but somewhere between 1843, and 1845." See Allan, "Reminiscences of an Ordinary Life," Pt. 1: 6.

9. The Campbell House was between the homes of John Letcher and Capt. William Willson, south of today's Willson-Walker House. For Preston's purchase of the house on November 26, 1844, see deed from William and Susan Preston McDowell Taylor to J.T.L. Preston for $2,000 for land with house on Main Street adjoined on one side by house of John Letcher and other side by Capt. William Willson's house (at 30 N. Main) with alley purchased by Taylor from Willson in 1817 ten or twelve feet wide from Main Street to the back street at the foot of the lots and between the house and Willson's house, in Deed Bk. Y, 226.

For Preston's sale of the house to Nannie Jordan on July 29, 1871, see deed from J.T.L. and Margaret Preston to Mary Dosey Jordan, Nannie A. Jordan, and James R. Jordan of Lexington and Rachel and George Baker of Baltimore, all heirs of Dr. James R. Jordan for $2,000 for a lot and house on Main Street between the house of John Letcher, where Odd Fellows Hall and the house of Charles Deaver are now located, and house of William Willson's heirs, now property of Samuel J. Campbell and A. M. Glasgow, together with alley bought by Taylor in 1817, being lot bought by J.T.L. Preston from William Taylor November 26, 1844, in Deed Book Y, 226 between Main Street and the back street. See Deed Bk. RR, 191. Note: Odd Fellows Hall was Lexington's entertainment center at the corner of Main and Henry Streets, belonged to the Jordan heirs in 1871, and was later the shoe factory of Thomas H. Deaver, a skating rink in 1885, a movie hall, and Washington and Lee Troubadour Workshop by 1936.

10. Royster Lyle, Jr., and Pamela Hemenway Simpson, *The Architecture of Historic Lexington* (Charlottesville, Va.: University Press of Virginia, 1977), 10.

11. Ibid., 285.

12. James W. Alexander, D.D., *Life of Archibald Alexander, D.D. LL.D.: First Professor in the Theological Seminary at Princeton, New Jersey* (Philadelphia: Presbyterian Board of Publications, 1856), 33.

13. Dr. Leslie Lyle Campbell, quoted in Leslie L. Campbell, "The Old Jordan House," Rockbridge County, Virginia, Rockbridge Historical Society Manuscripts, Washington and Lee Special Collections. The 26¾ acres of farmland on which this house sat was originally owned by Isaac Campbell's father, who had come with Borden and owned the present VMI grounds.

14. Ruth A. McCulloch, quoted in Royster and Simpson, *The Architecture of Historic Lexington*, 285.

15. Allan, *March Past*, 32.

16. Ibid., 87.

17. See J.T.L. Preston, "A Philosophy of Man Impossible without Aid from Revelation," *Southern Presbyterian Review* 29 No. 4 (October 1878): 740.

18. Allan, *March Past*, 19–20.

19. Ibid., 20.

20. Henry Ruffner assumed the chair of ancient languages at Washington College in 1819, the year he married Sally Lyle. But when the college constructed a president's house on campus in 1841, he sold his property to Preston's brother-in-law, Dr. Alfred Leyburn. On January 27, 1844, before Leyburn could pay off his mortgage to Ruffner, Preston paid both Ruffner and Leyburn $3,250 for full possession of the house. For Preston's purchase at today's 110 Preston Street, see deed of January 27, 1844, from Henry and Sarah Ruffner and Alfred and Ann P. Leyburn to J.T.L. Preston for $3,250 for lot lying on Woods Creek and partly within Lexington containing five acres, bounded by same as in John Robinson's deed to Ruffner in 1820, Deed Bk. Y, 309. See also *Preservation Master Plan for Washington and Lee University, Lexington, Virginia* (Charlottesville: John Milner Associates, October 2005), Chap. 2, "A Brief History of Washington and Lee," 9. And see Lyle and Simpson, *Architecture of Historic Lexington*, 80–81, and Allison Hyko, "The Preston House," April 1, 1994, an excellent, well-documented paper written for

Prof. Pamela Simpson's class in American architecture, in Architecture Papers: Pam Simpson's Class, Washington and Lee Special Collections.

21. Elizabeth's description of the house at today's 110 Preston Street in Allan, *March Past*, 35.

22. Allan, "Reminiscences of an Ordinary Life," Pt. 1: 19.

23. Dr. William Henry Ruffner, "Col. J.T.L. Preston," *Washington and Lee University Historical Papers* 4 (1893): 138–139.

24. William Couper, "Remarks at the Preston Library Dedication, November 4, 1939," Box: Faculty and Staff; Folder: Preston Clippings and Articles, 6, VMI Archives.

25. Ibid., 138.

26. William Couper, "Remarks at the Preston Library Dedication," 6.

27. J.T.L. Preston, *Removing to a New Charge: Letters to a Young Minister* (Richmond: Presbyterian Committee of Publication, 1890), 44.

28. William Ruffner, "Col. J.T.L. Preston," 138.

29. For Preston's love of ornithology, see his review of a biography of Thomas Edward in J.T.L. Preston, "The Study of Natural History," *Southern Presbyterian Review* 28, No. 4 (October 1877): 685–88. The quote comes from 686–87.

30. William Henry Ruffner, "Col. J.T.L. Preston," *Washington and Lee University Historical Papers* 4 (1893): 140.

31. J.T.L. Preston, as quoted in Allan, *March Past*, 13.

32. Ibid.

33. William Henry Ruffner's description of Edmonia Preston in "Gov. James McDowell," *Washington and Lee University Historical Papers* 4 (1893): 136.

Chapter 10

1. William Bean, "Half-forgotten Bits of Local History—'The Skinner Case': Presbyterian Church Trial of 1850s Had Unusual and Interesting Angles," *Lexington Gazette*, October 25, 1933.

2. James G. Leyburn, "Lexington Presbyterians, 1819–1882: Personalities, Problems, Peculiarities," *Proceedings of the Rockbridge Historical Society* 8 (1970–74): 35.

3. Royster Lyle, Jr., "John Blair Lyle of Lexington and His 'Automatic Bookstore,'" *Virginia Cavalcade* 21 (Autumn 1971): 23.

4. J.T.L. Preston, "A Card, dated November 8, 1847," *Richmond Enquirer*, November 19, 1847, 3.

5. Skinner, Rev. John, ed. "The Pastoral Relation—What are its Securities? Case of the Rev. John Skinner, D.D., and the Presbyterian Church of Lexington Before the Presbytery of Lexington" (Lexington, Va.: Winn and Carter, 1847), 20.

6. For a lively and thoroughly detailed account of the Skinner War, see William G. Bean, "The Skinner Case," manuscript copy of a paper delivered before the Rockbridge Historical Society, October 1947.

7. Leyburn, "Lexington Presbyterians," 35–36.

8. J.T.L. Preston, as quoted in *Record of the Presbytery of Lexington, Convened for the Trial of the Rev. Jno. Skinner, D.D.* (Lexington, Va.: Robert C. Noel, 1848), 67–68, Washington and Lee Special Collections. Preston's response, which became legendary, is misquoted in various sources, as in Elizabeth Randolph Preston Allan, *A March Past: Reminiscences of Elizabeth Randolph Preston Allan*, ed. Janet Allan Bryan (Richmond: Dietz Press, 1938), 20: "Mr. Moderator, Dr. Skinner will at once withdraw his statement and apologize, or I will come over and knock him down." And in a handwritten recollection, Preston's grandson Edmund Randolph Preston quoted Skinner as accusing Sally of being "blood proud, purse proud and neglecting her poor kin," and Preston, with "open knife in hand, though he was the ruling elder, jumping over the church benches and muttering, 'I will cut the d— scoundrel's tongue out.' He had to be held till he cooled off." See Edmund Randolph Preston, "Grandfather Preston (Col. J.T.L. Preston, founder of Virginia Military Institute)," handwritten manuscript.

9. Ibid.

10. *Record of the Presbytery*, 98.

11. Bean, "Half-Forgotten Bits of Local History," November 29, 1848.

12. James G. Leyburn, "Dr. Alfred Leyburn (1803–1878), A Lexington Whig, Legislator, and Man of Affairs," *Proceedings of the Rockbridge Historical Society* 6 (1961–65): 28. For the Presbytery's record of Skinner's relationship with the Lexington Church, see Presbyterian Church in the U.S.A., "Minutes of the Lexington Presbytery," 12: 557–58, October 6, 1841, when he is installed as minister; 647–49, August 21, 1847, when he is released from pastoral duties; 650–51, when he resigns and announces his intent to appeal to the Virginia Synod; and Vol. 13, May 3, 1848, when he presents his "Final Protest," Washington and Lee Special Collections.

13. Leyburn, "Lexington Presbyterians," 37.

14. Robert F. Hunter, *Lexington Presbyterian Church*, 1789–1989 (Lexington, Va.: Lexington Presbyterian Church, 1991), 54.

15. William Bean, "Dr. Bean Reads Historical Paper," *Rockbridge County News*, November 15, 22, and 29, 1945.

16. For the introduction of the Bible into VMI's curriculum in 1848, see "Minutes of the Board of Visitors" 1: 222, VMI Archives.

17. Gov. James H. Price, quoting John Wise in "Remarks of the Governor at the Exercises Commemorating the Centennial of the V.M.I. and the Twenty-first Armistice of the First World War, Lexington, Va., November 11, 1939," Price Speeches: July–December 1939, Washington and Lee Special Collections.

18. William Couper, *One Hundred Years at V.M.I.* (Richmond: Garrett and Massie, 1939), 1: 179.

19. For accounts of Ben Ficklin, see "Memories of Maj. Ben. Ficklin '49," VMI Cadet 2 (January 1872): 137–39, also May 3, 1948; John G. Barrett and Richard M. McMurry "VMI in the Civil War," in Davis, ed., *A Crowd of Honorable Youths*, 33; W. R. Austerman, "The Brash Reinsman: Ben Ficklin's Adventures," *Virginia Cavalcade* 33: 114–15; and Rick Britton, "Benjamin F. Ficklin, Monticello's Colorful Confederate Owner," *Monticello Newsletter* 17, No. 2 (Winter 2006): 1–5. See his photograph ca. 1855–60 with bow tie and hat in Richard M. McMurry, *Virginia Military Institute Alumni in the Civil War: In Bello Praesidium* (Lynchburg, Va.: H. E. Howard, 1999), 76.

20. Couper, *One Hundred Years at V.M.I.* 1: 163.

21. Henry Alexander Wise, Jr., *Drawing Out the Man: The VMI Story* (Charlottesville: University Press of Virginia, 1978), 22.

22. "Minutes of the Board of Visitors," 1: 211.

23. Wise, *Drawing Out the Man*, 23.

24. Couper, *One Hundred Years at V.M.I.* 2: 29–31.

25. Ibid., 248. On March 27, 1863, the board of visitors authorized the invaluable use of Ficklin's services.

26. Superintendent Francis Smith, "Annual Report, July 1, 1847," VMI Archives.
27. "Minutes of the Board of Visitors" 1: 259, June 22, 1849.
28. Ibid., 315–16, September 24, 1850. The board of visitors approved commissioning Superintendent Smith as colonel, the professors as major, assistant professors as lieutenant, and instructors as captain.
29. Ibid., 295, July 5, 1850.
30. Couper, *One Hundred Years at V.M.I.* 1: 238.
31. For the mutiny of the corps on April 21, 1851, see "Minutes of the Board of Visitors" 1: 318–22. See also William Couper, *One Hundred Years at V.M.I.* 1: 237–39.
32. Henry Wise, *Drawing Out the Man*, 24.
33. Letter of September 9, 1858, from Gen. Richardson to J.T.L. as acting superintendent, quoted in Couper, *One Hundred Years at V.M.I.* 1: 337–38.
34. J.T.L. Preston, "A Philosophy of Man Impossible without Aid from Revelation," *Southern Presbyterian Review* 29, No. 4 (October 1878): 736. See also Preston's illustration of the young girl seeking advice from her pastor, in J.T.L. Preston, "The Christian Life," *Southern Presbyterian Review* 28, No. 4 (October 1877): 718.
35. J.T.L. Preston, "Jottings," the name given to "John T. L. Preston Diary, 1861 July 24–September 22," MSS 17,264, p. 19, September 13, 1861, Manuscript Division, Library of Congress, Washington, D.C.
36. Ibid., 21, September 18, 1861.

Chapter 11

1. Although Preston's "London Journal" covered only the last month of his trip to Europe, from July 30 to August 27, 1851, his visa of May 11 specified the various countries he visited. Preston's passport, issued May 11, 1851, described him as age 40, 5 feet, 10 inches tall, medium forehead, blue eyes, large nose, large mouth, projecting chin, gray hair, ruddy complexion, and oval face. See his passport in Box: Preston, John T. L., Folder MS 0240, VMI Archives.
2. William Couper, *One Hundred Years at V.M.I.* (Richmond: Garrett and Massie, 1939), 1: 248–50.
3. For the nicknames of VMI's early professors, see John S. Wise, *The End of an Era* (Boston: Houghton Mifflin, 1899), 261; Henry Wise, *Drawing Out the Man: The VMI Story* (Charlottesville: University Press of Virginia, 1978), 18; and Edwin L. Dooley, "A New Look at the Old Guard," *VMI Alumni Review* 48 (Winter 1972): 9. John Wise gives different spellings: Smith as "Old Spex," Preston as "Old Bald," and Colston as "Old Polly," and includes nicknames for prominent cadets. Robertson, *Stonewall Jackson*, 117, follows John Wise's "Old Spex" for Smith and "Old Bald" for Preston.
4. Quoted in the Rev. J. C. Hiden, "Stonewall Jackson: Reminiscences of Him as a Professor in the Virginia Military Institute," *Southern Historical Society Papers* 20: 306. See also Montgomery, Alabama, *Advertiser*, November 27, 1892.
5. For the court-martial of Cadet James A. Walker, see Court-martial Book, May 2, 1852, VMI Archives. See also *Withrow Scrapbook 7*: 60, Washington and Lee Special Collections. A full account of the incident is given by Robertson, *Stonewall Jackson*, 140–41. During his outstanding service during the Civil War, Walker, class of 1852, would receive his diploma retroactively at Jackson's request and would go on to command, ironically, Jackson's own brigade long after Stonewall's death.

6. Hiden, "Stonewall Jackson," 309.
7. Letter of November 27, 1892, from James H. Lane to the editor of the *Richmond Advertiser*, in *Southern Historical Society Papers* 20: 310–11.
8. Mary Anna Morrison, *Memoirs of "Stonewall" Jackson by His Widow* (Dayton, Ohio: Morningside Bookshop, 1976), 81.
9. J.T.L. Preston, "General Jackson as a Professor, Extract of a lecture recently by Col. J.T.L. Preston, of the V. M. Institute," *Lexington Banner and Gazette*, May 16, 1866.
10. Elizabeth Preston Allan, "Reminiscences of an Ordinary Life," original manuscript of *A March Past*, which includes information omitted from the book, Collection 2764: William Allan Papers, Box 2, Folder 12, Pt. 1: 13, Southern Historical Collection, University of North Carolina, Chapel Hill. The *Preston Family Genealogy* lists the youngest child by Sally as John T. L. Preston. See William Bowker Preston, *Preston Family Genealogy*, tracing the history of the family from about 1040, A.D., in Great Britain, in the New England states, and in Virginia, to the present time, ed. L. A. Wilson, (Salt Lake City: Desert News, 1900), 202, index No. 124.
11. For John Lyle's love of Sally, see Dr. William Ruffner's account in Elizabeth Randolph Preston Allan, *A March Past: Reminiscences of Elizabeth Randolph Preston Allan*, ed. Janet Allan Bryan (Richmond: Dietz Press, 1938), 39. Sally was actually named after John Lyle's sister, Sarah "Sally" Lyle Ruffner, William's mother.
12. George West Diehl, "Preston Saga," in *Rockbridge County, Virginia Notebook* (Utica, Ky.: McDowell, 1982), 13–14.
13. Mary Anna Jackson, *Memoirs of "Stonewall" Jackson by His Widow* (Dayton, Ohio: Morningside Bookshop, 1976), 79–80.
14. Royster Lyle, Jr., "John Blair Lyle of Lexington and His 'Automatic Bookstore,'" *Virginia Cavalcade* 21, No. 2 (Autumn 1971): 20.
15. Henry Boley, *Lexington in Old Virginia* (Richmond: Garrett and Massie, 1936), 158–60.
16. Allan, "Reminiscences of an Ordinary Life," Pt. 1: 13.

Chapter 12

1. Willie, quoted in Margaret Junkin Preston, "William C. Preston," Collection 101B: Margaret Junkin Papers, 1837–72, Box 1, Folder 7: Scrapbook, Washington and Lee Special Collections.
2. Elizabeth Randolph Preston Allan, *A March Past: Reminiscences of Elizabeth Randolph Preston Allan*, ed. Janet Allan Bryan (Richmond: Dietz Press, 1938), 44.
3. J.T.L. Preston, "Jottings," the name given to "John T. L. Preston Diary, 1861 July 24–September 22," MSS 17,264, p. 5, August 2, 1861, Manuscript Division, Library of Congress, Washington, D.C.
4. William Ruffner, "Col. J.T.L. Preston," *Washington and Lee University Historical Papers* 4 (1893): 141, 113.
5. William Couper, *One Hundred Years at V.M.I.* (Richmond: Garrett and Massie, 1939), 1: 301. See also James Irvin Robertson, Jr., *Stonewall Jackson: The Man, the Soldier, The Legend* (New York: Macmillan, 1997), 169.
6. Allan, *March Past*, 44.
7. Mrs. W. J. Bryan, quoted in Curtis Carroll Davis,

Chronicler of the Cavaliers: A Life of William A. Caruthers (Richmond: Dietz Press, 1953), 517 n. 41. See also n. 42 and pp. 390, 523: Col. J.T.L. Preston, "Reminiscences of Sally Lyle Caruthers Preston, 1856, MS pp. ca. 150." Preston's reminiscences of nearly 150 pages somehow survived the family's burning of Preston papers after his own death and was in the possession of his granddaughter, Janet Allan Bryan, wife of Sen. William James Bryan of Florida, as late as September 18, 1949. Presumably it passed to her daughter, Betty Bryan Stockton, whose son, James Roosevelt Stockton, Jr., received it stored in a trunk, which unfortunately burned, he reported, in a recent house fire.
    8. Allan, *March Past*, 43–44.
    9. Elizabeth Randolph Preston Allan, *Life and Letters of Margaret Junkin Preston* (Boston: Riverside Press, 1903), 120. Included in the correspondence, according to Curtis Davis, were also items relating to George Washington. See Davis, *Chronicler of the Cavaliers*, 517 n. 41.
    10. Margaret Junkin Preston, "William C. Preston."
    11. Ibid.
    12. Allan, *March Past*, 48.
    13. Elizabeth Preston Allan, "Reminiscences of an Ordinary Life," the original manuscript of *March Past*, which includes information omitted from the book, Collection 2764: William Allan Papers, Box 2, Folder 12, Pt. 2: 1, Southern Historical Collection, University of North Carolina, Chapel Hill. If this is the Kentucky property that Preston sold in 1848, then Elizabeth's income was actually "$12,000 over ten years or two $6,000 payments with 6 percent interest paid annually," which is how Deed Bk. AA, 250, dated September 13, 1848, reads.
    14. Margaret J. Preston, "Personal Reminiscences of Stonewall Jackson," *Century Magazine* 32 (1886): 927.
    15. Ibid., 932–33.
    16. Laura C. Holloway, "Margaret J. Preston: A Famous American Poet," *Withrow Scrapbook* 19: 107, Washington and Lee Special Collections.
    17. Allan, *Life and Letters*, 353–55.
    18. Ibid., 4–5.
    19. D. X. Junkin, *The Reverend George Junkin, D.D., L.L.D.: A Historical Biography* (Philadelphia: J. B. Lippincott, 1871), 42.
    20. Allan, *Life and Letters*, 7.
    21. Ibid., 89.
    22. For the Presbyterian law, see James I. Robertson, Jr., *Stonewall Jackson: The Man, the Soldier, The Legend* (New York: Macmillan, 1997), 174, 817 n. 63.

Chapter 13

    1. Elizabeth Randolph Preston Allan, *Life and Letters of Margaret Junkin Preston* (Boston: Riverside Press, 1903), 93–94.
    2. Ibid., 93.
    3. Letter of 1857 from Margaret Junkin in Philadelphia to J.T.L. Preston, in Allan, *Life and Letters*, 97.
    4. Elizabeth Randolph Preston Allan, *A March Past: Reminiscences of Elizabeth Randolph Preston Allan*, ed. Janet Allan Bryan (Richmond: Dietz Press, 1938), 89.
    5. Ibid.
    6. Ibid.
    7. "John T. L. Preston Diary, 1861 July 24–September 22," MSS 17,264, p. 5, Manuscript Division, Library of Congress.
    8. The two novellas by Nerval were "Sylvie" and "Aurélia."
    9. "John T. L. Preston Diary, 1861," 5.
    10. Letter of December 27, 1861, from J.T.L. Preston in Richmond to Margaret Junkin in Lexington, in Allan, *March Past*, 136.
    11. Allan, *March Past*, 87.
    12. Edmund Randolph Preston, "Misfortunes in Pleasant Disguise," manuscript, Washington, D.C., October 15, 1950. An assessment of J.T.L. Preston's shortcomings by his daughter via his grandson.
    13. Allan, *March Past*, 94.
    14. Allan, *Life and Letters*, 101.

Chapter 14

    1. Letter of June 12, 1856, from J.T.L. Preston to Francis Smith, Superintendent's Incoming Correspondence, #0565, VMI Archives. See also William Couper, *One Hundred Years at V.M.I.* (Richmond: Garrett and Massie, 1939), 1: 304–09.
    2. "Progress of Education in Virginia: The University and the Colleges," *Southern Literary Messenger* 24 (March 1857): 161–69.
    3. που στω (pronounced "pooh stow"), translated from Doric Greek, is a vantage point, standing place, or place on which to stand. From Archimedes: "Give me a place to stand, and I'll move the earth."
    4. [J.T.L. Preston], "Progress of Education in Virginia: The University and the Colleges," *Southern Literary Messenger* 24 (April 1857): 241–47.
    5. Ibid., 24 (June 1857): 401–09.
    6. "Progress of Education in Virginia," *Southern Literary Messenger* 25 (July 1857): 55–62.
    7. Ibid., 25 (August 1857): 131–33.
    8. For the request for a professor of agriculture at VMI by the farmers of Virginia on July 7, 1855, see "Minutes of the Board of Visitors" 2: 80, VMI Archives. For the establishment of the Cocke Professor of Agriculture on July 2, 1859, see 2: 213. A second chair of agriculture was endowed for $10,000 by Dr. Wm. Newton Mercer of Louisiana and was titled Professor of Natural History and Animal and Vegetable Physiology, which was held by Dr. Robert L. Madison, who became the school surgeon.
    9. Olin and Preston Institute, founded in 1851 as a school for boys, and renamed in 1869 Preston and Olin Institute, was named after the Rev. Stephen Olin and William Preston's grandson Col. William Ballard Preston. The school's grounds stood northeast and adjacent to William Preston's "Smithfield Plantation." The school purchased "Solitude," the oldest building on today's campus, surrounded by 250 acres of farmland, which at the time belonged to another of William Preston's grandsons, Robert T. Preston. See Duncan Lyle Kinnear, *The First 100 Years: A History of the Virginia Polytechnic Institute and State University* (Blacksburg, Va.: VPI Educational Foundation, 1972), 11–59.
    10. VMI Archives, "Superintendent's Annual Report, July 1860," 31–33. The fourteen faculty members in 1860 were Col. Francis H. Smith, superintendent and professor of mathematics; Maj. Preston, professor of languages and English literature; Maj. Wm. Gilham, professor of chemistry; Maj. (later Gen.) Thomas Williamson, professor of drawing (later engineering); Maj. Thomas J. Jackson, professor of natural and experimental philosophy; Maj. (later Brig. Gen.) Raleigh Colston, professor of French, history, and political

economy; Maj. Stapleton Crutchfield, professor of mathematics (later physics); Maj. Robert Madison, post surgeon and professor of agriculture; Capt. Mark Hardin, adjunct professor of chemistry, mineralogy, and geology; Capt. (later Brig. Gen.) John McCausland, assistant professor of mathematics; Lt. Joseph H. Chenoweth (later Maj.), assistant professor of Mathematics; Lt. Scott Ship (Shipp after 1888) (later Brig. Gen.), 2nd superintendent in 1890; Lt. Daniel Trueheart, assistant professor of mathematics; and Lt. Octavius Henderson, instructor of French. For the list of faculty on April 16, 1860, see Couper, *One Hundred Years at V.M.I.* 2: 41, or Henry A. Wise, Jr., *Drawing Out the Man: The VMI Story* (Charlottesville: University Press of Virginia, 1978), 30.

Chapter 15

1. "Secretary's Books, 1830–45," May 11, 1816, Collection 103: Franklin Society, Box 40, Washington and Lee Special Collections.
2. Ibid., September 6–October 11, 1834; April 18, November 7, December 5 and 12, 1835; April 2, 1836; and April 1, 1837.
3. "Colonization Meeting in Lexington, Va.," *African Repository, and Colonial Journal* 26, No. 8 (August 1850): 246.
4. J.T.L. Preston, "The Colored Man in the South," *Southern Presbyterian Review* 28, No. 1 (January 1877): 97.
5. "Departure of Emigrants for Liberia," *Lexington Gazette*, December 22, 1849.
6. "Colonization Meeting in Lexington, Va.," *African Repository, and Colonial Journal* 26, No. 8 (August 1850): 246.
7. Superintendent Francis H. Smith, "Semi-Annual Report, July 9, 1856," in VMI Archives, Report of the Board of Visitors of the Virginia Military Institute, July 1856, 4.
8. Henry Ruffner, "Address to the People of West Virginia: Shewing that Slavery is Injurious to the Public Welfare, and that it May Be Gradually Abolished Without Detriment to the Rights and Interests of Slaveholders—By a Slaveholder of West Virginia," Lexington: R. C. Noel, 1847.
9. Dr. W. H. Ruffner, "The Ruffners. No. IV. Henry: Second Article," *West Virginia Historical Magazine Quarterly* 2, No. 3 (July 1903): 40. See Henry Boley, *Lexington in Old Virginia* (Richmond: Garrett and Massie, 1936), 60, for Rockbridge County agreement with Ruffner's economic argument.
10. John Sargeant Wise, *The End of an Era* (Boston: Houghton Mifflin, 1899), 113.
11. Dr. Junkin and President Lincoln corresponded about their shared belief that slavery should be abolished on a gradual scale. See Richard D. and Elisabeth C. Robinson, *Repassing at My Side: A Story of the Junkins* (Blacksburg, Va.: Southern Printing, 1975), 11–12. For Lincoln's position on slavery before his Emancipation Proclamation, see Eric Foner, *The Fiery Trail: Abraham Lincoln and American Slavery* (New York: W. W. Norton, 2010).
12. General Lee's 1846 Will. See also Boley, 129–30.
13. Col. Francis Smith, "Confidential Order No. 112, December 24, 1856," in William Couper, *One Hundred Years at V.M.I.* (Richmond: Garrett and Massie, 1939), 1: 318.
14. "Slave Schedules" in *1860 Census, Town of Lexington, Virginia*, transcribed, corrected, and annotated by Col. Edwin L. Dooley, Jr., updated May 29, 2008.
15. "A Family Poisoned, Lexington, Va., March 31," *Richmond Dispatch*, April 4, 1859.
16. Ollinger Crenshaw, "General Lee's College: Rise and Growth of Washington and Lee," unpublished typescript in two volumes (Lexington, Va.: Washington and Lee, 1973), 1: 464.
17. James I. Robertson, Jr., *Stonewall Jackson: The Man, the Soldier, The Legend* (New York: Macmillan, 1997), 197, quoting John Tidball in "Getting Through West Point," John Caldwell Tidball Papers, 18, United States Military Academy.
18. For Booth's attendance at John Brown's hanging, see Michael W. Kauffman, *American Brutus: John Wilkes Booth and the Lincoln Conspiracies* (New York: Random House, 2004), 105. See also Thomas Goodrich, *The Darkest Dawn* (Bloomington: Indiana University Press, 2005), 60–61.
19. William Couper, "Remarks at the Preston Library Dedication, November 4, 1939," Box: Faculty and Staff; Folder: Preston Clippings and Articles, 11, VMI Archives. Letter of December 2, 1859, from J.T.L. Preston to Margaret Preston, in Elizabeth Randolph Preston Allan, *Life and Letters of Margaret Junkin Preston* (Boston: Riverside Press, 1903), 111–17. It was reprinted as "On the Execution of John Brown" in *Lexington* (Va.) *Gazette*, December 15, 1859. See also *Withrow Scrapbook* 7: 64–65, Washington and Lee Special Collections, and J.T.L. Preston, "Execution of Capt. John Brown," *Southern Bivouac*, 5, 187–89, also repr. as "The Execution of John Brown, J.T.L. Preston in August Bivouac," *Wisconsin Labor Advocate*, September 17, 1886, 4.
20. Stephen Vincent Binét's quote of Colonel Preston appears near the end of Bk. 1 of *John Brown's Body* (Garden City, N.Y.: Doubleday, Doran, 1928). The tune of "John Brown's Song" and the "Battle Hymn of the Republic" originated with "Say, Brothers, Will You Meet Us," which itself may have sprung from the American tradition of camp meeting music during the early to mid 1800s or from an Afro-American wedding song in Georgia or from a Swedish drinking song that evolved into a British sea shanty. The "John Brown's Song" was played, probably for the first time in public, at a flag-raising ceremony near Boston on May 12, 1861, a month after the beginning of the Civil War.
21. Ralph Waldo Emerson's "gallows glorious" statement in his speech on "Courage," as quoted in David S. Reynolds, *John Brown, Abolitionist: The Man Who Killed Slavery, Sparked the Civil War, and Seeded Civil Rights* (New York: Vintage Books, 2005), 366.
22. For a summary of the North's praise of John Brown, see Wise, *The End of an Era*, 133–35.
23. "Arms for Virginia on the Eve of the Civil War: The Armory Commission Letters of Col. Francis H. Smith," transcribed and annotated by Col. Edwin L. Dooley, Jr., 1, VMI Archives. See also, Couper, *One Hundred Years at V.M.I.* 2: 42, January 21, 1860.
24. "Secretary's Books, 1830–45," March 1, 1851, Collection 103: Franklin Society, Box 40, Washington and Lee Special Collections.
25. Oren F. Morton, "The Franklin Society," *A History of Rockbridge County, Virginia* (Baltimore: Regional Publishing, 1980), 215.
26. "Secretary's Books, 1830–45," August 25, 1860, Collection 103: Franklin Society, Box 40, Washington and Lee Special Collections. For the Franklin Society's overwhelming opposition to secession, see Philip

Williams, Jr., "The Franklin Society: A Study of the Debates 1850–61," master's thesis (Lexington, Va.: Washington and Lee University, 1941), 37–39.

27. "Public Meeting in Rockbridge, Lexington, Va., December 4," *Richmond Dispatch*, December 6, 1860. See also letter of December 4, 1860, from Francis Smith to Col. P. S. Geo. Cocke, in Col. Edwin L. Dooley, Jr., "Francis H. Smith and the Secession Crisis of 1860–1861: The letters of VMI Superintendent Francis H. Smith," with transcription, annotation, and commentary, 9, VMI Archives.

28. William Couper, *One Hundred Years at V.M.I.* 2: 62–63.

29. Preston's reading list at the Franklin Society Library shows that he had read Richard Hildreth's and George Bancroft's histories of the United States, the works of John C. Calhoun, and John Taylor's *Construction Construed and Constitutions Vindicated*, which defended a strict states-rights interpretation of the U.S. Constitution and advocated limited republican government. See "John T. L. Preston's Reading List at the Franklin Society, 1827–78, in "Franklin Society, Library Book 1840–78," Collection 103: Franklin Society Library Book, Box 12L (Vol. 2): 241, Washington and Lee Special Collections.

30. William Couper, *One Hundred Years at V.M.I.* 2: 62.

31. Elizabeth Randolph Preston Allan, *A March Past: Reminiscences of Elizabeth Randolph Preston Allan*, ed. Janet Allan Bryan (Richmond: Dietz Press, 1938), 111. Thomas "Tad" Lincoln (1853–1871) was the youngest son of Abraham and Mary Lincoln. His father gave him the nickname "Tad" when he was a baby and "as wriggly as a tadpole." Impulsive and unrestrained, he refused to attend school and had free reign of the White House, where he would interrupt presidential meetings and even charge visitors to see his father.

32. Letter of December 30, 1860, from J.T.L. Preston to Samuel McDowell Reid, Reid Family Papers 027, Washington and Lee Special Collections.

33. "Lincoln's First Inaugural Address," March 4, 1861.

34. Williams, Jr., "The Franklin Society," 40.

35. Letter of April 1, 1861, from J.T.L. Preston to Col. Smith, "Smith's Incoming Letters," #0278, April 1, 1861, VMI Archives.

Chapter 16

1. William Couper, *One Hundred Years at V.M.I.* (Richmond: Garrett and Massie, 1939), 2: 79, and James Robertson, Jr., *Stonewall Jackson: The Man, the Soldier, The Legend* (New York: Macmillan, 1997), 208.

2. William Couper, "Benjamin Azariah Colonna—1864," in *The V.M.I. New Market Cadets: Biographical Sketches of All Members of the Virginia Military Institute Corps of Cadets Who Fought in the Battle of New Market, May 15, 1864* (Charlottesville, Va.: Michie, 1933), 46. See also "Who Did Stop the Cadets on Their March Against Lexington," *County News*, in Margaret and Lucy Withrow, *Withrow Scrapbook* (Lexington, Va.: Rockbridge Historical Society), 7: 53, Washington and Lee Special Collections.

3. For the flag-pole incident, see Couper, *One Hundred Years at V.M.I.* 2: 79–86, and Robertson, *Stonewall Jackson*, 209–11. There are many accounts of this incident and Jackson's scabbard speech, which are noted by Couper, but in the end Couper's account subsumes them all as the most reliable. See also James H. Wood, *The War: "Stonewall" Jackson, His Campaigns, and Battles, the Regiment As I Saw Them* (Cumberland, Md.: Eddy Press, 1910), 11.

4. F. N. Boney, *John Letcher of Virginia* (Tuscaloosa: University of Alabama Press, 1966), 92–93. See also Meridith G. Hays, "Our Once Glorious Union: The Secession Crisis in Lexington, Virginia, 1860–1861," *Proceedings of the Rockbridge Historical Society* 12 (1995–2002): 378–79.

5. Reply of April 16, 1861, from John Letcher to Abraham Lincoln, *The War of the Rebellion: A Compilation of the Official Records of the Union and Confederate Armies* (Washington, D.C.: Government Printing Office, 1897), Ser. 3, 1: 76.

6. Cf. Daniel W. Crofts, *Reluctant Confederates: Upper South Unionists in the Secession Crisis* (Chapel Hill: University of North Carolina Press, 1989).

7. Rev. H. M. White, ed. *Rev. William S. White, D. D., and His Times (1800–73): An Autobiography* (Richmond: Presbyterian Committee on Publications, 1891), 171.

8. Letter of May 2, 1861, from James D. Davidson to Honorable Robert M. T. Hunter, in Bruce S. Greenwait, ed., "Life Behind Confederate Lines in Virginia: The Correspondence of James Dorman Davidson," *Civil War History* 16 (September 1970): 210.

9. Letter of April 26, 1861, from Edward Echols to James D. Davidson, in ibid., 209.

10. Elizabeth Randolph Preston Allan, *A March Past: Reminiscences of Elizabeth Randolph Preston Allan*, ed. Janet Allan Bryan (Richmond: Dietz Press, 1938), 112.

11. Ibid., 115.

12. Ibid., 118.

13. "Faculty Minutes," Washington College, April 17, 1861, Washington and Lee Special Collections.

14. Ollinger Crenshaw, "General Lee's College: Rise and Growth of Washington and Lee," unpublished typescript in two volumes (Lexington, Va.: Washington and Lee University, 1973), 1: 480.

15. Letter of April 18, 1861, from J.T.L. Preston to Col. Francis Smith, "Smith's Incoming Letters," #0277, VMI Archives.

16. Order Book, Order No. 63, April 21, 1861, VMI Archives.

17. Ibid.

18. Couper, *One Hundred Years at V.M.I.* 2: 97.

19. Letter of April 20, 1861, from J.T.L. Preston to Col. Francis Smith, "Smith's Incoming Letters," #0276.

20. Charles W. Turner, ed. *Lieutenant John Newton Lyle: The Career of the Liberty Hall Volunteers* (Verona, Va.: McClure Press, 1906), 7–8.

21. Letter of February 17, 1865, from J.T.L. Preston to Hon. J. C. Breckinridge, Secretary of War, in *War of the Rebellion*, Ser. 4, 3, 1093.

22. *Richmond Daily Examiner*, April 27, 1861.

23. George Bagby, quoted in Couper, *One Hundred Years at V.M.I.* 2: 101.

Chapter 17

1. Capt. John D. Imboden, quoted in Robert Underwood Johnson and Clarence Clough Buel, ed., *Battles and Leaders of the Civil War, Being for the Most Part Contributions by Union and Confederate Officers* (New York: Century, 1887), 1: 121.

2. J.T.L. Preston, *Removing to a New Charge: Letters*

to a Young Minister (Richmond: Presbyterian Committee of Publication, 1890), 20.

3. Letter of May 12, 1861, from J.T.L. Preston to Margaret Preston, in Elizabeth Randolph Preston Allan, *A March Past: Reminiscences of Elizabeth Randolph Preston Allan*, ed. Janet Allan Bryan (Richmond: Dietz Press, 1938), 132.

4. Letter, n.d., from J.T.L. Preston to Margaret Preston, in ibid.

5. Letter of May 20, 1861, from J.T.L. Preston to Col. Francis Smith, "Smith's Incoming Letters," #0292, VMI Archives.

6. James Robertson, Jr., *Stonewall Jackson: The Man, the Soldier, The Legend* (New York: Macmillan, 1997), 239–40.

7. Letter of May 30, 1861, from Tom L. Preston to Col. Francis Smith, "Smith's Incoming Letters," #0291.

8. John G. Barrett and Richard M. McMurry "VMI in the Civil War," in Thomas W. Davis, ed., *A Crowd of Honorable Youths: Historical Essays on the First 150 Years of the Virginia Military Institute* (Lexington: VMI Sesquicentennial Committee, 1988), 42.

9. Letter of June 4, 1861, from J.T.L. Preston to Col. Francis Smith, "Smith's Incoming Letters," #0285.

10. Letter of June 18, 1861, from J.T.L. Preston to Col. Francis Smith, ibid., #0281.

11. Letter of June 20, 1861, from J.T.L. Preston to Col. Francis Smith, ibid., #0286.

12. Letter of June 22, 1861, from J.T.L. Preston to Col. Francis Smith, ibid., #0289.

13. William Couper, *One Hundred Years at V.M.I.* (Richmond: Garrett and Massie, 1939), 3: 120.

14. Letter of end of June 1861, from J.T.L. Preston to Col. Francis Smith, "Smith's Incoming Letters," #0271.

15. Letter of July 1, 1861, from J.T.L. Preston to Col. Francis Smith about Elisha "Frank" Paxton's declining his commission, ibid., #0272.

16. Letter of July 6, 1861, from J.T.L. Preston to Col. Francis Smith, ibid., #0273.

17. Benjamin H. Trask, *9th Virginia Infantry* (Lynchburg, Va.: H. E. Howard, 1984), 86. Preston's service record shows that he was commissioned lieutenant colonel on July 7, 1861.

18. Allan, *March Past*, 116. West Virginia unofficially seceded from Virginia on June 20, 1861, when it formed a rival state government and elected two U.S. senators, but it didn't officially become a state, the 35th, until two years later on June 20, 1863.

19. "Minutes of the Board of Visitors" 2: 302, VMI Archives. In April 1860, the board set the superintendent's salary at $3,000 and professors' salaries at $1,800 plus $100 for each of five years of faithful service, which for Preston amounted to $2,200.

20. Trask, *9th Virginia*, 86. Preston's service record shows that he was paid $306 for one month and 24 days from July 7 to August 31 and $340 for two months from September 1 to October 31.

21. Mrs. John H. Moore, *Memories of a Long Life in Virginia* (Staunton, Va.: McClure, 1920), 59.

22. Elizabeth Preston Allan, "Reminiscences of an Ordinary Life," original manuscript of *A March Past*, which includes information omitted from the book, Collection 2764: William Allan Papers, Box 2, Folder 12, pt 5: 20, Southern Historical Collection, University of North Carolina, Chapel Hill.

23. Letter of May 29, 1919, from Junius Lackland Hempstead, in William Couper, *One Hundred Years at V.M.I.* 2: 109.

24. Allan, "Reminiscences of an Ordinary Life," Pt. 5: 22.

Chapter 18

1. Craney Island is situated at the mouths of the James and Elizabeth rivers where they empty into the natural harbor of Hampton Roads on their way to Chesapeake Bay and the Atlantic Ocean. It was named for the birds that early English settlers saw there and believed to be cranes but were actually the blue and white herons, which still inhabit the island.

2. Benjamin H. Trask, *9th Virginia Infantry* (Lynchburg, Va.: H. E. Howard, 1984), 3–4.

3. J.T.L. Preston, "Jottings," the name given to "John T. L. Preston Diary, 1861 July 24–September 22," MSS 17,264, p. 4, Manuscript Division, Library of Congress, Washington, D.C. A second volume of "Jottings," which is mentioned on p. 16 and is missing, covered August 17 through September 8.

4. Preston, "Jottings," 12, August 13, 1861.

5. Preston, "Jottings," 9, August 9, 1861.

6. Ibid.

7. John E. Talmadge, "A Peace Movement in Civil War Connecticut," *New England Quarterly* 28, No. 3 (September 1964): 306–21.

8. Preston, "Jottings," 20–21, September 17, 1861.

9. Preston, "Jottings," 22, September 19, 1861.

10. Preston, "Jottings," 24, September 21, 1861.

11. Preston, "Jottings," 22, September 19, 1861.

12. Preston, "Jottings," 22, September 18, 1861. Tom L. Preston married, on May 22, 1861, Lucy Gordon Waddell, a descendent of James Waddell, the noted "Blind Preacher," whom Patrick Henry called "the greatest orator he ever heard."

13. Preston, "Jottings," 23, September 20, 1861.

Chapter 19

1. "Preston, John Thomas Lewis," in Robert E. L. Crick, *Staff Officers in Gray: A Biographical Register of the Staff Officers in the Army of Northern Virginia* (Chapel Hill: University of North Carolina Press, 2003), 246. See also *List of Staff Officers of the Confederate States Army, 1861–65* (Washington, D.C.: Government Printing Office, 1891), 133; and Joseph H. Crute, Jr. *Confederate Staff Officers, 1861–1865* (Powhatan, Va.: Dewent Books, 1982), 97. Preston would hold the position of chief of staff until February 1, 1862.

2. Letter of October 22, 1861, from T. J. Jackson to Mary Jackson, in Mary Anna Jackson, *Memoirs of "Stonewall" Jackson by His Widow* (Dayton, Ohio: Morningside Bookshop, 1976. Original printing by Courier-Journal Job Printing Co., Louisville, Ky., 1895), 197.

3. Letter of October 23, 1861, from T. J. Jackson to Margaret Preston, in Elizabeth Randolph Preston Allan, *A March Past: Reminiscences of Elizabeth Randolph Preston Allan*, ed. Janet Allan Bryan (Richmond: Dietz Press, 1938), 133.

4. William Couper, *One Hundred Years at V.M.I.* (Richmond: Garrett and Massie, 1939), 2: 135.

5. Jackson's farewell to the Stonewall Brigade, as quoted in James Robertson, Jr., *Stonewall Jackson: The Man, the Soldier, The Legend* (New York: Macmillan, 1997), 282–83.

6. William G. Bean, *Stonewall's Man: Sandie*

Pendleton (Chapel Hill: University of North Carolina Press, 1959), 49.

7. Letter of November 5, 1861, from T. J. Jackson to J. P. Benjamin, in *The War of the Rebellion: A Compilation of the Official Records of the Union and Confederate Armies* (Washington, D.C.: Government Printing Office, 1897), Ser. 1, 5, Pt. 1: 937. See also Robertson, *Stonewall Jackson*, 288.

8. Robertson, *Stonewall Jackson*, 292. See also letter of December 5, 1861, from J.T.L. Preston to Margaret Preston, in Allan, *March Past*, 135.

9. Letter of November 11, 1861, from T. J. Jackson to Margaret Preston, in Allan, *March Past*, 134.

10. Letter of November 20, 1861, from T. J. Jackson to J. P. Benjamin, Secretary of War, in *War of the Rebellion*, Ser. 1, 5, Pt. 1: 965.

11. Letter of December 8, 1861, from J.T.L. Preston to Margaret Preston, in Elizabeth Randolph Preston Allan, *Life and Letters of Margaret Junkin Preston* (Boston: Riverside Press, 1903), 125.

12. Ibid., 63–64.

13. Letter of December 27, 1861, from J.T.L. Preston to Margaret Preston, in ibid., 127–28. The Col. Preston whom Jefferson Davis had mistaken for J.T.L. Preston was the latter's first cousin Col. James Francis Preston, commander of 4th Virginia. He's the one to whom Jackson said at Manassas, "Reserve your fire, and give them the bayonet."

14. Letter of December 27, 1861, from J.T.L. Preston to Gen. Francis Smith, "Smith's Incoming Letters," #0274, VMI Archives. Francis Smith was relieved from his post at Craney Island and given the brevet commission of major general on December 18, 1861. See Couper, *One Hundred Years at V.M.I.* 2: 136–37.

15. T. J. Jackson, "Report of Operations, February 21, 1862," *War of the Rebellion*, Ser. 1, 5, 394.

16. Letter of January 11, 1862, from J.T.L. Preston to Hon. Alexander R. Boteler in Richmond, in ibid., Ser. 1, 51, Pt. 2: 435.

17. Couper, *One Hundred Years at V.M.I.* 2: 138.

18. Allan, *Life and Letters*, 134–35, April 3, 1862. Maggie's journal of the war, covering three years from April 1862 through April 1865, has disappeared in its original form. Some quotations from it appear in Allan, *Life and Letters* and *March Past*.

19. Ibid., 134.

20. Ibid., 133.

21. William G. Bean, *Stonewall's Man: Sandie Pendleton* (Chapel Hill: University of North Carolina Press, 1959), 50.

22. Allan, *Life and Letters*, 137, April 10, 1862.

23. Ibid., 138, April 22, 1862. See also Allan, *March Past*, 142.

24. John G. Barrett and Richard M. McMurry, "VMI in the Civil War," in Davis, ed., *A Crowd of Honorable Youths: Historical Essays on the First 150 Years of the Virginia Military Institute* (Lexington: VMI Sesquicentennial Committee, 1988), 34.

25. Allan, *March Past*, 138.

26. Letter of May 6, 1862, from T. J. Jackson to Gen. F. H. Smith, in Couper, *One Hundred Years at V.M.I.* 2: 153.

27. Ibid., 2: 70, 148.

28. Allan, *Life and Letters*, 139, May 10, 1862.

29. Ibid., 140, May 17, 1862. See also Robertson, *Stonewall Jackson*, 378, and *War of the Rebellion*, Ser. 1, 12, Pt. 1: 473, "Report of T. J. Jackson of operations in Battle of McDowell, May 8, 1862."

30. Robert Lewis Dabney, *Life and Campaigns of Lieut.-Gen. Thomas J. Jackson (Stonewall Jackson)* (Richmond: Blelock, 1866), 341, also quoted in Couper, *One Hundred Years at V.M.I.* 2: 155.

31. Letter of May 1, 1862, from the board of visitors in Richmond to Gen. Richardson, in Couper, *One Hundred Years at V.M.I.* 2: 149–50.

32. William Couper, *The V.M.I. New Market Cadets: Biographical Sketches of All Members of the Virginia Military Institute Corps of Cadets Who Fought in the Battle of New Market, May 15, 1864* (Charlottesville, Va.: Michie, 1933), 160.

33. Allan, *March Past*, 144. See also Allan, *Life and Letters*, 142, May 30; 144, June 6; 145, June 22, 1862. *March Past* is the only source that specifies Frank's left arm as the one injured and amputated. No other source identifies which arm.

34. Ibid., 145.

35. Ibid., 145–46.

36. Ibid., 146.

Chapter 20

1. William C. Preston, quoted by Margaret Junkin Preston, "William C. Preston," Collection 101B: Margaret Junkin Papers, 1837–72, Box 1, Folder 7: Scrapbook, Washington and Lee Special Collections. Willie's "best friend" was William "Willie" Nelson Page, Jr., four years his elder, who died at First Manassas on July 21, 1861. See Elizabeth Randolph Preston Allan, *A March Past: Reminiscences of Elizabeth Randolph Preston Allan*, ed. Janet Allan Bryan (Richmond: Dietz Press, 1938), 133.

2. For the description of "bucking" at VMI during the Civil War, see Joseph Gutmann and Stanley F. Chyet, ed., *Moses Jacob Ezekiel: Memoirs from the Baths of Diocletian* (Detroit: Wayne State University Press, 1975), 104.

3. Allan, *March Past*, 138–39.

4. Ibid., 140.

5. According to Tucker Shields, great-great-grandson of William Nelson Page, a photo of two Liberty Hall Volunteers was found "in the collection of Fanny Page Meredith's descendants, and inserted in its protective case is a death notice for Willie Preston—to whom Fanny Page is said to have been engaged." (Tucker Shields, letter of February 14, 2014, to Randolph Shaffner, "Re: W. N. Page—J.T.L. Preston matters—photographic images of mid-nineteenth century.") The image is currently in the collection of Shields's cousin Page McLemore.

Also inserted in the case, but much later by a member of the Page family, was a handwritten attempt to identify the two soldiers, one of whom was said to be "Willie Preston," who was "Fanny Page's fiancé," and the other Willie Page. Willie Page, however, was never a Liberty Hall Volunteer, unlike his brother Coupland, who might or might not be the other recruit in the image. (Randolph Tucker Shields III, "Re: Photo of Confederate Soldiers [Liberty Hall Volunteers?], January 2002.")

At the time that Willie Preston mustered in the Liberty Hall Volunteers on June 6, 1862, his age was seventeen and a half. From a facial comparison with Willie's brother Frank (see Frank Preston's image in Chapter 24), the author believes the soldier on the right to be Willie Preston.

6. William Couper, *One Hundred Years at V.M.I.* (Richmond: Garrett and Massie, 1939), 2: 163.

7. Letter of August 10, 1862, from William C. Preston to J.T.L. Preston, in Allan, *March Past*, 148. For a description of this battle and Willie's role in it, see James Robertson, Jr., *Stonewall Jackson: The Man, the Soldier, The Legend* (New York: Macmillan, 1997), 533–34.

8. Ibid.

9. Ibid., 149.

10. Ibid.

11. Allan, *March Past*, 146, August 23, 1862. See also James Robertson, Jr., *Stonewall Jackson: The Man, the Soldier, The Legend* (New York: Macmillan, 1997), 533–34.

12. McGuire, Hunter, "Address by Dr. Hunter McGuire, Delivered on 23rd Day of June 1897, at the Virginia Military Institute, in the presence of a vast audience, upon the occasion of the Inauguration of the Stonewall Jackson Memorial Building" (Lynchburg, Va.: J. P. Bell, 1897), 17.

13. Margaret Junkin Preston, "William C. Preston," Collection 101B: Margaret Junkin Papers, 1837–72, Box 1, Folder 7: Scrapbook, Washington and Lee Special Collections.

14. William Preston, as quoted in Charles D. Walker, "William C. Preston," *Memorial, Virginia Military Institute: Biographical Sketches of the Graduates and Élèves of the Virginia Military Institute Who Fell During the War Between the States* (Philadelphia: J. B. Lippincott, 1875), 434.

15. McGuire, "Address," 17–18.

16. Letter of mid October 1862, from T. J. Jackson at Bunker Hill to Maggie, in Elizabeth Randolph Preston Allan, *Life and Letters of Margaret Junkin Preston* (Boston: Riverside Press, 1903), 152.

17. Ibid., 147, September 4, 1862. For other accounts of Willie's death, see Joseph A. Waddell, *Annals of Augusta County, Virginia, from 1726 to 1871* (Harrisonburg, Va.: C. J. Carrier, 1972), Thursday, September 11, 1862; Martha M. Boltz, "A Gentle Rebel Youth Slain in Battle," *Washington Times* (Washington, D.C.), August 23, 1997; Preston Nuttall, "The Young Soldier and His General," *Old War Horse: The Voice of General James Longstreet Camp #1247, Sons of Confederate Veterans*, Vol. 6, Issue 10 (November 2004), "Willie Preston."

18. Robertson, *Stonewall Jackson*, 575–76.

19. Allan, *Life and Letters*, 149.

20. William C. Preston of Preston and Leake Law Office in Richmond, "Willie C. Preston," Collection 1543: Margaret Junkin Papers, Box 1, Folder 1, Southern Historical Collection, University of North Carolina, Chapel Hill.

21. Allan, *Life and Letters*, 149.

22. See photograph of Willie's grave in Folder: Preston, Mr. Herbert R., VMI Museum, which includes letter of April 3, 1979, about the photograph from June F. Cunningham to Herbert Preston. The grave is located at 16850 Sudley Road near Centreville, Virginia. Its coordinates are 38.84.7256–77.530744.The GPS coordinates of the gravesite are Latitude +38.847256 Longitude −77.530744.

23. Charles D. Walker, "William C. Preston," *Memorial, Virginia Military Institute: Biographical Sketches of the Graduates and Élèves of the Virginia Military Institute Who Fell During the War Between the States* (Philadelphia: J. B. Lippincott, 1875), 434, note penciled into the margins of this copy by John A. Preston. See Rare Books Collection, Z986 J14 W177 1875, Virginia Historical Society.

24. Margaret Junkin Preston, "W.C.P. Slain in Battle—August 28th, 1862," Collection 1543: Margaret Junkin Papers, Box 1, Folder 1, Southern Historical Collection, University of North Carolina, Chapel Hill. This poem, which misses Willie's date of death by one day, was written by Maggie for her daughter Phoebe, who did not want it published, but Elizabeth Preston Allan copied it "from memory in 1879, not having seen it for seventeen years."

Chapter 21

1. Elizabeth Preston Allan, "Reminiscences of an Ordinary Life," original manuscript of *A March Past*, which includes information omitted from the book, Collection 2764: William Allan Papers, Box 2, Folder 12, Pt. 6: 13–14, Southern Historical Collection, University of North Carolina, Chapel Hill.

2. Elizabeth Randolph Preston Allan, *Life and Letters of Margaret Junkin Preston* (Boston: Riverside Press, 1903), 157, December 19, 1862.

3. Ibid., 154.

4. Elizabeth Randolph Preston Allan, *A March Past: Reminiscences of Elizabeth Randolph Preston Allan*, ed. Janet Allan Bryan (Richmond: Dietz Press, 1938), 150.

5. Allan, *Life and Letters*, 154–55.

6. Allan, *March Past*, 150–51.

7. Letter of December 22, 1862, from T. J. Jackson to Col. Preston, in Allan, *Life and Letters*, 153–54. Jackson's farm was located a mile southeast of his home, at today's Quarry Lane off U.S. 60 East. Preston ran an ad in the *Lexington Gazette* on January 22, 1863, and sold the farm at auction to John Miller for $620. See Deed Bk. II, 267, March 12, 1863.

8. Ibid., 158, December 24, 1862.

9. Ibid., 156, December 19, 1862. Jackson met Dr. John Junkin on December 15, 1862, the last day of the Battle of Fredericksburg.

10. Dr. Junkin, as quoted by overland mail in "Atlantic Intelligence," *Sacramento Daily Union* 25, No. 3772, April 24, 1863. Also published in Philadelphia *Sunday School Times*.

11. "Review of Political Fallacies," *Christian Examiner* 74, Ser. 5, 12, No. 3 (May 1863): 456.

12. "Political Fallacies," in "Literary Notices," *Continental Monthly: Devoted to Literature and National Policy* 3, Issue 6 (June 1863).

13. James Power Smith, "The Religious Character of Stonewall Jackson," delivered at the inauguration of the Stonewall Jackson Memorial Building, Virginia Military Institute, June 23, 1897 (Lynchburg: Virginia Military Institute, 1897), 8. The actual title of Junkin's book was *Political Fallacies*, but Smith misquotes it as Political Heresies and has Jackson reply, "I expect it is well named, Captain; that's just what the book contains, 'Political Heresies.'"

14. Allan, *Life and Letters*, 158–59, January 9, 1863.

15. Letter of January 19, 1863, from T. J. Jackson to J.T.L. Preston, Collection 1543: Margaret Junkin Preston Papers, Box 1, Folder 1, Southern Historical Collection, University of North Carolina, Chapel Hill.

16. Allan, *Life and Letters*, 163, May 5, 1863.

17. Deed Bk. PP, 15, December 19, 1862: William L. and Mary S. Ayers to William Gilham, J.T.L. Preston, George W. Shields, and Jacob Fuller for $2,601 for land on Guys Run adjoining Preston, W. W. Davis, et al., for 289 acres as part of 769 acres known as Mayberry Tract near Furnace Tract near the mouth of the mill.

18. Deed Bk. II: 237, January 16, 1863: William W. Mason sells for $1,280 "with general warranty" to Jacob Fuller, Thos. J. Jackson, Wm. Gilham, and J.T.L. Preston "a parcel of land supposedly to contain 320 acres" lying in the Blue Ridge Mountains adjoining lands of Elisha Paxton, James Camden, et al., being Wm. A. Ready's Hart's Bottom estates with right to survey and reduce price if less than 320 acres and retain same price if more than 320 acres. In addition, they are given the privilege to deposit their tan bark in any amount not exceeding 20 cords at any one time at a convenient spot on Mason's land on the banks of the canal, "all rents for the terms of their leases to be paid to the said Mason."

19. The deed for the Lexington Tannery was not recorded until 1869, where it was referenced in Deed Bk. KK, 434, September 10, 1869, at the sale of the Lexington Tannery, which Jacob Fuller, T. J. Jackson, William Gilham, and J.T.L. Preston had previously purchased on April 12, 1860, from a Mr. W. (the estate of Andrew Withrow at auction) for $4,889.86 the Lexington Tannery, located at the corner of Henry and Randolph streets, at the foot of the hill below Blandome. See also Blandome national registration nomination, 11, and Katharine L. Brown, "Stonewall Jackson in Lexington," *Proceedings of the Rockbridge Historical Society* 9 (1975–79): 207. For purchase of the tannery lot from William A. and Susannah Rhodes on November 2, 1860, for $1,050, see Deed Bk. KK, 191. For Fuller's earlier purchase of the house that later became Blandome on January 28, 1854, from Preston's in-laws, John and Phebe Wilson, for $5,000, see Deed Bk. KK, 179.

20. "Minutes of the Board of Visitors" 2: 252, April 25, 1860, VMI Archives.

21. Letter of April 28, 1863, from J.T.L. Preston to T. J. Jackson, Box: Preston, John T. L., Folder MS 0240, VMI Archives.

22. Ibid.

23. Letter of April 27, 1863, from T. J. Jackson at Fredericksburg to J.T.L. Preston, Collection 1543: Margaret Junkin Papers, Box 1, Folder 1.

Chapter 22

1. See the list of VMI officers and soldiers in Jackson's corps in William Couper, *One Hundred Years at V.M.I.* (Richmond: Garrett and Massie, 1939), 2: 171–72.

2. Elizabeth Randolph Preston Allan, *Life and Letters of Margaret Junkin Preston* (Boston: Riverside Press, 1903), 163.

3. Ibid.

4. Ibid., 165.

5. Elizabeth Randolph Preston Allan, *A March Past: Reminiscences of Elizabeth Randolph Preston Allan*, ed. Janet Allan Bryan (Richmond: Dietz Press, 1938), 152.

6. Margaret Junkin Preston, "The Shade of the Trees," *Cartoons* (Boston: Roberts Brothers, 1875), 182–83.

7. Allan, *Life and Letters*, 143, June 3, 1862.

8. Ibid., 178, June 24 and July 1, 1863.

9. Superintendent Francis Smith, "24th Annual Report," in "Minutes of the Board of Visitors, 1853–64" 2: 371, 374, June 26, 1863, VMI Archives.

10. Letter of June 19, 1863, from J.T.L. Preston to VMI Board of Visitors, "Smith's Incoming Letters," #0290, VMI Archives.

11. Allan, *Life and Letters*, 168, April 11, 1863.

12. Ibid., 172, December 11, 1863. See also Allan, *March Past*, 155.

13. For the list of VMI men serving in Pickett's division, see Couper, *One Hundred Years at V.M.I.* 2: 200. For the losses suffered by the 26th N.C. Regiment, see 198–99. For the Confederate casualties incurred in the Pickett-Pettigrew Charge, see George R. Stewart, *Pickett's Charge, A Micro-History of the Final Attack at Gettysburg, July 3, 1863* (New York: Houghton Mifflin, 1959).

14. Allan, *March Past*, 154.

15. Allan, *Life and Letters*, 168 n. 1.

16. Couper, *One Hundred Years at V.M.I.* 2: 213–14.

17. Ibid., 204–05.

18. Letter of October 16, 1863, from J.T.L. Preston to General Francis Smith, "Smith's Incoming Letters," #0286.

19. Allan, *Life and Letters*, 168, November 6–7, 1863.

20. Concerning the spelling of Scott Ship's surname, it was changed from Ship to Shipp ca. 1883, according to Couper, *One Hundred Years at V.M.I.* 1: 315, and William Couper, *The V.M.I. New Market Cadets: Biographical Sketches of All Members of the Virginia Military Institute Corps of Cadets Who Fought in the Battle of New Market, May 15, 1864* (Charlottesville, Va.: Michie, 1933), 182. It was changed in 1888, according to Henry Alexander, Jr., *Drawing Out the Man: The VMI Story* (Charlottesville: University Press of Virginia, 1978), 68. Col. Ship, Class of 1859, known as "Old Billy," was born August 2, 1839, entered VMI as a cadet in 1856, was commandant 1862–90, commander of the corps during the war, and VMI's second superintendent 1890–1907. He died December 4, 1917.

21. Allan, *Life and Letters*, 173–74, December 6 (misprint for 16), 1863.

22. Ibid., 174, December 19, 1863.

Chapter 23

1. Shelby Foote, *The Civil War: A Narrative* (New York: Random House, 1974), 3: 247.

2. Gen. John Breckinridge would later become the last Confederate secretary of war.

3. Elizabeth Randolph Preston Allan, *Life and Letters of Margaret Junkin Preston* (Boston: Riverside Press, 1903), 179, May 11, 1864. See also William Charles Davis, *Battle of New Market* (Baton Rouge: Louisiana State University Press, 1975), 49.

4. Henry Alexander, Jr., *Drawing Out the Man: The VMI Story* (Charlottesville: University Press of Virginia, 1978), 37.

5. John Sargeant Wise, Chap. 19, "The Most Glorious Day of My Life," in *The End of An Era* (Boston: Houghton Mifflin, 1901), 293.

6. The lines "the bravest are the tenderest, the loving are the daring," describing the poet's hero, come from Bayard Taylor's "Song of the Camp."

7. Edmund Raymond Turner, *The New Market Campaign, May 1864* (Richmond: Whittet and Shepperson, 1912), ix.

8. Wise, *The End of an Era*, 294.

9. Ibid., 297. John Sargeant Wise was son of Governor Henry Alexander Wise, brother of Capt. Henry A. "Old Chinook" Wise, Jr., and father of Jennings Cropper Wise.

10. Ibid.

11. Ibid., 299–300.

12. [Franklin "Frank" C. Preston], "Battle of New

Market," *Lexington Gazette and General Advocate*, May 25, 1864. All the quotes from Frank Preston's description of the battle are from this account in the *Gazette and Advocate*.

13. Preston Cocke, *Battle of New Market and the Cadets of the Virginia Military Institute: May 15, 1864* (Richmond: May 15, 1914), 3.

14. As the grandson of Thomas Jefferson's brother, John G. Jefferson, Sr., Thomas Garland Jefferson III, born January 1, 1847, was President Thomas Jefferson's great-great-nephew.

15. See also Davis, *Battle of New Market*, 136, who, taking Preston's letter as his source, contends, "The cadets spring from behind the fence, Henry Wise and Frank Preston simultaneously ordering the charge." Henry Wise of A Company, as cadet senior tactical officer, had replaced Lieutenant Colonel Ship in command.

16. J. H. Wartmann, *Rockingham Register* (Harrisonburg, Va.), May 20, 1864.

17. Edmund R. Turner, Chap. 5, "The Part of the Cadets," *The New Market Campaign, May 1864*, 66–89. Turner was professor of European history at the University of Michigan.

18. Ibid., 72.

19. Ibid., 66, 72.

20. Ibid., 83–85.

21. Letter of April 14, 1909, from Benjamin A. Colonna to Henry A. Wise, in Turner, *New Market Campaign*, 85.

22. Turner, 87.

23. Although there is agreement about the number of cadets killed and mortally wounded, that number being 10, there is some confusion among scholars about the number wounded and the total number engaged in the battle. The confusion occurs when the number includes or omits officers. Of 257 cadets engaged in the battle, 45 were wounded. But of 263 cadets and officers engaged in the battle, 47 cadets and officers were wounded. In *The V.M.I. New Market Cadets: Biographical Sketches of All Members of the Virginia Military Institute Corps of Cadets Who Fought in the Battle of New Market, May 15, 1864* (Charlottesville, Va.: Michie, 1933), Couper lists five cadets killed and five mortally wounded for a total of 10. He then combines 45 cadets and two officers for a total of 47 cadets and officers wounded (p. 6). The two officers were Battalion Commander Lt. Col. Scott Ship and Capt. Govan Hill of C Company. He combines 257 cadets and six officers for a total of 263 cadets and officers leaving Lexington (p. 253). The number at this point in the text applies only to cadets: 45 wounded of the 257 engaged.

24. Frank Preston, in Elizabeth Randolph Preston Allan, *A March Past: Reminiscences of Elizabeth Randolph Preston Allan*, ed. Janet Allan Bryan (Richmond: Dietz Press, 1938), 160. See also Wise, *The End of an Era*, 302; and Couper, *The V.M.I. New Market Cadet*, 160: Quote from a letter of March 27, 1909, by Francis Lee Smith: "I remember distinctly the fact of our lying down in this position, because I was immediately next to Captain Preston, who, having lost one of his arms at the first battle of Manassas [Winchester], protected the other as well as he could by keeping it under his body."

25. Col. Bennett H. Young, "John Cabell Breckinridge," *Confederate Veteran* 13, No. 6 (June 1905): 260.

26. Benjamin A. Colonna, "The Battle of New Market," *Journal of the Military Service Institution of the United States* 51 (November–December 1912): 347.

27. An Englishman, quoted in Henry Boley, *Lexington in Old Virginia* (Richmond: Garrett and Massie, 1936), 74.

28. For the origin and practice of the New Market Day ceremony, see William Couper, *One Hundred Years at V.M.I.* (Richmond: Garrett and Massie, 1939), 2: 323–25.

29. Couper, *One Hundred Years at V.M.I.* 3: 17–18.

30. The handwritten date on the typed copy of Preston's speech at the VMI Archives is May 15, 1872, and page 8 alludes to "eight years ago," but the speech was actually published in its entirety in the July 1871 issue of *The Cadet: A Monthly Magazine of Science, Literature and Art* 1, No. 5 (July 1871): 213–17, so it was given, not on the eighth anniversary in 1872, but on the seventh anniversary in 1871 and the tenth anniversary of VMI's entry into the war. See the typed copy at VMI Archives, Box: VMI Faculty and Staff, 19th Cent., Preston, John T. L., Folder 2: Material from the VMI and National archives.

Chapter 24

1. The corps assembled at Camp Lee on October 1, 1864, moved to Poe's Farm on October 27, and quartered at the Alms House on December 12, where academic work resumed on December 28. See William Couper, *One Hundred Years at V.M.I.* (Richmond: Garrett and Massie, 1939), 2: 71, and *The V.M.I. New Market Cadets: Biographical Sketches of All Members of the Virginia Military Institute Corps of Cadets Who Fought in the Battle of New Market, May 15, 1864* (Charlottesville, Va.: Michie, 1933), x–xi.

2. Elizabeth Randolph Preston Allan, *A March Past: Reminiscences of Elizabeth Randolph Preston Allan*, ed. Janet Allan Bryan (Richmond: Dietz Press, 1938), 177–79. John J. Williams would return home after the war eventually to become mayor of Winchester.

3. Elizabeth Randolph Preston Allan, *Life and Letters of Margaret Junkin Preston* (Boston: Riverside Press, 1903), 199, winter of 1864–65.

4. Allan, *March Past*, 182.

5. Allan, *Life and Letters*, 203, winter of 1864–65.

6. J.T.L. Preston registered a Confederate copyright for *Beechenbrook* in late March of 1865. See "Confederate Copyrights," *Virginia Magazine of History and Biography* 20 (1912): 425. Preston was granted leave of absence for two months by the board of visitors on March 20, 1865. "Minutes of the Board of Visitors" 3: 34, VMI Archives.

7. Preston's mother had worried about Preston's lungs when he was only a child at age ten. His own son Frank would die in 1869 at age 28 of consumption; and his son Tom, on May 28, 1895, at age 59 after five years of grippe and Bright's disease. See letter of February 22, 1831, from Edmonia Preston to Susan Preston McDowell, Smithfield-Preston Foundation MS97–002, Box 1, Folder 11, VPI Special Collections: "This symptom of cough gives me peculiar uneasiness with him, owing to my fears for his lungs, which have harassed me for some time."

8. Letter of March 13, 1865, from Governor William Smith to J.T.L. Preston, Acting Superintendent, "Smith's Incoming Letters," #0242, VMI Archives.

9. Couper, *One Hundred Years at V.M.I.* 1: 178. See also James F. Dittrich, "Horses at VMI," in Thomas W. Davis, ed., *A Crowd of Honorable Youths: Historical Essays on the First 150 Years of the Virginia Military In-*

stitute (Lexington: VMI Sesquicentennial Committee, 1988), 164.

10. Copy of letter of March 15, 1865, sent from J.T.L. Preston to Governor William Smith, "Smith's Incoming Letters," #0242. Cavalry mounts were not furnished at VMI until 1919 during the World War.

11. Allan, *Life and Letters*, 207–08, April 10, 1865.

12. Elizabeth Preston Allan, "Reminiscences of an Ordinary Life," original manuscript of *A March Past*, which includes information omitted from the book, Collection 2764: William Allan Papers, Box 2, Folder 12, Pt. 8: 6–7, Southern Historical Collection, University of North Carolina, Chapel Hill.

13. Allan, *March Past*, 186.

14. Ibid., 187.

15. Allan, *Life and Letters*, 208, July 4, 1865.

16. Ibid., 132. See also Allan, *March Past*, 115.

17. For Preston's dismissal of four servants, including Anakee and Old Uncle Young, see Allan, *Life and Letters*, 208. For Phil and Coralie, see also *March Past*, 178–79.

18. Helen Dickey, who lived in Oxford, Pennsylvania, was Maggie's first cousin and longtime confidante.

19. Allan, *Life and Letters*, 208, July 10, 1865. Presumably the four servants were Uncle Young, Phil, Anakee, and Sandy, the latter two in trust with Preston since 1835. See Deed Bk. S, 505, June 23, 1835, and Deed Bk. U, 80, September 13, 1837, for J.T.L. Preston as trustee of Anakee, about twenty-one, and Sandy, about twenty-four.

20. Allan, *March Past*, 230.

21. Couper, *One Hundred Years at V.M.I.* 2: 8, 72, 119–20. See also June F. Cunningham, "Colonel John Thomas Lewis Preston," in Davis, ed., *A Crowd of Honorable Youths*, 58.

22. J.T.L. Preston, "The Atlantic Cable," *Southern Review* 2, No. 3 (July 1867): 39.

23. F. H. Smith, Jr., ed., *History of the Virginia Military Institute: Its Building and Rebuilding* (Lynchburg, Va.: J. P. Bell, 1912), 219.

24. J.T.L. Preston, "The Atlantic Cable," *Southern Review* 2, No. 3 (July 1867): 38.

25. Smith, Jr., ed., *History of the Virginia Military Institute*, 220.

26. Allan, *March Past*, 197. See also Allan, *Life and Letters*, 215. Derwent, in Powhatan, Virginia, is part of today's Civil War Trails program.

27. Ibid., 213–14.

28. "General Robert E. Lee as College President," *Southern Historical Society Papers* 28 (1900): 246. See also *Richmond Dispatch*, January 27, 1901.

Chapter 25

1. William Couper, "Remarks at the Preston Library Dedication, November 4, 1939," Box: Faculty and Staff; Folder: Preston Clippings and Articles, 7, VMI Archives.

2. William Ruffner, "Col. J.T.L. Preston," *Washington and Lee University Historical Papers* 4 (1893): 140.

3. Stowe, *Uncle Tom's Cabin*, Chap. 45, "Concluding Remarks."

4. J.T.L. Preston, "The Colored Man in the South," *Southern Presbyterian Review* 28, No. 1 (January 1877): 84–85.

5. Ibid., 85–86.

6. Ibid., 87–88.

7. Ibid., 88–89.

8. Ibid., 90.

9. Ibid., 97.

10. Stowe, *Uncle Tom's Cabin*, Chap. 1.

11. Elizabeth Randolph Preston Allan, *A March Past: Reminiscences of Elizabeth Randolph Preston Allan*, ed. Janet Allan Bryan (Richmond: Dietz Press, 1938), 21.

12. Quoting Augustine St. Clare, in Stowe, *Uncle Tom's Cabin*, Chap. 19.

13. Preston, "The Colored Man in the South," 102.

14. Ibid., 97.

15. Stowe, *Uncle Tom's Cabin*, Chap. 19.

16. Ibid.

17. Allan, *March Past*, 78.

18. Preston, "The Colored Man in the South," 89.

19. Stowe, *Uncle Tom's Cabin*, Chap. 45, "Concluding Remarks."

20. Preston, "The Colored Man in the South," 93.

21. Stowe, *Uncle Tom's Cabin*, Chap. 19.

22. Preston, "The Colored Man in the South," 97.

23. For Preston's holding the slave Anakee in trust for his brother-in-law John Caruthers, see Deed Book S, 505, where on June 23, 1835, he acted as trustee in settling William H. Alexander's debt to John Caruthers, which included the sale of land and two Negro slaves, a man named Sandy, about age 24, and a woman named Annaky, about age 21. See also Elizabeth Preston Allan's mention of Anakee as one of Preston's servants, who lived with him for twenty-five years before he reluctantly dismissed her and three other servants in July 1865, in *Life and Letters of Margaret Junkin Preston* (Boston: Riverside Press, 1903), 208. She noted that he thought it best to change but "was grieved to give her up, and she wanted to stay."

24. Preston hired Sylvia and Isaac from his mother, who had hired them from her cousin Col. Samuel McDowell Reid until he sold them in 1835 to Mr. Garland of Lynchburg. Mr. Garland had wished to keep the Hants-Bottom family together. See Allan, *March Past*, 33. See also Elizabeth Preston Allan, "Reminiscences of an Ordinary Life," original manuscript of *A March Past*, which includes information omitted from the book, Collection 2764: William Allan Papers, Box 2, Folder 12, Pt. 2: 18, Southern Historical Collection, University of North Carolina, Chapel Hill: "Father never owned slaves, and the servants (hired servants) in his house were mature men and women: there were no negro children."

25. For Preston's guardianship of the slave Jane, see Deed Bk. DD, 375, November 14, 1849. John Ramsey's heirs appointed Preston as their attorney to set free a girl, Jane, daughter of a Negro woman, Mary, who was the property of the deceased John Ramsey. The act of manumission was to take place when Jane would be 21, until which time she was to remain in the possession of Preston, who had brought her up from a child. If Jane should have a child or children, then Preston might defer her manumission for a period not exceeding four years.

26. Soon after Preston's marriage to Maggie, Aunt Coralie was hired as a middle-aged maid, who nursed Libbie through a bout with typhoid fever. Allan, *March Past*, 96.

27. For Preston's purchase of the slave John, see Receipt of December 12, 1864, in Collection 1543: Margaret Junkin Papers, Box 1, Folder 1, Southern Historical Collection, University of North Carolina, Chapel Hill.

28. Henry Boley, *Lexington in Old Virginia* (Richmond: Garrett and Massie, 1936), 141.
29. J.T.L. Preston, "Religious Education of the Colored People in the South," *New Englander and Yale Review* 37, No. 146 (September 1878): 681.
30. Ibid., 682.
31. Preston, quoted in Oren F. Morton, *A History of Rockbridge County, Virginia* (Baltimore: Regional Publishing, 1980), 142.
32. Preston, "The Colored Man in the South," 102.
33. Preston, "Religious Education of the Colored People," 682.
34. Ibid., 683.
35. Ibid.
36. Ibid., 686.
37. Ibid.
38. Ibid., 680.
39. Anne H. R. Barclay, "William Henry Ruffner, LL.D., by his Daughter," *West Virginia Historical Magazine Quarterly* 2, No. 4 (October 1902): 36. See also Theodore C. DeLaney, Jr., "Aspects of Black Religious and Educational Development in Lexington, Virginia, 1840–1928," *Proceedings of the Rockbridge Historical Society* 10 (1980–89): 140.
40. For Maggie's suggestion of a servants' Sunday school, see Margaret J. Preston, "The General's Colored Sunday School," *Sunday School Times* 29 (December 3, 1887): 771.
41. Preston took over as superintendent of the Colored Sabbath school on July 9, 1864. See Records of Session, Presbyterian Church, Lexington, Virginia 3, 75.
42. Preston, "The General's Colored Sunday School," 772.
43. Ibid.
44. The two black churches that formed in 1864 and 1867 were Randolph Street Methodist Church and Lexington African Baptist Church (today's First Baptist Church).
45. DeLaney, Jr., 143.
46. "Personal," *New York Evening Post*, January 22, 1895, 7.
47. Richard G. Williams, Jr., "Jackson's 'colored Sunday school' Class," *Washington Times*, May 6, 2006.
48. Ibid. See also Kathleen Shelor, "Dr. D. L. Downing, Colored Pastor, Honors Stonewall Jackson," *Richmond Times-Dispatch*, May 10, 1936; and *Roanoke World-News*, from scrapbook, n.d., Folder: Mr. Herbert R. Preston, VMI Museum Archives.

Chapter 26

1. Margaret Preston, as quoted in Henry Boley, *Lexington in Old Virginia* (Richmond: Garrett and Massie, 1936), 182–84.
2. J.T.L. Preston, *Removing to a New Charge: Letters to a Young Minister* (Richmond: Presbyterian Committee of Publication, 1890), 44.
3. William Couper, "Remarks at the Preston Library Dedication, November 4, 1939," Box: Faculty and Staff; Folder: Preston Clippings and Articles, 8, VMI Archives.
4. J.T.L. Preston, "Address Delivered Before the Franklin Society of Lexington, at Its Semi-centenary Anniversary, February 1866, Lexington, Virginia," Collection 103: Franklin Society Library Book Collection (FSL/F/234/.LS/P74/1866), Washington and Lee Special Collections. All quotes in the text are from this address.
5. J.T.L. Preston, "General Jackson as a Professor, Extract of a lecture recently by Col. J.T.L. Preston, of the V. M. Institute," *Lexington Banner and Gazette*, May 16, 1866. All quotes from this lecture are from the *Lexington Banner and Gazette*.
6. Allan, "Reminiscences of an Ordinary Life," Pt. 6: 20.
7. William Ruffner, "History of Washington College," *Washington and Lee Historical Papers* 4 (1893): 142–43.
8. College of William and Mary, "Faculty Minutes," 1861–83, 233.
9. Letter of November 20, 1869, from J.T.L. Preston to Gen. Smith, "Smith's Incoming Letters," #0277, VMI Archives.
10. Capt. Robert E. Lee, Recollections and Letters of General Robert E. Lee, by His Son Captain Robert E. Lee (New York: Doubleday, Page, 1904), 374–75.
11. "A Year in Heaven," in *Old Song and New* (Philadelphia: J. B. Lippincott, 1870), 157–58, 160.
12. Elizabeth Randolph Preston Allan, *Life and Letters of Margaret Junkin Preston* (Boston: Riverside Press, 1903), 236, August 27, 1870, and 231, January 24, 1870.
13. "Afternoon," in *Old Song and New*, 130–32, 161–63.
14. Phoebe Alexander Preston Cocke died on August 5, 1873.
15. "Afternoon," in *Old Song and New*, 161–63. The line "Too vaguely wrapped your young ideal" is a later revision of "Made large and luminous life's ideal." See Margaret J. Preston, "Afternoon," *Land We Love* 3, No. 2 (June 1867), 109–10.

Chapter 27

1. Elizabeth Preston married Col. William Allan on May 12, 1874. See William Allan's diary in Bryan, ed., "Reminiscences of Elizabeth Preston Allan," Collection 2764: William Allan Papers, Box 2, Folder 18, Southern Historical Collection, University of North Carolina, Chapel Hill.
2. Elizabeth Randolph Preston Allan, *Life and Letters of Margaret Junkin Preston* (Boston: Riverside Press, 1903), 305.
3. Royster Lyle, Jr., and Pamela Hemenway Simpson, *The Architecture of Historic Lexington* (Charlottesville, Va.: University Press of Virginia, 1977), 119.
4. Margaret J. Preston, "We Two," *Colonial Ballads, Sonnets and Other Verse* (Boston: Houghton Mifflin, 1887), 202.
5. James A. Harrison, "Margaret J. Preston, An Appreciation," in Allan, *Life and Letters*, 361.
6. Ibid., 272.
7. Letter of December 23, 1873, from Paul Hayne to Margaret J. Preston, in Accession 2000–073, Box 1, Folder December 23, 1873, David M. Rubenstein Rare Book and Manuscript Library, Duke University, Durham, N.C.
8. Ibid.
9. Hon. J. M. Daniells, *A Virginian* [John Moncure Daniel]: *The Life of Stonewall Jackson from Official Papers, Contemporary Narratives, and Personal Acquaintance* (London and New York: Sampson Low, Son, 1863).
10. Elizabeth Randolph Preston Allan, *A March Past: Reminiscences of Elizabeth Randolph Preston Allan*, ed. Janet Allan Bryan (Richmond: Dietz Press, 1938), 143.

11. "Minutes of the Board of Visitors" 3: 264, June 26, 1876, VMI Archives, for Preston's resignation from teaching, 267 (June 28, 1876) for the board's regretful acceptance, and 268 for Preston's appointment as emeritus professor.

12. Ibid., 290, June 30, 1877.

13. Edmund Randolph Preston, "Col. J.T.L. Preston of Lexington, Virginia (1811–1890)," comments at the dedication of the Preston Memorial Library at VMI, November 11, 1939. Regarding Preston's letter declining the rank of brigadier general, many of Governor Kemper's records for the 1870s were lost or destroyed, and a search for Preston's letter in the Office of the Governor, James L. Kemper, Executive Papers, 1877 March–December, Barcode 1056066, Box 4, Special Collections, Library of Virginia, proved futile. But see William Couper, *One Hundred Years at V.M.I.* (Richmond: Garrett and Massie, 1939), 3: 355, who claims regarding Preston, "Apparently no action was taken on this order so far as Colonel Preston was concerned."

14. For Preston's nomination by the General Assembly in Savannah, see *Georgia Weekly Telegraph*, May 30, 1876, 7. For his participation as a delegate, see Howard McKnight Wilson, *Lexington Presbyterian Heritage* (Verona, Va.: McClure Press, 1971), 349.

15. Rev. J. Thomson, ed., *Report of Proceedings of the First General Presbyterian Council Convened at Edinburgh, July 1877, with Relative Documents Bearing on the Affairs of the Council, and the State of the Presbyterian Churches Throughout the World* (Edinburgh: Thomas and Archibald Constable, 1877).

16. William Couper, quoting Preston's grandchildren, in "Remarks at the Preston Library Dedication, November 4, 1939," Box: Faculty and Staff; Folder: Preston Clippings and Articles, 7, VMI Archives. See also Edmund Randolph Preston, "Grandfather Preston (Col. J.T.L. Preston, founder of Virginia Military Institute)," handwritten manuscript.

17. J.T.L. Preston, "Annual Report," Box: Superintendent 19th Cent. Subject Files, Annual Reports, Departments, June 15, 1881, VMI Archives.

18. Terence, *Andria*, Act 5, Scene. 2: Davus to Chremes, 166 BC.

19. *Catalogue of the Officers and Alumni of Washington and Lee* (Baltimore: John Murphy, 1888), 213.

Chapter 28

1. Elizabeth Randolph Preston Allan, *Life and Letters of Margaret Junkin Preston* (Boston: Riverside Press, 1903), 303.

2. Letter of October 27, 1952, from Janet Allan Bryan to VMI Public Relations Director Robert W. Jeffrey, Box: VMI Faculty and Staff, 19th Cent., Preston, John T. L., VMI Archives.

3. Allan, *Life and Letters*, 303.

4. Letter of January 15, 1880, from Paul Hayne to Margaret J. Preston, in Accession 2000-073, Box 1, Folder January 15, 1880, David M. Rubenstein Rare Book and Manuscript Library, Duke University, Durham, N.C.

5. Allan, *Life and Letters*, 303.

6. J.T.L. Preston, "Silver Wedding Day," Collection 1543: Margaret Junkin Preston Papers, Box 2, Southern Historical Collection, University of North Carolina, Chapel Hill.

7. Letter of December 1, 1881, from Margaret J. Preston to Paul Hayne, in Allan, *Life and Letters*, 301–02.

8. "Jottings," the name given to "John T. L. Preston Diary, 1861 July 24–September 22," MSS 17,264, p. 9, August 9, 1861, Manuscript Division, Library of Congress, Washington, D.C.

9. Allan, *Life and Letters*, 307.

10. Letters of June 28 through August 20, 1884, from Margaret J. Preston to Paul Hayne, in ibid., 308–12.

11. Ibid., 312.

12. *Catalogue of Officers and Alumni of Washington and Lee University* (Baltimore: John Murphy, 1888), 41.

13. Leslie Lyle Campbell, "The Hunter is Home From the Hill: Picture of Col. J.T.L. Preston is found after long search." *Rockbridge County News*, March 18, 1948, 5.

14. "Washington and Lee, Annual Commencement, Lexington, Va., June 17," *Philadelphia Inquirer*, June 18, 1885, 5.

15. Margaret J. Preston, *Centennial Poem for Washington and Lee: 1775–1885* (New York: Putnam's, 1885), 24. The dates indicated for the "Centennial" are 1775–1885. Liberty Hall Academy was founded around 1775, which was the date chosen in Preston's time as the birth year of the university, but today Washington and Lee traces its history back to the Rev. Robert Alexander's School at Larkin Spring in Augusta County, which was opened in 1749 as the first classical school west of the Blue Ridge and evolved in 1775 under William Graham into Mount Pleasant Academy, the embryo of a college patterned after his alma mater, Princeton College, and changing its name the following year to Liberty Hall in celebration of the Revolution. See John McDaniel with Charles N. Watson and David T. Moore, *Liberty Hall Academy: The Early History of the Institutions Which Evolved into Washington and Lee University* (Lexington, Va.: Liberty Hall Press, 1979).

16. Campbell, "The Hunter is Home From the Hill," 5.

17. William H. Ruffner, "Col. J.T.L. Preston," *Washington and Lee University Historical Papers* 4 (1893): 138.

18. Letter of July 4, 1889, from J.T.L. Preston at McDonogh School in Baltimore to F. H. Smith, handwritten original in possession of A. H. Morrison; copy at McDonogh School; typed copy at MSS2 P9263a1, Virginia Historical Society.

19. Ibid.

20. J.T.L. Preston, "Historical Sketch of the Establishment and Organization of the Virginia Military Institute, prepared, at the request of the Board of Visitors, by Col. John Thomas Lewis Preston, Professor Emeritus V.M.I., July 4, 1889," Box: Preston, John T. L., Folder MS 0240, 1, VMI Archives.

21. William Couper, *One Hundred Years at V.M.I.* (Richmond: Garrett and Massie, 1939), 4: 20.

22. Preston, "Historical Sketch," 2.

23. Ibid., 5

24. Ibid., 5.

25. Ibid., 6.

26. Couper, *One Hundred Years at V.M.I.* 4: 16.

27. Margaret J. Preston, *Semi-Centennial Ode for the Virginia Military Institute, Lexington, Virginia 1839–1889* (New York: Putnam's, 1889).

28. Couper, *One Hundred Years at V.M.I.* 4: 18.

29. Allan, *Life and Letters*, 321.

30. Ibid., 322.

31. "Died" (Col. J.T.L. Preston), *Lexington Gazette*, July 17, 1890. Preston's death is noted at "12 o'clock, midnight." See also *Roanoke Times*, July 18, 1890.

32. Although Willie's grave was at Manassas, a duplicate stone was erected in Lexington.
33. "Funeral of Colonel J.T.L. Preston," *Lexington Gazette*, July 24, 1890.
34. 2 Timothy 4: 7.
35. "Laus Deo is the signet legend on my heart," wrote Preston in "Journal of a Trip Abroad in 1884," 21, June 24, 1884.

Epilogue

1. Elizabeth Randolph Preston Allan, *Life and Letters of Margaret Junkin Preston* (Boston: Riverside Press, 1903), 324.
2. The population of Lexington, Virginia, in 1890 was 3,059. See William Couper, *One Hundred Years at V.M.I.* (Richmond: Garrett and Massie, 1939), 1: 236 n. 29.
3. "Col. John L. Preston Dead," *Roanoke Times*, July 18, 1890. See also "Col. John L. Preston," *Peninsula Enterprise* (Accomac, Va.), July 19, 1890, 2, col. 1.
4. J.T.L. Preston's obituary, July 17, 1890, in *Withrow Scrapbook* 19: 104, Washington and Lee Special Collections.
5. William Couper, "Remarks at the Preston Library Dedication, November 4, 1939." Box: Faculty and Staff; Folder: Preston Clippings and Articles, 7, VMI Archives.
6. "Funeral of Colonel J.T.L. Preston," *Lexington Gazette*, July 24, 1890.
7. James A. Harrison, "Margaret J. Preston: An Appreciation," in Allan, *Life and Letters*, app., 345–46.
8. Ibid., 351.
9. "Memorial of Col. J.T.L. Preston," Records of Session, Presbyterian Church, Lexington, Virginia 4, 159–62. Preston was admitted to church membership July 31, 1831, and was ordained ruling elder March 5, 1843.
10. Ibid.
11. "Minutes of the Board of Visitors" 4: 164, VMI Archives.
12. Will of J.T.L. Preston, dated March 15, 1883, in Will Book No. 2 (1874–1904), 246, Rockbridge Old Circuit Court. See also 247–48, Codicils 2, 3, 4, 6, and 7 between 1885 and 1889. Preston bought the Fair Ground Lot, amounting to 8.91 acres, at public auction on December 1, 1873, for $525 but didn't finish his payments with interest until October 12, 1889. See Deed Bk. 54, 113. The Fair Ground Lot adjoined Rockbridge Agricultural Society.
13. The 2012 figures are based on the income index of per-capita GDP as calculated by MeasuringWorth.com, a service for comparing income or wealth over time.
14. Letter of January 13, 1891, from Margaret J. Preston to S. G. [Sophia Gilman], quoted in Allan, *Life and Letters*, 323.
15. Deed Bk. 73, 53, of February 28, 1891, from Herbert and Thomas Preston, executors, to Henry H. Myers for $6,860 for Preston home. For a list of new homes see *Rockbridge County News*, February 19 and July 16, 1891, also March 30, 1922.
16. For all the changes that Myers made to the Preston home, see *Lexington Gazette*, April 23, 1891. Subsequent owners of the home after Myers's death were Gen. Scott Shipp in 1906, his daughter Lucy Shipp Huger when he died in 1917, and then her children, known as the Huger family; Sigma Phi Epsilon in 1963; and Washington and Lee University in 1992. See Allison Hyko, "The Preston House," a paper written for Professor Pamela Simpson's class in American Architecture, Washington and Lee Architectural Papers, April 1, 1994, Washington and Lee Special Collections. For the "yellow brick" of the original house, see Allan, "Reminiscences of an Ordinary Life," original manuscript of *March Past*, which includes information omitted from the book, Collection 2764: William Allan Papers, Box 2, Folder 12, Pt. 7: 16, Southern Historical Collection, University of North Carolina, Chapel Hill.
17. Allan, *Life and Letters*, 325.
18. Elizabeth Allen's home, which she purchased in July 1890, was at today's 503 South Main Street, previously occupied by Thomas Semmes, professor of French and tactics at VMI from 1860 to 1904. See Deed Bk. 63, 88.
19. Letter of late 1893 from M.J.P. to A. deF. (deForest), in Allan, *Life and Letters*, 328.
20. Letter of November 20, 1893, from M.J.P. to A. deF. (deForest), in ibid., 331.
21. Margaret J. Preston, "Who Knoweth? A Sonnet," *For Love's Sake: Poems of Faith and Comfort* (New York: Anson D. F. Randolph, 1886), 143.
22. James A. Harrison, "Margaret J. Preston," *The Critic* 27, No. 792 (April 24, 1897): 291.
23. "Margaret Preston Oak," in J. Elton Lodewick and Mrs. Lynwood R. Holmes, *Notable Trees of Virginia: Bulletin of the Virginia Polytechnic Institute* 24, No. 7 (March 15, 1931): 12. "The space covered by her family burying ground in Lexington Cemetery is said by old inhabitants to be almost the exact spot occupied by the Little Brick Church which was the first home of Presbyterianism in Lexington, in what was then known as Taylor's Grove." In 1931 the tree was conservatively estimated to be over 130 years old.
24. "Mrs. Margaret J. Preston: Death of This Well-known Southern Poetess in Baltimore," *Lexington Gazette*, March 31, 1897. Thomas L. Preston died at age 59 on May 28, 1895, and John A. Preston at age 43 on September 13, 1896.
25. The birth date on Maggie's gravestone is incorrect. She was born May 19, 1820. See Allan, *Life and Letters*, 6 and 229, which quote Maggie herself on the date of "my birthday."
26. "Minutes of the Board of Visitors" 4: 396, June 24, 1901.
27. Memo of William Couper to Superintendent Charles Kilborne, June 3, 1939, Records of the Superintendent, Memoranda, 1939, VMI Archives. For a history of the libraries at VMI, including the Preston Library, see James E. Gaines, Jr., "A Brief History of VMI's Libraries," in Thomas W. Davis, ed., *A Crowd of Honorable Youths: Historical Essays on the First 150 Years of the Virginia Military Institute* (Lexington: VMI Sesquicentennial Committee, 1988), 169–83.
28. Gov. James H. Price, "Remarks of the Governor at the Exercises Commemorating the Centennial of the V.M.I. and the Twenty-first Armistice of the First World War, Lexington, Va., November 11, 1939," Price Speeches: July–December 1939, Washington and Lee Special Collections. All quotes from this address are from these remarks.
29. General J. H. Binford Peay, III, "Remarks at Founders Day Convocation: Superintendent's speech on anniversary of founding of VMI," November 9, 2007.

Bibliography

Acts of the Virginia General Assembly, Session Laws, 1794–1812, film 358/reel 4, and 1846–51, film 358a/reel 2. Archives Division, Library of Virginia, Richmond.

"Address of the President and Trustees of Washington College to the Cincinnati Society of Virginia," Washington and Lee University Trustees Papers, Cabinet C, Drawer 4, Washington and Lee University Scrapbook, "Original Papers Relating to Early History of Washington and Lee College and Society of the Cincinnati," No. 11 1/2. Washington and Lee University Special Collections.

Alexander, James W. *Life of Archibald Alexander, D.D. LL.D.: First Professor in the Theological Seminary at Princeton, New Jersey.* Philadelphia: Presbyterian Board of Publications, 1856.

Allan, Elizabeth Preston. *Life and Letters of Margaret Junkin Preston.* Boston: Riverside Press, 1903.

———. "Notes on William Alexander Caruthers," *William and Mary College Quarterly,* Series 2, 9, No. 4 (October 1929): 294–97.

———. "Reminiscences of an Ordinary Life." Ed. Janet Allan Bryan. Collection 2764: William Allan Papers, Box 2, Folders 12–13. Southern Historical Collection, University of North Carolina, Chapel Hill. Contains original manuscript of *A March Past* in ten parts, including material omitted from the book.

Allan, Elizabeth Randolph Preston. *A March Past: Reminiscences of Elizabeth Randolph Preston Allan.* Ed. Janet Allan Bryan. Richmond: Dietz Press, 1938.

Allardice, Bruce. "West Points of the Confederacy: Southern Military Schools and the Confederate Army," *Civil War History* 43, No. 4 (December 1997): 310–31.

Ambler, Charles Henry. *Thomas Ritchie: A Study in Virginia Politics.* Richmond: Bell Book and Stationery, 1913.

Anderson, Col. James A. "The Founding of VMI and Its Early Years," in J. Eston Johnston, ed., *Echoes of Virginia Military Institute.* Lexington: Virginia Military Institute, 1937, 1–11.

Anderson, Col. Joseph R. "Col. Preston as Teacher," a one-page remembrance written ca. 1891. Box: Virginia Military Institute Faculty and Staff, 19th century, Preston, John T. L., Folder: Miscellaneous. Virginia Military Institute Archives.

Anderson, William. "Preston," *The Scottish Nation, or the Surnames, Families, Literature, Honors and Biographical History of the People of Scotland.* London: A. Fullarton, 1863, 3: 303–05.

Andrew, Rod, Jr. *Long Gray Lines: The Southern Military School Tradition, 1839–1915.* Chapel Hill: University of North Carolina Press, 2001 [mistakes J.T.L. Preston for Barclay, who visited West Point].

Armstrong, Richard L. *The Battle of McDowell, March 11–May 18, 1862.* Lynchburg, Va.: H. E. Howard, 1990.

Arnold, Thomas Jackson. *Early Life and Letters of General Thomas J. Jackson ("Stonewall") by His Nephew, Thomas Jackson Arnold.* New York: Fleming H. Revell, 1916.

Askew, Amanda. "207 North Randolph Street, Lexington, Virginia: A Study of Vernacular Architecture," a paper written for Prof. Pamela Simpson's class in American architecture, Washington and Lee Architectural Papers, April 2007. Washington and Lee University Special Collections.

"Atlantic Intelligence," *Sacramento Daily Union* 25, No. 3772, April 24, 1863. Quotes the Rev. George Junkin re General T. J. Jackson and Col. J.T.L. Preston.

Aubrey, Thomas. *Travels Through the Interior Parts of America in a Series of Letters.* 2 vols. London: Printed for William Lane, 1789.

Baldwin, Cornelius C. "Lexington Arsenal," *Lexington Gazette,* December 25, 1835.

Barclay, Anne H. R. "William Henry Ruffner, LL.D., by his Daughter," *West Virginia Historical Magazine Quarterly* 2, No. 4 (October 1902): 33–43.

Barrett, John G., and Richard M. McMurry. "VMI in the Civil War," in Thomas W. Davis, ed., *A Crowd of Honorable Youths: Historical Essays on the First 150 Years of the Virginia Military Institute.* Lexington: Virginia Military Institute Sesquicentennial Committee, 1988, 31–45.

Baylor, George. *Bull Run to Bull Run; or Four Years in the Army of Northern Virginia.* Richmond: B. F. Johnson, 1900.

Bean, William G. *The Liberty Hall Volunteers: Stonewall's College Boys.* Charlottesville: University Press of Virginia, 1964; 2nd ed., 2005.

———. "The Skinner Case," manuscript copy of a paper delivered before the Rockbridge Historical Society, October 1947. See "Dr. Bean Reads Historical Paper," *Rockbridge County News,* Nov. 15, 22, and 29, 1945.

———. *Stonewall's Man: Sandie Pendleton.* Chapel Hill: University of North Carolina Press, 1959.

Beck, Bandon H., and Charles S. Grunder. *The First Battle of Winchester, May 25, 1862.* Lynchburg, Va.: H. E. Howard, 1992.

Becker, Trudy Harrington. "Broadening Access to a Classical Education: State Universities in Virginia in the Nineteenth Century," *Classical Journal* 96, No. 3 (2001): 309–22.

Benét, Stephen Vincent. *John Brown's Body.* Garden City, N.Y.: Doubleday, Doran, 1928.

Blair, Hugh. *Lectures on Rhetoric and Belles Lettres*, Vol. 1 of 3. London: T. Cadell and W. Davies, 1812.

Blandome. Final Nomination to the National Register of Historic Places, Record No. 348532, NRIS No. 01001520, VDHR File No. 117–8027–0127. Washington, D.C.: National Park Service, January 24, 2002.

"Blue Tide Engulfed Lexington," *Withrow Scrapbook* 7: 74. Washington and Lee University Special Collections.

Bodie, Charles A. *Remarkable Rockbridge: The Story of Rockbridge County, Virginia*. Lexington, Va.: Rockbridge Historical Society, 2011.

———, ed. *Rockbridge County, Virginia, Manuscripts: A Guide to Collections in the United States*. Lexington, Va.: Rockbridge Historical Society, 1998.

Boley, Henry. *Lexington in Old Virginia*. Richmond: Garrett and Massie, 1936.

Boltz, Martha M. "A Gentle Rebel Youth Slain in Battle," *Washington Times* (Washington, D.C.), August 23, 1997.

Boney, F. N. *John Letcher of Virginia*. Tuscaloosa: University of Alabama Press, 1966.

Bowen, Cawthon A. "Col. J.T.L. Preston, Original Spirit of V.M.I.," *Roanoke Times*, November 5, 1939, 1, 14–15.

Boyd, Thomas Massie. "General Stonewall Jackson," *Southern Bivouac* 5 (1885–86): 355–60.

Britton, Rick. "Benjamin F. Ficklin, Monticello's Colorful Confederate Owner," *Monticello Newsletter* 17, No. 2 (Winter 2006): 1–5.

Brock, Robert Alonzo, and Virgil Anson Lewis. *Virginia and Virginians*. Richmond: H. H. Hardesty, 1888.

Brown, Katharine L. "Stonewall Jackson in Lexington," *Proceedings of the Rockbridge Historical Society* 9 (1975–79): 197–210.

Brown, Orlando. *Memoranda of the Preston Family*. Albany: J. Munsell, 1864. 1st ed. was privately printed in 1842. A record compiled by his father, John Mason Brown, before his death in 1837.

Brown, Rev. James Moore. *Captives of Abb's Valley: A Legend of Frontier Life*. Staunton, Va.: McClure, 1942.

Bruce, William Cabell. *John Randolph of Roanoke, 1773–1833: A Biography Based Largely on New Material*. 2 vols. New York: Putnam's, 1922.

Brundage, Fitzhugh. "Shifting Attitudes Towards Slavery in Antebellum Rockbridge County," *Proceedings of the Rockbridge Historical Society* 10 (1980–89): 333–44.

Bryan, Janet Allan. "Looking Backward: Reminiscences of the Family of Colonel J.T.L. Preston." Jacksonville, Florida, 1947. Manuscript describing the individuals in the photograph of Col. J.T.L. Preston's family ca. 1890.

Burke, John Bernard. *Genealogical and Heraldic History of the Extinct and Dormant Baronetcies of England, Ireland, and Scotland*, 2nd ed. London: John Russell Smith, 1844. Esp. "Preston," 424–27.

Butler, Stuart Lee. *A Guide to Virginia Military Units in the War of 1812*. Athens, Ga.: Iberian, 1988.

———. *Virginia Soldiers in the United States Army, 1800–1815*. Athens, Ga.: Iberian, 1986.

C [pseud.]. "The Arsenal," *Lexington Gazette*, January 13, 1837.

"Cadets of Lexington," *Richmond Enquirer*, January 11, 1842. The first showing of the cadets in Richmond, Virginia.

Campbell, Leslie Lyle. "207 North Randolph Street," *Rockbridge County, Virginia*, Rockbridge Historical Society Manuscripts. Washington and Lee University Special Collections.

———. "The Hunter is Home From the Hill: Picture of Col. J.T.L. Preston is found after long search," *Rockbridge County News*, March 18, 1948.

———. "The Old Jordan House," *Rockbridge County, Virginia*, Rockbridge Historical Society Manuscripts. Washington and Lee University Special Collections.

Cappon, Lester J. *Virginia Newspapers 1821–1935: A Bibliography with Historical Introduction and Notes*. New York: D. Appleton–Century, 1936.

"Capt. Thomas L. Preston," *Washington and Lee Historical Papers* 4 (1893): 137.

Carton, Evan. *Patriotic Treason: John Brown and the Soul of America*. New York: Free Press, 2006. A portrayal of the human side of John Brown.

Casler, John Overton. *Four Years in the Stonewall Brigade*. Dayton, Ohio: Morningside Bookshop, 1971.

Catalogue of the Officers and Alumni of Washington and Lee University, Lexington, Virginia, 1749–1888. Baltimore: John Murphy, 1888.

Census, 1860, Town of Lexington, Virginia. Transcribed, corrected, and annotated by Col. Edwin L. Dooley, Jr., updated May 29, 2008.

Census, 1870, Town of Lexington and Township of Lexington, Virginia. Transcribed, corrected, and annotated by Col. Edwin L. Dooley, Jr.

Chalkley, Lyman. *Chronicles of the Scotch-Irish Settlement in Virginia, Extracted from the Original Court Records of Augusta County, 1745–1800*. 3 vols. 1912. Baltimore: Genealogical Publishing, 1980. Esp. 1: 17, May 12, 1746, No. 44: "John Preston proved his importation."

Chambers, Lenoir. *Stonewall Jackson and the Virginia Military Institute: The Lexington Years*. Lexington, Va.: Historic Lexington Foundation, 1959. Photographically reproduced from Lenoir Chambers, *Stonewall Jackson*. New York: William Morrow, 1959.

Chowder, Ken. "The Father of American Terrorism," in *American Heritage Magazine* 51, Issue 1 (February–March 2000). A reassessment of John Brown 200 years after his birth.

Citizen of Lexington [pseud.]. "Communication," *Lexington Gazette*, January 8, 1836.

———. "Lexington Arsenal," *Lexington Gazette*, December 18, 1835; January 1; February 5 and 26, 1836. Four articles rebutting the plan by Cives [J.T.L. Preston] for converting the arsenal into an educational institution.

Cocke, Elizabeth Randolph. "A Beautiful Life," MSS1 C6458 d FA2. Virginia Historical Society. Taken from *Southern Churchman* of January 31, 1889.

Cocke Family Papers, 1794–1981, MSS1 C6458d FA2. Virginia Historical Society. Represented are Thomas Lewis Preston (1781–1812) of Rockbridge County, his daughter Elizabeth Randolph (Preston) Cocke (1808–1889) of Powhatan County, her son John Preston Cocke (1845–1917) of Richmond, and his daughter Elizabeth Preston Cocke (1891–1981) of Richmond.

Cocke, Preston. *Battle of New Market and the Cadets of the Virginia Military Institute: May 15, 1864.* Richmond: May 15, 1914, 12 pp. No. E476.64 C66 1914. Albert and Shirley Small Special Collections Library, University of Virginia.

"Col. John L. Preston," *Peninsula Enterprise* (Accomac, Va.), July 19, 1890, 2, col. 1. Obituary.

"Col. S. [J.] M. Schoonmaker, A Union Officer and Gentleman," *Withrow Scrapbook* 7:86. Washington and Lee University Special Collections.

"Colonization Meeting in Lexington, Va.," *African Repository, and Colonial Journal* 26, No. 8 (August 1850): 246.

Colonna, Benjamin A. "The Battle of New Market," *Journal of the Military Service Institution of the United States* 51 (November–December 1912): 344–49.

Conrad, James Lee. *The Young Lions: Confederate Cadets at War.* Mechanicsburg, Pa.: Stackpole Books, 1997. A history of military colleges as background to a lucid view of the Confederate cadet's wartime world.

Coulling, Mary Price. *Margaret Junkin Preston: A Biography.* Winston-Salem, N.C.: John F. Blair, 1993.

Couper, William. *Claudius Crozet: Soldier-Scholar-Educator-Engineer (1789–1964).* Charlottesville, Va.: Historical Publishing, 1936.

_____. Letter of August 28, 1939, from William Couper to Maj. J. W. McClung, in Box: Virginia Military Institute Faculty and Staff, 19th cent., Folder 1: Preston, John T. L. Virginia Military Institute Archives. Letter about J.T.L. Preston.

_____. *One Hundred Years at V.M.I.* 4 vols. Richmond: Garrett and Massie, 1939.

_____. "Remarks at the Preston Library Dedication, Nov. 4, 1939." 12 pp. Box: Faculty and Staff; Folder: Preston Clippings and Articles. Virginia Military Institute Archives.

_____. *The V.M.I. New Market Cadets: Biographical Sketches of All Members of the Virginia Military Institute Corps of Cadets Who Fought in the Battle of New Market, May 15, 1864.* Charlottesville, Va.: Michie, 1933.

Crenshaw, Ollinger. *General Lee's College: The Rise and Growth of Washington and Lee University.* New York: Random House, 1969.

_____. "General Lee's College: The Rise and Growth of Washington and Lee," unpublished typescript in two volumes. Lexington, Va.: Washington and Lee University, 1973.

Crofts, Daniel W. *Reluctant Confederates: Upper South Unionists in the Secession Crisis.* Chapel Hill: University of North Carolina Press, 1989.

Crute, Joseph H., Jr. *Confederate Staff Officers, 1861–1865.* Powhatan, Va.: Derwent Books, 1982.

Cunningham, June F. "Col. J.T.L. Preston," *Main Street Magazine* 2, No. 9 (November 1975): 7–11. In Virginia Military Institute Museum Archives.

Current, Richard Nelson, ed. *Encyclopedia of the Confederacy.* 4 vols. New York: Simon & Schuster, 1993.

Dabney, Robert Lewis. *Life and Campaigns of Lieut.-Gen. Thomas J. Jackson (Stonewall Jackson).* Richmond: Blelock, 1866.

Daniells, Hon. J. M., A Virginian [John Moncure Daniel]. *The Life of Stonewall Jackson from Official Papers, Contemporary Narratives, and Personal Acquaintance.* London and New York: Sampson Low, Son, 1863.

Daniels, Jonathan. *The Randolphs of Virginia.* Garden City, N.Y.: Doubleday, 1972.

Davis, Curtis Carroll. *Chronicler of the Cavaliers: A Life of William A. Caruthers.* Richmond: Dietz Press, 1953.

Davis, Thomas W., ed. *A Crowd of Honorable Youths: Historical Essays on the First 150 Years of the Virginia Military Institute.* Lexington: Virginia Military Institute Sesquicentennial Committee, 1988. Eighteen Essays, esp. including Thomas W. Davis, "The Initial Corps: An Overview of Virginia Military Institute's First Cadets and their Subsequent Careers"; Edwin L. Dooley, Jr., "Francis H. Smith and VMI on the Eve of the Civil War"; John G. Barrett and Richard M. McMurry, "Virginia Military Institute in the Civil War"; June F. Cunningham, "Colonel John Thomas Lewis Preston"; George M. Brooke, Jr., "Virginia Military Institute's Semicentennial Year"; Royster Lyle, Jr., "The Architecture of Virginia Military Institute"; James F. Dittrich, "Horses at VMI"; James E. Gaines, Jr., "A Brief History of Virginia Military Institute's Libraries"; and John W. Knapp's "A Short Academic History of the Virginia Military Institute."

Davis, William Charles. *Battle at Bull Run.* Garden City, N.Y.: Doubleday, 1977.

_____. *Battle of New Market.* Baton Rouge: Louisiana State University Press, 1975.

"Death of Col. J.T.L. Preston: He Passes Peacefully Away in His 80th Year; Sketch of His Life," *Lexington Gazette*, 24 July 1890. Also in *Withrow Scrapbook* 19: 104–05. Washington and Lee University Special Collections.

"Death of Col. Preston," *The Week* (Baltimore: McDonogh School), July 19, 1890.

"Death of Thomas L. Preston, Esq.," *Richmond Enquirer*, August 18, 1812. Obituary of J.T.L. Preston's father by Thomas Ritchie.

"Deaths" [Col. J.T.L. Preston], *Richmond Enquirer*, August 27, 1849, 1, col. 7. False obituary of J.T.L. Preston and retraction, "Gross and Malicious Imposition," 2, col. 3.

Deed Books E–Z, AA–ZZ, 52–72. Lexington, Va.: Rockbridge County Courthouse, 1778–1892.

DeLaney, Theodore C., Jr. "Aspects of Black Religious and Educational Development in Lexington, Virginia, 1840–1928." *Proceedings of the Rockbridge Historical Society* 10 (1980–89). 139–151.

Delautier, Roger U., Jr. *Winchester in the Civil War.* Lynchburg, Va.: H. E. Howard, 1992.

"Departure of Emigrants for Liberia." *Lexington Gazette*, December 22, 1849. Repr. as "News of One Hundred Years Ago," *Withrow Scrapbook* 19: 113. Washington and Lee University Special Collections.

"Died" [Col. J.T.L. Preston], *Lexington Gazette*, July 17, 1890.

Diehl, George West. "Caruthers Clan," *Rockbridge County, Virginia Notebook* [articles written by Dr. George West Diehl in the *News Gazette*, Lexington, Va.; comp. by Maxim A. Coppage III, with additional charts and notes added as well as surname index]. Utica, Ky.: McDowell, 1982, 15–18.

_____. "Forgotten Glories," *Rockbridge County, Virginia Notebook*, 229–31. Ann Smith Academy.

_____. "Preston Saga," *Rockbridge County, Virginia Notebook*, 69–73.

_____, comp. *A Brief History of Public Education in Rockbridge County, Lexington. Buena Vista, 1748–1980.* Lexington and Buena Vista, Va.: Rockbridge Retired Teachers Association, 1980.

Dooley, Edwin L. "Arms for Virginia on the Eve of the Civil War: The Armory Commission Letters of Col. Francis H. Smith," with transcription and annotation. 87 pp. Virginia Military Institute Archives.

_____. "Francis H. Smith and the Secession Crisis of 1860–1861: The Letters of VMI Superintendent Francis H. Smith," with transcription, annotation, and commentary. 75 pp. Virginia Military Institute Archives.

_____. "Lexington in the 1860 Census," in *Proceedings of the Rockbridge Historical Society* 9 (1982): 189–96.

_____. "A New Look at the Old Guard," *Virginia Military Institute Alumni Review* 48 (Winter 1972): 9–11.

Dorman, Charles P. Legislative bill establishing Virginia Military Institute, April 3, 1839. Charles P. Dorman Collection, MS#066, Folder 3. Virginia Military Institute Archives.

Dorman, John Frederick. *The Prestons of Smithfield and Greenfield in Virginia: Descendants of John and Elizabeth (Patton) Preston Through Five Generations.* Louisville, Ky.: Filson Club, 1982.

Driver, R. J., Jr. *The 1st and 2nd Rockbridge Artillery*, 2nd ed. (*Virginia Regimental Histories Series*). Lynchburg, Va.: H. E. Howard, 1987. Listing for "Franklin C. Preston."

Driver, Robert J., Jr. *Guide to Published Material on the History and Genealogy of Rockbridge County, Virginia, and Vicinity.* Lexington, Va.: Rockbridge Historical Society, 1997.

_____. *Lexington and Rockbridge County in the Civil War.* Lynchburg, Va.: H. E. Howard, 1989.

Early, Jubal Anderson. *Lieutenant General Jubal Anderson Early, C.S.A.: Autobiographical Sketch and Narrative of the War Between the States.* Philadelphia: J. B. Lippincott, 1912.

Eby, Cecil D., Jr. "David Hunter: Villain of the Valley: The Sack of the Virginia Military Institute," *Iron Worker* 28, No. 2 (Spring 1964): 1–9.

Eckenrode, H. J. *The Randolphs: The Story of a Virginia Family.* Indianapolis: Bobbs-Merrill, 1946.

"Education in the Antebellum Era," in Virginius Dabney, *Virginia: The New Dominion.* Garden City, N.Y.: Doubleday, 1971, 245–53.

Ellis, William Arba, and Grenville M. Dodge. *Norwich University, 1819–1911: Her History, Her Graduates, Her Roll of Honor.* 3 vols. Montpelier, Vt.: Capital City Press, 1911.

"Faculty Minutes," Washington College. Washington and Lee University Special Collections.

"A Family Poisoned, Lexington, Va., March 31," *Richmond Dispatch*, April 4, 1859. Attempted poisoning of Dr. Junkin's family.

Fishwick, Marshall W. "Margaret J. Preston: Virginia Poetess," *Commonwealth*, in *Withrow Scrapbook* 19: 109–10. Washington and Lee University Special Collections.

Follett, John. D. "Alumnus Explains Old Shot in East Wall of Barracks: John D. Follet, '22, Adds to Story of Colonel Schoonmaker, Says Orders Were Not Disobeyed," *The Cadet*, April 25, 1932.

Foner, Eric. *Fiery Trial: Abraham Lincoln and American Slavery.* New York: W. W. Norton, 2010.

Foote, Shelby. *The Civil War: A Narrative.* 3 vols. New York: Random House, 1974.

Foote, William Henry. *Sketches of Virginia, Historical and Biographical.* Philadelphia: W. S. Martien, 1850.

"Franklin Society, Library Book 1840–78." 3 vols. Collection 103: Franklin Society, Boxes 11L (1827–45), 12L (1846–65), 13L (1865–78). Washington and Lee University Special Collections. Lists the books withdrawn by the society's members by name.

French, Samuel Bassett. Handwritten notes for a planned biographical dictionary to be called Annals of Prominent Virginians of the XIX Century, compiled information on over 14,000 men. Also available on microfilm: S. Bassett French Biographical Sketches, 4 reels. Archives Division, Library of Virginia.

"From an Old Scottish Paper." Manuscript owned by Mrs. William Allan, daughter-in-law of Elizabeth Preston Allan.

"Funeral of Colonel J.T.L. Preston," *Lexington Gazette*, July 24, 1890.

Gaines, James E., Jr. "A Brief History of Virginia Military Institute's Libraries," in Thomas W. Davis, ed., *A Crowd of Honorable Youths: Historical Essays on the First 150 Years of the Virginia Military Institute.* Lexington: Virginia Military Institute Sesquicentennial Committee, 1988, 169–83.

_____. "Virginia Military Institute's Library, 1839–1939: Its History as Shown in Local Records," *Proceedings of the Rockbridge Historical Society* 10 (1980–89): 287–97.

Geiger, Robert L. "The Rise and Fall of Useful Knowledge: Higher Education for Science, Agriculture, and the Mechanical Arts, 1850–1875," *History of Higher Education Annual* 18 (1998): 47–65. Also in Roger Geiger, ed., *The American College in the Nineteenth Century.* Nashville, Tenn.: Vanderbilt University Press, 2000, 153–68.

"Gen. Robert E. Lee as College President," *Southern Historical Society Papers* 28 (1900): 243–46, esp. 246 about Preston on campus. Also in *Richmond Dispatch*, Jan. 27, 1901.

Gibson, Keith E. *Virginia Military Institute: The Campus History Series.* Charleston, S.C.: Arcadia, 2010.

"Glimpses of Old College Life," *William and Mary College Quarterly* 8, No. 4 (April 1900): 213–27. Letters from Thomas L. Preston to Andrew Reid, Jr., in Williamsburg, January and February 1802, p. 216.

Goodrich, Thomas. *The Darkest Dawn.* Bloomington: Indiana University, 2005.

"Governor David Campbell Tells the Legislature of Virginia about the Importance of Free Schools in That State," *Journal of the House of Delegates of the Commonwealth of Virginia*, 1839, 7–10. Repr. in Edgar W. Knight, ed., *A Documentary History of Education in the South Before 1860.* Chapel Hill: University of North Carolina Press, 1949, 5: 85–89.

Gray, Garland. "A History of the Franklin Society and Library Company of Lexington, Virginia." Thesis, Washington and Lee University, 1922.

Green, Jennifer R. "Networks of Military Educators: Middle-class Stability and Professionalization in the Late Antebellum South," *Journal of Southern History* 73, No. 1 (February 2007): 39–74.

Greenwait, Bruce S., ed. "Life Behind Confederate Lines in Virginia: The Correspondence of James Dorman Davidson," *Civil War History* 16 (September 1970): 205–26.

Grey, John Hugh. "Margaret Junkin Preston: Virginia's Poetess of the Old South." Thesis, Washington and Lee University, 1933.

Gutmann, Joseph, and Stanley F. Chyet, eds. *Moses Jacob Ezekiel: Memoirs from the Baths of Diocletian.* Detroit: Wayne State University Press, 1975.

Hadsel, Winifred. "Preston Street," in *The Streets of Lexington, Virginia: A Guide to the Origins and History of Their Names.* Lexington, Va.: Rockbridge Historical Society, 1985, 113–25.

———. *The Streets of Lexington.* Lexington, Va.: Rockbridge Historical Society, 1985.

"Half-forgotten Bits of Local History—"The Skinner Case": Presbyterian Church Trial of 1850s had Unusual and Interesting Angles," *Lexington Gazette*, Oct. 25, 1933.

Harrel, T. H., and L. M. Caperton. *Fragments of V.M.I. History.* Lexington, Va.: Virginia Military Institute, 1933. A series of lectures on the history of V.M.I. for the Corps of Cadets.

Harrison, James A. "Margaret J. Preston: An Appreciation," in Elizabeth Preston Allan, *Margaret J. Preston: Life and Letters.* New York: Houghton Mifflin, 1903, 341–78.

Hart, Freeman H. "Preston Defended Virginia's Frontier," *Commonwealth* (December 1960), 33–35. Life of Col. William Preston.

Hayes, Rutherford B. *Diary and Letters of Rutherford Birchard Hayes, Nineteenth President of the United States:1834–1860.* Ed. C. R. Williams. 4 vols. Columbus: Ohio State Archeological and Historical Society, 1922–26.

Hays, Meridith G. "'Our Once Glorious Union': The Secession Crisis in Lexington, Virginia, 1860–61." *Proceedings of the Rockbridge Historical Society* 12 (1995–2002): 353–382.

Heatwole, Cornelius J. *A History of Education in Virginia.* New York: Macmillan, 1916.

Hennessy, John. *The First Battle of Manassas: An End to Innocence, July 18–21, 1861.* Lynchburg, Va.: H. E. Howard, 1989.

———. *Return to Bull Run: The Campaign and Battle of Second Manassas.* New York: Simon & Schuster, 1993.

Herbst, Jurgen. "American Higher Education in the Age of the College," *History of Universities* 7 (1988): 37–59.

Hiden, Rev. J. C. "Stonewall Jackson: Reminiscences of Him as a Professor in the Virginia Military Institute," *Southern Historical Society Papers* 20: 306–11. See also Montgomery, Alabama, *Advertiser*, Nov. 27, 1892.

Hill, Daniel H. "The Real Stonewall Jackson," *Century Magazine* 47, No. 4 (February 1894): 623–28.

"History of the Virginia Military Institute," *The Cadet: A Monthly Magazine of Science, Literature and Art* 1, No. 1 (March 1871): 26–30, No. 2 (April 1871): 83–86, No. 3 (May 1871): 123–29, No. 4 (June 1871): 176–82; 2, No. 5 (December 1871): 85–90; No. 6 (April 1872): 298–303, No. 7 (May 1872): 350–54. A seven-part historical sketch on the early history of V.M.I., 1839–1872.

Holland, Lynwood M. "Georgia Military Institute: The West Point of Georgia, 1851–1864," *Georgia Historical Quarterly* 43, No. 3 (September 1959): 225–47, esp. 241.

Hopkins, Luther Wesley. *From Bull Run to Appomattox: A Boy's View.* Baltimore: Fleet-McGinley, 1908.

Horace. *The Odes and Carmen Saeculare of Horace*, trans. John Conington. London: George Bell and Sons, 1882.

Hunter, Robert F. *Lexington Presbyterian Church, 1789–1989.* Lexington, Va.: Lexington Presbyterian Church, 1991. A well-written and carefully documented bicentennial history of the church.

Hunter, Robert F., and Edwin L. Dooley, Jr. *Claudius Crozet: French Engineer in America, 1790–1864.* Charlottesville: University Press of Virginia, 1989.

Hyko, Allison. "The Preston House," a paper written for Professor Pamela Simpson's class in American architecture, Washington and Lee Architectural Papers, April 1, 1994. Washington and Lee University Special Collections. An excellent, well-documented paper.

In Memoriam: Francis H. Smith, Father and Founder of the Virginia Military Institute. New York: Knickerbocker Press, 1890.

Ingram, John H. *Edgar Allan Poe: His Life, Letters, and Opinions.* New York: AMS Press, 1965. 1st ed., London, 1880. Esp. Preston's friendship with Poe, 16–20.

"J.T.L. Preston's Estate," in *Southwestern Reporter.* St. Paul, Minn.: West Publishing, 1899, 51: 593–98.

Jackson, Mary Anna. *Life and Letters of General Thomas J. Jackson (Stonewall Jackson), by His Wife, Mary Anna Jackson.* New York: Harper and Brothers, 1892.

———. *Memoirs of "Stonewall" Jackson by His Widow.* Dayton, Ohio: Morningside Bookshop, 1976. Original printing by Courier-Journal Job Printing Co., Louisville, Ky., 1895.

Jacob, Diane B., and Judith M. Arnold. *A Virginia Military Institute Album, 1839–1910.* Charlottesville: University Press of Virginia, 1982.

Jeffrey, Robert W. "Virginia Military Institute," *Iron Worker* 16 (Summer 1952): 1–15.

"John Cabell Breckinridge," *Confederate Veteran* 13, No. 6 (June 1905): 257–61.

Johnson, Robert Underwood, and Clarence Clough Buel, eds. *Battles and Leaders of the Civil War, Being for the Most Part Contributions by Union and Confederate Officers.* 4 vols. New York: Century, 1887.

Johnson, Thomas Cary. *A History of the Southern Presbyterian Church.* New York: Christian Literature, 1894.

———. *The Life and Letters of Robert Lewis Dabney.* Richmond: Presbyterian Committee of Publication, 1903.

Johnston, Eston, ed. *Echoes of V.M.I.* Lexington: Virginia Military Institute, 1937.

Journal of the House of Delegates of the Commonwealth of Virginia, in Records of the States of the United States, Cabinet: Va. General Assembly, House Journals, etc., 1835–39, Film 331, Reels 15–18. Archives Division, Library of Virginia, Richmond. See also *Journal of the House of Delegates of the Commonwealth of Virginia*. Richmond: Thomas Ritchie, 1835–36.

Junkin, David Xavier. *The Reverend George Junkin, D.D., LL.D.: A Historical Biography*. Philadelphia: J. B. Lippincott, 1871.

Junkin, George. *Political Fallacies: An Examination of the False Assumptions, and Refutation of the Sophistical Reasonings, Which Have Brought on This Civil War*. New York: Scribner, 1863.

Kauffman, Michael W. *American Brutus: John Wilkes Booth and the Lincoln Conspiracies*. New York: Random House, 2004.

King, Fannie Bayly (Mrs. W. W). "Augusta County Early Settlers, Importations, 1739–1740," in Michael Tepper, ed., *New World Immigrants: A Consolidation of Ship Passenger Lists and Associated Data from Periodical Literature*. Baltimore: Genealogical Publishing, 1979, 2: 133–35. Also in *National Genealogical Society Quarterly* 25, No. 2 (June 1937): 46–50.

Kinnear, Duncan Lyle. *The First 100 Years: A History of the Virginia Polytechnic Institute and State University*. Blacksburg, Va.: VPI Educational Foundation, 1972.

Klein, Stacey Jean. *Margaret Junkin Preston: Poet of the Confederacy, A Literary Life*. Columbia: University of South Carolina Press, 2007.

_____. "Wielding the pen: Margaret Preston, Confederate nationalistic literature, and the expansion of a woman's place in the South." *Civil War History* 49, No. 3 (September 2003): 221–34.

Knight, Edgar W., ed. *A Documentary History of Education in the South Before 1860*. Vols. 1, 4, and 5 of 5. Chapel Hill: University of North Carolina Press, 1949. See "William C. Preston's Account of His Education, 1800–1812," in 1: 649–51. William C. Preston was J.T.L. Preston's first cousin. See also "Captain Alden Partridge's Arguments for Military Education, 1825," in 4: 153–62, and acts, petitions, and reports relating to Virginia Military Institute, 164–80. And see "Governor David Campbell Tells the Legislature of Virginia about the Importance of Free Schools in That State, 1839," in 5: 45–79.

Knox [pseud.]. "Beginnings of V.M.I., Report by Eye Witness of First Commencement Held and the Honor Graduates," *Lexington Gazette*, June 3, 1841.

_____. "Virginia Military Institute," *Lexington Gazette*, May 20, 1841.

Koch, Adrienne, and Harry Ammon. "The Virginia and Kentucky Resolutions: An Episode in Jefferson's and Madison's Defense of Civil Liberties," *William and Mary Quarterly*, Series 3, 5, No. 2 (April 1948): 145–76.

Lee, Capt. Robert E. Lee. *Recollections and Letters of General Robert E. Lee, by His Son Captain Robert E. Lee*. New York: Doubleday, Page, 1904.

Leonard, Cynthia Miller, comp. *General Assembly of Virginia, July 30, 1619–January 11, 1978: A Bicentennial Register of Members*. Richmond: General Assembly of Virginia, 1978.

"Lexington Arsenal," *Lexington Gazette*, December 25, 1835.

"Lexington: Thursday Morning," *The* (Lexington) *Intelligencer*, May 11, 1826.

Leyburn, James G. "Dr. Alfred Leyburn (1803–1878): A Lexington Whig, Legislator, and Man of Affairs," *Proceedings of the Rockbridge Historical Society* 6 (1961–65): 22–30.

_____. "Lexington Presbyterians, 1819–1882: Personalities, Problems, Peculiarities," *Proceedings of the Rockbridge Historical Society* 8 (1970–74): 29–44.

_____. *The Scotch-Irish: A Social History*. Chapel Hill: University of North Carolina Press, 1962.

Link, Eugene P. *Democratic-Republican Societies, 1790–1800*. New York: Columbia University Press, 1942.

List of Staff Officers of the Confederate States Army, 1861–65. Washington, D.C.: Government Printing Office, 1891.

Loope, David Roger. "A Wealth of Hallowed Memories: The Development of Mission, Saga, and Distinctiveness at the Virginia Military Institute." Dissertation. Williamsburg: College of William and Mary, 1993.

Lord, Gary Thomas. "Alden Partridge's Proposal for a National System of Education: A Model for the Morrill Land-Grant Act," in Roger Geiger, ed., *History of Higher Education Annual* 18 (1998): 11–24. See Partridge's open letter to Col. Dorman in *Lexington Gazette*, Jan. 22, 1836.

Lyle, Prof. Duncan C., comp. at McDonogh School. "Caruthers Family Genealogical Notes," MSS6502. Albert and Shirley Small Special Collections Library, University of Virginia.

Lyle, Royster, Jr. "John Blair Lyle of Lexington and His 'Automatic Bookstore,'" *Virginia Cavalcade* 21 (Autumn 1971): 20–27.

Lyle, Royster, Jr., and Matthew W. Paxton, Jr. "The V.M.I. Barracks," *Virginia Cavalcade* 23, No. 3 (Winter 1974): 14–29.

Lyle, Royster, Jr., and Pamela Hemenway Simpson. *The Architecture of Historic Lexington*. Charlottesville, Va.: University Press of Virginia, 1977.

Maddox, William Arthur. *The Free School Idea in Virginia Before the Civil War*. New York: Teachers College, Columbia University, 1918.

Map: *Borden Grant*. J. R. Hildebrand version, 1964. Map showing 92,100-acre grant from George II to Benjamin Borden lying on the west side of the Blue Ridge and on north and northeast branches of the James River, between the Blue Ridge and North Mountain, in the County of Augusta, Nov. 6, 1739. Rockbridge Historical Society Miscellaneous, Oversize maps. Washington and Lee University Special Collections.

Map: *County of Rockbridge, 1859*, by William Gilham at Virginia Military Institute. Rockbridge Historical Society Miscellaneous, Oversize maps. Washington and Lee University Special Collections.

Map: *County of Rockbridge, 1883*, by John Carmichael. Based on the maps of William Gilham and Jedediah Hotchkiss. Rockbridge Historical Society Miscellaneous, Oversize maps. Washington and Lee University Special Collections.

Map: *Gray's New Map of Lexington, Rockingham* [sic] *County, Virginia, Drawn from Special Surveys*, by O. W. Gray and Son. Philadelphia: O. W. Gray and Son, Geographers, 1877.

Map: *Historical Map of Rockbridge County, Virginia 1778–1865*, by J. R. Hildebrand, Roanoke Valley Historical Society. Rockbridge Historical Society Miscellaneous, Oversize maps. Washington and Lee University Special Collections.

Map: J.T.L. Preston's seven lots on Randolph Street. Preston Collection 1980.023.0012, Oct. 7, 1856. Stonewall Jackson House (now at Virginia Military Institute Archives).

Map: *Plan of the Town of Lexington in Rockbridge from the Record in the Surveyors Office, June 5, 1787*, plat drawn apparently by Andrew Reid, Clerk. Copy from Will Book 1, p. 304, Rockbridge County Courthouse. All surveyors' records were destroyed by Gen. Hunter's Army during the Civil War. See also Dr. E. P. Tompkins, *A Copy from Will Book 1, Page 304: A Plan of the Town of Lexington in Rockbridge County from the Record in the Surveyors Office*, includes original lot owner data, courtesy Dr. E. P. Tompkins, August 1944. Rockbridge Historical Society Miscellaneous, Oversize maps. Washington and Lee University Special Collections.

Map: *Prestonia*. John E. Kleber, ed., *Encyclopedia of Louisville*. Lexington: University Press of Kentucky, 2001, 728.

Map: *Property of the Lexington Development Company, Lexington, Rockbridge County, Virginia, August 15, 1891*, by D. C. Humphries. Rockbridge Historical Society Miscellaneous, Oversize maps. Washington and Lee University Special Collections.

Map: *Sewer and Water Pipe Connections*, Sheets No. 1–7, Lexington, Va., Jan. 1, 1902. Rockbridge Historical Society Miscellaneous, Oversize maps. Washington and Lee University Special Collections.

Map: Thomas Lewis Preston's 21 acres he bought from John Galbraith in 1808. Preston Collection, Folder 1980.23.0019. Stonewall Jackson House (now at Virginia Military Institute Archives).

Maps: Edmund Randolph's property in Richmond, 1809 and 1810, in Mutual Assurance Society Policy for Mr. Comfort (Spring Farm), Declarations, 41, reel 4, No. 1227; reel 5, No. 355.

Maps: The Rev. Thomas L. Preston's land in Kentucky, 1858 and 1879; Iowa, 1894; and Wisconsin, 1895. In possession of Lois Strange, Louisville, Ky.

Maps: William Preston's 1,000 acres in Louisville, Ky. Three maps of 1858, 1879, and 1907. In possession of Lois Strange, Louisville, Ky.

"Margaret J. Preston," *The Critic* 27, No. 792 (April 24, 1897): 291. Obituary by James A. Harrison.

"Margaret J. Preston: A Famous American Poet; Her Works, Her Life and Her Books—Home Life in Virginia," written for the *Washington Post*, Withrow Scrapbook 19: 107–08. Washington and Lee University Special Collections.

"Margaret Preston Oak," in J. Elton Lodewick and Mrs. Lynwood R. Holmes, *Notable Trees of Virginia: Bulletin of the Virginia Polytechnic Institute* 24, No. 7 (March 15, 1931): 12.

Marr, Col. Robert A., Jr. "V.M.I. in the Civil War," in J. Eston Johnston, ed., *Echoes of Virginia Military Institute*. Lexington: Virginia Military Institute, 1937, 12–20.

McCausland, Gen. John. "The Burning of Chambersburg, Penn.: Ordered by General Early in Retaliation or the Wanton Destruction of the Private Property of Citizens of Virginia," repr. from New Orleans, La., *Picayune*, August 2, 1908, in *Southern Historical Society Papers* 31: 266–70.

McCulloch, Mrs. Charles. "Rockbridge and Its County Seat," *Proceedings of the Rockbridge Historical Society* 1 (1939–41): 62–77.

McCulloch, Ruth. *Mrs. McCulloch's Stories of Ole Lexington*, ed. Charles W. Turner. Verona, Va.: McClure, 1972.

———. "Rockbridge and Its County Seat," *Proceedings of the Rockbridge Historical Society* 1 (1939–1941): 62–77.

McDaniel, John, with Charles N. Watson and David T. Moore. *Liberty Hall Academy: The Early History of the Institutions Which Evolved into Washington and Lee University*. Lexington, Va.: Liberty Hall Press, 1979.

McGuire, Hunter. "Address Delivered on 23d day of June, 1897, at the Virginia Military Institute, in the presence of a vast audience, upon the occasion of the inauguration of the Stonewall Jackson memorial building." Lynchburg, Va.: J. P. Bell, 1897.

[McKeever, William.] "A Few Plain Words About the Lexington Development Company." A pamphlet distributed to the stockholders, said to be by William McKeever, citing deception and mismanagement. Washington and Lee University Special Collections.

McLachlan, James. "The American College in the Nineteenth Century: Toward a Reappraisal." *Teachers College Record* 80 (1978–79): 287–306.

McMurry, Richard M. *Virginia Military Institute Alumni in the Civil War: In Bello Praesidium*. Lynchburg, Va.: H. E. Howard, 1999.

McPherson, James M., David J. Coles, David Stephen Heidler, Jeanne T. Heidler. *Encyclopedia of the American Civil War: A Political, Social, and Military History*. New York: W. W. Norton, 2002.

McWhorter, Lucullus Virgil. *The Border Settlers of Northwestern Virginia from 1768 to 1795*. Hamilton, Ohio: Republican, 1915.

"Memorial of Col. J.T.L. Preston," Records of Session 4, 159–62. Lexington Presbyterian Church Vault, Lexington, Virginia.

Miller, Jonson W. *Citizen Soldiers and Professional Engineers: The Antebellum Engineering Culture of the Virginia Military Institute*. Dissertation. Blacksburg: Virginia Polytechnic Institute and State University, 2008.

"Minutes of the Board of Visitors," Virginia Military Institute. Virginia Military Institute Archives.

"Minutes of the Society of Cincinnati of Virginia," Richmond, Washington and Lee University Scrapbook, "Original Papers Relating to Early History of Washington and Lee College and Society of the Cincinnati," No. 5, December 13, 1802. Washington and Lee University Special Collections.

Moore, Mrs. John H. *Memories of a Long Life in Virginia*. Staunton, Va.: McClure, 1920.

Moore, Stuart. "Greater Lexington—1890," *Rockbridge Historical Society Proceedings* 5 (1954–60): 70–79. An address delivered before the society in January 1959.

Morgan, Col. James M., Jr. "The Changing Face of the VMI," *Rockbridge Historical Society Proceedings* 7 (1966–69): 141–47.

Morton, Oren F. *A History of Rockbridge County, Virginia*. Staunton, Va., 1920; repr. Baltimore: Regional Publishing, 1973, 1980.

"Mrs. Margaret J. Preston: Death of This Well-known Southern Poetess in Baltimore," *Lexington Gazette*, March 31, 1897.

Naisawald, L. VanLoan. "Little Devils with the White Flag." *Civil War Times* 3, No. 10 (February 1962): 1–8, 23–24. Account of the cadets at New Market.

"Networks of military educators: middle-class stability and professionalization in the late antebellum South," *Journal of Southern History*, February 2007.

Nichols, E. W. *Fifty Years of Service and Other Papers*. Lexington, Va.: Rockbridge County News Print, 1926.

Nuttall, Preston. "Echoes of Our Ancestors: The Young Soldier and His General," in *The Old War Horse: The Voice of General James Longstreet Camp 1247, Sons of Confederate Veterans* 6, Issue 10 (November 2004). Death of J.T.L. Preston's son Willie at Manassas.

_____. "The Young Soldier and His General," *Old War Horse: The Voice of General James Longstreet Camp 1247, Sons of Confederate Veterans*, Vol. 6, Issue 10 (November 2004), "Willie Preston."

Obenchain, William A. "Jackson's Scabbard Speech," *Southern Historical Society Papers* 16 (1888): 36–47.

Oram, Richard W. "John W. Fuller and the Franklin Society Library of Lexington," *Virginia Magazine of History and Biography* 93, No. 3 (July 1985): 323–40.

"Origin of the State Military Academies," *Russell's Magazine* 4, No. 3 (December 1858): 219–26.

Osborn, Richard Charles. *William Preston of Virginia, 1727–1783: The Making of a Frontier Elite*. Dissertation. College Park: University of Maryland, 1990.

Paine, R. A. "A Southern Gentleman," *Richmond Times-Dispatch*, Nov. 15, 1908. An account of "Colonel Preston and the Watch."

Parish, Mrs. T. T. "Col. William Preston Founded One of Most Famous and Patriotic Families of State," the third in a series of articles prepared by Daughters of American Revolution chapters in honor of American History Month, Feb. 27, 1959. Virginia Military Institute Archives.

Partridge, Alden. *Discourse on Education*, Part 2: "Correspondence Between a Cadet and His Father," 216–62, and "Captain Partridge's Lecture on Education," 263–80. Middletown, Conn.: E.&H. Clark, 1926.

_____. "Military Academy," *Lexington Gazette*, Jan. 22, 1836. A letter to C. P. Dorman of the House of Delegates, dated Richmond, Dec. 31, 1835.

_____. "Open letter to Col. Dorman," *Lexington Gazette*, Jan. 26, 1836.

_____. "Plan of Establishing Additional Military Academies," April 1915. Alden Partridge Records, Box 3: Papers and Financial Records; Writings, Bound Manuscripts 1810–1817. Norwich University Archives, Kreitzberg Library, Northfield, VT.; microfilmed by the Library of Congress in 1969 as Alden Partridge Records, 1807–1950 (MS 68–2061).

Paxton, Matthew W., Jr. "Bringing the Railroad to Lexington, 1866–1883," *Proceedings of the Rockbridge Historical Society* 10 (1980–89): 180–89.

[Paxton, Matthew W., Jr., editor], "When the Virginia Military Institute Was Founded," *Rockbridge County News*, October 14, 1926.

Payne, Leonidas Warren. "Margaret Junkin Preston," in *Southern Literary Readings*. Chicago: Rand McNally, 1913, 184–92.

Peay, Gen. J. H. Binford, III. "Remarks at the Founders Day Convocation: Superintendent's Speech on Anniversary of Founding of Virginia Military Institute," November 9, 2007.

Pendleton, Edmund. "Early Days at the Virginia Military Institute." *The Bomb, The Virginia Military Institute, Lexington, Virginia*, 12–16. Philadelphia: Huston, Ashmead, Wilson, 1896.

Pendleton, Rose Page. "General David Hunter's Sack of Lexington, Virginia, June 10–14, 1864: An Account by Rose Page Pendleton," ed. Charles W. Turner, *Virginia Magazine of History and Biography* 83, No. 2 (April 1975): 173–83.

Perkins, John Earle, IV. "The Documented History of 'Blandome,'" December 10, 1989, Architectural Papers, Pam Simpson's Class. Washington and Lee University Special Collections.

Peyton, J. Lewis. *History of Augusta County, Virginia*. Staunton, Va.: Samuel M. Yost and Son, 1882, esp. 303–07, "The Preston Family."

Pickett, La Salle Corbell. "Woman and Poet: Margaret Junkin Preston," in *Literary Hearthstones of Dixie*. Philadelphia: J. B. Lippincott, 1912, 64–71.

Poe, Edgar Allan. "William Wilson," in *The Prose Tales of Edgar Allan Poe, Second Series* (Boston: Dana Estes, 1876), 44–74.

"Political Fallacies," in "Literary Notices," *Continental Monthly: Devoted to Literature and National Policy* 3, Issue 6 (June 1863).

Presbyterian Church in the U.S.A. "Minutes of the Lexington Presbytery." Vols. 12 and 13. Richmond: Whittet and Shepperson, 1786–1880.

Preservation Master Plan for Washington and Lee University, Lexington, Virginia. Charlottesville, Va.: John Milner Associates, October 2005, Chap. 2, "A Brief History of Washington and Lee." 26 pp.

Preston and Virginia Papers of the Draper Collection of Manuscripts, comp. Lyman C. Draper. Madison, Wis.: Publications of the State Historical Society of Wisconsin, 1915.

Preston, Edmonia Madison Randolph. "Music Album, ca. 1805–08, hand-copied piano music for two and four hands, and piano and voice, as well as exercises and scales," MSS5:5 P9267:1. 48 pp. Virginia Historical Society. Inside cover bears signatures "Edmonia Randolph" and "Eddy M. Preston."

Preston, Edmund Randolph. "Col. J.T.L. Preston of Lexington, Virginia (1811–1890)." Comments of Preston's grandson at the dedication of the Preston Memorial Library at Virginia Military Institute, Nov. 11, 1939.

_____. "Cosmopolitan Culture," manuscript ca. May 1955.

_____. "Farm Account Book," manuscript, Stonewall Jackson House (now at Virginia Military Institute Archives).

_____. "General Lee at Oakland," manuscript, Washington, D.C.: Feb. 16, 1954.

_____. "Grandfather Preston (Col. J.T.L. Preston, founder of Virginia Military Institute)," handwritten manuscript.

_____. *Memoirs and Memories of My Life and Family*, ed. James McAfee. Richmond: Privately published, 2010.

_____. "Miseducation of a Southerner," manuscript, Washington, D.C., ca. 1955. J.T.L. Preston's grandson regrets that he wasn't educated in practical matters.

_____. "Misfortunes in Pleasant Disguise," manuscript, Washington, D.C., Oct. 15, 1950. An assessment of J.T.L. Preston's shortcomings by his daughter via his grandson.

_____. "The Name Thomas Lewis Preston and Some of Those Who Have Borne It," manuscript, Chicago, June 24, 1945.

_____. "The Name William Preston," manuscript written for Edmund Randolph Preston's grandson, William Edmund Preston, Washington, D.C., ca. 1955.

_____. "Preston Homes in the Valley of Virginia," manuscript intended as an attachment to the Greenfield article in the *Roanoke Times*, August 28, 1955.

"The Preston Family," in J. Lewis Peyton, *History of Augusta County, Virginia*. Staunton, Va.: Samuel M. Yost and Son, 1882, 302–07.

Preston Family Bible Record, 1729–1837, Bible Records Collection, *Holy Bible*. New York: Daniel D. Smith, 1828, Accession 26190, State Government Records Collection. Archives Division, Library of Virginia, Richmond.

Preston Family Genealogical Notes, Accession 26160, State Government Records Collection, Archives Division, Library of Virginia, Richmond.

"Preston Family of Virginia," 14 reels of microfilm, covering 1727–1896, AC 6288a. Manuscript Division, Library of Congress, Washington, D.C. Reel 1 includes an annotated list of 3,510 papers in the collection, also available in loose-leaf notebooks 1: 1–251 and 2: 252–420, which are indexed in Vol. 3 by Names of Persons and Places of the Papers of the Preston Family of Virginia (1727–1896). Deposited in the Division of Manuscripts by Preston Davie, Esq. Original manuscripts now located at Virginia Historical Society, Richmond.

[Preston, Franklin "Frank" C.] "Battle of New Market," *Lexington Gazette and General Advocate*, May 25, 1864. A participant's account on May 19 of the New Market battle of May 15.

Preston, Herbert, Jr. "Family Recollections of Col. J.T.L. Preston," manuscript, Baltimore, Md., November 14, 1989.

Preston, John. John Preston Papers, 1806–30, 1844, MS 94–034. VPI Special Collections.

Preston, John Thomas Lewis. "Address of Col. Preston," May 15, 1871, *The Cadet: A Monthly Magazine of Science, Literature and Art* 1, No. 5 (July 1871): 213–17. Repr. of an address delivered to the Corps of Cadets on the 7th anniversary of the Battle of New Market and the 10th anniversary of VMI's entry into the war. Virginia Military Institute Archives.

_____. "Address Delivered Before the Franklin Society of Lexington, at Its Semi-centenary Anniversary, February 1866, Lexington, Virginia," Collection 103: Franklin Society Library Book Collection, FSL/F/234/.LS/P74/1866. Washington and Lee University Special Collections. Repr. in *Lexington Gazette*, Feb. 21 and 28, 1873.

_____. "Alumni Address [June 25, 1878]," *Southern Collegian*, Washington and Lee University, 10, No. 18 (July 6, 1878): 3, 6.

_____. "Baker's African Explorations," *Southern Review* 2, No. 4 (October 1867): 330–58.

_____. "Caleb, a Bible Study," *Southern Presbyterian Review* 35, No. 2 (April 1884): 251–65.

_____. "A Century of Presbytery," *Southern Presbyterian Review* 32, No. 4 (October 1881): 665–82.

_____. "The Christian Life," *Southern Presbyterian Review* 28, No. 4 (October 1877): 712–21.

_____. "The Colored Man in the South," *Southern Presbyterian Review* 28, No. 1 (January 1877): 83–102.

_____. "Examination List for John T. L. Preston, October 1823–March 1828, Washington College." Virginia Military Institute Archives.

_____. "Execution of Capt. John Brown," *Southern Bivouac*, 5, 187–89.

_____. "Execution of John Brown, J.T.L. Preston in *August Bivouac*," *Wisconsin Labor Advocate*, Sept. 17, 1886, 4.

_____. "Froude's Bunyan," *Southern Presbyterian Review* 30, No. 4 (October 1880): 717–30. A book review.

_____. "General Jackson as a Professor, Extract of a lecture recently by Col. J.T.L. Preston, of the V. M. Institute," *Lexington Banner and Gazette*, May 16, 1866. Delivered before the Graham Philanthropic Society of Washington College.

_____. "Historical Sketch of the Establishment and Organization of the Virginia Military Institute, prepared at the request of the Board of Visitors, by Col. John Thomas Lewis Preston, Professor Emeritus V.M.I., July 4, 1889," Box: Preston, John T. L., Folder MS 0240. Virginia Military Institute Archives. Also quoted as Chap. 1 of Major General Francis Henney Smith, *Virginia Military Institute—Building and Rebuilding*.

_____. Incoming Letters from J.T.L. Preston, Records of the Superintendent (Smith), 1839–1870. Virginia Military Institute Archives.

_____. John Thomas Lewis Preston's Passport, May 11, 1851. Virginia Military Institute Archives.

_____. "John T. L. Preston's Reading List at the Franklin Society, 1827–78," Collection 103: Franklin Society, "Franklin Society Library Book" llL [Vol. 1]: 11, 24, 71, 108, and 142; 12L [Vol. 2]: 31, 188, 241, and 309–10; and 13L [Vol. 3]: 7, 192, and 291–92. Washington and Lee University Special Collections.

_____. "Jottings," the name given to "John T. L. Preston Diary, 1861 July 24–Sept 22." MSS 17,264. Manuscript Division, Library of Congress, Washington, D.C. A 65-page handwritten journal, also available on microfilm, describing Lt. Col. Preston's Civil War activities while with the 9th Regiment of the Virginia Volunteers at Craney Island, Va. A transcription from the original by June F. Cunningham, director, Virginia Military Institute Museum, 1986, is also available at the Virginia Military Institute Archives. A second volume, covering August 17 through September 8, is mentioned on p. 16 but is missing.

_____. "Journal of a Trip Abroad in 1884 by J.T.L. Preston of Lexington, Virginia," Ed. Janet Allan Bryan. A 48-page notebook covering a tour of England, Brussels, the Netherlands, Germany, and Switzerland by J.T.L. and Margaret Preston, her son Dr. George Preston, and her sister Julia Junkin Fishburn from June 14 to August 5, breaking off before Italy, for the trip ended on September 24.

_____. Letter to Gen. Francis H. Smith, July 4, 1889, from McDonogh School re Smith's retirement.

Preston, John Thomas Lewis, MSS2 P9263 a 1. Virginia Historical Society.

———. Letter to Prof. George Frederick Holmes, Richmond College, April 16, 1846, Johnson Family Papers, 1821–85, Section 3, MSS1 J6496 d 19. Virginia Historical Society. Letter about the need for a physics professor at VMI.

———. Letter to James McDowell, Jr., September 10, 1835, Smithfield-Preston Foundation, MS 97–002, Box 1, Folder 20. VPI Special Collections.

———. Letter to James McDowell, Jr., May 28, 1836, Smithfield-Preston Foundation, MS 97–002, Box 1, Folder 20. VPI Special Collections.

———. Letters in *The War of the Rebellion: A Compilation of the Official Records of the Union and Confederate Armies.* Washington, D.C.: Government Printing Office, 1897. Letter to Assistant Adjutant-General Hon. A. R. Boteler, Jan. 11, 1862, Series 1, 51, pt. 2: 435; letter to Hon. J. C. Breckinridge, Secretary of War, Feb. 17, 1865, Series 4, 3: 1093.

———. Letters to and from Francis H. Smith, April 29–August 20, 1839. Virginia Military Institute Archives.

———. Letters to John A. Preston about not naming his son John Thomas Lewis Preston, June 7 and 9, 1880.

——— [as Cives]. "The Lexington Arsenal," *Lexington Gazette*, August 28, September 4, and September 11, 1835. A series of three articles proposing pseudonymously that the arsenal be converted into an educational institution.

———. "Life of Horace Mann," *Southern Presbyterian Review* 30, No. 2 (April 1879): 385–400.

———. "Light of Asia, and Buddhism," *Southern Presbyterian Review* 34, No. 4 (October 1883): 745–60.

———. "London Journal," written on a European tour in 1851 by Col. J.T.L. Preston of Lexington, Virginia. An 85-page notebook covering the month of August, which he spent largely in England, enjoying the Great Exhibition (Crystal Palace), subsequent to his travels on the Continent to France, Switzerland, Italy, the Netherlands, and Prussia. Typed copy with notes by his granddaughter Janet Allan Bryan in 1952.

———. "Marcus Aurelius," *Southern Presbyterian Review* 28, No. 2 (April 1877): 340–52.

———. "The Mind of Man, The Image of God," *Southern Presbyterian Review* 11, No. 2 (July 1858): 228–45.

———. "On the Execution of John Brown," Letter of John T. L. Preston, December 2, 1859, in *Lexington Gazette*, December 15, 1859.

———. "Philosophy and Poetry of Tears," *Atlantic Monthly* 63, No. 379 (May 1889): 650–56.

———. "A Philosophy of Man Impossible without Aid from Revelation," *Southern Presbyterian Review* 29, No. 4 (October 1878): 732–41.

———. "Philosophy of Tears: Valuable Information That May Prove Uncomfortable to Some Young Men," *Evening News* [San Jose, Calif.], Sept. 20, 1889. Published originally in *Atlantic*.

[———.] "Progress of Education in Virginia," *Southern Literary Messenger* 24 (April 1857): 241–47. J.T.L. Preston's anonymous defense of Smith's portrayal of Virginia Military Institute.

[———.] "Progress of Education in Virginia," *Southern Literary Messenger* 25 (July 1857): 55–62. Preston's anonymous refutation of the rebuttal.

———. *Pulpit Manner, As Seen From the Pew.* Richmond: Presbyterian Committee of Publication, 1890. Washington and Lee University Special Collections.

———. "Religious Education of the Colored People in the South," *New Englander and Yale Review* 37, No. 146 (September 1878): 680–97.

———. "Reminiscences of Sally Lyle Caruthers Preston, 1856, MS pp. ca. 150." Col. Preston's account of his distress over the loss of his first wife. A 150-page document that was in the possession of Col. Preston's granddaughter, Mrs. William J. Bryan of Jacksonville, Florida, on Sept. 18, 1949, but reportedly perished later in a house fire.

———. *Removing to a New Charge: Letters to a Young Minister.* Richmond: Presbyterian Committee of Publication, 1890, also in Washington and Lee University Special Collections. Advice probably directed originally to Preston's son John, a young minister taking charge of Tinkling Springs Presbyterian Church in Staunton, Virginia, and having two young boys, Ran and Ben, when the pamphlet was written.

———. Reports of the Professor of Languages on the Progress of His Classes, June 13, 1844–June 15, 1881. Virginia Military Institute Archives.

———. "Sketch of John Howe Peyton," by Col. John T. L. Preston, A.M., of Yale, Professor of Modern Languages etc., in the V. M. Institute, in Ann M. Peyton, *Memoir of John Howe Peyton, in Sketches by His Contemporaries.* Staunton, Va.: A. B. Blackburn, 1894, also Boston: D. Clapp and Son, 1881, 160–68. 14 pp. See also "John H. Peyton," in J. Lewis Peyton, *History of Augusta County, Virginia.* Staunton, Va.: Samuel M. Yost and Son, 1882, 361–65.

———. "Some Reminiscences of Edgar A. Poe as a Schoolboy," in Sara Sigourney Rice, *Edgar Allan Poe: A Memorial Volume.* Baltimore, Turnbull Brothers, 1876, 37–42.

———. "The Study of Natural History," *Southern Presbyterian Review* 28, No. 4 (October 1877): 679–88.

———. "Whitefield and his Times," *Southern Presbyterian Review* 29, No. 2 (April 1878): 298–313.

———. "Will of J.T.L. Preston, Rockbridge County, Va.," in Will Book No. 2 (1874–1904), Rockbridge Old Circuit Court, 246–49; plus four Estate Settlements, 269–74 for 1891, 291–94 for 1892, 322–27 for 1893, and 338–41 for 1894; also Jefferson County, Ky., Will Book No. 16, 500–04.

Preston, John Thomas Lewis, and the Rev. C. R. Vaughn, "The Evangelist in Foreign Fields," *Southern Presbyterian Review* 35, No. 3 (April 1884): 500–20.

"Preston, John Thomas Lewis," in *Catalogue of the Officers and Students in Yale College, 1829–1830.* New Haven: Yale College, 1830, 7: Resident Graduates.

"Preston, John Thomas Lewis," in Robert E. L. Crick, *Staff Officers in Gray: A Biographical Register of the Staff Officers in the Army of Northern Virginia.* Chapel Hill: University of North Carolina Press, 2003, 246.

"Preston, John Thomas Lewis," in Nathaniel Cheairs Hughes, Jr., *Yale's Confederates: A Biographical Dictionary.* Knoxville: University of Tennessee Press, 2008, 163.

"Preston, John Thomas Lewis," in Robert K. Krick, *Lee's Colonels: A Biographical Register of the Field Officers of the Army of Northern Virginia*. Wilmington: Broadfoot, 2009, 311.

"Preston, John Thomas Lewis," in Robert K. Krick, *Staff Officers in Gray: A Biographical Register of the Staff Officers in the Army of Northern Virginia*. Chapel Hill: University of North Carolina Press, 2003, 246.

"Preston, John Thomas Lewis," *National Cyclopedia of American Biography*. New York: James T. White, 1940, 28: 245.

Preston, Margaret Junkin. "Afternoon," *Land We Love* 3, No. 2 (June 1867), 109–10.

———. *Beechenbrook: A Rhyme of the War*. Richmond: J. W. Randolph, 1865, repr. Baltimore: Kelly and Piet, 1866.

———. *Cartoons*. Boston: Roberts Brothers, 1875.

———. Collection 101: Margaret Junkin Papers, 1837–73, Box 1, Folder 7: Scrapbook. Washington and Lee University Special Collections.

———. *Colonial Ballads, Sonnets, and Other Verses*. Boston: Houghton Mifflin, 1887. A collection of sonnets, ballads, and poetic sketches of famous artists.

———. *For Love's Sake*. New York: Anson D. F. Randolph, 1886. A collection of religious and devotional poems.

———. "General Lee After the War," *Century Magazine* 38 (May 1889): 271–76.

———. "The General's Colored Sunday School," *Sunday School Times* 29 (December 3, 1887): 771–72.

———. "Giving Children Right Impressions of Death," *Sunday School Times* 33 (Nov. 7, 1891): 707–08.

———. *A Handful of Monographs: Continental and English*. New York: Anson D. F. Randolph, 1886. Sketches about her tour of Europe in 1884.

———. Journals, April 1862–April 1865. These journals have not been found.

———. "The Literary Profession in the South," *Library Magazine of American and Foreign Thought* 8 (1881): 60–74.

———. Margaret Junkin Preston Papers, Collection 1543: Box 1, Folders 1–6. Southern Historical Collection, University of North Carolina, Chapel Hill.

———. *Old Song and New*. Philadelphia: Lippincott, 1870.

———. Paul H. Hayne Papers, Correspondence, Box 1: 1831 May 10; Box 4: 1886 Nov. 13, Accession 2000–073. David M. Rubenstein Rare Book and Manuscript Library, Duke University, Durham, N.C.

———. "Personal Reminiscences of Stonewall Jackson," *Century Magazine* 32 (1886): 927–36.

———. Poem: *At Unveiling of Marble Bust of Col. William Allan McDonogh School*. Printed pamphlet, 1891.

———. "President George Junkin, D.D., 1848–1861," in *The Scotch-Irish in America: Proceedings and Addresses of the Seventh Congress at Lexington, Va., June 20–23, 1895*. Nashville, Tenn.: Scotch-Irish Society of America, 1895, 115–18.

———. *Semi-centennial Ode for the Virginia Military Institute, Lexington, Virginia 1839–1889*. New York: G. P. Putnam's Sons, 1889, repr. in part in *Withrow Scrapbook* 19: 114–15. Washington and Lee University Special Collections.

[———.] *Silverwood*. New York: Derby and Jackson, 1856. Margaret Preston's only novel, published anonymously.

———. "William C. Preston," Collection 101B: Margaret Junkin Papers, 1837–72, Box 1, Folder 7: Scrapbook. Washington and Lee University Special Collections.

Preston, Sarah C. "Obituary," by Francis H. Smith, *Lexington Gazette*, January 10, 1856, 3, col. 1.

Preston, Thomas L. *Historical Sketches and Reminiscences of an Octogenarian*. Richmond: B. F. Johnson, 1900. Personal reminiscences of the earliest settlers of Southwest Virginia from 1732 until 1900 by J.T.L. Preston's first cousin.

———. Letter of July 16, 1945, from Assistant General Counsel Thomas L. Preston in Washington, D.C., to Edmund Randolph Preston.

Preston, Thomas L. Letter of February 15, 1810, to James McDowell, in James D. Davidson Collection. McCormick Historical Association Library, Chicago. Request by J.T.L. Preston's father for a military school at Washington College.

———. "Petition to the Congress of the United States by the Rector and Trustees of Washington Academy," no date, in Washington and Lee University Trustees Papers, Cabinet C, Drawer 4, Washington and Lee University Scrapbook, "Original Papers Relating to Early History of Washington and Lee College and Society of the Cincinnati," No. 7. Washington and Lee University Special Collections. Petition by J.T.L. Preston's father for a military school at Washington College.

Preston, William. "An Account of Property William Preston Owned When He Died on June 28, 1783," APVA MS 62–001, Box 12, Folder 21. VPI Special Collections. A two-page typed copy.

Preston, William Bowker. *Preston Family Genealogy, tracing the history of the family from about 1040, A.D., in Great Britain, in the New England states, and in Virginia, to the present time*, ed. L. A. Wilson. Salt Lake City: Desert News, 1900.

"The Prestons," *Washington and Lee Historical Papers* 4 (1893): 117–28, esp. John and William Preston, and 5 (1895): 39–49.

Price, Gov. James H. "Remarks of the Governor at the Exercises Commemorating the Centennial of the V.M.I. and the Twenty-first Armistice of the First World War, Lexington, Va., Nov. 11, 1939." Price Speeches: July–December 1939. Washington and Lee University Special Collections.

"Progress of Education, Again," *Southern Literary Messenger* 25 (August 1857): 131–33. Anonymous counter rebuttal of Preston's defense.

"Progress of Education in Virginia: The University and the Colleges," *Southern Literary Messenger* 24 (March 1857): 161–69. Anonymous attack on F. H. Smith's speech to the cadets at the opening of the 1857 session regarding Virginia Military Institute's leading role in Virginia education.

"Progress of Education in Virginia: The University, the Colleges, the Military Institute," *Southern Literary Messenger* 24 (June 1857): 401–09. Anonymous rebuttal of J.T.L. Preston's defense of Smith.

"A Proud Record," *St. Louis Republic*, Sept. 6, 1891, repr. in William Bowker Preston, *The Preston Genealogy*. Salt Lake City: Desert News, 1900, 209–18. A list of prominent descendants of John Preston, the paterfamilias, through three generations.

Pusey, William W., III. *Elusive Aspirations: The History of the Female Academy in Lexington, Virginia.* Lexington, Va.: Washington and Lee University, 1983.

———. "Lexington's Female Academy," *Virginia Cavalcade* 32 (Summer 1982): 40–47.

Putnam, Sallie A. Brock. *Richmond During the War: Four Years of Personal Observations.* New York: G. W. Carleton, 1867.

Randolph, Edmund. *A Vindication of Edmund Randolph, Written by Himself, and Published in 1795*, new ed., with preface by P. V. Daniel, Jr. 82 pp. Richmond: Charles H. Wynne, 1855.

Randolph, Robert Isham. *The Randolphs of Virginia, a Compilation of the Descendants of William Randolph of Turkey Island, and His Wife Mary Isham of Bermuda Hundred.* Chicago, 1936.

"Randolph Tree—Sir John Randolph" (ca. 1889). A 69-page manuscript.

Randolph, Wassell. *William Randolph I of Turkey Island, Henrico County, Virginia, and his Immediate Descendants.* Memphis: Seebode Mimeo Service, 1949.

Record of the Presbytery of Lexington, Convened for the Trial of the Rev. Jno. Skinner, D.D. Lexington, Va.: Robert C. Noel, 1848.

Records of Session, Presbyterian Church, Lexington, Virginia. 4 vols. (1833–96). Stored in the vault of the Lexington Presbyterian Church.

Register of the Officers and Cadets of the Virginia Military Institute, 1856. Richmond: Macfarlane and Fergusson, 1856.

Regulations of the Virginia Military Institute, 1848. Richmond: Macfarlane and Ferguson, 1848.

Regulations of the Virginia Military Institute, 1854. Richmond: Macfarlane and Ferguson, 1854.

"Resolution of the Society of Cincinnati of Virginia," Richmond, Washington and Lee University Scrapbook, "Original Papers Relating to Early History of Washington and Lee College and Society of the Cincinnati," No. 8, December 16, 1807. Washington and Lee University Collections.

"Review of *Political Fallacies*," *Christian Examiner* 74, Series 5, 12, No. 3 (May 1863): 456.

Reynolds, David S. *John Brown, Abolitionist: The Man Who Killed Slavery, Sparked the Civil War, and Seeded Civil Rights.* New York: Vintage Books, 2005.

Reynolds, Terry S. "The Education of Engineers in America before the Morrill Act of 1862," *History of Education Quarterly* 32 (1992): 459–82.

———. "The Engineer in 19th-century America," *The Engineer in America: A Historical Anthology from Technology and Culture* (Chicago: University of Chicago Press, 1991), 7–26.

Robertson, James Irvin, Jr. "The Council of Three: Advisors to Governor 'Honest John' Letcher." *Virginia Cavalcade* 26 (Spring 1977): 176–83.

———. *4th Virginia Infantry.* Lynchburg, Va.: H. E. Howard, 1882.

———. *The Stonewall Brigade.* Baton Rouge: Louisiana State University Press, 1963.

———. *Stonewall Jackson: The Man, the Soldier, The Legend.* New York: Macmillan, 1997.

Robinson, Richard D. and Elisabeth C. *Repassing at My Side: A Story of the Junkins.* Blacksburg, Va.: Southern Printing, 1975.

Rockbridge County chancery, deed, tax, and will records. Rockbridge County Courthouse, Lexington, Va. Covers the first half of the nineteenth century.

Rockbridge County, Virginia, Heritage Book. Rockbridge Baths, Va.: Rockbridge Area Genealogical Society, 1997.

Ruff, William A. "Reminiscences of Lexington 65 and 70 Years Ago," *Rockbridge County News*, February 6, 20, and 27; March 13, 1902. A series of articles about Lexington in 1945.

Ruffner, Dr. Henry. "Address to the People of West Virginia: Shewing That Slavery is Injurious to the Public Welfare, and That It May Be Gradually Abolished Without Detriment to the Rights and Interests of Slaveholders—By a Slaveholder of West Virginia." Lexington: R. C. Noel, 1847.

———. "The Laying of the Washington College Cornerstone," John Robinson of Hart's Bottom Scrapbook, 11. Washington and Lee University Special Collections.

Ruffner, Dr. William Henry. "Capt. Thomas L. Preston," *Washington and Lee University Historical Papers* 4 (1893): 137.

———. "Col. J.T.L. Preston," *Washington and Lee University Historical Papers* 4 (1893): 138–145.

———. "Gov. James McDowell," *Washington and Lee University Historical Papers* 4 (1893): 128–34.

———. "The Prestons," *Washington and Lee University Historical Papers* 4 (1893): 117–28; also 5 (1895): 39–49.

———. "The Ruffners. No. IV. Henry: First Article," *West Virginia Historical Magazine Quarterly* 2, No. 2 (April 1902): 60–74.

———. "The Ruffners. No. IV. Henry: Second Article," *West Virginia Historical Magazine Quarterly* 2, No. 3 (July 1902): 36–44.

———. "The Society of the Cincinnati," *Washington and Lee University Historical Papers* 4 (1893): 66–79.

"Savannah, May 27," *Georgia Weekly Telegraph*, May 30, 1876, 7. General Assembly nominates Preston as delegate to Pan Presbyterian Council.

Schneck, Benjamin Schroder. *The Burning of Chambersburg, Pennsylvania.* Philadelphia: Lindsay and Blackiston, 1865.

"Secretary's Books, 1830–45." Collection 103: Franklin Society, Box 40. Washington and Lee University Special Collections.

Semi-annual Report of the Board of Visitors of the Virginia Military Institute, July 1856. Includes Superintendent Francis H. Smith's Semi-annual Report, June 24, 1856; and Gov. Wise's Address Delivered at the Ceremonies of Erecting, at the Virginia Military Institute, Hubbard's Bronze Cast of Houdon's Statue of Washington, July 3, 1856. Virginia Military Institute Archives.

Shanks, Henry T. *The Secession Movement in Virginia 1847–1861*, esp. 85–102. Richmond: Garrett and Massie, 1934.

Shields, R. Tucker, III. "Re: Photo of Confederate Soldiers (Liberty Hall Volunteers?), January 2002," manuscript, an attempt to identify the two CSA soldiers in the old photograph that belonged to the family of Fanny Page, namely William C. Preston and another Liberty Hall Volunteer.

———. Letter of February 14, 2014, to Randolph

Shaffner, "Re: W. N. Page—J.T.L. Preston matters—photographic images of mid-nineteenth century."
Shoop, Michael I., comp. *Genealogies of the Jackson, Junkin, and Morrison Families*. Lexington, Va.: Garland Gray Memorial Research Center, Stonewall Jackson House, Historic Lexington Foundation, 1981.
Skinner, Rev. John. John Skinner Papers, Rockbridge Historical Society. Washington and Lee University Special Collections.
____, ed. *The Pastoral Relation—What are its Securities? Case of the Rev. John Skinner, D.D., and the Presbyterian Church of Lexington Before the Presbytery of Lexington*. Lexington, Va.: Winn and Carter, 1847.
Slave Census for Rockbridge County, 1860.
Smith, Francis H. "Annual Report, Superintendent, V.M.I., 1843," *Richmond Enquirer*, February 1, 1844.
____. *College Reform*. Philadelphia: Thomas Cowperthwait, 1851.
____. *Elements of Descriptive Geometry with its Applications to Shades, Shadows, and Perspective and to Topography*. Baltimore: Kelly, Piet, 1868, esp. the "Dedication to Colonel John T. L. Preston, Professor of Latin Language and English Literature, Virginia Military Institute," November 11, 1867 (28th anniversary of Virginia Military Institute).
____. *History of the Virginia Military Institute: Its Building and Rebuilding*, ed. F. H. Smith, Jr. Lynchburg, Va.: J. P. Bell, 1912. Smith's posthumously published memoirs.
____. Letter to J.T.L. Preston, August 28, 1844, Superintendent Francis H. Smith, Outgoing Correspondence Letter Book 1844—48. Virginia Military Institute Archives.
Smith, James Power. "The Religious Character of Stonewall Jackson," Delivered at the Inauguration of the Stonewall Jackson Memorial Building, Virginia Military Institute, June 23d, 1897. Lynchburg: Virginia Military Institute, 1897. Also appended to Robert Lewis Dabney, *Life and Campaigns of Lieut.-Gen. Thomas J. Jackson (Stonewall Jackson)*. Harrisonburg, Va.: Sprinkle, 1976, 1–10.
Smith, Laura Katz. "Union Catalog of Manuscript Collections of the Preston Family," *Smithfield Review: Studies in the History of the Region West of the Blue Ridge* 2 (1998): 53–64.
Smithfield Preston Foundation Papers, 1784–1881. MS97–002. VPI Special Collections.
"Soldier Scholar." *Southern Literary Messenger* 16 (May 1850): 266–67. A poem by S.L.C. about a Virginia Military Institute cadet, the ideal sought by Adelaide and found in Ashton.
Stagg, J.C.A., Jeanne Kerr Cross, and Susan Holbrook Perdue. *Papers of James Madison, Presidential Series*. Vol. 2 of 23 vols. Charlottesville: University of Virginia, 1992.
Stanard, Beverly. *Letters of a New Market Cadet*, eds. John G. Barrett and Robert K. Turner, Jr. Chapel Hill: University of North Carolina Press, 1961.
Stanard, Mary Newton. *The Dreamer: A Romantic Rendering of the Life Story of Edgar Allan Poe*. Richmond: Bell Book and Stationery, 1909.
Stewart, George R. *Pickett's Charge, A Micro-history of the Final Attack at Gettysburg, July 3, 1863*. New York: Houghton Mifflin, 1959.
Stoddard, Richard Henry. "Life of Edgar Allan Poe," in *Poems and Essays of Edgar Allan Poe*. Boston: Dana Estes, 1876.
Stowe, Harriet Beecher. *Uncle Tom's Cabin, or, Life Among the Lowly*. Boston: John P. Jewett, 1852.
Swem, Earl G., and John W. Williams. *A Register of the General Assembly of Virginia, 1776–1918*. Richmond, 1918.
Tachau, Mary K. Bonesteel. "George Washington and the Reputation of Edmund Randolph," *Journal of American History* 73, No. 1 (June 1986): 15–34.
Thompkins, Edmund Pendleton. *Rockbridge County, Virginia: An Informal History*. Richmond: Whittet and Shepperson, 1952, esp. Michael Miley's composite picture of many Rockbridge County personalities, facing 158, in "To See Ourselves As Others See Us," 158–66.
Thomson, Rev. J., ed. *Report of Proceedings of the First General Presbyterian Council Convened at Edinburgh, July 1877, with Relative Documents Bearing on the Affairs of the Council, and the State of the Presbyterian Churches Throughout the World*. Edinburgh: Thomas and Archibald Constable, 1877.
Trask, Benjamin H. *9th Virginia Infantry*. Lynchburg, Va.: H. E. Howard, 1984.
Trout, William E., III. *Maury River Atlas: Historic Sites on the North River Navigation*. Virginia Canals and Navigation Society, 1991.
Turner, Charles W. "The Franklin Society, 1800–1891." *Virginia Magazine of History and Biography* 66, No. 5 (October 1958): 432–47. Also in *Stories of Ole Lexington: A Sequel to Mrs. McCulloch's Stories*, 45–62.
____. *Stories of Ole Lexington: A Sequel to Mrs. McCulloch's Stories*. Verona, Va.: McClure Press, 1977.
____, ed. *Lieutenant John Newton Lyle: The Career of the Liberty Hall Volunteers*. Verona, Va.: McClure, 1906.
Turner, Edward Raymond. *The New Market Campaign, May, 1864*. Richmond: Whittet and Shepperson, 1912. Chap. 5, "The Part of the Cadets," attempts to demythologize the role played by the cadets.
Tuttle, Bruce Douglas. *Colonel William Preston, 1729–1783*. Master's thesis. Blacksburg: Virginia Polytechnic Institute and State University, 1971.
"Virginia Military Institute," in Oren F. Morton, *A History of Rockbridge County, Virginia*. Staunton: McClure, 1920, 199–206.
Virginia Military Institute Alumni Association. *The 1989 Register of Former Cadets of the Virginia Military Institute: Sesquicentennial Ed*. Lexington, Va.: 1989.
Virginia Military Institute Faculty and Staff Correspondence regarding J.T.L. Preston, May 6, 1938–April 8, 1980. Virginia Military Institute Archives.
Virginia Military Institute Historic District. Final Nomination to the National Register of Historic Places, Record No. 431843, NHLS No. 74002219. Washington, D.C.: National Park Service, May 30, 1974.
Virginia Military Institute Records, 1837–45, 1848, and 1850, Accession 36739, State Government Records Collection. Archives Division, Library of Virginia, Richmond.
Waddell, Joseph A. *Annals of Augusta County, Virginia, from 1726 to 1871*. Harrisonburg, Va.: C. J. Carrier, 1972.

Wade, Benjamin F. "Reminiscences of Early Lexington," *Rockbridge County News*, Feb. 27, 1936, 6.
Walker, Charles Duy. *Memorial, Virginia Military Institute: Biographical Sketches of the Graduates and Élèves of the Virginia Military Institute Who Fell During the War Between the States.* Philadelphia: J. B. Lippincott, 1875. Biographical sketches of 170 former V.M.I. cadets who lost their lives in military service during the Civil War.
_____. "William C. Preston, of Lexington, Virginia," *Memorial: Virginia Military Institute* (Philadelphia: J. B. Lippincott, 1875), 453–54, in Rare Books, Z986 J14 W177 1875. Virginia Historical Society. J.T.L. Preston's copy, esp. the description of Willie's death penciled in the margins by his brother John A. Preston.
Wallace, Michael M. *Use of the Virginia Military Institute Corps of Cadets as a Military Unit Before and During the War Between the States.* Master's thesis. New Orleans: Tulane University, 1999.
The War of the Rebellion: A Compilation of the Official Records of the Union and Confederate Armies. Washington, D.C.: Government Printing Office, 1897.
Warren, Robert Penn. *John Brown: The Making of a Martyr*, esp. 447–62. New York: Payson and Clarke, 1929.
Washington and Lee University Historical Papers. 5 vols. Baltimore: John Murphy, 1890–95.
Washington and Lee University Records of Board of Trustees: Jan. 15, 1811–Oct. 1, 1844, Washington and Lee University Trustees Papers, Cabinet B, Drawer 1. Washington and Lee University Special Collections.
Washington and Lee University Scrapbook, "Original Papers Relating to Early History of Washington and Lee College and Society of the Cincinnati," Washington and Lee University Trustees Papers, Cabinet C, Drawer 4. Washington and Lee University Special Collections.
Weaver, Ethan Allen. "Margaret Junkin Preston: An Easton Lass of Long Ago, Who Achieved Distinction in Literature and Art," a memoir read at meeting of Northampton County, Pa., Historical and Genealogical Society, Sept. 20, 1921. Virginia Military Institute Archives.
White, Rev. H. M., ed. *Rev. William S. White, D. D., and His Times (1800–73): An Autobiography.* Richmond: Whittet and Shepperson, 1891.
"Who Did Stop the Cadets on Their March Against Lexington," *County News*, in Margaret and Lucy Withrow, *Withrow Scrapbook* (Lexington, Va.: Rockbridge Historical Society) 7: 53. Washington and Lee University Special Collections.
Williams, Philip, Jr., "The Franklin Society: A Study of the Debates 1850–61." Master's thesis. Lexington, Va.: Washington and Lee University, 1941.
Williams, Richard G., Jr., "Jackson's 'colored Sunday school' class," *Washington Times*, May 6, 2006.
"Willie," *The Cadet: A Monthly Magazine of Science, Literature and Art* 1, No. 4 (July 1871): 208–09. Poem on the death of Willie Preston by a fellow cadet, if not actual brother.
Wilson, Howard McKnight. *Lexington Presbyterian Heritage.* Verona, Va.: McClure Press, 1971.
Wineman, Bradford Alexander. *Francis H. Smith: Architect of Antebellum Southern Military Schools and Educational Reform.* Dissertation. Texas A&M, 2006.
_____. "J.T.L. Preston and the Origins of the Virginia Military Institute, 1834–42," *Virginia Magazine of History and Biography* 114, No. 2 (2006): 226–61.
_____. "Military Schools," in Maggi M. Morehouse and Zoe Trod, eds., *Civil War America: A Social and Cultural History.* New York: Routledge, 2012, 121–30.
Wise, Henry Alexander, Jr. *Drawing Out the Man: The VMI Story.* Charlottesville: University Press of Virginia, 1978, esp. 11–12 for a brief life sketch of J.T.L. Preston.
Wise, Jennings Cropper. *Long Arm of Lee: The History of the Artillery of the Army of Northern Virginia*, Vol. 1. Lynchburg, Va.: J. P. Bell, 1915. Covers Bull Run to Fredericksburg.
_____. *Military History of the Virginia Military Institute From 1839 to 1865.* Lynchburg, Va.: J. P. Bell, 1915.
Wise, John Sargeant. "Battle of New Market, Va., May 15, 1864: An Address, Repeated Before the Virginia Military Institute, May 13, 1882." Speeches, Box 1: New Market Speeches. Virginia Military Institute Archives.
_____. *The End of an Era.* Boston: Houghton Mifflin, 1899.
Withrow, Margaret, and Lucy Withrow. *Withrow Scrapbooks.* Vols. 7, 13, and 19 of 20. Rockbridge Historical Society. Washington and Lee University Special Collections. A collection of 20th-century clippings relating to Virginia Military Institute.
Wood, Alexander Barbour. "Alexander Barbour Wood: A [sic] Oral History," interview by Richard C. Halseth. Rockbridge Historical Society, 2001–02. Washington and Lee University Special Collections.
Wood, James H. *The War: "Stonewall" Jackson, His Campaigns, and Battles, the Regiment As I Saw Them.* Cumberland, Md.: Eddy Press, 1910.
Young, Col. Bennett H. "John Cabell Breckinridge," *Confederate Veteran* 13, No. 6 (June 1905): 257–61.

Index

Numbers in ***bold italics*** indicate pages with photographs.

abolitionist movement 127–28, 130–31
African Colonization Society 126
Albemarle Military Institute 57
Alexander, Abbott 118
Alexander, Andrew 67–68, 70, 72
Alexander, Archibald 27, 31, 90, 113, 214
Alexander, Elizabeth "Betty" 162
Alexander, H.C. 205
Alexander, Margaret (Mrs. Edward Graham) 27
Allan, Elizabeth Randolph Preston "Libbie" 29, 89, 92, 96, 108–9, ***110***–11, 113, 115–18, 132, 144, 162, 177, 182–85, 192, 204, 206, 210, 213–14, 216, 218–19, 246*ch*27*n*1, 248*n*18; *Life and Letters of Margaret Junkin Preston* 93; *A March Past: Reminiscences of Elizabeth Randolph Preston Allan* 110, 183, 188
Allan, John 22, 24
Allan, William 204, 246*ch*27*n*1
Allen, John J. 137
Alumnus [pseud.] 86
American Literary, Scientific, and Military College *see* Norwich University
Anakee 185, 192, 245*ch*24*n*17, 245*ch*24*n*19, 245*ch*25*n*23
Anderson, Joseph A. 82
Anderson, Joseph Reid 55
Anderson, Robert A. 132
Anderson, Sara Eliza Archer 55
Anderson, William A. 68
Ann Smith Academy 42, 54, 197
Antietam (Sharpsburg), Battle of 162
Appomattox 184
Arkwright, Richard 41
Armstrong, the Rev. George 81, 85
Arnold, Laura Ann Jackson 164
asylum for deaf and dumb 49
Atkinson, the Rev. William M. 55
Averell, William 5, 7, 169–71
Avon Hill 18

Bagby, George 138
Baker, Samuel 190
Balcony Falls 6
Baldwin, Cornelius C. 47, 50

Banks, Nathaniel 152–53, 157, 171
Baptist Church 86, 232*ch*6*n*11; Colored Baptist Association of Virginia 190; Lexington African Baptist Church 246*n*44
Barclay, Hugh 37–38, 53, 56, 68, 70, 72, 132, 229*n*34
"Battle Hymn of the Republic" 131, 238*n*20; *see also* "John Brown's Song"
Baxter, the Rev. George 25
Baylor, William S.H. 160
Bean, William G. 98
Beauregard, P.G.T. 143
Beechenbrook see Preston, Margaret
Beechenbrook Chapel 204, ***205***
Belmead 86
Benét, Stephen Vincent: *John Brown's Body* 131
Benjamin, Judah P. 149–51
Berea College 194
Berlin University 201
Blain, the Rev. Daniel 27; Daniel Blain House ***26***
Blain, Mary Hanna "Polly" 27
Blair, William B. ***186***
Blandome 29–***30***, 90, 165; naming 226*n*16(9), 227*n*18; title line 225*n*16; vs. Little Blandome 226*n*16(2)*Note* 243*ch*21*n*19
Bledsoe, Margaret 198
Boley, Henry 65, 107, 128, 193; *Lexington in Old Virginia* 64
Booth, John Wilkes 129
Boteler, Alexander 151
Botts, Thomas H. 229*n*34
Boude, John C. 9, 118–19
Bowen, the Rev. Thomas Jefferson 190
Boyd, Thomas Massie 36
Brady, Mathew 106
Breckinridge, John 10, 171–72, 176–77, 243*ch*23*n*2
Brockenbrough, John 127
Brooke, John Mercer 186; Brooke Rifle 186
Brown, John 128–31, 139; execution ***130***
Brown, William G. 52
Browning, Elizabeth Barrett 219
Brownson, Dr. and Mrs. James I. 196
Bryan, Janet Allan 109

Buchanan, James 131, 171
Buckner, Simon 213
Burgwyn, Harry 169
Burnside, Ambrose 162
Butler, Benjamin 171

C [pseud.] 51
Cabel, William 174
Calhoun, John C. 164
Camp Lee 10, 137, 139, 224*prologuen*25
Campbell, David 51–54, 56
Campbell, Isaac 14, 90, 234*n*13
Campbell, Leslie Lyle 91, 198, 210–11
Campbell-Jordan House 90, ***92***, 234*n*8–9, 234*n*13
Cartoons: Little Pictures or Imaginary; Conversations 205
Caruthers, John Franklin 27, 31, 52, 60, 89, 192, 227*n*33, 245*ch*25*n*23
Caruthers, Louisa Catherine Gibson 29
Caruthers, Phoebe Alexander 21
Caruthers, Sarah Lyle *see* Preston, Sarah
Caruthers, William Alexander, Jr. 29–31, 226*n*16(3), 227*n*24; *Cavaliers of Virginia* 30; *Kentuckian in New York* 30; *Knights of the Golden Horseshoe* 30, 227*n*20
Caruthers, William Alexander, Sr. 21, 27
Cavaliers of Virginia 30
Cave Spring 197
Cedar Mountain, Battle of 157
Chambersburg, Pennsylvania 9
Chancellorsville, Battle of 167, 182
Charge of the VMI Cadets, mural ***178***
Chenoweth, Joseph H. 238*ch*14*n*10
Cherry Grove Mansion 76
Christian, Julia Jackson *see* Preston, Julia
Christian, Thomas Jonathan Jackson, Sr. "Jack" 218
Cincinnati Fund 81, 83, 87, 233*n*16
Cincinnatus Monument 221
Citizen of Lexington [pseud.] 47–49

263

INDEX

Citizen-soldier 41, 46, 49–50, 71, 81, 221
Cives letters 38–47, 60–61, 65, 69–70, 72, 80, 123, 138, 228*ch*3*n*12; first letter 39–40; second letter 40–43; third letter 43–46
Clarke, John 22
Clay, Henry 126
Clinedinst, Benjamin 177–78
Clinton, DeWitt 41
Cocke, Edmund Randolph 118, 168, 202
Cocke, Elizabeth Randolph Preston (Mrs. William Armistead Cocke, Sr.) 17, 19–20, 22, 29, 76–77, 95, 104, 110–11, 168, 187, 237*ch*12*n*13; appearance 95
Cocke, J. Preston 143, 168, 173, 184
Cocke, Philip St. George 86–87, 123
Cocke, Sally Lyle Preston 202
Cocke, Thomas Lewis Preston 118
Cocke, William Armistead, Jr. 111
Cocke, William Armistead, Sr. 77
Cocke, William Fauntleroy 118, 168–69, 185, 202
Cocke, William H. 46
Col Alto 104
College Reform 80
Colonna, Benjamin A. 176–77, 239*ch*16*n*2
Colston, Raleigh E. 99, 104–5, 167, 237*ch*14*n*10
Coralie 193, 245*ch*25*n*26
Couper, William 28, 54–55, 62, 73, 94, 129, 132, 189, 192–93, 213, 220; *One Hundred Years at V.M.I.* 68–69
Craney Island 101, 145–48, *146*, 240*ch*18*n*1
Creigh, David 5
Crockett, Charles 174
Crook, George 5–7, 171
"Crowd of honorable youths" 46
Crozet, Claudius 51–*52*, 55, 64–68, 70, 72–73, 228*n*26, 229*n*34, 230*n*21; first to call VMI by its initials 230*n*21; letter to Francis Smith *66*
Crutchfield, Oscar Minor 51, 228*ch*4*n*17
Crutchfield, Stapleton 51, 139, 143, 145, 167, 228*ch*4*n*17, 238*ch*14*n*10
Crystal Palace 100
Cuffee, Paul 126
Cumings, John Agnew 29, 225*n*16(1)

Dame, Mr. 20
Dame's School 21, 89, 93
Daniel, John Moncure 206
Davidson, the Rev. Andrew B. 29, 225*n*16(2)
Davidson, James D. 37–38, 135

Davidson College 210
Davis, Alexander J. 87
Davis, Jefferson 132, 143, 151, 165, 177
"Dedication to J.T.L. Preston" *see* Smith, Francis
Derrick, Clarence 176
Derwent 187, 245*ch*24*n*26
Deyerle, Charles P. 59
Diamond Hill 20, 78, 224*n*11
Dickey, Helen 185, 245*ch*24*n*18
Dooley, Edwin 82
Dorman, Charles P. 17, 50–51, 53, 56, 71, 132, 135, 229*n*34
Dorman, Cornelius 17, 225*n*16(1), 227*n*33
Downing, Lylburn Liggin 195–96
Dunbar, Douglas 183
DuPont, Henry Algernon 7–8, 223*n*16

Early, Jubal 9, 148
Eastman, Seth 15, 32
Echols, Edward 135
Edgar, George 173, 176
Edward, Thomas 94
Elements of Descriptive Geometry 63
Emancipation Proclamation 162
Emerson, Ralph Waldo 131
End of an Era 128
Episcopal Church 86, 98
Estill, Cecil 167
Estill, Harry 167
Estill, Mrs. Henry M. (Mary J. Patrick) 167
Estill, John Livingston 167
Estill, Robert Kyle 167
Estill House *26*
Evans, Nathan 149
Ewell, Richard S. 153, 204
Ezekiel, Moses 177

Fair Ground Lot 216, 248*n*12
Fairchild, Henry 194
Fairfield, Virginia 21, 76
Fanny Randolph Page *see* Meredith
Ficklin, Benjamin Franklin 99, 105
Fifth Avenue Presbyterian Church of Roanoke *see* Presbyterian Church
Fishburn, Julia Rush Junkin 113, 136, 147, 170, 210
Flag of New Market *180*
flag of secession 134, 136
Floyd, John B. 100
Foxwood 77, 232*ch*6*n*11
Franklin Society 33, *37–38*, 40, 56, 60–61, 64, 68, 72, 77, 126, 128, 131, 197–99, 227*n*33; debates 33, 37–38; on secession 131–32, 238*n*26; on slavery 127
Fredericksburg, Battle of 163
Freedman's Hill 78, 224*n*11
Frémont, John, 149, 152
Fugitive Slave Law 189, 195
Fulkerson, Abe 105

Fuller, Jacob 7, 163, 165, 226*n*16(7)-(8), 243*ch*21*n*18–19
Fulton, Robert 41

Garnett, Richard B. 150
Garrison, William Lloyd 128, 131
Gilham, William T. 7, 84, 99, 100, 104–5, 122–23, 129, 142, 165, 172, 237*ch*14*n*10, 243*ch*21*n*18–19; *Manual of Instruction for the Vounteers and Militia of the United States* (1861) 138
Gladstone, William 205
Glasgow House *92*
Graham, Archibald A., Jr. 167
Graham, Archibald A., Sr. 153
Graham, Mrs. Archibald, Sr. (Martha Lyle) 167
Graham, the Rev. Edward 25
Graham, James McDowell 167
Graham, John Alexander 167
Graham Philanthropic Society 199
Grant, Ulysses S. 5, 10, 168, 171, 185
Gray, Gabriel 106

Hagerstown, Maryland 9
Halleck, Henry 169, 171
Hampden-Sydney 54–55
Hampton, Wade 8
Hampton Roads, Battle of *146*
Hardin, Mark B. *186*, 238*ch*14*n*10
Harper, Kenton 139
Harpers Ferry 14, 129–30, 139–41, 143, 149, 152–53
Harrison, James A. 205, 215, 219
Hart's Bottom Estates 243*ch*21*n*18
Haugawout, John 28
Hayes, Rutherford B. 7
Hayne, Paul 206, 209–10
Hempstead, Junius 143
Henderson, Octavius 238*ch*14*n*10
Henry, Patrick 14
Herbert, Henry William 197
Hill, Ambrose Powell 157, 159, 167
Hill, Daniel H. 104
Hill, Govan 244*n*23
History of the Virginia Military Institute: Its Building and Rebuilding see Smith, Francis
Holliday, Frederick 212
Holmes, George Frederick 83
Hooker, Joseph 164, 166–67
Houdon, Jean-Antoine 119
Houghawout, J.W. *198*
Howard, Nat 22–23
Hubbard, William J. 12, 119
Hunter, David 5, 119, 149; burning of VMI 7–8; raid on Lexington 5–8, 96, 182
Hunter, Robert 135
"Hunter Is Home from the Hill" *198*
Hutchinson, William 197

Index

Imboden, John D. 170–71
Isaac 192, 245*ch*25*n*24

Jackson, Andrew 132
Jackson, Elinor Junkin "Ellie" 111, 113, 150
Jackson, Julia Laura 168
Jackson, Laura Ann *see* Arnold
Jackson, Mary Anna Morrison 106–7, 114, 168, 174, 195
Jackson, Thomas Jonathan "Stonewall" 6, 100, 102, **106**, 111–12, 116, 128–29, 132, 137, 164–65, 169, 177, 180, 185, 199–201, 204, 206, 237*ch*14*n*10, 243*ch*21*n*18, 243*ch*21*n*19; at Battle of Winchester 153; begins teaching at VMI 104–6; commands First Virginia Brigade 141–44; commands Harpers Ferry 140–41; conducts McDowell Campaign 152; conducts Romney Campaign 150–5; death at Chancellorsville 167; farm 163, 242*ch*21*n*7; at First Battle of Manassas 143; gives scabbard speech 134, 200, 239*n*3; at Kernstown 152; at Second Battle of Manassas 156–60; statue 218; sword 8; takes leave of First Brigade 149–50, 200; teaches Slave Sabbath School 194–96
Jackson, William L. "Mudwall" 169–70
Jackson Memorial Hall 8, 177
Jane 193, 245*ch*25*n*25
Jefferson, Thomas 14, 30, 71–72, 99, 227*n*21, 244*n*14
Jefferson, Thomas Garfield, III, "Tom" 174, 244*n*14
Jefferson College 112
Jeffrey, Robert W. 72
John 193
John Brown's Body 131
"John Brown's Song" 238*n*20; *see also* "Battle Hymn of the Republic"
Johnston, Joseph E. 141, 143, 157
Johnston, Peter C. 52, 228*n*26, 229*n*34
Jones, Henry 174
Jordan, Nannie A. 234*n*9
"Jottings" *see* Preston, John Thomas Lewis "J.T.L."
Junkin, Agnes Penick 165
Junkin, the Rev. Ebenezer Dickey "Eben" 137
Junkin, George, Jr. 115, 137, 210
Junkin, the Rev. George, Sr. 112–**13**, 116–17, 120, 127–29, 135–36, 188, 202, 238*n*11; *Political Fallacies* 164, 242*ch*21*n*13
Junkin, John Miller 137, 164, 167, 242*ch*21*n*9
Junkin, Julia Rush *see* Fishburn
Junkin, Julia Rush Miller 113
Junkin, Margaret *see* Preston, Margaret

Junkin, William Finney "Willy" 137, 210

Kahle, Matthew 38, 136
Kemper, James L. 207, 247*ch*27*n*13
Kentuckian in New York 30
Kirkpatrick, the Rev. John L. 210
Knights of the Golden Horseshoe 30
Knox [pseud.] 60

Ladies of Rockbridge County 138
Lafayette College 113
Lane, James 105
Lee, Custis **186**
Lee, Fitzhugh 8, 213
Lee, Robert E. 128–29, 135, 137, 139–40, 143, 147, 157, 162, 167–68, 171–72, 177, 184–**88**, 201, 211, 232*ch*6*n*11
Lee, Mrs. Robert E. (Mary Anna Custis) 187
Leesburg, Battle of 149
Letcher, John 7, 128, 131, 135, 137–38, 142, 151, 177, **186**
Levy, Benjamin 67
Lewis, William C. 38
Lexington, Virginia **10**, 12, 14–**15**, 27, 42, 48, 54, 87, **91**, 97, 128–29, 131, 134–37, 184, 187, 197, 199, 204, 215, **217**, 248*n*2
Lexington Arsenal 21, **32–33**, 36, 39, 40–41, 43–44, 47, 50–51, 53, 60, 67–69, 71, 90, 197
Lexington Tannery 165, 243*ch*21*n*19
Leyburn, Alfred 49, 56, 67, 93, 96–97, 234*n*20
Leyburn, Ann Eliza Caruthers 230*n*25, 234*n*20
Leyburn, James G. 53, 65
Leyburn, John 21, 227*n*33, 229*n*34
Liberia 126–27
Liberty Hall 197, 247*ch*28*n*15
"Liberty Hall Volunteers" (4th Virginia Infantry, Company I) 136, 138, 157, 241*n*5
Ligon, William 52, 228*n*26, 229*n*34
Lincoln, Abraham 5, 128, 131–33, 136, 152–53, 182, 185, 238*n*11; call for Virginia troops 134–35; Emancipation Proclamation 162
Lincoln, Thomas "Tad," III 132, 239*n*31
Literary Fund 51, 54
"London Journal" *see* Preston, John Thomas Lewis "J.T.L."
Longfellow, Henry Wadsworth 131, 205
Longstreet, James 159, 168–69
Loring, William W. 150–51
Lyle, John Blair 31, 87, 106–7, 236*n*11
Lyle, John Newton 138
Lyle, Royster, Jr. 96, 107

Madison, Eliza Preston 18
Madison, Robert L. **186**, 237*ch*14*n*8, 238*ch*14*n*9
Manassas, First Battle of 138, 142–45, 149, 184; Second Battle of 157–60, 162; battlefield map **158**
Manchester, Edwin H. 23
Manual of Instruction for the Volunteers and Militia of the United States see Gilham, William
Marr, John Quincy 142
Marshall, George C. 221
Marshall, Louis 52
Massachusetts Historical Society 206
Massie, James W. 134, **186**
Matthew, Mark, Luke, and John **141**
Maury, Matthew Fontaine 137; "geographer of the seas" **186–87**
Maury River *see* North River
McCausland, John 6, 9, 142, 238*ch*14*n*10
McCay, Charles F. 113
McClellan, George 149, 153, 162, 169
McClung, C.L. 130
McClung, Elizabeth Alexander 27
McClung, Henry 27
McClung, James W. 26, 225*n*16(2)*Note* 231*n*3
McCrum, Barton **198**
McCulloch, Ruth A. 91
McDonald, James 62
McDonald, Marshall **186**
McDonogh, John 204
McDonogh School 204, 211
McDowell, Dudley **198**
McDowell, Irvin 143, 157
McDowell, James, Jr. 53, 77, 85, 104, 229*n*34
McDowell, James, Sr. 76, 231*n*3
McDowell, Susan Preston 29
McDowell, William 174
McDowell Campaign 182
McGuire, Hunter 159
McKinley, William 7
Meade, George 171
Meredith, Fanny Randolph Page 157, 241*n*5
USS *Merrimack* **186**; *see also* CSS *Virginia*
Methodist Church 86; Randolph Street Methodist Church 246*n*44
Mexican War 84, 104, 111, 149
Miami University of Ohio 112–13
Michie, Thomas J. 100
Miley, Michael 26, 37, 77, 118–19, 188, 212, 217
Mills, Daniel 36
Minis, Raymond 55
"Minks" *see* Virginia Military Institute
USS *Monitor* 146

Moore, David Evans, Sr. 36, 41
Moore, David Evans, Jr. 167
Moore, Mrs. David Evans, Sr. (Elizabeth M. Harvey) 167
Moore, Edward Alexander "Ned" 167
Moore, Mrs. John H. (Sallie Alexander Moore) 67–68, 143
Moore, Samuel McDowell 69, 128
Moore, William 81
Morgan, James, Jr. 69
Morgan, W.H. 138
Morrill Act 123
Morrison, Frances Henderson Smith 7, 223*n*11
Morrison, Francis Henney Smith 7, 223*n*11
Morrison, the Rev. James 5
Morton, Oren 193; *History of Rockbridge County* 36, 65
Moseley, John 36
Munford, Thomas 167
Myers, Henry M. 216

National Cyclopedia of American Biography 28
National Register of Historic Places 67, 227*n*16(13)
Nelson, Alexander L. 138
New Market, Battle of 5–6, 168, 173–76, 184; battlefield *174–75*; cadet biographies 239*ch*16*n*2; cadet casualties 176, 244*n*23; field of lost shoes *175*
New Market Campaign see Turner, Edward
Nicholas, Elizabeth *see* Randolph, Elizabeth
Nicholas, Wilson Cary 21, 36, 69
Nichols, Edward West 67–68
North Carolina troops: Infantry, 26th 169
North River 6, 28, 36, 94, 136, 197; covered bridge on 6
Norwich University 71

Oakland 77, 104, 110–11, 117, 193
Odd Fellows Hall *92*, 234*n*9
Old Song and New 202–3
Olin and Preston Institute *see* Virginia Polytechnic Institute

Page, William Nelson, Jr., "Willie" 156, 241*n*1
Page, William Nelson, Sr. 241*n*5
Paine, Henry Ruffner 160
Parapet inscription at VMI *45*; original wording 228*n*17
Partridge, Alden 49, 50, *70*–72, 231*n*48
Patrick, William 160
Patton, John Mercer, Class of 1880 207
Paxton, Elisha Franklin "Bull" 68, 142, 150, 167
Paxton, James 36
Paxton, Matthew W. 68

Peaks of Otter 95
Peasant Reform of 1861 129
Peay, J.H. Binford 221
Pendleton, Alexander Swift "Sandie" 150
Pendleton, Edmund 79, 213
Pendleton, the Rev. William Nelson 138, 141
Penn, Davidson 105
Pennsylvania Manual Labor Academy 112
Pettigrew, Matt *198*
Peyton, Bernard 52, 228*n*26, 229*n*34
Peyton, John Howe 18, 38
Phil 193, 245*ch*24*n*17, 245*ch*24*n*19
Phillips, Wendell 131
Pickett, George Edward 168; Pickett's charge 169, *178*
Plecker, A.H. 10
Poe, Edgar Allan 22–24, *23*, 224*n*20; "William Wilson" 24
Poe's Farm 10
Political Fallacies see Junkin, the Rev. George
Pope, John 157, 159
Presbyterian Church 85–86, 96, 98, 197, 202, 215, 219; Fifth Avenue Presbyterian Church of Roanoke 195–*196*; General Assembly 97, 143, 165, 171, 184; Presbyterian Council 207; Presbytery 94, 96–97; Record of the Presbytery 97
Preston, Edmonia Madison Randolph (daughter) 78, 89, 95, 214
Preston, Edmonia Madison Randolph (mother) 16–20, 22, 24, 27, 29, 76–78, 234*n*2, 244*n*7
Preston, Edmund Randolph "Ran" (grandson) 117, 207, 218, 235*n*8
Preston, Edmund Randolph "Ran" (son) 93, 111, 117–18, 161–62, 169, 185, 214
Preston, Elizabeth Randolph (daughter) *see* Allan, Elizabeth
Preston, Elizabeth Randolph (great-grandchild) 214
Preston, Elizabeth Randolph (sister) *see* Cocke, Elizabeth
Preston, Emma Heinrichs 218
Preston, Franklin "Frank" 6, 8, 10, 89, 110, 118, 143, 148, 151, 153, 156, 162–63, 169, *175*, 182, 184, 214, 241*n*33, 244*n*7, 244*n*24, describes Battle of New Market 172–77; middle name 234*n*1
Preston, George Heinrichs 218
Preston, George Junkin 76, *93*, 118, 148, 151, 164, 202, 210, 214, 216, 218–19, 231*n*1
Preston, Herbert Rush "Bert" *93*, 148, 164–65, 202, 214, 216, 218–19
Preston, James Francis 141, 143, 151, 241*n*13

Preston, James Patton 36
Preston, John (great-grandfather) 17, 30
Preston, John (uncle) 18, 27
Preston, John Alexander 107, 110–11, 118, 161, 197–*98*, 217, 219, 236*n*10, 248*n*24
Preston, John Thomas Lewis "J.T.L." *186*, *198*; ancestry 17, 31, 215–16, 236*n*10; anecdote of value of Latin 29; appearance *3*, 111, 115, 215, 236*ch*11*n*1; argues for creation of military school 38; attends Richmond Academy 24; attends Washington College 25–26; begins career as attorney in Lexington 33, 38, 78; begins career as teacher 57; birth 17; birthplace *19*; called "Lexington's Demosthenes" 38; called "spasmodically social" 94; choice of surrogate father 77, 231*n*3; "Colored Man in the South" 189; commissioned Lt. Col. in 9th Virginia Infantry 142, 240*n*17; composes history of VMI 61, 212; death 214, 247*n*31; declines post of inspector-general 152; declines rank of brigadier general 207, 247*ch*27*n*13; defends against Averell's raids of western Virginia 169–71; defense of Superintendent Smith 86, 119–23; disclaims originating VMI 39, 62, 70; dogs, horses, and hunting, fondness for 21, 27, 77, 94, 197–*98*, 215; elected delegate to first world-wide Presbyterian Council 207; elected delegate to Presbyterian General Assembly 165; faces first mutiny 100; false obituary 88; farming, love of 77, 94; goes to Dame's School 20; grieves the death of four children 201–2; health 32, 115, 184, 209, 213, 244*n*7; joins Franklin Society 33; joins VMI Board of Visitors 53; "Jottings" 236*n*35, 240*ch*18*n*1; landowner 6, 30, 32, 38, 77–78, 95, 165, 216, 227*n*21, 232*ch*6*n*8, 232*ch*6*n*11, 242*ch*21*n*17, 243*ch*21*n*18–19, 248*n*12; leads the charge in the Skinner War 96–97, 235*n*8; "London Journal" 225*n*5, 225*n*14, 232*ch*6*n*15, 232*ch*7*n*8, 236*ch*11*n*1; manual labor, advocate of 77, 112; marries Sally Caruthers 30, 227*n*24; mourns death of Sally 108–9, 237*ch*12*n*7; moves to Blandome 29–*30*, 226*n*16(4), 227*n*18; moves to Campbell-Jordan House 90, *92*; moves to Ruffner House *93*, 234*n*20; nature, love of 94–95, 197; nicknames 22, 38, 105; opinions on agriculture 77–78, 122–23;

opinions on balanced education 40, 56, 70, 72–73, 79, 84, 121–22; opinions on Battle of New Market 177–80; opinions on charities 40, 42; opinions on citizen-soldier 41, 46, 79; opinions on cursing 92, 165; opinions on democracy 70; opinions on earning an education 39–40, 42–44; opinions on education of the poor 41–42, 54, 83, 122–123; opinions on emancipation 193–94; opinions on fishing 94; opinions on genius 41–42; opinions on Gettysburg 169; opinions on honesty and truth 46; opinions on hope 199; opinions on idleness 41, 165; opinions on Jackson as teacher 201; opinions on military discipline 40, 43, 56, 62, 70, 72, 91, 101–2, 121, 123, 140; opinions on moral character 41, 43–44, 46, 79–80, 82, 192, 200, 215–16; opinions on normal school 40, 43–44, 82, 121–123; opinions on patronage 42; opinions on practice of law 78; opinions on religion 31, 61, 89, 91–92, 95, 98, 101, 112, 115, 117, 131, 137, 144, 160, 163, 165, 179, 194, 199, 207, 214, 216, 248*n*35; opinions on secession 132, 135; opinions on slavery 127, 163, 189–96; opinions on state of education in the contemporary U.S., 42, 54, 121–22; opinions on teaching 80, 82, 200–201, 210; opinions on Virginia's militia 40–41, 138; opinions on West Point vs. VMI 38, 41, 56, 62, 68, 212; opinions on women 42, 89–91, 97, 117, 191; ordained ruling elder of Presbyterian Church 92, 248*n*9; ornithology, interest in 95, 235*n*29; passport 236*ch*11*n*1; physical exercise, love of 27, 77; portrait, *frontispiece 3*, 220; prepares VMI for war 133, 137; promoted to major (full professor) 99; provides homes for working class 78, 232*ch*6*n*11, 204; *Pulpit Manner, as Seen from the Pew* 213; reading list 239*n*29; receives LL.D. degree 208; recounts history of Lexington 197; rejoins Jackson at McDowell Campaign 152; "Religious Education of the Colored People of the South" 193; reluctance to mention father 76, 231*n*1, 231*n*3; *Removing to a New Charge:Letters to a Young Minister* 213; retires from teaching at VMI 206, 247*ch*27*n*11; returns to teach at VMI 151; salary 57, 79, 143, 165, 186, 240*n*19–20; serves as Jackson's adjutant general 149; serves as Jackson's chief of staff 139, 240*ch*19*n*1; speaks on Battle of New Market 177–80, 244*n*30; stationed on Craney Island 145; studies languages at University of Virginia 28; studies Latin at Fairfield 22; studies law at Yale College 28; teaches part-time at VMI 207; teaches Slave Sabbath School 195, 246*n*41; teaches at Washington College 210; teaching, love of 78; travels in Europe 28, 104, 210; war 145–46, 163, 179, 185; will of 216, 248*n*12; witnesses John Brown's execution 129–31; writes Cives letters 38–47, 61, 228*n*12; writes ministerial guide books 213

Preston, Julia Jackson Christian 218

Preston, Lewis McDowell [pseud.] 88

Preston, Lucy Gordon Waddell 148, 240*ch*18*n*12

Preston, Margaret Junkin (granddaughter) 218

Preston, Margaret Junkin "Maggie" *93*, *118*, 127, 129, 131, 148–49, 164–65, 171, 187, 195, 197, 202–6, 209–11, 213; appearance 111, 117–18; *Beechenbrook: A Rhyme of the War 9, 183*, 204; birth 248*n*25; *Cartoons: Little Pictures or Imaginary; Conversations* 205; composes *Beechenbrook* 182–84, 244*n*6; death 219; on death of Frank 202; on death of Phoebe 202; on death of Ran 162–63; on death of Willie 158–61, 242*n*24; divided loyalties 136–37, 151, 163, 167–68; on hardships of war 151–53, 163, 167–70; on Hunter's raid 6–9; introduction to J.T.L. Preston 111–14; last days 215–19; on Lee's surrender 184–85; Margaret Preston Oak 219, 248*n*23; marriage to J.T.L. Preston 115–17; *Old Song and New* 202–3; "Poetess of the Confederacy" 9, 183; poetry 115–16, 161, 202–3, 205, 211, 219; on sale of Preston home 216; "Sandringham" 205; *Semi-centennial Ode for the Virginia Military Institute* 213; *Silverwood: A Book of Memories* 112; writes journal of the war 6, 9, 151–2, 160, 162–64, 167, 184–85, 241*n*18

Preston, Phoebe Alexander 78, 111, 118, 161–62, 169, 202, 214, 246*n*14

Preston, Sarah Lyle Caruthers "Sally" 30–31, 76, 78, 80, 89, 93–94, 97, 104, 106–10, 113, 115–18, 202, 214, 227*n*24, 227*n*33, 230*n*25, 234*n*20, 236*n*11; appearance 21, 27; "fountain of happiness" 31

Preston, Susanna Smith 18, 19

Preston, Thomas Lewis (father) 16–17, 33, 68, 72, 76–77, 81, 88, 224*n*6, 234*ch*8*n*17; town lot 19–*20*, 29, 224*n*11

Preston, Thomas Lewis "Tom" (son) 76, 110, 118, 141, 143, 148, 161, 202, 212, 214, 216, 219, 240*ch*18*n*12, 244*n*7, 248*n*24

Preston, William (grandfather) 76, 123, 227*n*21, 237*ch*14*n*10

Preston, William Ballard 237*ch*14*n*9; Preston Resolution 133

Preston, William Campbell 118, 227*n*18

Preston, William Caruthers "Willie" (son) 90, 108, 110–11, 118, 136, 156–61, *157*, 169, 185, 214, 241*n*5; gravestone *160*, 248*n*32; name, spelling 234*n*7

Preston, William Caruthers (grandson) 148, 161

Preston and Olin Institute *see* Virginia Polytechnic Institute

Preston family plot *218*; family portrait *217*

Preston home 93, *109*, 161, 216, 248*n*15–16

Preston Library 69, 73, *220*, 221; history 81, 248*n*27

Preston Resolution *see* Preston, William Ballard

Preston Row 78, 232*ch*6*n*14

Preston Street 78, 232*ch*6*n*13, 234*n*20

Price, James H. 221

Princeton Theological Seminary 27, 214

"Progress of Education in Virginia" 120–23

Randolph, Edmonia Madison *see* Preston, Edmonia (mother)

Randolph, Edmund Jennings 18, 22, 95

Randolph, Elizabeth Nicholas 17

Randolph, John, of Roanoke 126

Randolph, Joseph W. 183

Randolph, Peyton 14

Randolph, William 143

"Rats" *see* Virginia Military Institute

Reconstruction Act of 1867 187

Rees, C.R. 175

Reid, Mayne 197

Reid, Samuel McDowell, Jr. 202

Reid, Samuel McDowell, Sr. 245*ch*25*n*24

"Reluctant Confederates" 135

Richardson, William Harvie, Jr. 81

Richardson, William Harvie, Sr. 81–82, 101, 169, *186*

Richmond, Virginia 5–6, 8, 10, 17–18, 21–22, 26–27, 36, 77,

81–83, 87, 95, 101, 119, 137–41, 143, 150–53, 157, 160, 165, 172, 177–78, 182–84, 186–87, 193, 201–2, 213, 224*prologuen*25, 224*ch*1*n*3, 242*n*20
Richmond Academy 22, 88
Richmond College (University of Richmond) 83
Ritchie, Thomas, Jr. 88
Ritchie, Thomas, Sr. 88, 234*ch*8*n*17
Ritchie, William 88
Robertson, James I., Jr. 60, 114, 129
Robinson, John 147–48
Rockbridge [pseud.] 50
Rockbridge Artillery *see* Virginia Troops
Rockbridge County 14–15, 17, 21, 36, 50, 53, 68, 87, 135, 147, 193–94
"Rockbridge Dragoons" (1st Virginia Cavalry, Company C) 136
"Rockbridge Grays" (4th Virginia Infantry, Company H) 138
Rockbridge Historical Society 91
"Rockbridge Rifles" (27th Virginia Infantry, Company H) 136
Rockwood, James 38
Rodes, Robert 167
Romney Campaign 150–51
Roosevelt, Franklin 221
Ruff, Jacob 28
Ruff, John 33
Ruffin, Edmund 122
Ruffner, Sarah Lyle "Sally" 27, 93, 234*n*20, 236*n*11
Ruffner, W. Henry 25, 27, 31, 52, 86, 93, 113, 128–29; "Ruffner Pamphlet" 128, 234*n*20
Ruffner, William H. 17, 94–95, 107–8, 189, 192–93, 195, 201, 211
"Ruffner Pamphlet" *see* Ruffner, W. Henry
Rust, George, Jr. 52–53, 228*n*26

Sandy 245*ch*24*n*19, 245*ch*25*n*23
School House Lot 232*ch*6*n*11
Schoonmaker, James 7
Scots-Irish 14, 16, 17
Scott, Winfield 149
secession 131–33, 164; of Virginia 135
Semi-centennial Ode for the Virginia Military Institute 213
Semmes, Thomas M. *186*, 248*n*18
Shenandoah Valley 5, *10*, 16, 143, 171–72, 182; "breadbasket of the Confederacy" 10
Shenandoah Valley Campaign 182
Sheridan, Philip 8, 10, 182, 184
Sherman, William Tecumseh 171, 182, 229*n*57
Shields, Alexander 225*n*16(1), 227*n*33, 232*ch*6*n*12
Shields, George W. 165

Shields, James 153
Shields, Walsh *198*
Shields' Hill 224*n*11, 232*ch*6*n*12
Ship, Scott *see* Shipp, Scott
Shipp, Scott 62, 64–65, 170, 172, 174, *186*, 207, 220, 243, 238*ch*14*n*10, 248*n*16; name, spelling 243*ch*22*n*20
Sigel, Franz 5, 171–72, 176
Silliman, Benjamin 28
Silverwood: A Book of Memories 112
Skinner, the Rev. John 96, 235*n*12
Skinner War *see* Skinner, the Rev. John
Slave Sabbath Schools 195
slavery 104, 126–29, 162, 189–96, 245*ch*24*n*17, 245*ch*24*n*19, 245*ch*25*n*23–27
Smith, Francis Henney 7, 36, 54–57, *55*, 60, 62–65, 72–73, 79–80, 82, 85–87, 97–98, 100–101, 104–5, 119–23, 127, 129–32, 134, 137, 142, 145, 168–69, 171, *186*, 201, 207, *212*, 211–13, 237*ch*14*n*10, 241*n*14; *College Reform* 80; "Dedication to J.T.L. Preston" *63*; *Elements of Descriptive Geometry* 63; "History of the Origin and Progress of the Virginia Military Institute" 62–63, 230n14; *History of the Virginia Military Institute: Its Building and Rebuilding* 36, 55, 87, 187; nickname 64, 105; rebuilding of VMI 187
Smith, H.W. 70
Smith, Sarah Henderson 55, 87
Smith, William 177, 184
Smithfield Plantation 18, 19, 237*ch*14*n*9
Stanard, Jack 174
Staples, John 36
Staunton Artillery 140
Stewart, Alexander P. 104
Stonewall Brigade 138, 142, 144, 148–50, 160, 167
Stonewall Jackson House 17, *19*
Stonewall Jackson Memorial Cemetery 218
Stowe, Harriet Beecher *see Uncle Tom's Cabin*
Strange, John Bowie 57, 229*n*55
Sudley Plantation 160
Sylvia 192, 245*ch*25*n*24

Taylor, Bayard 190
Taylor, Susan Preston McDowell 89, 90, 226*n*16(5), 234*n*9
Taylor, Susan Randolph 18
Taylor, William F. 89–90, 226*n*16(5), 234*n*9
Taylor, Zachary 133
Taylor's Grove 93, 199, 248*n*23
Thompson, John R. 6
Tidd, Charles 20–21, 27, 93
Town lot *see* Preston, Thomas Lewis (father)
Trueheart, Daniel 238*ch*14*n*10

Troubadour Theatre *92*
Tuckahoe Plantation 193
Tucker, John Randolph 226*n*16(9), 227*n*18
Turner, Edward Raymond: *New Market Campaign* 176, 244*n*17
Turner, Nat 126, 128
Tyler, John F. 132, 213

Uncle Tom's Cabin 104, 189, 191–93
Union Theological Seminary 118, 205
University of Richmond 83
University of Virginia 24, 28, 72, 111, 120–23, 201, 205, 215, 233*n*21

Valentine, Edward V. 218
Valley Campaign 157
CSS *Virginia* 146, 186
Virginia, Colony of 14, *16*
Virginia Military Institute 9, *59*, *74*, 121–22; agriculture, chair 123, 237*ch*14*n*8; board of visitors *see* VMI Board of Visitors; burning by Hunter 7; corps of cadets *see* VMI Corps of Cadets; curriculum 39–40, 55, 64, 81–83, 100, 104, 120–24, 221; disorderly conduct 80, 98–102; faculty nicknames 64, 98, 105, 236*n*11*n*3, 243*ch*22*n*20; first day of school 57, 229*n*54; first superintendent 56; first to call VMI by its initials 230*n*21; graduates 56, 82, 99, 147–48, 152, 167–68, 212–13, 229*n*55, 233*n*24; hazing 101, 156; lack of a cavalry 184, 245*ch*24*n*10; legislative acts establishing 47–53, 229*n*33; mantra 46; mission 59, 221; naming 53; new barracks 87, 104; proposal to move the school 86, 87; "rats" vs. "minks" 81, 101, 233*n*17, 233*n*18; schools modeled after 57, 70, 82, 121–22, 212, 229–30*n*57; "that pesky little military school" 152; unique characteristics 56–58, 73, 123
Virginia Mourning Her Dead, statue of 177
Virginia Polytechnic Institute 123; Olin and Preston Institute 237*ch*14*n*9
Virginia troops: artillery, Rockbridge 136, 141, 148, 151, 153; Cavalry, 1st 136; Infantry, 4th 141, 157, 159–60; 9th 142, 145; 22nd 176; 23rd 176; 26th 173; 27th 141, 148; 51st 174–76; 62nd 174–76
VMI Board of Visitors 52, 60–61, 64–68, 73, 80, 83–87, 94, 98–101, 104, 122–23, 143, 168, 206–7, 212, 216, 220–21, 229*n*34; approves commissioning professors 207, 232*n*7,

236n28; first board 51–52; second board 53; third board 53, 56
VMI class ring 98
VMI Corps of Cadets 81, 89, 108, 123, 134, 142, 213, 219; at execution of John Brown 129–31; on parade *220*; war service chronology: at Camp Lee near Richmond as drill instructors (April 21, 1861) 10, 137–38; at McDowell Campaign (May 1–20, 1861) 152–53, 162; at Jackson's funeral (May 15, 1863) 168; at Averell's first raid at Goshen (Aug. 25, 1863) 169; at Averell's second raid at Covington (Nov. 6–11, 1863) 170; at Averell's third raid at Rockbridge Baths (Dec. 15–19, 1863) 170; at Battle of New Market (May 11–15, 1864) 5, 171–77, 239*ch*16*n*2; at Richmond guarding the city (May 22–June 7, 1864) 6, 177; at Lexington during Hunter's raid (June 9–11, 1864) 5–6; in camp at Balcony Falls (June 12–14, 1864) 6; at Lynchburg in the trenches (June 15–24, 1864) 10; furloughed (June 27–Sept. 30, 1864) 10; at Camp Lee near Richmond (Oct. 1–26, 1864) 10; at Poe's Farm for infantry support (Oct. 27–Dec. 12, 1864) 10; at Alms House for academic work (Dec. 28–March 10, 1865) 182; at defense of Richmond (March 11–April 1, 1865) 182–84; disbanded at fall of Richmond (April 2, 1865) 185; resumption of academic work at VMI (Oct. 17, 1865) 186

Waddell, James 240*ch*18*n*12
Walker, Charles D. 160
Walker, Eliza Bannister 227*n*16(13)
Walker, Harry Lee 226*n*16(13)
Walker, James A. 105, 236*ch*11*n*5
Washington, George 14, 71, 81, 180; statue of, at VMI 12, *119*, 224*n*28; statue of, at Washington College 136
Washington, William D. 186
Washington Academy *see* Washington College
Washington & Lee University *see* Washington College
Washington College 25–*26*, 39, 42, 50, 52–54, 60–61, 81, 83, 85–87, 93–94, 106, 110, 113, 118, 120, 123, 129, 136, 138, 156, 159, 187, 199, 201–2, 204; history 247*ch*28*n*15; vs. VMI 85; as Washington Academy 14, 27, 72, 81; as Washington and Lee University 90, 198, 208, 210–11, 248*n*16
"Washington Institute of Virginia" 86
West Point 37–38, 41, 49, 52, 54–56, 61, 65, 67–68, 70–71, 73, 81, 84, 86, 105, 120, 138, 212
West Point of the South 67, 120, 221
West Virginia 147, 240*n*18
West Virginia troops: Infantry Mounted, 8th 169

White, Hugh A. 159, 160
White, James J. 138
White, Joe *198*
White, the Rev. William Spottswood 7, 97, 135, 160
Whittier, John Greenleaf 131, 205
Wiley, John F. 229*n*34
William and Mary College 201
Williams, Adele 3
Williams, John James 153, 182, 244*n*2
Williams, Mrs. Philip (Mary Louise Dunbar) 153
Williamson, Thomas H. 7, 81, 104–5, *186*, 207, 220, 237*ch*14*n*10
Wilson, John Mark 225*n*6, 226*n*16(6)
Wilson, Phoebe Shields Caruthers 225*n*6, 226*n*16(6)
Wilson, Mrs. Samuel R. 225*n*6
Winchester, Battle of 153, 182
Wineman, Bradford 69, 80
Wise, Henry Alexander, Jr., "Old Chinook" 243*ch*23*n*9
Wise, Henry Alexander, Sr. 101, 129, 172, 243*ch*23*n*9
Wise, Jennings Cropper 55, 64–65; claim for Claudius Crozet *66*, 243*ch*23*n*9
Wise, John Sargeant 57, 173, 175, 243*ch*23*n*9; *End of an Era* 128
Withrow, Andrew 165
World's Fair 104

Yale College 28
Young, Uncle 185, 245*ch*24*n*17, 245*ch*24*n*19

www.ingramcontent.com/pod-product-compliance
Lightning Source LLC
Chambersburg PA
CBHW081545300426

44116CB00015B/2761